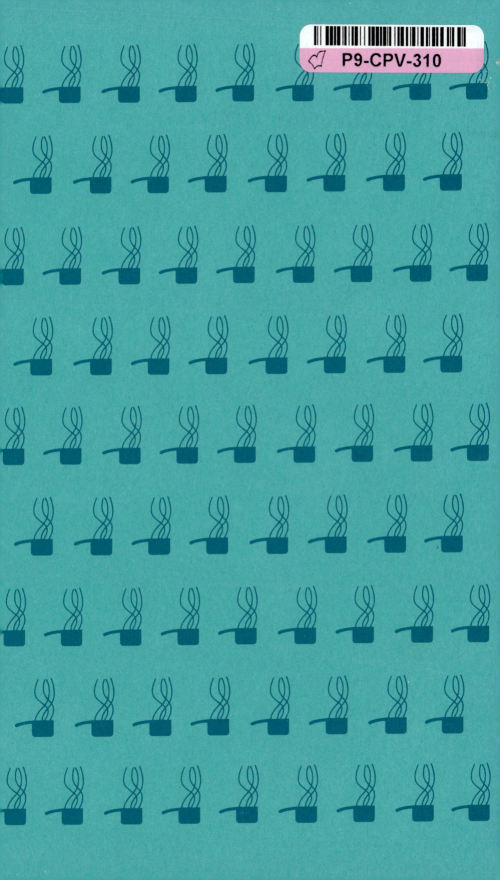

# ALPHⱭBET SⰝUP

## JEWISH FAMILY COOKING
## FROM A TO Z

PUBLISHED FOR THE BENEFIT OF THE
SOLOMON SCHECHTER DAY SCHOOLS

Additional copies of
**ALPHABET SOUP**
Jewish Family Cooking from A to Z
may be obtained by writing:

Solomon Schechter Day Schools
350 Maxine Cohen Memorial Drive
Northbrook, Illinois 60062
Attention: Cookbook Sales

First Edition, First Printing, January, 1990.

Printed in the United States of America
Saltzman Printers, Inc.
50 Madison Street
Maywood, Illinois 60153

To the students
of the
Solomon Schechter Day Schools,
past, present and future;
to our children and to your children;
to the future of our people,
in their hands.

# TaBLe oF COnTENtS

*Editor*
Karen Sager
*Co-editor*
Chris Erenberg
*Design Editor*
Jennifer Gritton
*Illustration*
Jackie Siegel

*Food & Testing Editors*
Myra Dorf
Hannah Engelman
Janet Resnick
Sybil Zimmerman

*Additional Illustration*
The Students of the
Solomon Schechter Day Schools
Jennifer Gritton
*Additional Design*
James Knippen

*Proofreading*
Barbara Wohlstadter
Carol Levenberg
*Word-processing*
Toni McGuire
Deborah Nathan
*Index*
Sharon Cramer

*Consultant & Sales Chairman*
Judy Schuster
*Publicity & Marketing*
Dotty Fiedler
Carol Levenberg
Jay Levenberg
Lewis Saltzman
Mark Siegel

*Committee*
Bonny Barezky
Elayne Baum
Fortunee Belilos
Dorene Benuck
Lois Berkson
Anne Bielenberg
Helene Blivaiss
William Branda
Debby Braun
Hilary Braun
Marleen Chesler
Adele Cohen
Helen Dredze
Rachel Engler
Naomi Fisher
Fran Fogel
Beverly Fox
Sonia Frazin
Barbara Goldman
Jan Goldman
Nancy Goldstein
Janet Grossman
Ahouva Hatzbani
Diane Hoffman
Gail Isaacson
Rebecca Isenberg
Chana Kaufman
Joanne Kestnbaum
Barbara Lavin
Naomi Levi
Arlene Levin
Judy Miller
Carol Minkus
Faye Newman
Sheila Patt
Jona Peretz
Linda Pilloff
Naomi Pollak
Aviva Rodin
Susan Rosenberg
Judi Rosenthal
Beth Sair
Terri Schwartz
Shoshana Seidman
Jane Shapiro
Hope Sheppard
Naomi Strauss
Irene Sufrin
Gail Taxy
Ruth Taxy
Dahlia Tesher
Larry Wasserman
Jeanne Weinstein
Judy Wolkin

this art
by
Schechter
Students

# INTRODUCTION & ACKNOWLEDGEMENTS

*ALPHABET SOUP: Jewish Family Cooking From A to Z* is the culmination of four years of work by devoted parents and friends of the Chicago Area Solomon Schechter Day Schools. They have pooled their professional expertise in many fields to create a sophisticated and innovative kosher cookbook which they hope will be a welcome addition to every Jewish kitchen.

The editors began by collecting recipes from the Solomon Schechter community of parents, teachers, students, grandparents, alumni, and friends. They were pleased to find not only "heirloom" recipes and old favorites, but also many new dishes created for a modern culinary approach, as well as gourmet specialties donated by professional chefs, cooks, and caterers. These include exciting international cuisine; recipes for the food processor, wok, and microwave oven; healthy and easy snacks for kids; vegetarian and calorie-trimmed dishes; and authentic, diverse holiday traditions.

A large committee of experienced cooks took great care to test, taste, and where necessary, revise, each recipe in kosher kitchens. The editors selected and, in some cases, combined or expanded, the most savory and successful entries. The *Holiday and Special Menus* bring together a wide variety of recipes from all the chapters, as well as special holiday dishes and notes; Pesach recipes are keyed throughout the book; and *Kids* has its own key to safety and age-level for budding chefs. The editor, co-editor, design editor and illustrator worked closely together to co-ordinate the content and graphic design for ease and pleasure of use, and to create a book that would reflect both the sophistication and the *hamischness* of the Solomon Schechter community, as well as the charm and imagination of its students.

The Solomon Schechter Day Schools offer a unique education through an integrated curriculum of Jewish and general studies.

The schools enroll all children regardless of family income or ability to pay tuition. Indeed, more than thirty-five per cent of the families receive some form of tuition scholarship. All proceeds from the sale of *ALPHABET SOUP* will provide scholarship assistance and help maintain the high educational standards of the Solomon Schechter Day Schools.

The editor and co-editor wish to gratefully acknowledge Rabbi Samuel Fraint of Moriah Congregation of Deerfield and Jay Leberman, Director of the Sager Solomon Schechter Day School of Northbrook, for reading *Holidays* and *Key to Kashrut* and making helpful suggestions to Karen Sager in her preparation of these sections; Miriam Lobstein, art teacher at the schools, for directing the projects that provided the delightful student drawings throughout the book; Toni McGuire for the long hours spent in typing the first draft; James Knippen of *Jennifer and James: Graphic Design*, for his valuable contributions to the book design; Barry Sufrin, for his legal advice and assistance; Barbara Wohlstatder and her editors at *Word for Word, Inc.;* and Robert Hartle of *MediaWorks* for his computer expertise. We also thank Judy Wolkin, co-editor of *Essabissel—and a Whole Lot More!*, and Sybil Zimmerman, author of three Israeli cookbooks, for their advice in the early phases of the book; and Judy Schuster, Director of Development for the schools, for her encouragement and support from the beginning of the project. We further thank Mr. Weiner, the head of catering at The King David, Jerusalem; and the Chicago Rabbinical Council, Joel Jacobs of *The Kosher Gourmet*, Selig's Delicatessan, and Sunset Foods for their time and assistance. Last, but always first in our hearts, we thank our children, who served as our inspiration as well as our purpose in undertaking this project.

We hope you enjoy using *ALPHABET SOUP* as much as we have enjoyed making it. *B'tayavon!*

# KEY TO KASHRUT

Each recipe is marked with at least one of the following symbols:

**D** DAIRY RECIPE: Contains milk or milk products.

**M** MEAT RECIPE: Contains meat or meat products.

**P** PAREVE RECIPE: Contains neither milk nor meat products.

**KP** KOSHER FOR PASSOVER: In accordance with the special dietary laws for Pesach. "KP" recipes are marked throughout the book, as well as in the PESACH section.

*The recipes in this book have been tested in kosher kitchens.*

*"Thou shalt not seethe a kid in its mother's milk."*
—Exodus 23:19

Throughout their history, Jews have adapted the various local cuisines of the many countries they have inhabited to the laws of *kashrut*, creating a wealth of diverse and delicious culinary traditions. The laws of *kashrut* present a unique and exciting challenge to the modern Jewish American cook, who is concerned about health and speed of preparation as well as taste and religious identity.

The laws of *kashrut* are the dietary rules of Judaism. Rabbi Samuel Dresner defines *kashrut* "... as a part of Judaism's attempt to hallow the act of eating by teaching us reverence for life." The laws may be divided into the following categories:

1. Separation of meat from milk products.
2. Permitted and forbidden foods.
3. Proper ritual slaughtering of animals, *sh'chitah*, designed to cause the animal the least amount of pain.
4. Proper preparation or *kashering* of meat to remove blood.

The latter two categories govern the meat which may be eaten by Jews. The former two categories give kosher cuisine its particular character. In addition, the festival of Pesach has its own dietary laws, largely derived from the added prohibition against *hametz* (leavening), which is central to observance of the holiday.

It is fascinating to note that in an age in which authenticity is associated with individual freedom and choice, the word *kosher*—denoting accordance with an elaborate system of dietary rules and obligations—has entered the English language with the additional meanings of "genuine" or "authentic." It suffices to say, the only authentically Jewish cuisine is kosher. We think you will find the recipes in this book appealing, and we hope they will serve to encourage and enrich the observance of *kashrut*.

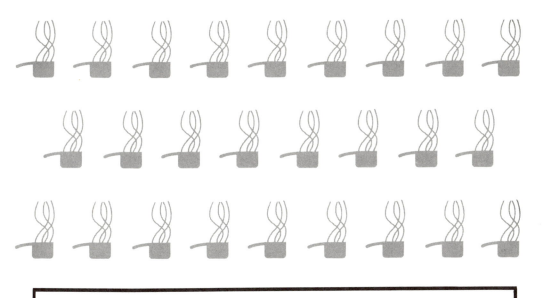

# APPETIZERS

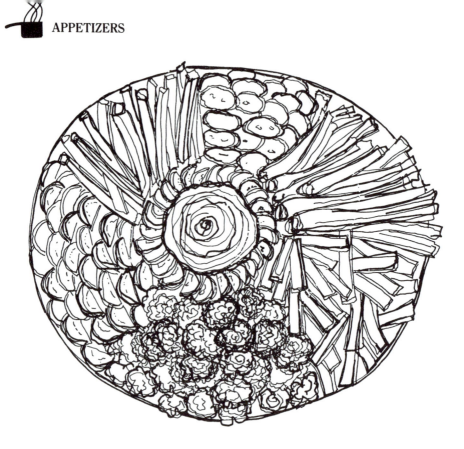

# "BON APPÉTIT" VEGETABLE DIP  *Bonnie Krbec*

1 cup mayonnaise
1 cup sour cream
1½ Tbsps. grated
  dehydrated onion
1 Tbsp. fresh or dry
  parsley
1 tsp. dill
1 tsp. "Bon Appétit"
  seasoning

1. Mix all ingredients together well.
2. Chill 4 to 6 hours before serving.
Serve with any raw vegetable.
*(Best with fresh, finely minced onion.)*
*The main seasonings in "Bon Appétit" are*
*celery seed, onion, and salt, which, in*
*combination, give this dip its distinctive flavor.*

# MY MOTHER'S DIP  *Bonny Barezky*

8 ounces cream cheese
3 Tbsps. whipping cream
1 small can black olives,
  chopped
4 Tbsps. onions, chopped
½ tsp. garlic powder

Combine all ingredients and mix.
Serve with wheat crackers or vegetables.

# TANGY VEGETABLE DIP *Ruth Aberman* Ⓓ

8 ounces cream cheese
½ cup tomato juice
1 package dry Italian salad
  dressing

1. Soften cream cheese.
2. Blend with tomato juice and dressing.
3. Chill.
*Delicious with raw vegetables—arrange a beautiful platter of broccoli, cauliflower, zucchini, cherry tomatoes, mushrooms, radishes, and other vegetables.*

# SPINACH DIP *Ruth Aberman* Ⓓ

1 10-ounce package frozen
  spinach
1 8-ounce can water
  chestnuts
3 green onions, chopped
  fine
1 cup mayonnaise
1 cup sour cream

1. Defrost and squeeze moisture from spinach.
2. Drain and chop water chestnuts.
3. Thoroughly blend all ingredients.
4. Chill.
Serve as a dip or as a stuffing for mushrooms and cherry tomatoes.
*Calorie conscious? Substitute low calorie mayonnaise and sour cream.*

# DILL DIP *Ruth Aberman* Ⓓ

1 pint sour cream
1 pint mayonnaise
3 Tbsps. dehydrated
  minced onion
3 tsps. dill seed
3 tsps. "Nature's Seasons"

1. Blend all ingredients thoroughly.
2. Chill overnight.
*Serve with RYE BREAD BASKET (see below) and/or raw vegetables.*

# RYE BREAD BASKET *Ruth Aberman* ◆P

1. Take 2 pounds unsliced rye bread (day-old is better) and cut in half horizontally.
2. Carve along inside of bottom half and scoop out inside as much as possible.
3. Cube inside. Then cube top half of rye also.
4. Fill rye bread shell with cubes and serve as accompaniment to DILL DIP, above.
*A bread basket like this adds a festive touch to many different dips and appetizers.*

## ⓓ TUNA - ARTICHOKE DIP  *Janet Resnick*

1 cup sour cream
1 cup mayonnaise
1 7-ounce can tuna, flaked
1 Tbsp. Worcestershire
  sauce
1 can artichokes, drained
  and sliced
1 medium red onion, sliced
Chili sauce
Tabasco sauce, dash

1. Mix together sour cream, mayonnaise, tuna, Worcestershire sauce, artichokes, and onion.
2. Add chili sauce until mixture turns pink.
3. Add dash of Tabasco, to taste.

## ⓓ BAKED ARTICHOKE SPREAD  *Irit Jacobson*

1 small jar marinated
  artichokes
1 cup mayonnaise
1 cup Parmesan cheese
2 to 3 cloves garlic
Tabasco sauce, dash

1. Blend all ingredients in food processor.
2. Put into a small casserole dish. Bake in 350 degree oven for 20 to 25 minutes. Serve with crackers.
Makes 6 servings.
*Different and delicious!*

# HOT ARTICHOKE APPETIZERS *Ruth Taxy* **D**

2 cups mayonnaise
1¼ cups Parmesan cheese
1 tsp. Dijon mustard
½ tsp. onion, grated
Worcestershire sauce, dash
2 cans artichoke hearts,
  quartered and drained

1. Mix together mayonnaise, Parmesan cheese, mustard, onion, and Worcestershire sauce. Place artichokes in shallow dish (quiche pan or Pyrex dish).
2. Pour mixture over artichokes and spread evenly. Bake in 350 degree oven for 15 to 20 minutes or until golden brown and puffy. Serve hot on buttered, toasted bread triangles, crackers, or rye slices.

# CURRY DIP *Catherine Akiva* **P**

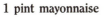

1 pint mayonnaise
3 Tbsps. chili sauce
1 Tbsp. onion, grated
¼ tsp. salt
¼ tsp. pepper
1 Tbsp. Worcestershire
  sauce
1 Tbsp. curry powder or
  to taste
1 or 2 cloves of garlic,
  pressed or ⅛ to ¼ tsp.
  garlic powder

1. Mix all ingredients together at least 24 hours before serving.
2. Chill.

# DIP FOR FRESH VEGETABLES *Irene Sufrin* **D**

1 cup mayonnaise
1 cup sour cream
¼ cup onion, grated
¼ cup parsley, chopped
5 ounces water chestnuts,
  grated
2 Tbsps. candied ginger,
  chopped
2 cloves garlic, pressed
1 tsp. soy sauce
Tabasco sauce, dash

1. Mix in order listed.
2. Chill 24 hours before serving.

13

#  MARIANA'S SPINACH DIP  *Eva Sideman*

| | |
|---|---|
| 1 10-ounce package frozen chopped spinach | 1. Thaw the spinach. Drain for several hours. |
| ½ cup parsley, chopped | 2. Mix with parsley, green onions, salt, pepper, and mayonnaise. |
| ½ cup green onions with tops, chopped | 3. Chill to blend flavors. |
| ½ tsp. salt | Makes 12 servings. |
| ½ tsp. pepper | |
| 2 cups mayonnaise | |

# ANCHOVY DIP  *Karen Sager*

1½ cups mayonnaise
1 2-ounce tube anchovy paste
1 4-ounce can chopped ripe olives

1. Measure mayonnaise into a small bowl. Add anchovy paste. Whip together with a fork.
2. Add olives and blend.
3. Refrigerate overnight.
Serve as a dip with crudités (carrot sticks, celery sticks, cucumber slices, broccoli and cauliflower flowerettes, and cherry tomatoes).
*This recipe has been kept a carefully guarded family secret for many years. Why? Because it is so easy!*

# EGGPLANT CAVIAR  *Irene Sufrin*

1 large eggplant
2 cloves garlic, crushed
1 large onion, chopped
2 ripe tomatoes, chopped
1 green pepper, chopped
¼ pound mushrooms, chopped
½ cup olive oil (or vegetable oil)
1 15-ounce can tomato sauce
2 tsps. wine vinegar
½ tsp. oregano
½ tsp. basil
Salt, to taste

1. Cut a large oval out of top of eggplant and cut out the "meat," leaving a shell about ½-inch thick. Wrap the shell and keep it chilled in refrigerator.
2. Chop eggplant "meat." Put chopped eggplant, garlic, onion, tomatoes, green pepper, mushrooms, and oil in frying pan. Stir over high heat about 5 minutes.
3. Lower heat and add tomato sauce, vinegar, and seasonings. Simmer uncovered, stirring occasionally for 25 to 30 minutes, until thick and tender. Cool.
4. Put in food processor to chop the mixture (4 or 5 pulses). Season with salt. Chill.
5. When ready to serve, fill the shell with the "caviar." Serve with crackers, pita, celery sticks, or mushrooms.
*Very festive and appropriate for Sukkot. Can be served beautifully in an eggplant shell "basket."*

# QUICK BLENDER HUMMUS   *Chris Erenberg*   P

3 Tbsps. sesame seeds
2 cloves garlic, chopped
½ cup vegetable oil
1 19-ounce can chick peas,
  drained and rinsed
¼ cup lemon juice
2 Tbsps. parsley, chopped
Salt and pepper, to taste

1. Gently roast sesame seeds in small skillet about 5 minutes until golden brown.
2. In blender, pureé sesame seeds, garlic, salt, pepper, and ¼ cup of the oil. Slowly add chick peas.
3. Alternately add the oil and the lemon juice until all ingredients are added and mixture is smooth.
4. Add chopped parsley as a garnish.
Makes 2 cups.
*Serve with toasted pita bread wedges.*
*Very good if made with olive oil.*

# MIRIAM'S EGGPLANT SALAD   *Miriam Spun*   P

2 medium eggplants
1 clove garlic, finely
  minced
2 Tbsps. lemon juice
2 Tbsps. fresh parsley,
  finely minced
1½ tsps. salt
¼ tsp. pepper
⅔ cup mayonnaise

1. Pierce eggplants and place on a baking sheet in oven turned onto "broil."
2. Broil 45 minutes to an hour until soft to the touch. Turn once, approximately half way through the cooking time.
3. Cool eggplants until warm to the touch; peel them.
4. Combine eggplants with garlic in blender or food processor, or mash together with a spoon.
5. Add lemon juice, parsley, salt, and pepper.
6. Stir in mayonnaise last by hand, adding more or less for taste and consistency.
*Serve as a dip with raw vegetables, crackers, or chips. Miriam has been keeping customers at "Selig's Delicatessen" well supplied with her delicious eggplant salad for many years. We thank her for sharing her secret recipe!*

##  HERRING SALAD  Sonia Frazin

1 large jar herring,
  drained and diced
1 large green pepper, diced
1 large purple onion,
  thinly sliced
2 carrots, grated
1 small can pitted black
  olives, sliced
1 cup sour cream
½ cup mayonnaise
1 Tbsp. celery seed
2 tsps. lemon juice
¼ cup sugar (scant)

1. Drain and dice one large jar of herring. Add green pepper, purple onion, carrots, and black olives. Drain everything and mix.
2. Add sour cream, mayonnaise, celery seed, lemon juice, and sugar.
Keeps about one week.
*Be sure to make it a day ahead so the flavors can blend.*

## CHOPPED ("GEHAGDE") HERRING  Hannah Engelman

2 schmaltz herrings, bones
  removed
1 big Granny Smith apple
1 onion
2 slices white bread,
  soaked in vinegar
2 hard boiled eggs,
  chopped
Sugar, to taste
  (about 4 Tbsps.)
Parsley

1. Clean herring with sharp knife. Soak overnight in cold water.
2. Drain herring. Chop in food processor, bit by bit.
3. Cut, peel, and pare apple. Chop in food processor.
4. Peel and chop onion and add to mixture in food processor.
5. Place herring mixture in bowl. Add soaked bread. Mix. Add one of the chopped eggs.
6. Add sugar to taste. Spread on platter.
7. Separate white and yolk of remaining hard-boiled egg. Chop each part separately.
*For holidays, garnish herring spread with parsley and chopped white and yellow of egg as desired, e.g., in shape of Mogen David or Menorah (use more than one hard-boiled egg for this if necessary). This is a special South African recipe.*

## HERRING APPETIZER  Nancy Shapiro

1 7½-ounce jar herring
  salad
1 tart apple, grated
1 hard boiled egg, mashed

1. Put herring salad in a bowl. Add mashed egg and grated apple.
2. Mix all ingredients together and chill.
Makes 4 servings.

16

Carrot

## PICKLED HERRING  *Hannah Engelman*  Ⓟ

2 Schmaltz herrings (bones removed)
White vinegar
Water
½ cup sugar
10 bay leaves
Peppercorns

1. Clean herrings and soak in bowl of cold water overnight.
2. Slice herrings in 2-inch pieces.
3. Make a solution of ½ water, ½ white vinegar —enough to fill 2 large jars. Add sugar, bay leaves, and peppercorns.
4. Divide herring pieces into 2 jars. Pour mixture into both jars. Add extra sugar and vinegar if desired to taste. Let stand for at least 2 days.

## LOX INCOGNITO HORS D'OEUVRES  *Karen Sager*  Ⓓ

2 ounces lox, nova or belly, as preferred
8 ounces cream cheese
Lemon juice from fresh wedge
White pepper, dash
2 large cucumbers, seedless English are preferable, when available
Watercress leaves, 1 bunch

1. Prepare a "mousse" by blending the lox, cream cheese, lemon juice, and white pepper in a food processor. Chill 1 hour or longer.
2. Peel cucumbers or run fork prongs lengthwise down cucumber peel for a "flowery" look. Slice cucumbers approximately ¼-inch thick. Cucumber slices may be cut into fancy shapes with cookie cutters, if desired.
3. One hour before serving, soften lox "mousse" with a wooden spoon. Press into a pastry bag with a leaf tip.
4. Squeeze out two lox leaves onto each cucumber slice. Add a watercress leaf for decoration.
Makes approximately 40 hors d'oeuvres.
*Martha Stewart calls this "Smoked Salmon Mousse"!*

## ❶ TUNA SPREAD *Helene Blivaiss*

1 8-ounce package cream
  cheese, softened
3 Tbsps. chili sauce
2 dashes Tabasco sauce
1 Tbsp. onion, minced
2 6½-ounce cans tuna,
  drained and flaked

1. Mix all ingredients except tuna in food
processor or blender.
2. Add tuna. Turn processor on and off to
lightly mix.
3. Put into greased mold. Refrigerate until ready
to serve.
Unmold and serve with crackers or vegetables.

## ❶ TUNA MOUSSE *Lois Wallace*

1 can tomato soup,
  undiluted
1 package unflavored
  gelatin, dissolved in
  ⅓ cup warm water
  (may be omitted for
  soft spread)
1 cup mayonnaise
8 ounces cream cheese,
  softened
1 cup celery, finely
  chopped
1 cup onion, finely
  chopped
2 7-ounce cans tuna,
  drained

1. Heat soup in a sauce pan.
2. Add gelatin.
3. Pour into food processor. Add mayonnaise
and cream cheese. Process until blended.
3. Add celery and onion and process 1 or 2
seconds.
4. Add tuna and process again 1 or 2 seconds
until mixed. Do not overblend.
May be mixed by hand.
Serve with crackers.

## ❶ SALMON BALL *Philip Waitzman*

1 7-ounce can salmon
  (bones removed)
2 to 3 Tbsps. red
  horseradish
1 to 2 Tbsps. dried instant
  minced onions (to taste)
1 Tbsp. lemon juice
1 8-ounce package cream
  cheese, softened
1 2-ounce package pecans,
  chopped (optional)

1. Bone salmon and mash.
2. Add horseradish, onions and lemon juice;
blend together.
3. Soften and mash cream cheese.
4. Add all ingredients to cream cheese and mix
thoroughly.
Roll into a ball, sprinkle chopped pecans on
top, and refrigerate until firm. Serve with
crackers or matzah or as a spread on bagels.

# SALMON MOUSSE  *Mitchell Taxy*   Ⓓ

½ cup tomato soup
1 package unflavored
  gelatin
½ tsp. salt
¾ cup mayonnaise
3 ounces cream cheese
½ cup celery, chopped
½ cup onion, finely
  chopped
1 large can salmon, well
  drained

Dill Sauce:
1 cup sour cream
1 cup mayonnaise
2 Tbsps. dill weed

1. Heat tomato soup, gelatin, and salt slowly until gelatin is dissolved. Cool.
2. Mix mayonnaise, cream cheese, celery, onion, and salmon in separate bowl.
3. Mix together tomato mixture with salmon mixture and chill overnight. This can be molded in greased 1-quart mold.
4. For sauce, combine sour cream, mayonnaise, and dill.
Garnish with parsley, olives, pimento, and cucumbers.
*This also makes a delicious main course when served with the dill sauce.*

# CAVIAR MOLD  *Laurel Feldman*   ◆P

1 jar black lumpfish caviar
½ onion, grated
6 hard boiled eggs
1 envelope unflavored
  gelatin
2 Tbsps. lemon juice
2 Tbsps. water
1 cup mayonnaise
1 tsp. Worcestershire sauce
1 Tbsp. anchovy paste

1. Grate onions with steel blade of food processor.
2. Chop hard boiled eggs in food processor.
3. Dissolve gelatin in lemon juice and water in small bowl.
4. Add to food processor with Worcestershire sauce, mayonnaise, and anchovy paste.
5. Fold in caviar.
6. Place in well greased mold. Cover with wax paper. Chill.
7. Unmold onto bed of romaine lettuce. When unmolded, decorate with olives (fish eyes) and pimento (fish fins). Serve with cocktail rye.
*Very festive in a fish-shaped mold.*

## P EGG SALAD MOLD Nancy Goldstein

2 dozen hard boiled eggs
1 green pepper (optional)
1 small jar pimento
(drained)
2 Tbsps. chili sauce
2 to 4 Tbsps. mayonnaise
½ onion, grated
1 tsp. salt
Olives to garnish

1. Grind egg, pepper, and pimento.
2. Add all other ingredients and mix well.
3. Pour into greased mold and chill.
4. To serve, unmold and garnish.
Serve with crackers or rye bread.
A 4-cup mold holds ¾ recipe.
*This is a molded salad that can be used for an appetizer.*

## P TEA EGGS Miriam Steinberg

1 dozen small eggs
1 tsp. kosher salt
1 Tbsp. light soy sauce
1 Tbsp. dark soy sauce
¼ tsp. kosher salt
2 whole star anise
2 Tbsps. black tea leaves
1 cinnamon stick
2 slices fresh or dried
orange peel, *or* 2 Tbsps.
spiced dark tea leaves

1. Hard cook eggs with salt, cool and drain. Tap each egg lightly with a spoon until it is covered with many fine cracks.
2. Place cracked eggs in saucepan; add enough water to cover. Add remaining ingredients and heat to a boil, stirring near the top to submerge the tea leaves. Reduce heat to a steady slow simmer; cover pot and simmer 2 hours.
3. Add more water, sparingly, if needed. Remove from heat.
4. Keep eggs in steeping liquid up to 2 days; the longer the steeping time, the richer the flavor.
5. Peel eggs just before serving. Store unpeeled eggs in the refrigerator for up to 5 days.
Makes 12 to 18 servings.
*Looks gorgeous! Very unusual taste.*

# GEFILTE FISH

P

So closely identified with Ashkenazi cuisine that folk stories have been written about its origins and significance, Gefilte Fish, literally "stuffed" fish, derives its name from the fact that the ground fish mixture was traditionally stuffed back into the fish skin for cooking. Today it is commonly prepared in a way similar to the French *quenelle*: the ground mixture is formed into balls and simmered in a stock made from the heads, skins, and bones of the fish. Traditionally eaten on so many holidays, (see HOLIDAYS, pp. 360-381, for menus) recipes for this delicacy are often kept secret and treasured like family heirlooms. We thank our four contributors for sharing theirs with us.

*Hints for preparation:*
*1. Figure a yield of ½ pound filleted, ground fish per pound whole, raw fish.*
*2. Reserve fish bones, heads, and skins to make the stock.*
*3. Most fish markets will fillet and grind the fish for you.*

## DORIS'S GEFILTE FISH *Doris Roskin*

P

KP

3 pounds white fish
1 to 2 pounds lake trout
1 to 2 pounds pike
(Ground fish total weight:
   approximately 3 pounds)
1 Tbsp. matzah meal
1 Tbsp. salt
2 tsps. white pepper
Sugar, pinch
2 medium onions, chopped
3 eggs

Stock:
Fish bones, heads, skins
2 quarts water
2 to 3 carrots
2 onions
2 ribs celery
1 to 2 sprigs dill
   (optional)
Salt, to taste
White pepper, to taste

1. Grind or chop filleted fish; reserve bones, heads and skins.
2. Mix together chopped fish, matzah meal, salt, pepper, sugar, chopped onions, and eggs.
3. Place the fish bones, skins, and heads in a large pot. Add 2 quarts water, carrots, onions, celery, and dill (optional). When mixture has come to a boil, remove the fish parts from the stock, and skim the top of the soup. Add salt and white pepper to taste.
4. Using an ice cream scoop, scoop up fish mixture and form into a ball in your hand. Place gently into the boiling stock. When all the mixture is formed and in the soup, cover the pot and simmer 2 hours.
5. Uncover and simmer 2 hours more. Cool and refrigerate.
Makes 10 to 12 pieces.

21

## ⬥ PHYLLIS'S GEFILTE FISH *Phyllis Cantor*

KP 6 pounds (weight ground)
whitefish, buffalo,
pike, and trout, ground
3 onions, grated
2 carrots, grated
1 stalk celery, grated
4 extra large eggs
¼ cup matzah meal
1 cup water (more may be
needed)
1 tsp. white pepper
2 tsps. black pepper
6 tsps. salt
3 to 4 carrots

Broth (stock):
Fish bones and heads
2 onions, sliced
2 carrots, sliced
1 tsp. black pepper
2 tsps. salt

1. Mix fish, grated vegetables, eggs, water, and seasonings in electric mixer for 10 minutes. (I mix in small batches.) Add more water if mixture is too thick.
2. Wash bones and heads and lay on bottom of large pot.
3. Add sliced carrots and onions to bottom of pot on top of bones. Cover with water (just enough so that pot is ¼ full). Bring to boil.
4. Make fish balls. Before cooking fish, slice carrots. Indent top of each fish ball and put carrot slice in the indentation. Carrots will remain in fish during cooking.
5. Lay fish balls in pot as stock is boiling. Return to a boil, cover and simmer for 3 hours. Allow steam to escape last 2 hours.
6. Strain stock, throw away bones. Fish will settle in pot shortly before fish is done.

*This recipe makes 30 pieces of fish. Even that may not be enough. Family and friends love it!*

## ⬥ ARLENE'S GEFILTE FISH *Arlene Levin*

KP 3 pounds (weight ground)
of 3 varieties of fish
(whitefish, trout, and
pike)
1 carrot
1 onion
2 eggs
3 tsps. salt
1½ tsps. white pepper
2½ Tbsps. matzah meal
1 cup ice cold water

Stock:
Fish heads, bones, and
skins
2 quarts water
1 tsp. salt
½ tsp. pepper
Sugar, pinch
2 carrots, sliced
1 onion

1. Place heads, bones, and skins in large pot and add 2 quarts of water, 1 tsp. salt, ½ tsp. pepper, and a pinch of sugar. Boil for 30 minutes.
2. Meanwhile grind or put in food processor 1 carrot and 1 onion. Add fish, eggs, 3 tsps. salt, and 1½ tsps. white pepper.
3. Add matzah meal and water, a little at a time; adjust salt and pepper to taste.
4. Remove heads and bones from pot, and add 1 whole onion and 2 sliced carrots to pot.
5. Gently add fish balls into broth. Add warm water to covered fish balls, if necessary. Cover and bring to a boil.
6. Uncover, reduce heat and simmer for 2½ hours. (Stock will be reduced by half.) Carefully remove fish when cool. Place fish in a single-layer pan or casserole. Add 1 carrot slice on top of each piece. Cover and refrigerate.
Makes 12 to 15 pieces.

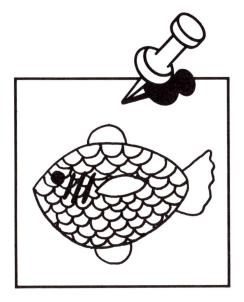

# GRANDMA AND GRANDPA KAY'S
# GEFILTE FISH *Barbara Ament*

**P**

2 pounds buffalo fish
2 pounds whitefish
2 pounds pike
2 pounds red snapper
2 pounds trout
(ground fish total weight:
4½ to 5 pounds)
3 pounds onions, ground
(may grind with fish)
6 eggs
½ cup water
⅓ to ½ cup matzah meal
1½ Tbsps. salt
White pepper, to taste

Stock:
3 ribs celery
1 pound carrots, sliced
in rounds
3 large onions, sliced
Fish bones and heads
2 cups water

KP

1. Place celery ribs and sliced carrots and onions in large stock pot. (Amount of stock increases during cooking; be sure pot is deep enough to accommodate.) Add bones and heads. Add 2 cups water, salt, and pepper to taste. Simmer.
2. To the ground fish, add ground onions, eggs, ½ cup water, matzah meal, salt, and white pepper to taste. Mix well.
3. Drop a small fish ball in simmering salt water and cook for 10 to 15 minutes to see if amount of matzah meal is enough to make it firm. Add fish patties, about 2½ to 3 inches in diameter, to stock. Simmer, covered, approximately 2 hours. Baste with soup stock periodically during cooking.
4. Strain and reserve stock; reserve carrots; refrigerate fish, carrots, and stock. (It is best to remove cooked gefilte fish to plate while still hot so patties do not stick together.)
Makes approximately 2 dozen.
*When serving, place fish on lettuce leaf. Top each piece with a carrot slice and 1 Tbsp. of soup stock. Best when left out for 15 minutes to remove chill.*

## ❖ MOCK SHRIMP TOAST *Arlene Levin*

½ pound sole fillets, finely chopped
½ tsp. salt
½ tsp. sugar
1 Tbsp. cornstarch
4 water chestnuts, chopped
2 green onions, chopped
1 egg, beaten
6 slices stale bread
Peanut oil for frying

1. Sprinkle fish with salt, sugar, and cornstarch. Mix in the water chestnuts and green onions, then the beaten egg. If mixture seems too wet to hold together, cover it well and refrigerate it for an hour or two.
2. Trim crusts off bread. Divide the mixture into 6 equal parts and spread the mixture on the 6 slices of trimmed bread, covering the tops completely.
3. With sharp knife, cut each piece of bread into 4 triangles. If fish is very fresh, the "shrimp toast" may now be refrigerated overnight. Place in a single layer, and cover well with foil over dish.
4. To fry, heat at least ½ inch of oil in a large deep skillet or 2 inches of oil in a pot. When hot, drop the bread, fish side down, adding one piece at a time to prevent the pieces from sticking to each other. When fish is light brown (2 minutes), turn the bread over with tongs and fry other side until dark brown but not burned. Drain.

## ❖ KREPLACH WITH A SLANT *Bonny Barezky*

1 6½ ounce can of white tuna, drained and flaked
½ cup walnuts, finely chopped
¼ cup green onion, minced
1 egg
2 tsps. soy sauce
½ tsp. sugar
1 Tbsp. fresh ginger, grated
Garlic powder, dash
Wonton wrappers*
Cooking oil

1. Mix together tuna, walnuts, green onion, egg, soy sauce, sugar, ginger, and garlic powder.
2. Place 1 tsp. of the mixture in the center of each wonton wrapper. Moisten the edges with water. Fold once into a rectangle, and pinch to seal edges.
3. Heat oil to 375 degrees. Deep fry several at a time in hot oil until lightly browned.
Drain on paper towels.
Serve with sweet and sour sauce.
Makes 36 wontons.
*See EGG ROLL AND WONTON SKINS, p. 328.
For Purim, fold kreplach in triangles (see p. 376).*

# FRIED EGG ROLLS *Debbie Stern*

**P**

1 large onion, diced
6 cloves garlic, sliced
1 cup carrots, grated
1 cup bamboo shoots, diced
1 package oriental or regular mushrooms
Soy sauce, to taste
Bay leaf, to taste
Salt and pepper, to taste
1 cup bean sprouts
2 packages tofu, sliced ½-inch thick
8 hard boiled eggs, diced
1 package egg roll skins*
Oil for frying

1. Sauté onion, garlic, carrots, bamboo shoots, and sliced mushrooms in a frying pan. Add soy sauce, bay leaf, salt, and pepper. Add bean sprouts at the last minute so they do not overcook.
2. Sauté tofu separately until golden brown.
3. To wrap egg rolls: Lay out a single wrapper on a plate. Have a bowl of clean water nearby. Place one spoonful of vegetable filling, half a spoonful of tofu cubes and half a teaspoon of diced hard boiled egg on the wrapper. Wrap the contents, folding the sides to keep filling in. To seal, dip fingers in water and spread on wrapper.
4. Fry in hot oil until golden brown. Serve with sweet and sour or mustard sauce.
*See EGG ROLL AND WONTON SKINS, p. 328.*

# BALI-BALI BEEF *Bonny Barezky*

**M**

6 ounces of rib roast, sliced (by butcher) ⅛-inch thick
1 cup soy sauce
2 cloves garlic, crushed
2 inches ginger root, peeled and chopped
⅓ cup sugar

1. Cut meat slices into 3 x 1 inch rectangles.
2. Put soy sauce, garlic, ginger, and sugar in a bowl. Add meat rectangles. Marinate 15 minutes.
3. Thread rectangles on bamboo skewers.
Broil 2 minutes on each side.
Makes 6 servings.
*Fast, easy and elegant!*

# MAHOGANY CHICKEN WINGS *Marla Dorf*

**M**

1½ cups soy sauce
¾ cup sherry
1⅛ cups Hoisin sauce*
¾ cup plum sauce*
18 green onions, minced
¾ cup cider vinegar
½ cup honey
6 to 7 pounds chicken wings (clip ends and disjoint)

1. Night before serving: In 3-quart saucepan, combine all ingredients except chicken. Bring to a boil, then cool.
2. Marinate chicken in cooled sauce overnight in a covered pan.
3. Next day: Place oven racks in upper and lower third of oven. Preheat to 375 degrees.
4. Oil 2 large roasting pans. Drain wings.
5. Divide wings between the 2 pans and bake uncovered for 1½ hours, basting every 20 minutes. Switch pans halfway through cooking.
6. Cool wings in layers on aluminum foil sheets.
Makes 20 servings.
*These may be difficult to find with kosher certification; see pp. 326 & 327.*

25

## D ZUCCHINI PIZZA *Janet Grossman*

2 cups zucchini, grated
½ tsp. salt
2 medium eggs
1 ounce Parmesan cheese, grated
2 Tbsps. flour
1 cup mozzarella cheese, grated (divided)
½ cup pizza sauce
½ onion (if desired)
¼ tsp. oregano
Non-stick cooking spray

1. Place zucchini in colander, sprinkle with salt, and let stand for 30 minutes.
2. Rinse and dry with paper towel.
3. Mix zucchini with eggs.
4. Add Parmesan, flour and ½ cup mozzarella.
5. Spray a quiche dish with non-stick cooking oil, then spread mixture.
6. Bake in a 350 degree oven for 20 minutes or until firm.
7. Broil for 3 minutes.
8. Top with pizza sauce, onion, oregano, and the remaining mozzarella.
9. Bake in 350 degree oven for 5 minutes.
Makes 2 to 3 servings.
*Low calorie pizza.*

## P EGGPLANT *Fran Fogel*

1 medium eggplant, sliced
1 cup matzah meal
1 cup bread crumbs or cornflake crumbs
1 Tbsp. garlic powder
1 Tbsp. onion powder
2 tsps. "Bon Appétit" seasoning
1 to 1½ tsps. freshly ground pepper
1 jumbo egg, whipped
½ cup olive oil
Dairy option: 3 Tbsps. Parmesan cheese

1. Peel the eggplant and slice very thin. Then depending on size, cut each slice in ½ or ⅓.
2. Place matzah meal, bread crumbs, garlic and onion powders, seasoning, pepper (and optional cheese) in shallow bowl. Beat eggs in another bowl.
3. Heat oil on medium to high flame.
4. Dip eggplant in egg, then dip in dry ingredients.
5. Fry until golden. Then turn and fry on other side. Drain on paper bag(s). Place on warming tray or in oven on very low heat until time to serve.
*When cooking with dairy option, sprinkle additional Parmesan cheese on cooked eggplant. Make sure to use the eggplant fast. The longer it sits, the more bitter it becomes. Paper bags are the most efficient material for draining fried foods; you may wish to cut and turn them inside-out.*

# MUSHROOM TARTLETS *Lois Wallace*

Pastry of 1 pie crust
2 Tbsps. butter
½ pound mushrooms,
  finely chopped
2 Tbsps. onion,
  finely chopped
½ tsp. salt
¼ tsp. pepper
1 Tbsp. flour
½ cup heavy cream or
  half and half
Olives, optional

1. Press small pieces of pie dough to line miniature muffin tins.
2. Heat butter in medium skillet over low heat. Add mushrooms, onions, salt and pepper. Cook until soft.
3. Sprinkle with flour. Cook 1 minute until liquid is absorbed.
4. Add cream and stir until mixture thickens.
5. Put a heaping teaspoonful of mixture in each tart shell.
6. Bake at 450 degrees for 15 to 20 minutes or until filling is firm and crust is brown.
Garnish with olive slices, if desired.
Makes 24 tartlets.

# SAM'S APPETIZER *Samantha Schuster*

2 packages of large
  capped mushrooms
Garlic salt, to taste
Margarine
3 ladle spoons buckwheat
  honey
Juice of 1 large orange

1. Heat margarine in frying pan.
2. Clean mushrooms. Cut out stem, place mushrooms top down in pan and season with garlic salt. Cook until mushrooms turn soft.
3. Add buckwheat honey and stir.
4. Squeeze in orange juice. Stir. Simmer about 10 minutes.
5. Set on low flame; when honey boils, it's ready to serve.

# CHOPPED LIVER *Arlene Levin*

1 pound beef liver
4 large onions, chopped
3 Tbsps. oil
3 hard boiled eggs
Salt, to taste

1. Salt liver on both sides. Broil just until done.
2. Sauté onions in oil until translucent.
3. Grind (using a food processor, if you have one) liver and onions with the oil and eggs. Add salt to taste.
*Easy delicious version of traditional favorite.*

# M SWEET AND SOUR MEATBALLS *Joyce Kamen*

4 pounds ground meat
2 packages onion soup mix
½ cup grape jam
2 cups brown sugar
24 ounces chili sauce
Juice of 1 lemon

1. Combine meat with onion soup.
2. Prepare sauce by mixing jam, brown sugar, chili sauce, and lemon juice in a pot; bring to a low boil.
3. Make meatballs and add to sauce. Simmer for 30 to 40 minutes.
4. Let sit overnight in refrigerator. Skim off top fat. Heat and serve. Makes 25+ servings.
*These meatballs are easy and freeze well.*

# UNCLE SY AND JEFF'S
# M FAVORITE MEATBALLS *Arlene Levin*

1¼ pounds ground beef
1 egg
¼ cup bread crumbs
½ tsp. salt

Sauce:
2 cups water
1 Tbsp. pickling spice
3 medium bay leaves
2 large celery ribs, diced
3 tsps. onion, chopped
1 cup ketchup
3 Tbsps. brown sugar

1. Combine the beef, egg, bread crumbs, and salt. Shape into meatballs.
2. Place water, pickling spice, bay leaves, celery, and onion into an 8-quart pot. Bring the mixture to a boil.
3. Add meatballs, cover and cook for 10 minutes.
4. Add ketchup and brown sugar to pot and mix. Cover and simmer for 10 minutes.
5. Uncover and simmer for 45 minutes. Makes 6 servings.

# M SESAME CHICKEN NUGGETS *Arlene Levin*

1½ pounds boneless, skinless chicken breasts
1 Tbsp. salad oil
1 Tbsp. light soy sauce
2 Tbsps. dry sherry
2 egg whites
½ tsp. ground ginger
4 Tbsps. bread crumbs
4 Tbsps. sesame seeds

1. Cut chicken into bite-sized cubes.
2. Stir in salad oil, soy sauce, sherry, egg whites, and ginger. Marinate 1 hour.
3. Combine bread crumbs and sesame seeds; roll chicken cubes in this mixture or shake in closed plastic bag.
4. Spray 9 x 13 inch baking pan with non-stick cooking spray. Arrange in single layer.
5. Bake uncovered in preheated 475 degree oven about 8 minutes.

## LECHO *Susie Weiss* `M`

6 tomatoes, sliced in chunks
3 green peppers, sliced
1 large onion, sliced
½ cup rice
Salt, to taste
6 hot dogs, sliced

1. Combine all ingredients in a sauce pan. Cook on medium to high flame, stirring constantly. Bring to a boil.
2. Cover and simmer 20 minutes, stirring frequently. Let stand 15 minutes to thicken.
*Great way to use the summer crop of tomatoes and green peppers. Kids love it!*

## GRANDMA GUSSIE'S STUFFED CABBAGE *Barbara Wohlstadter* `M`

2 large heads cabbage, parboiled
2 to 3 medium onions, sliced
6 ounces tomato paste
1 tsp. salt
6 Tbsps. brown sugar
2 pounds ground beef
2 eggs
½ cup bread crumbs or matzah meal
¼ cup onion, minced
Garlic powder
Parsley, chopped
1 Tbsp. cornstarch or potato starch

`KP`

1. Remove leaves of the cabbage. In a large stock pot (larger than 6 quarts, if possible) combine sliced onions, tomato paste, and 3 cups of water. Add salt and brown sugar.
2. Combine meat, eggs, bread crumbs or matzah meal, onion, and seasonings.
3. Place about 2 to 3 Tbsps. of meat mixture inside each cabbage leaf and roll tightly. Place in pot. Cook 2 hours on medium to low heat. If gravy is watery, mix 5 Tbsps. gravy with 1 Tbsp. cornstarch or potato starch and pour back into gravy; adjust seasoning.
Makes 9 servings.
*If rolls are made small, this is a lovely Shabbat appetizer. For Pesach, substitute matzah meal for bread crumbs and potato starch for cornstarch.*

## SALAMI - YOMMY *Bonny Barezky* `M`

3 pounds salami
12 ounces Dijon mustard
12 ounces apricot preserves
12 ounces "sweet 'n tart" sauce
Non-stick cooking spray

1. Score the salami ⅓-inch deep at ½-inch intervals.
2. Combine mustard, apricot preserves, and "sweet 'n tart" sauce.
3. Line a cookie sheet with foil and spray with non-stick cooking spray.
4. Spread salami with sauce mixture and place on cookie sheet.
5. Bake in 350 degree oven for 1½ hours, rotating every 20 minutes.
Serve in slices.
*Kids and men love this! For a variation, make two smaller salamis and/or try grilling.*

## M "EMPANADAS CRIOLLAS" Shoshana Eselevsky

1½ cups onions, minced
½ cup shortening
1 pound ground beef
¼ cup seedless raisins (optional)
¼ cup pine nuts (optional)
½ cup sweet red pepper, finely chopped
4 tsps. salt
⅛ tsp. pepper
¼ tsp. oregano
6 hard boiled eggs, cooled and chopped
5 cups flour (all-purpose)
¾ cup pareve margarine
1 cup water
2 dozen stuffed green olives
1 egg, slightly beaten

1. In a skillet, sauté onions in shortening until golden. Add meat and cook, stirring frequently, until lightly browned.

2. Add raisins, pine nuts, red pepper, 1½ tsps. salt, pepper, and oregano. Blend thoroughly. Cool. Add hard boiled eggs. Chill for at least one hour.

3. Sift together flour and remaining 2½ tsps. salt. Mix in pareve margarine until mixture resembles coarse meal. Add water, a little at a time, stirring lightly with a fork, using just enough water to hold ingredients together.

4. Shape into a ball. Chill for 30 minutes. Roll dough ⅛-inch thick on lightly floured surface. Cut into circles about 3½ inches in diameter.

5. On half of each round, place an olive and a rounded tablespoon of the meat mixture. Fold dough over meat and moisten edges. Seal edges securely by pinching with lightly floured fingers or fork.

6. Place on ungreased baking sheet. Brush over pastries with lightly beaten egg. Bake in 450 degree oven for 20 minutes.

Makes 2 dozen servings.

*"Empanadas" are traditional in Argentina and almost always served at cocktail parties and barbecues. They are best hot, but may be served cold as well. The bite-sized is best for hors d'oeuvres, but they also make an excellent luncheon dish in a larger size. Enjoy!*

OREGANO

# GOUGERE RING  *Janet Resnick*  Ⓓ

1 stick salted butter,
  cut into small pieces
½ tsp. salt
¼ tsp. pepper
1 cup all-purpose flour
4 whole eggs, at room
  temperature
Pinch of nutmeg
1½ cups Gruyere cheese,
  grated
1 egg yolk
1 Tbsp. milk (optional)
½ cup slivered almonds

1. Preheat oven to 375 degrees.
2. In saucepan combine butter, salt and pepper with 1 cup water. Boil over high heat until butter has melted.
3. Remove from heat and add flour all at one time. Return to low heat and mix for one minute. Remove from heat and cool for about a minute.
4. Beat in eggs one at a time, making sure each is completely mixed before adding the next.
5. Stir in nutmeg and 1¼ cups cheese (reserve remaining ¼ cup).
6. Heap large spoonfuls of dough on a buttered baking sheet to form a ring (the inside circle measuring about 7 inches).
7. Beat egg yolk with milk and spoon over top of the ring. Sprinkle the remaining cheese and almonds over the dough.
8. Bake for 15 minutes at 375 degrees, then reduce heat to 350 degrees and bake circle for another 40 to 45 minutes, or until golden brown and firm to the touch.
9. Cool at least 15 minutes. Fill center with a dip or just sprigs of fresh parsley. Break off pieces to eat.

# MEXICAN FUDGE  *Karen Barron*  Ⓓ

½ pound Cheddar cheese,
  grated
½ pound Monterey Jack
  cheese, grated
3 eggs
½ cup green taco or
  enchilada sauce
Tortilla or nacho chips

1. Combine grated cheeses and spread half the cheese in bottom of 9 x 9 inch baking pan.
2. Beat eggs and mix with taco sauce. Pour over cheese.
3. Spread remaining cheese on top and bake at 350 degrees for 30 minutes, until eggs are set and cheese is golden.
4. Remove from oven and cool slightly (so that eggs and cheese are firm enough to slice).
5. Cut into 1-inch squares and serve on corn chips.

## TART OF "IT'S NOT SHRIMP,"
**D** GOAT CHEESE AND PESTO *Janet Resnick*

**Crust:**
1½ lightly packed cups
  of flour
6 Tbsps. cold butter
2 Tbsps. solid shortening
2 to 3 Tbsps. ice water

**Filling:**
6 ounces imitation shrimp
2 Tbsps. goat cheese (or
  ½ cup Parmesan cheese)
2 Tbsps. prepared pesto
  sauce (see below)
1 medium tomato, thinly
  sliced

**Pesto:**
1 cup fresh basil leaves
1 Tbsp. pine nuts
½ tsp. minced garlic
3 Tbsps. olive oil

1. In processor bowl, blend flour, butter, and shortening with a few on/off pulses until crumbly. Through feed tube, slowly add ice water, one tablespoon at a time. Process until a ball forms. If a ball does not form and the dough is sticky, add a tablespoon of flour a little at a time and continue to process. If it is crumbly, add a little more water.

2. If time allows, wrap and refrigerate dough about one hour. When ready to use, roll it out on a floured surface and spread it in a 9 x 12 inch buttered baking dish, preferably with removable bottom.

3. Place aluminum foil over the dough and cover with baking weights. Bake in preheated 375 degree oven for 12 to 15 minutes or until edges start to brown. Remove foil and weights and bake another 5 to 6 minutes. Make sure the crust is crisp.

4. Prepare pesto by processing basil leaves, pine nuts, and garlic in processor bowl. Add oil through feed tube slowly, and puree until smooth.

5. Mix about 2 Tbsps. of the pesto with 2 ounces of goat cheese (or Parmesan, if substituting it for goat cheese). Set aside.

6. Pat dry the imitation shrimp, chop in small pieces and spread over the baked dough. Cover fish pieces with tomato and then spread pesto and goat cheese mixture over the tomatoes.

7. Bake in preheated 375 degree oven about 10 minutes or until the cheese and pesto are soft. Cool a few minutes and cut into squares. This can be served warm or at room temperature. Makes approximately 6 appetizer servings.

*The standard recipe for pesto sauce calls for Parmesan cheese; however, the Parmesan is too strong to use with goat cheese. If you wish to make more pesto than the 2 tablespoons required for this recipe, freeze the pesto and add Parmesan later as needed.*

# BEVERAGES

##  STRAWBERRY DAIQUIRI *Marla Dorf*

3 4-ounce cans frozen
pink lemonade
3 4-ounce cans water
1 4-ounce can frozen
orange juice
1 pint fresh strawberries,
hulls removed
⅓ of a fifth of light rum

1. Place all ingredients in a blender and puree.
2. Pour into an empty ½ gallon juice carton.
3. Freeze overnight or longer.
4. Defrost approximately 30 minutes and serve.
*This is a great party recipe because it may be made ahead in multiple batches—just be sure to have enough empty juice cartons on hand. A strawberry with stem left on makes a festive garnish for each glass.*

## HOT SANGRIA *Sybil Zimmerman*

1 pink grapefruit, cut into
sections
4 cups dry red wine
3 cups apple juice
1 6-ounce can orange
juice concentrate
1 small lemon, sliced
2 small oranges, sliced
2 Tbsps. brown sugar

1. Seven hours before serving: Combine in a pot grapefruit, wine, apple juice, and orange juice concentrate.
2. Let stand 7 hours.
3. Add lemon, orange slices, and brown sugar.
4. Heat and stir.
Makes approximately 8 to 10 servings.

## MULLED WINE *Sybil Zimmerman*

2 quarts dry red wine
1½ cups sugar
4½ tsps. lemon peel
½ cup water
2 cups lemon juice
1 whole nutmeg
24 cloves
3 cinnamon sticks
Peel of 1 orange

1. In a piece of cheesecloth, tie together nutmeg and cloves.
2. In a large pot, combine wine, sugar, lemon peel, water, and lemon juice. Bring to a boil.
3. Add cinnamon sticks, cheesecloth bag, and orange peel.
Bring to a boil. Serve warm.
Makes 16 servings.

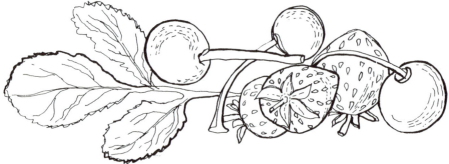

# PIMM'S HOLIDAY PUNCH  *Fran Fogel*

P

10 ounces "Pimm's No. 1
  Cup" (liquor)
1 liter "7-Up"
½ liter gingerale
½ liter cranberry-apple
  juice
1 lemon, sliced
1 lime, sliced
1 orange, sliced

1. Freeze water in a ring mold smaller than
your punch bowl.
2. Mix liquid ingredients together in punch bowl.
3. Float ice mold and fruit slices on top.
Makes approximately 8 servings.
*When doubling or tripling recipe, add 3 or 4*
*extra ounces "Pimm's."*

# PARTY PUNCH
# (FOR LITTLE OR BIG PEOPLE)  *Cele Benensohn*

D

½ gallon vanilla ice cream
  (*or* New York Cherry)
1 46-ounce can pineapple-
  grapefruit juice
1 quart gingerale
Strawberries *or* maraschino
  cherries *or* any decorative
  fruit for ice mold

1. Make a decorative ice mold by filling a ring
mold smaller than your punch bowl with water.
2. When water is partially frozen, but still
slushy, place fruit in any decorative fashion.
Return to freezer and freeze solid. (Best done at
least a day before serving.)
3. Just before serving, place ice cream in
punch bowl.
4. Pour juice and gingerale over ice cream and
stir. (Ice cream does not have to melt entirely.)
5. Float decorated ice mold on top. As the ice
melts, the fruit will float in the punch.
Makes approximately 8 servings.
*Doubles and triples easily.*

# LEMON LIMEADE  *Sybil Zimmerman*

P

⅓ cup juice of lemons
  and limes
⅓ cup sugar
⅓ cup boiling water
10 ice cubes
2½ cups cold water

1. In a non-breakable container, combine lemon
and lime juice, sugar, and boiling water. Stir
until sugar is dissolved.
2. Add ice cubes and cold water.
Makes 2 to 4 servings.

# ⓓ CAPPUCCINO *Bonny Barezky*

2 cups brewed coffee
2 cups milk
1 Tbsp. sugar
1 Tbsp. cocoa
1 shot brandy
1 shot Crème de Cocoa
Whipped cream
2 cinnamon sticks

1. Combine coffee, milk, sugar, cocoa, brandy, and Crème de Cocoa in a pot and bring to a boil.
2. Pour into cups and garnish with whipped cream and a cinnamon stick.
Makes 2 servings.
*Dessert, coffee, and after-dinner-drink in one!*

# ⓓ MOCHA CAPPUCCINO *Sybil Zimmerman*

4 tsps. chocolate chips
4 tsps. dried coffee
granules
1 cup milk
3 cups boiling water
¾ tsp. vanilla
6 tsps. sugar
½ tsp. cinnamon
⅛ tsp. allspice
1 tsp. brandy extract
Whipped cream

1. Combine boiling water and milk in a saucepan.
2. Stir in chocolate chips and coffee to dissolve.
3. Add vanilla, sugar, cinnamon, allspice, and brandy extract, and stir.
4. Pour into cups or mugs and garnish with whipped cream.
Makes 4 servings.

# ⓟ ISRAELI "TURKISH" COFFEE *Sybil Zimmerman*

2 cups water
2 Tbsps. coffee
(strong, espresso is best)
2 tsps. sugar
2 cardamon pods
(*Hel* in Hebrew)

1. Boil water in a coffee pot.
2. Add coffee grounds, sugar, and cardamon pods. Return to boil.
3. Remove from heat and let settle.
4. Return to heat; bring to boil; remove from heat; let settle. Repeat this process *seven* times total.
5. Pour into demitasse coffee cups.
Makes 6 servings.

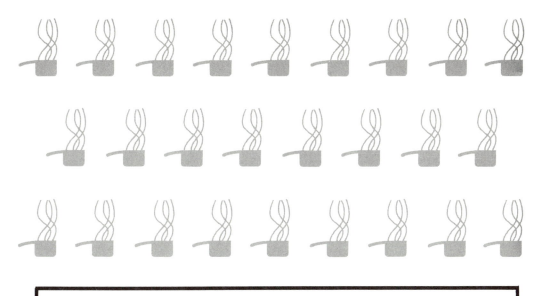

# BREADS

## ⓓ RAISIN - OAT BRAN MUFFINS *Florence Sager*

2½ cups oat bran cereal
(quick cooking or regular)
2 tsps. baking powder
½ tsp. baking soda
1 cup yogurt, buttermilk,
or skim milk, *or*
combination
2 eggs, *or* egg whites, *or*
½ cup egg-substitute
¼ cup brown sugar or
honey
2 Tbsps. vegetable oil
¼ cup nuts
¼ cup raisins or coconut
1 tsp. cinnamon, optional

1. Grease muffin tins lightly or use paper liners. Preheat oven to 400 degrees.
2. In large bowl, mix oat bran cereal with baking powder and baking soda.
3. In separate bowl, mix yogurt or milk, eggs, sugar or honey, and oil. Blend well with spoon or whisk.
4. Add liquid mixture to dry ingredients. Mix well. Add nuts and raisins or coconut.
5. Pour into muffin cups approximately ⅔ full. Bake in preheated oven approximately 15 minutes.
Makes 12 to 18 muffins.
*These tasty muffins are especially healthful for people on a low-cholesterol diet.*

# OAT BRAN BREAD *Sarita Blau*

**For "sponge"*:**
2 cups oat bran
4 cups flour
1 Tbsp. or 1 package dry
  yeast
5 cups water

**Add to "sponge":**
2 to 3 tsps. salt
½ cup sugar
½ cup wheat germ
½ cup shortening or
  margarine
2 to 4 eggs
5 to 6 cups flour,
  or enough to make a
  good dough

1. In a very large bowl or pan, mix together the 2 cups oat bran, 4 cups flour, and 1 Tbsp. dry yeast. Add the 5 cups water and stir well. Cover bowl with towel and let rise until mixture is bubbly and greater in bulk. This is called a "sponge" mixture, and, when ready, is used as a "starter" for the bread dough.

2. When the sponge has risen, stir it down, and add the salt, sugar, wheat germ, shortening, and eggs. Stir this mixture very well, then start adding flour. Add enough flour to make a dough that holds together for kneading, but is not stiff or dry. Knead well, about 10 to 15 minutes. If pan or bowl is large enough, knead right in pan or bowl. Otherwise, knead on floured surface.

3. Grease kneaded dough well and let rise about an hour, covered with towel, in bowl or pan.

4. While dough is rising, grease bread pans. You will need two or three large pans, or use two 9 x 5 inch loaf pans and two smaller ones.

5. When dough has doubled in bulk, punch down and divide to fit pans. Shape into loaves, or braid dough. Bread pans should be about half-filled with dough to make well-shaped loaves.

6. Let loaves rise in pans until doubled in bulk. Glaze, if desired, with egg white, egg yolk or whole beaten egg. Sprinkle glaze with poppy or sesame seeds, if desired.

7. Bake loaves at 350 to 375 degrees for 30 to 45 minutes, or until done.

8. Cut around pan and shake out loaves. Cool on rack or place crosswise over pans.

*The "sponge" method helps develop sufficient gluten to hold the bread together. Mix flour, yeast and liquid together first and let that rise. Next add the rest of the ingredients, including the eggs, then knead, and let rise. After much experimentation, I discovered that a large Rubbermaid dish pan allows room for both rising and kneading. This eliminates a lot of the flour mess usually connected with baking bread!*

## Ⓓ CINNAMON TWISTS Barbara Ament

Dough:
1 package yeast
¼ cup warm water
2 eggs, slightly beaten
1 cup margarine, melted
1 cup sour cream
4 cups flour
1 tsp. salt
1 tsp. vanilla

Topping:
1 cup sugar
1 tsp. cinnamon

1. Dissolve yeast in ¼ cup warm water.
2. Mix remaining dough ingredients together in a bowl until blended.
3. Add dissolved yeast and mix until smooth. Cover dough with damp cloth and refrigerate at least 2 hours or up to 2 days.
4. Combine 1 cup sugar and 1 tsp. cinnamon and sprinkle on board. Roll dough into 15 x 18 inch rectangle, and turn so both sides are covered. Fold in thirds. Cut slices and roll each in cinnamon-sugar. Twist.
5. Place on greased cookie sheet. Place ½ inch apart since they spread. Bake in 350 degree oven 15 minutes. These freeze well.
*Excellent!*

## GRANDMA ROSE'S
## Ⓓ CINNAMON ROLLS Gail Taxy

1 package yeast
1 cup sweet cream, lukewarm
1 cup lightly salted butter
5 egg yolks
½ cup granulated sugar
3 cups flour

Filling:
¼ cup butter, melted
2 tsps. cinnamon (or more)
½ cup sugar
½ to 1 cup raisins
½ to 1 cup nuts

1. Dissolve yeast in cream which has been gently heated to lukewarm.
2. Cream butter, yolks, and sugar in a large bowl, preferably with a lid. Add yeast and cream. Add flour.
3. Cover with lid and refrigerate for 4 hours or overnight.
4. Roll dough into a rectangular sheet, ¼-inch thick. Brush with melted butter. Mix together cinnamon and sugar and sprinkle on dough. Add raisins and nuts.
5. Grease six 8-inch round aluminum foil tins.
6. Cut roll into ½-inch slices and place 5 flat in each tin. Let rise 20 minutes.
7. Bake in 325 degree oven 20 to 30 minutes or until browned.
Can reheat or freeze in the same tins.
Yields 24 to 30 rolls.
*Easy and delicious. Tops may be brushed with melted butter and sprinkled with cinnamon and sugar, if desired. Cinnamon lovers may require more cinnamon—to taste!*

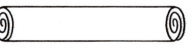

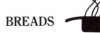

# CINNAMON COFFEECAKE BRAID  *Nancy Goldstein*  Ⓓ

4½ cups flour
½ to ¾ cup sugar
1½ tsps. salt
2 packages active dry yeast
¾ cup milk
½ cup water
1 cup margarine
3 egg yolks
2 tsps. ground cinnamon
Melted margarine

Glaze:
1 to 1½ cups powdered
  sugar
½ tsp. vanilla
¼ cup milk, warmed
Jelly (optional)

1. Combine 1½ cups flour, ¼ cup sugar, salt, and yeast in large bowl of electric mixer.
2. Heat milk, water, and 1 cup margarine. Add to dry ingredients.
3. Beat at medium speed 2 minutes. Add egg yolks and ½ cup flour. Beat at high speed for 2 minutes.
4. By hand, mix in remaining 2½ cups flour until stiff. Cover and refrigerate 4 hours.
5. Combine ¼ to ½ cup sugar and 2 tsps. cinammon, set aside.
6. On floured board, roll dough into 6 ropes 18 inches long. To make 2 coffee cakes, braid 3 ropes together. Seal ends. Place on greased cookie sheet.
7. Brush each braid with melted margarine. Sprinkle cinnamon mixture on top. Cover. Let rise until double in size (about 1 hour).
8. Bake uncovered in 375 degree oven 25 to 30 minutes.
9. To make glaze, mix powdered sugar, vanilla, and warm milk until smooth. Brush mixture over warm cake.
Optional: Before glazing, put spoonful of jelly (any flavor) in each "X" of braiding.
*Beautiful! Special for Yom Kippur break-fast.*

# BEST GUESS BANANA BREAD  *Sarita Blau*  Ⓓ

½ to ¾ cup vegetable
  shortening or margarine
½ cup sugar
1 Tbsp. molasses
3 eggs
4 cups flour, mixed with
½ tsp. baking soda
4 tsps. baking powder
6 to 8 bananas
At least 4 cups fruit
  and nuts, including:
  at least 1 cup chopped
  apricots or cranberries,
  1 cup walnuts, raisins,
  or dates

1. Cream shortening with sugar. Beat in molasses, then eggs, one at a time.
2. Stir in ⅓ of the flour; mash in ½ of bananas, then alternate flour and bananas.
3. Stir in dried fruits and nuts. Spoon batter evenly into two well greased loaf pans, and smooth tops.
4. Bake in 350 degree oven for 30 to 45 minutes. Cool out of pans and slice.

##  CHOCO - CHIP BANANA BREAD *Debbie Stern*

½ cup butter
¾ cup brown sugar
1 egg
1½ cups flour
1 tsp. baking soda
¾ tsp. salt
½ tsp. cinnamon
½ cup yogurt
1 to 1½ cups (2 to 3 ripe)
  bananas, mashed
1 cup chocolate chips
1 tsp. vanilla

1. Cream butter and brown sugar together until light and creamy. Beat in egg.
2. Sift together the flour, baking soda, salt, and cinnamon. Combine bananas and yogurt, stirring just enough to mix.
3. Add dry ingredients alternately with banana mixture to butter mixture, stirring just enough to combine well. Add chocolate chips and vanilla.
4. Pour into oiled 9 x 5 inch loaf pan. Bake in 350 degree oven 50 to 60 minutes or until done. Cool in pan 10 minutes.

## GERMAN HONEY BREAD *Charlotte Cleeland*

1¾ cups honey
½ cup sugar
1 Tbsp. butter, melted
¾ cup milk (approximately)
4 cups flour
4 tsps. baking powder
½ tsp. cinnamon
½ tsp. ground cloves
½ cup candied lemon and
  citron
¾ cup nuts, chopped

1. Mix honey and sugar. Add melted butter and milk.
2. Sift together flour, baking powder, cinnamon, and cloves. Add flour mixture by spoonfuls to honey mixture. Stir in candied lemon, citron, and chopped nuts. Batter should be fairly thick.
3. Fill well greased floured bread pans or three 1-pound coffee cans about ½ full. Bake slowly in 350 degree oven 1½ hours.
*This recipe was brought to the United States by a member of the Koenigsberger family who left Nazi Germany in the 1930's.*

## ZUCCHINI FRUIT BREAD *Sylvia Oliff*

1 cup oil
3 eggs
1 tsp. sugar
2 tsps. vanilla
8 ounces crushed
  pineapple, well drained
3 cups flour
1 tsp. salt
2 tsps. baking soda
1½ tsps. cinnamon
3 tsps. nutmeg
¼ tsp. baking powder
1 cup dates, chopped
1 cup pecans, chopped
2 cups zucchini, shredded

1. Beat together oil, eggs, sugar, and vanilla until thick. Add the pineapple, flour, salt, baking soda, cinnamon, nutmeg, baking powder, dates, nuts, and zucchini. Blend.
2. Place in two greased 9 x 5 x 3 inch loaf pans.
3. Bake in 350 degree oven for 45 minutes. Test with a toothpick. Turn off oven and let dry out about 5 minutes.
*Great for holidays — especially Sukkot.*

# SOUR CREAM COFFEECAKE   *Susan Markowitz*   **D**

¾ cup margarine or butter
1¼ cups sugar
2 eggs
1 tsp. vanilla
2 cups flour, sifted
1 tsp. baking powder
1 tsp. baking soda
½ tsp. salt
1 cup sour cream
¼ cup brown sugar
½ tsp. cinnamon

1. Cream margarine and 1 cup sugar until light and fluffy.
2. Beat in eggs, one at a time, then blend in the vanilla.
3. Sift together flour, baking powder, baking soda, and salt.
4. Add flour mixture to creamed mixture, alternately with sour cream, beginning and ending with the dry ingredients.
5. Spread batter evenly in a greased 9-inch square or tube pan.
6. Combine remaining ¼ cup sugar, brown sugar, and cinnamon. Sprinkle over top of the batter.
7. Bake in 350 degree oven 45 to 55 minutes or until top springs back when lightly touched with fingers.
8. Cool on wire rack before removing from pan.
*Yummy "quick" coffeecake!*

# SWEDISH SAFFRON BREAD   *Chris Erenberg*   **D**

3 yeast cakes, *or*
   2 envelopes dry yeast
   dissolved in ½ cup
   tepid water
¾ cup sugar
2 cups milk (warmed)
½ cup mashed potato
7 cups flour (approximately)
¾ cup butter or margarine
1 egg, beaten
1 tsp. saffron (or ⅛ tsp.
   ground cardamon)
1 tsp. salt
1 cup white raisins
½ cup candied citron,
   orange peel, and cherries
¼ cup ground almonds
   (optional)
1 tsp. almond extract

Icing:
1 cup powdered sugar
½ tsp. almond extract
2 to 3 Tbsps. water

1. Dissolve yeast and 1 Tbsp. sugar in water. When yeast mixture bubbles, add lukewarm milk and mashed potato.
2. Add 3 cups flour. Blend in dough. Let mixture rise until double in size.
3. Cream together butter and sugar. Add beaten egg. Combine with flour mixture. Add saffron and salt.
4. Add raisins, candied peels, almonds, and almond extract. Knead in rest of flour (add more if needed, to make a springy dough). Place in bowl. Let rise until double in size.
5. Push down dough and let rise again until more than double in size. Shape into circles or twisted strands and let rise in greased pans until double in size.
6. Bake in 350 degree oven for 45 to 50 minutes, or until done.
7. Add almond extract and water gradually to powdered sugar, stirring until a smooth icing forms. Ice bread while still warm, then sprinkle top with ground almonds.
*A wonderful coffeecake bread for holidays and entertaining.*

## ⓓ YOGURT AND HERB BREAD  *Marsha Arons*

1 cup unbleached
  white flour
1 cup whole wheat flour
1 tsp. baking powder
½ tsp. baking soda
½ tsp. salt
4 Tbsps. butter, melted
2 large eggs, beaten
1 cup firm plain yogurt
⅓ cup light honey
1 tsp. dried dill
½ tsp. dried oregano
½ tsp. dried basil
½ tsp. dried tarragon

1. Sift together flours, baking powder, baking soda, and salt. Make a well in the center of bowl.
2. Beat together melted butter, eggs, yogurt, and honey until foamy. Add the herbs. Beat well.
3. Pour liquid-herb mixture in the center of dry ingredients and mix with wooden spoon.
4. Pour into well-buttered loaf pan and bake in 350 degree oven 40 to 50 minutes or until knife inserted in center is clean.
*Best if left in refrigerator for a few days so herbs can mingle, but this rarely happens, because everyone loves it so much!*

## ⓟ ZUCCHINI BREAD  *Debbie Stern*

3 cups flour, sifted
1½ tsps. cinnamon
1 tsp. baking soda
1 tsp. salt
¼ tsp. baking powder
1 cup oil
2 cups sugar
3 eggs
1 Tbsp. vanilla
2 cups zucchini, grated
½ cup walnuts, chopped
  (optional)

1. Mix all the ingredients together in the listed order in a large bowl.
2. Place in two greased 9 x 5 x 3 inch loaf pans.
3. Bake in 350 degree oven for 1 hour.
Makes 2 loaves.
*Quick and easy!*

## Ⓜ MELBA TOAST  *Barbara Ament*

1 loaf white bread,
  sliced thin
½ cup margarine, soft
1 Tbsp. powdered beef
  bouillon
¼ tsp. Tabasco sauce
Onion salt, dash

1. Mix together margarine, bouillon, Tabasco, and onion salt.
2. Cut bread into squares. Spread mixture on bread. Place on baking sheet.
3. Bake in 300 degree oven for 30 minutes or until brown.

# DILL BREAD *Debbie Stern* **D**

1 package dry yeast
½ cup very warm water
1 cup cottage cheese
1 egg
2 Tbsps. sugar
1 Tbsp. onion chips, dry
1 tsp. salt
2 tsps. dill
2¼ cups flour
½ tsp. baking soda

1. Dissolve the yeast in the water.
2. Mix together cottage cheese, egg, sugar, onion chips, salt, and dill; allow to come to room temperature.
3. Add cottage cheese mixture, flour, and baking soda to yeast. (Dough will be sticky). Let rise in covered bowl in warm space for 1 hour. Knock down and punch a bit with a fork.
4. Put dough in teflon pan or well greased round casserole dish and let rise again about 1 hour.
5. Bake in 350 degree oven for 45 minutes. Brush with butter while hot and salt lightly. *Especially delicious served warm.*

# "QUICK" DILL BREAD *Marsha Arons* **D**

1 cup unbleached
  white flour
1 cup whole wheat flour
2 tsps. baking powder
½ tsp. baking soda
¼ tsp. salt
1 cup cottage cheese
2 large eggs, beaten
6 Tbsps. milk
1 Tbsp. honey
4 Tbsps. butter, melted
2 Tbsps. fresh dill weed,
  finely minced

1. Sift together flours, baking powder, baking soda, and salt.
2. Beat together cottage cheese, eggs, milk, honey, and butter. Add the dill.
3. Gradually sift dry ingredients into the wet. (Don't beat, just mix). Batter will be stiff. Spread into greased loaf pan carefully.
4. Bake in 350 degree oven 35 to 45 minutes.

DILL

# P CHALLAH IN THE FOOD PROCESSOR

2 envelopes dry yeast
2 tsps. sugar
¼ cup hot water
1 stick corn oil margarine,
　room temperature
½ cup sugar
2 tsps. salt
1¾ cups hot water
2 extra large eggs
7 cups unbleached flour
　(approximately)
1 egg yolk
Sesame or poppy seeds
　(optional topping)

## Braided Challah

**The basic rule is:
under two and over one,
alternating outside pieces
from right and left.**

1. Dissolve sugar and yeast in ¼ cup hot water. Set aside; yeast is ready when it is rising and puffy.
2. Place margarine, sugar, and salt in a mixing bowl; pour 1¾ cups hot water over them.
3. Crack eggs into large capacity food processor bowl with plastic dough blade, and pulse 30 seconds.
4. Add 1 cup flour and puffy yeast mixture to eggs. Pulse 30 seconds to blend.
5. Add margarine/sugar/salt/water mixture and 3 cups flour. Pulse 1 minute, scrape down sides of bowl, pulse 30 more seconds.
6. Add remaining flour, 1 cup at a time; pulse approximately 15 to 20 seconds after each addition. Dough will form a large, sticky ball around the blade. The food processor may not accomodate all 7 cups of flour.
7. Spread remaining flour or an extra ½ cup flour onto a board or pastry cloth. Turn dough onto floured surface.
8. Knead the dough 2 to 3 minutes, incorporating flour. (Humid days require more flour!) Ready dough will form a smooth, round ball and will bounce back when lightly touched.
9. Grease a large bowl. Place dough in it, and cover with a towel. Set in a warm place to rise until double in size (1 to 2 hours).
10. Punch down the dough; remove from bowl onto floured board. Let it rest 5 to 10 minutes.
*For 2 or 3 braided loaves:*
1. Divide dough in half or thirds.
2. Divide each portion into 4 long pieces; roll these between palms to make strips for braiding.

**2. Under two**

**3. Over one**

**4. Under two from
　opposite side**

*Karen Sager*

## Round Challah

**Bottom Coil**

**Middle Coil**

**Top Coil**

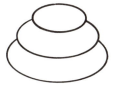

3. Pinch the 4 strips together at the top. Braid like a "lanyard"! Bring an outside strip under the 2 inside strips and back over one. Repeat, but alternate sides from which you start, until the entire loaf is braided. Pinch the ends together and tuck underneath. (See illustration.)

4. Place each loaf on a greased baking sheet or loaf pan. Cover with towels and allow to rise until double in size (approximately 2 hours).

*For 2 round holiday loaves:*

1. Divide dough in half. Divide each portion in half.

2. Roll one piece into a long, smooth strip. Coil this strip into a circle on a greased cookie sheet. Pinch the end under. (See illustration.)

3. Divide second portion into 2 unequal strips, about ⅔ and ⅓. Roll into smooth strips.

4. Take the larger of the 2 and make a second coil on top of the first. Take the last piece and make a third coil on top.

*Baking instructions:*

1. Preheat oven to 350 degrees. Mix 1 raw egg yolk with 1 tsp. water; brush the loaves for a shiny crust. Sprinkle with seeds, if desired.

2. Bake for 15 minutes to brown crust. Reduce heat to 325 degrees and bake 15 more minutes (30 minutes total). Cool and remove from pans.

*My mother-in-law taught me how to bake challah. Over the years I have adapted her method to the food processor. It is far more difficult to describe than to do, and well worth the effort. These loaves freeze very well. Bake ahead and heat just before the Shabbat or holiday meal.*

**5. Over one**

**6. Under two from opposite**

**7. Over one, and continue**

**8. Tuck ends under**

 **BREADS**

## ❶ CHALLAH "OOH - LA - LA" *Bonny Barezky*

1 1-pound loaf Challah,
  sliced (about 16 slices)
8 ounces cream cheese
1 egg yolk
½ cup sugar
1 tsp. vanilla
½ cup pecans, chopped
4 large eggs
¾ cup whipping cream
½ cup sugar
2 tsps. vanilla
Juice of 2 lemons *or*
  1 orange
Oil for frying
Powdered sugar to garnish

1. Cut crusts off entire loaf. Cut each slice diagonally into 2 triangles.
2. Combine cream cheese, egg yolk, ½ cup sugar, and 1 tsp. vanilla until smooth.
3. Spread one side of each triangle with cream cheese mixture. Sprinkle one side with pecans. Cover with the other side as for a sandwich. Repeat with the rest of the slices.
4. Place triangle sandwiches in an oblong pan.
5. Combine 4 eggs, whipping cream, ½ cup sugar, 2 tsps. vanilla, and the juice of 2 lemons (or 1 orange) until smooth. Pour over sandwiches. Cover pan with foil and refrigerate 30 minutes.
6. Turn sandwiches over with spatula. Cover again and refrigerate 30 more minutes. (Can be prepared the day before up to this point.)
7. Deep fry in oil on both sides until golden. Drain on paper towels.
8. Dust with powdered sugar.
Loosely covered, these can be kept warm in a 250 degree oven for 1 hour.
*Very popular and convenient brunch dish. May be served with warm maple syrup.*

## ❶ FRENCH CHALLAH *Bonny Barezky*

4 ¾-inch slices of 2 day
  old challah (slightly dry)
3 whole eggs and 2 yolks
1 tsp. orange peel, grated
1 Tbsp. honey
⅓ cup orange juice
2 Tbsps. orange liqueur
  (optional)
2 tsps. vanilla
4 Tbsps. butter for pan
4 Tbsps. powdered sugar

1. Remove crusts from challah. Cut each slice diagonally into 2 triangles.
2. Combine 3 eggs, 2 egg yolks, orange peel, honey, orange juice, orange liqueur, and vanilla. Mix well.
3. Dip challah into batter long enough to soak challah (at least 10 minutes). Remove pieces from batter with spatula.
4. In large skillet, fry challah pieces in butter on both sides until golden brown.
Sprinkle on powdered sugar before serving.
*Easy for brunch!*

48

# PIZZA DOUGH *Eve Erenberg*

2 envelopes quick-rising
   dry yeast
1 tsp. sugar
½ cup lukewarm water
1½ cups lukewarm water
1 tsp. salt
6 cups sifted flour
¼ cup olive oil

1. Dissolve yeast and sugar in ½ cup warm water. Let stand until foamy, about 10 minutes.
2. Mix salt in 1½ cups lukewarm water. Add to yeast mixture. Make sure water is not too hot, or it will destroy the rising ability of the yeast.
3. Gradually stir in flour. When flour forms a ball, work in ¼ cup olive oil. Turn dough ball onto floured work surface and knead until smooth and elastic, about 10 minutes.
4. Put back into floured bowl, cover and let rise until double in bulk. Quick-rise yeast cuts the rising time in half.
5. Divide dough in half. Roll and stretch each half until it fits a large, round pizza pan, with a nice edging of dough around each pan.
6. Top with tomato sauce and toppings of choice. Cook 20 minutes in a preheated 400 to 425 degree oven.
*Makes 2 large pizza crusts.*

# **D** ENGLISH MUFFIN BREAD *Roberta Bell*

6 cups flour, unsifted
2 packages dry yeast
1 Tbsp. sugar
2 tsps. salt
¼ tsp. baking soda
2 cups whole milk
½ cup water
Cornmeal

1. Combine 3 cups flour, undissolved yeast, sugar, salt, and baking soda.
2. Heat milk and water until very warm (120 to 130 degrees). Add to dry ingredients and beat well.
3. Stir in remaining 3 cups flour to make a stiff batter. Grease and sprinkle with cornmeal two 8½ x 4½ x 2½ inch loaf pans; spoon in batter.
4. Sprinkle tops with cornmeal. Cover. Let rise in a warm place, free from draft, for 45 minutes.
5. Bake in 400 degree oven for 25 minutes. Remove from pans and cool.

By adding these ingredients, you can also make:

**SOUR CREAM AND CHIVE ENGLISH MUFFIN BREAD**
3 Tbsps. freeze-dried chives
½ cup dairy sour cream (room temperature)

**GARLIC ENGLISH MUFFIN BREAD**
2 Tbsps. chopped parsley
1½ tsp. garlic powder

# **D** SQUASH MUFFINS *Jackie Siegel*

1½ cups unsifted flour
¼ cup firmly packed
  light brown sugar
1 Tbsp. baking powder
½ tsp. salt
½ tsp. cinnamon
¼ tsp. nutmeg
1 egg
1 cup cooked squash,
  pureed*
½ cup milk
¼ cup butter, melted

1. Preheat oven to 400 degrees.
2. Combine flour, sugar, baking powder, salt, cinnamon, and nutmeg in large bowl.
3. Combine egg, squash, milk, and melted butter in smaller bowl.
4. Add squash mixture to flour mixture. Stir just until dry ingredients are moistened.
5. Spoon into greased muffin cups; bake 15 to 20 minutes.
Makes 12 muffins.
*Any dry winter squash may be used in these spicy muffins. This recipe comes from the Playa Dorada Hotel in the Dominican Republic.*

# BLUEBERRY MUFFINS *Goldie Langer* Ⓓ

1 egg
½ cup milk
¼ cup oil
1½ cups flour
½ cup sugar
2 tsps. baking powder
¼ tsp. salt
1 cup fresh bluberries
  (or more, to taste)

1. Combine egg, milk, oil, and beat by hand.
2. Mix in remaining ingredients, except blueberries, until flour is moistened. Batter should be lumpy.
3. Add fruit.
4. Fill muffin cups ⅔ full of batter. Bake in 400 degree oven 20 to 25 minutes.
Makes 12 muffins.
*Quick and easy!*

# BLUEBERRY - LEMON MUFFINS *Bonny Barezky* Ⓓ

1¾ cups flour
¼ cup sugar
2½ tsps. baking powder
¾ tsp. salt
¾ cup light cream
1 egg
⅓ cup cooking oil
1 Tbsp. lemon juice
1 tsp. vanilla
1 cup blueberries
2 Tbsps. sugar
1 tsp. lemon peel, grated
3 Tbsps. butter, melted
⅓ cup sugar

1. Place flour, sugar, baking powder, and salt in food processor and pulse twice.
2. Add cream, egg, oil, vanilla, and lemon juice. Pulse 8 times or until blended.
3. Toss blueberries with sugar and lemon peel. Gently stir blueberries into batter.
4. Fill greased 2½ inch muffin tins ⅔ full with batter. Bake in 400 degree oven for 25 minutes.
5. While muffins are still warm, dip tops in melted butter and then sugar.
To make mini-muffins, reduce heat to 375 degrees and bake for 20 minutes or until golden brown on top. Makes 24 mini-muffins.
*A different topping may be preferred; instead of dipping in butter and sugar after baking, try sprinkling cinnamon and sugar on top before baking!*

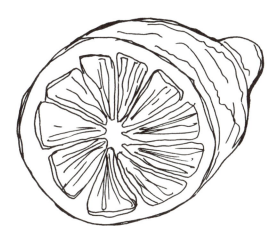

#  ORANGE - MACADAMIA MUFFINS *Bonny Barezky*

1 large naval orange
½ cup orange juice
1 cup butter, softened
2 tsps. vanilla
1 large egg
½ cup macadamia nuts, chopped
1½ cups flour
¾ cup sugar
1 tsp. baking soda
1 tsp. baking powder
1 tsp. salt

1. With a potato peeler, remove the orange part of the peel (rind). Chop and reserve rind.
2. Peel the orange (removing all the white), quarter it and remove seeds.
3. In food processor, place rind, orange quarters, orange juice, softened butter, vanilla, and egg. Process until smooth. Add macadamia nuts and pulse 2 times.
4. In a large bowl, place flour, sugar, baking soda, baking powder, and salt. Mix.
5. Add orange mixture to flour mixture. Stir together. Batter will be lumpy.
6. Spray muffin pan or muffin papers with non-stick cooking spray. Pour batter into muffin pans ½ full.
7. Bake in 400 degree oven 15 to 20 minutes (10 to 15 minutes for mini-muffins).
Makes 16 muffins, or about 30 mini-muffins.
*Excellent for a ladies luncheon!*

#  PUMPKIN MUFFINS *Barbara Ament*

1½ cups flour
½ cup sugar
2 tsps. baking powder
½ tsp. salt
½ tsp. cinnamon
½ tsp. nutmeg
½ cup canned pumpkin
½ cup non-dairy creamer*
¼ cup margarine, melted
1 egg
½ cup raisins

1. Preheat oven to 400 degrees. Grease muffin tins or use cupcake papers.
2. Mix all ingredients just until flour is moist and lumpy. Fill muffin tins ⅔ full with batter. If desired, sprinkle tops with sugar.
3. Bake in 400 degree oven 18 to 20 minutes.
1 16-ounce can of pumpkin makes 4 recipes (48 muffins).
*May also be made dairy by using milk instead of non-dairy creamer, but a good pareve muffin recipe is hard to find!*

# SOUPS

## Ⓜ VEGETABLE BEEF SOUP *Jackie Siegel*

4 pounds soup meat
2 to 3 pounds soup bones
6 quarts water
2 packages vegetable
soup mix
1 medium onion, chopped
1 sweet potato, sliced
3 ribs celery, sliced
3 carrots, sliced
½ pound fresh mushrooms,
sliced
1 pound fresh peas, shelled
1 zucchini, sliced
1 parsnip, sliced
1 small bunch dill,
chopped
1 small bunch parsley,
chopped
Kosher salt
Pepper

1. Remove fat from meat. Place in large soup pot with bones, and cover with water. Bring to boil and lower heat. Skim fat from top of water several times.
2. Add the 2 packages of vegetable soup mix and cook ½ hour.
3. Add remaining ingredients; cook, uncovered, 2 to 3 hours. Add small amounts of water if soup is too thick.
Season to taste with salt and pepper during cooking.
*The secret ingredient is the dill! This is a wonderful soup for Sukkot.*

## Ⓜ HANDFUL MINESTRONE *Gail Taxy*

2 handfuls Great Northern
white beans
1 handful barley
2 handfuls small lima
beans
2 handfuls black-eyed peas
1 28-ounce can tomatoes
1 cup onion, chopped
½ cup celery, chopped
1 10-ounce package frozen
green beans
½ cup macaroni, uncooked
¼ cup parsley, chopped
½ tsp. oregano
¼ tsp. thyme
½ tsp. basil
¼ tsp. salt
⅛ tsp. pepper

1. Two days before serving: Place beans, barley, lima beans, and black-eyed peas, by the handful into soup pot. Add 2 quarts of water, bring to a boil, simmer for 5 minutes, uncovered.
2. Let stand all day and overnight to soften. This will absorb most of the water.
3. Next day, pour off excess water. To softened beans, add 1 quart of water or soup starter broth*, tomatoes, and liquid. Mash tomatoes. Add onions, celery, frozen green beans, macaroni, and seasonings. Simmer covered 1 hour; add liquid as needed. Add more salt and pepper to taste, and serve.
*Save liquid from steaming green vegetables to use as enriched soup starter (can save for a maximum of 3 days).*
*As soup is used, add leftover vegetables, potatoes, or rice to enhance and change flavor slightly. Make recipe at least one day prior to serving; it needs to mellow overnight.*

# CREAMY MUSHROOM SOUP *Chana Kaufman* **D**

½ pound fresh mushrooms, sliced
1 medium onion, sliced
2 Tbsps. butter or margarine
1 Tbsp. vegetable oil
1 Tbsp. flour*
2 cups pareve "beef" broth
White pepper, to taste
Nutmeg, to taste
1 cup sour cream or yogurt or combination
Fresh parsley, chopped

**KP**

1. Melt butter or margarine in large saucepan. Cook mushrooms and onion until most of pan juices have evaporated.
2. Stir in flour and cook until flour is slightly browned.
3. Slowly stir in broth and bring to boil, stirring. Season with white pepper and nutmeg.
4. Purée soup with sour cream (or yogurt), a portion at a time, until smooth.
5. Reheat, without boiling. Garnish with parsley, if desired.
*Can be adapted easily for Pesach by substituting ½ Tbsp. potato starch for flour.*

# CURRIED PUMPKIN MUSHROOM SOUP *Aviva Rodin* **P**

½ pound mushrooms, sliced
½ cup onion, chopped
2 Tbsps. unsalted margarine
1 Tbsp. curry powder
2 Tbsps. flour
3 cups pareve "chicken" bouillon
1 1-pound can pumpkin purée
1 Tbsp. honey
Nutmeg, pinch
1 cup non-dairy creamer
Salt and pepper, to taste

1. Cook mushrooms and onions in margarine for 3 minutes or until onion is soft.
2. Add curry powder and flour, and cook mixture, stirring constantly for 5 minutes.
3. Remove from heat and stir in bouillon, pumpkin, honey, and nutmeg. Add salt and pepper to taste and simmer 15 minutes.
4. Add non-dairy creamer and reheat soup, but do not boil.
*Scrumptious adaption of recipe from "Turbacks Restaurant" in New York.*

# P YELLOW SPLIT PEA SOUP *Jackie Siegel*

1 bag yellow split peas
5 to 6 quarts water
1 package split pea soup
  mix
1 cup celery, chopped
1 cup onion, chopped
1 cup carrots, chopped
1 potato, sliced
1 parsnip, sliced
1 small bunch dill,
  chopped
1 bay leaf
1 clove garlic
1 to 2 vegetable bouillon
  cubes (optional)
Salt and pepper, to taste

1. Wash and drain split peas. Cover with water. Bring to a boil, then cook over low flame.
2. Add remaining ingredients and stir. Cook for 3 to 4 hours until desired consistency.
3. Add more water if soup becomes too thick. Season with salt and pepper, to taste, while cooking.

# P HUNGARIAN SPLIT PEA SOUP *Gail Taxy*

1 package dried, yellow
  split peas
1 to 1½ quarts water
2 medium onions, chopped
4 Tbsps. margarine
Salt and white pepper,
  to taste

Egg drop ("Ein brin"):
1 egg, beaten in
  ½ cup water
  (optional)

1. Day before serving: Place split peas in water in large pot. Bring to a boil. Allow to boil 3 minutes; remove from heat. Let stand uncovered overnight.
2. Cook peas 2 to 3 hours until soft. Simmer, stirring occasionally.
3. Sauté onions in margarine until brown on edges.
4. Add optional "Ein brin" to pea soup.* Simmer another ½ hour.
5. Add salt and white pepper to taste.
*If using egg drop, beat egg with water and drop mixture from spoon into simmering soup; stir. For smoother soup, purée in blender before adding egg drop. This was my grandmother's recipe!*

# TOMATO - EGGPLANT SOUP *Gail Taxy* **M**

3 small eggplants (not
  miniature)
5 Tbsps. margarine
1 28-ounce can tomatoes
1 large onion, chopped
2 cloves garlic, crushed
2 bay leaves, crushed
Marjoram, pinch
½ cup rice
2½ quarts beef stock
Salt and pepper, to taste

Meatballs: (optional)
½ pound ground veal
2 tsps. onion, chopped
⅛ tsp. nutmeg
⅛ tsp. oregano

For garnish:
½ cup garlic croutons
2 Tbsps. chives, chopped

1. Peel, cube, and soak eggplant in salted water for 20 minutes. Drain. In large Dutch oven, sauté eggplant in margarine 15 minutes until softened.
2. Add can of tomatoes, onion, garlic, bay leaves, and marjoram. Cook 15 minutes.
3. Add rice, beef stock, salt, and pepper. Simmer, covered, for 40 minutes.
4. Process soup in blender and return to pot.
5. For optional meatballs, mix ingredients, and form into balls. Add to soup in pot, and simmer 15 minutes or longer.
*Garnish with croutons and chives.*

# FRENCH ONION SOUP *Judy Miller* **D**

2 to 3 large onions,
  sliced
¼ cup margarine or butter
6 rounded tsps. pareve
  instant "beef" soup mix
Pepper, dash
1 tsp. sugar
6 cups water
½ cup dry white wine
  or dry sherry, optional
1 tsp. Worcestershire sauce
4 to 6 slices French bread
2 to 3 cups Monterey Jack
  cheese, grated
½ cup Parmesan cheese,
  grated

1. In large saucepan, cook onions in margarine until tender (golden).
2. Add soup mix, pepper, sugar, water, and Worcestershire sauce. Wine may be substituted for ½ cup of the water. (I do this only when serving adults. Kids don't like it.)
3. Heat to boiling. Reduce heat, cover, and simmer 20 to 25 minutes.
4. Pour into individual casseroles or heat-proof bowls. Float a slice of toasted French bread on each serving. Sprinkle generously with cheeses.
5. Bake in 375 degree oven or broil for 5 minutes, until cheese is bubbly.
*Serve with large tossed salad and more French bread for an easy supper.*

## **Ⓓ POTATO SOUP** *Charlotte Cleeland*

6 tsps. pareve "chicken" bouillon
6 cups water
3 to 4 potatoes, cut in chunks
1 small onion, cut in chunks
2 medium carrots, cut in chunks
½ tsp. salt
⅜ tsp. chervil
⅜ tsp. pepper
¼ tsp. onion salt
1 20-ounce can evaporated milk (can use whole milk or non-dairy creamer)
1 cup Cheddar cheese, grated
½ cup shell macaroni, cooked

1. Boil potatoes, onions, and carrots until tender in water with chicken-flavored bouillon. Add seasonings.
2. Cook macaroni in boiling water.
3. Add milk, Cheddar cheese, and cooked macaroni to potato mixture. Heat, but do not boil. Serve immediately.
*Rich enough for an evening supper with salad.*

## **Ⓓ CREAM OF SPINACH SOUP** *Jennifer Gritton*

1 pound spinach, fresh or frozen
1 cup water
1 potato, peeled
1 carrot, peeled
1 onion, peeled
⅓ cup butter
⅓ cup flour
2 cups milk
½ tsp. basil
Nutmeg, dash
Thyme, to taste

1. Steam spinach in 1 cup water. Purée in food processor; set aside.
2. Steam potato, carrot, and onion in enough water to cover; do not drain. Purée them in food processor with the cooking water; set aside.
3. Melt butter in a large saucepot over a very low flame. Whisk the flour into the butter to form a *roux*. Add the milk gradually, stirring continuously with whisk until smooth and thick.
4. Add the puréed spinach to the *roux* and continue stirring with a wooden spoon.
5. Add basil, nutmeg, and thyme to taste. Last add the puréed vegetables. Continue stirring over very low flame. Add more milk slowly if soup is too thick.
Makes 4 servings.
*Add a dash of sherry for a different flavor!*

# VICHYSSOISE *Karen Sager* ⒹD

6 pareve bouillon cubes, "chicken" or onion
1½ quarts water
3 cups potatoes, peeled and thickly sliced
3 cups whites of leek, sliced
½ to 1 cup whipping cream
Salt, to taste
White pepper, to taste
2 to 3 Tbsps. chives, minced

1. Prepare a broth by dissolving bouillon cubes in boiling water.
2. Add potatoes and leeks to broth, reduce heat, and simmer until tender (approximately 40 to 50 minutes). Cool.
3. Purée soup in food mill or processor. Press through a fine sieve into a heavy glass bowl.
4. Stir in the cream, varying amount according to thickness desired.
5. Season with salt and pepper. Chill in refrigerator several hours.
6. Check seasoning just before serving as saltiness will decrease during refrigeration.
Serve in chilled soup bowls. Sprinkle chives on top of each serving.
*This recipe was adapted from a recipe of Julia Child who explains that, despite the name, cold vichyssoise is an American version of French potato and leek—a hot soup.*

# BROCCOLI CREAM SOUP *Chris Erenberg* ⒹD

4 to 5 broccoli stalks
4 cups water
4 Tbsps. pareve "chicken" bouillon
4 Tbsps. butter
4 Tbsps. flour
1 cup half & half cream
Salt and pepper, to taste

1. Cut stems from the flowerets of the broccoli stalks. Slice stems into thin rondelles. Cut flowerets into bite-sized pieces. Set flowerets aside.
2. In a large saucepan, combine bouillon and water. Bring to a rolling boil. Add broccoli rondelles. Lower heat to medium and cover pan. Cook about 10 to 15 minutes or until broccoli is very soft. Let cool until lukewarm.
3. In food processor or blender, blend soup mixture until puréed. Soup will have cooked down somewhat, so you may have to add 1 or 2 cups of water to correct the amount of liquid. Set aside.
4. Melt butter over low heat. Stir in flour and cook until smooth, about 1 or 2 minutes. Gradually add puréed soup mixture, correct the seasoning, and cook on medium heat until thickened, about 5 minutes.
5. Add broccoli flowerets, cover, and cook until just tender. Lower heat to simmer. Add cream. Cook until just heated through. Do not boil. Serve immediately.
Makes 4 to 6 servings.
*If preparing soup ahead of time, do not add the cream until you reheat the soup for serving.*

## Ⓓ FISH CHOWDER *Gail Taxy*

1 quart water
4 medium-sized red new potatoes, cubed, but unpeeled
½ stick butter
2 medium onions, sliced
¼ cup green pepper, chopped
¼ cup celery, sliced
2 carrots, sliced
1½ pounds cod,* in chunks
1 tsp. salt
½ tsp. seasoned salt
¼ tsp. thyme
¼ tsp. white pepper
2 Tbsps. fresh parsley, chopped
2 dashes Worcestershire sauce
Tabasco, dash (optional)
1 quart cream or half & half

1. In soup pot, bring water to boil. Add potatoes and simmer for 15 minutes.
2. In frying pan, melt butter and sauté onions, green pepper, celery, and carrots for about 10 minutes, or until wilted.
3. Add sautéed vegetables and cod to pot and simmer 15 minutes. Add all seasonings.
4. Heat half & half in frying pan just until warm. Do not boil. Add to fish pot.
5. Remove half of fish chowder to blender and grate for 15 seconds. Pour back into pot. This will be a natural thickener for the soup. No flour is necessary.
*Any boneless fish may be substituted; for example, turbot, haddock, grouper.*

## CHICKEN SOUP
## Ⓜ WITH DILL AND LEEK *Jackie Siegel*

KP   1 5- to 6-pound pullet, quartered
Water
1 large onion
1 small leek, cleaned
3 to 4 carrots, peeled
2 to 3 parsnips, peeled
3 stalks celery
1 tomato
1 sweet potato, peeled
1 small bunch parsley, stems removed
1 small bunch dill, stems removed
1 bay leaf
2 cloves garlic, peeled
1 Tbsp. salt
¼ tsp. pepper

1. Clean chicken and place in stock pot. Cover with water. Bring to a boil.
2. Reduce heat and remove scum from the top.
3. Add onion, leek, carrots, parsnips, celery, whole tomato, sweet potato, parsley, dill, and seasonings. Simmer, covered, for 2 hours.
4. Strain soup in colander. Reserve chicken and vegetables.
5. Serve with meat from chicken, carrots, celery, parsnips, rice, noodles, soup nuts, or matzah balls, as desired.
Makes 12 servings.

# CHICKEN SOUP *Arlene Levin*  **M**

1 3-pound pullet
2 medium carrots
1 medium onion
3 ribs celery
1 medium parsnip
Water, 3 quarts, or more
   (enough to cover chicken)
1 Tbsp. salt
¼ tsp. pepper

**KP**

1. Clean chicken. Place in soup pot, cover with water, and bring to a boil.
2. Skim scum off top of water.
3. Add carrots, onion, celery, and parsnip. Add salt and pepper. Boil slowly for 2 hours or until tender.
Makes 8 servings.
*For matzah balls, see recipe below.*

# MATZAH BALLS *Arlene Levin*  **M**

4 eggs, beaten
½ cup cold chicken soup
⅓ cup oil
2 tsps. salt
Pepper, dash
1 cup matzah meal

**KP**

1. Combine eggs, soup, oil, salt, and pepper. Mix well.
2. Add matzah meal and stir thoroughly.
3. Let stand at least 20 minutes. (May refrigerate.)
4. Boil 1½ quarts water in a saucepot. Add 1 Tbsp. salt.
5. Form into balls; dip hands in ice water to prevent dough sticking.
6. Drop balls into the boiling water. Cover, reduce heat, and cook 20 minutes.
Serve in soup or as a side dish.
Makes 20 matzah balls.

*Chopped parsley adds color and flavor to both CHICKEN SOUP and MATZAH BALLS; it is especially appropriate and festive during Pesach.*

PARSLEY

## ▪ HOT AND SOUR SOUP  *Arlene Levin*

3 dried black mushrooms
4 cups chicken stock
¾ cup boneless chicken breast, cut into 2-inch long shreds
2 Tbsps. canned bamboo shoots, cut into 2-inch long shreds
1 tsp. water mixed with ½ tsp. cornstarch
½ cup tofu, cubed
1 large egg, beaten

Seasoning mixture:
¾ tsp. salt
¾ tsp. light soy sauce
1 Tbsp. dry sherry
1 Tbsp. Chinese red vinegar
½ tsp. white pepper

1. Soak the mushrooms in warm water for 25 minutes. Drain, dry well. Remove the stems and quarter the caps.
2. Combine the ingredients for the seasoning mixture and set aside.
3. Bring the stock to a boil in a large pot. Add the chicken and cook for about 1 minute over medium heat. Add the mushrooms and bamboo shoots. Cook 2 minutes.
4. Add the seasoning mixture and stir a bit.
5. Add the cornstarch mixture and stir until slightly thickened.
6. Add the tofu and egg. Stir several times and serve.
*This goes very well with dishes in the 7-COURSE ORIENTAL BANQUET, pp. 390-394.*

## SWEET AND SOUR
## ▪ CABBAGE BORSCHT  *Bonny Barezky*

KP 2 pounds brisket
Beef bones
1 35-ounce can tomatoes (broken up)
2 medium onions, chopped
3 pounds cabbage, shredded
2½ tsps. salt
1 tsp. pepper
¼ cup lemon juice
4 Tbsps. sugar
½ cup brown sugar
⅔ cup seedless white raisins

1. Place brisket and bones in soup pot with 2 quarts of water. When water comes to a boil, skim well.
2. Add tomatoes and onions. Cook uncovered for 1 hour.
3. Add cabbage, salt, and pepper. Cook for another hour.
4. Add lemon juice, sugar, brown sugar, and raisins. Cook for ½ hour. Adjust lemon juice and white sugar to your taste preference.
*Mm-mm! Even more delicious the next day!*

# HOT OR COLD CABBAGE BORSCHT *Jennifer Gritton* ◆P

`KP`

1 to 2 Tbsps. margarine
2 medium or 1 large onion, chopped
1 rib celery, sliced thin
2 large carrots, sliced thin
2 to 2½ cups cabbage, chopped or shredded
4½ cups vegetable stock *or* water
1 cup fresh or canned beets, sliced thin
1 large potato, sliced thin
1 cup tomato juice, tomato sauce, *or* tomato purée
¼ cup cider vinegar
¼ cup honey
¼ cup lemon juice
¼ cup sugar
Dill weed, to taste
Pepper, to taste (optional)

1. Melt margarine in a large kettle, and sauté onions until translucent. Add celery, carrots, and cabbage. Cook until cabbage gets tender.
2. Add vegetable stock or water, beets, potatoes, and tomato sauce. Cover and cook approximately 15 minutes.
3. Combine vinegar, honey, lemon juice, and sugar. Slowly add to soup. Adjust to desired taste. Add dill and pepper to taste.
4. Simmer, covered for 20 to 30 minutes.
Makes 8 servings.
*Serve hot with crusty bread.*
*Serve cold with sour cream for a delicious dairy variation.*

# EDA'S BEET BORSCHT *Harriet Chavis* ●D

`KP`

1 bunch beets
7 green onions
7 cups water
2 fresh lemons
1½ tsps. salt
Sugar, to taste
3 eggs
Sour cream

1. Break off stems from beets. Soak beets, stems, and green onions in pot of cold water for about 10 minutes to get dirt off. Then rinse.
2. Cut off leaves. Dice stems and green onions into ½-inch pieces. Throw all into a large pot.
3. Scrape skin off beets and rinse. Grate beets coarsely (not fine). Add beets to pot with 7 cups water. Bring to a boil and let simmer about 20 minutes covered (not too low a simmer).
4. Add juice and pulp from lemon, salt, and sugar. Bring to boil again and simmer a few minutes. Let cool for about 10 minutes.
5. Beat 3 eggs in separate bowl. Pour into borscht slowly, a little at a time. (The eggs should not cook.) Refrigerate.
Makes 4 servings.
*Serve cold with a large spoonful of sour cream in the center of each bowl.*

#  GAIL'S GAZPACHO  *Gail Lifshitz*

KP
2 large tomatoes
1 large cucumber, pared
   and halved
½ onion, peeled
½ green pepper, quartered
   and seeded
2 12-ounce cans tomato
   juice
½ cup red wine vinegar
1½ tsps. salt
2 cloves garlic
¼ tsp. Tabasco sauce
   (optional)*

1. In an electric blender, combine tomatoes, cucumber, onion, and green pepper with ½ to 1 cup tomato juice. Blend, covered, and at high speed, to purée the vegetables.
2. Combine with the remaining ingredients and refrigerate, covered, until well chilled. Serve with croutons.
Makes 6 servings.
*Omit optional Tabasco and use kosher for Pesach vinegar for a seasonal Pesach treat!*

# GAZPACHO  *Janet Resnick*

8 medium tomatoes, finely
   chopped
2 large cucumbers, chopped
2 green peppers, chopped
8 green onions, finely
   chopped
¼ cup parsley, minced
2 cloves garlic, minced
2 tsps. salt
1 tsp. pepper
1 quart Bloody Mary mix
½ cup red wine vinegar

1. Mix and chill. Serve.
*Great for a hot summer night!*

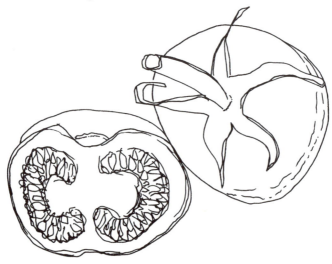

# WATERCRESS SOUP *Aviva Leberman*  **D**

¼ pound butter
1 cup flour
2 cups pareve "chicken" stock
2 bunches watercress
Cream, to taste
Nutmeg, dash
Salt, dash
Pepper, dash
Croutons

1. Melt butter in saucepot over low heat. Stir in flour. Add stock slowly, stirring constantly.
2. Wash and drain watercress. Add to stock mixture and simmer for ½ hour.
3. Add cream to taste. Season with nutmeg, salt, and pepper, to taste.
4. If desired, add 1 to 2 Tbsps. more butter.
Makes 4 servings.
*Garnish this lovely English soup with croutons and sprigs of fresh watercress.*

# COLD MELON "PUNCH" SOUP *Karen Sager* ◆ **P**

**KP**

3½ cups cantaloupe, coarsely chopped
3½ cups honeydew melon, coarsely chopped
1 cup fresh orange juice
¼ cup fresh lime juice
3 Tbsps. honey
2 cups dry champagne or dry white wine, chilled
Mint leaves (optional)

1. Purée 2 cups cantaloupe and 2 cups honeydew melon in processor. Add orange juice, lime juice, and honey, and process to blend.
2. Pour into large glass bowl.
3. Finely chop remaining cantaloupe and honeydew. Add to puréed fruit mixture.
4. Add chilled champagne or wine. Stir carefully to blend. Ladle into glass soup bowls or stemware; garnish with optional mint leaves. May be chilled in refrigerator, but best when served immediately.
Makes 6 to 8 servings.
*For a variation, substitute 1½ cups each cantaloupe and honeydew melon balls for the chopped melon; float these in the soup for a fruit cocktail effect.*

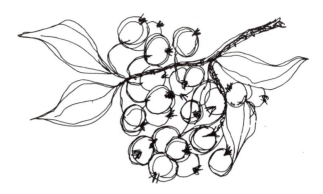

## 🅓 BERRIES & CREAM SOUP  *Karen Sager*

3 pints fresh strawberries,
washed and hulled
1 Tbsp. sugar
1 Tbsp. honey, *or*
2 Tbsps. brown sugar
2 Tbsps. lemon juice
2 cups buttermilk
1 cup yogurt
1 cup sour cream
Cinnamon, dash

1. In a food processor, purée 2 pints of berries.
2. Add sugar, honey or brown sugar, and lemon juice, and process until blended.
3. In a large bowl, whisk together buttermilk, yogurt, and sour cream.
4. Add puréed berry mixture to milk mixture and whisk together until well blended. Add a dash of cinnamon to taste. Chill in refrigerator.
5. Slice remaining pint of berries. Float in large bowl of chilled soup and ladle into serving dishes, or divide sliced berries among individual bowls, add soup, and serve.
Makes 4 to 6 servings.
*Sour cream, brown sugar, and extra berries may be served on the side for a dessert soup. Other berries may be substituted for strawberries. Yogurt may be substituted for sour cream for a less rich dish. Sweeten to taste; amount of sugar may have to be adjusted, depending on tartness of berries.*

## 🅓 COLD BLUEBERRY SOUP  *Harriet Chavis*

1 1-pound can blueberry pie
filling
1 cup dry sherry
¼ cup lemon juice,
fresh or bottled
½ cup water
1 cup sour cream
⅛ tsp. ground cinnamon
Blueberries, fresh, for garnish

1. Combine all ingredients in blender, put on high speed for 1 minute. Pour into jar or bowl.
2. Cover and refrigerate at least 3 hours or until totally cold.
Makes 4 to 6 servings.
*Serve in chilled bowls with fresh blueberries, if available, and a sprig of mint. Quick and easy!*

# SaLAds

## M ORIENTAL SALAD BUFFET *Miriam Steinberg*

Marinated Cucumbers (from
  HUNAN CHICKEN
  SALAD, p. 69)
Chicken in sauce (prepared
  according to HUNAN
  CHICKEN SALAD, p. 69)
Extra, plain boiled chicken
14 ounces noodles (either
  cellophane or vermicelli)
Sesame oil
Meat sauce (prepared for
  PEKING NOODLES,
  p. 137)

Garnishes, choose from:
  Radishes, bean sprouts,
  Water chestnuts, peanuts,
  Scallions, sesame seeds,
  Cashews, olives,
  Steamed vegetables

Additional suggestions:
  FRUIT FISH, p. 69
  TEA EGGS, p. 20
  TEA SMOKED FISH
  (cold), p. 150

1. The day before serving, prepare the marinated cucumbers, and cook the chicken (see p. 69).
2. The next day, cook noodles, drain, and toss with sesame oil.
3. Prepare the sauce for PEKING NOODLES (p. 137).
4. In separate bowls on the buffet table, serve the noodles, chicken, meat sauce, marinated cucumbers, and whatever garnishes you choose.
Makes 12 to 14 servings.

*This recipe explains how to assemble an elegant buffet using an assortment of garnishes as well as several recipes in this book. For an even more elaborate buffet, we suggest adding from among Miriam's other Oriental delicacies: FRUIT FISH, TEA EGGS, and/or TEA SMOKED FISH. You may also wish to consult recipes for CHILI PASTE and HOISIN SAUCE (pp. 326 & 327). This is fun and delicious entertaining!*

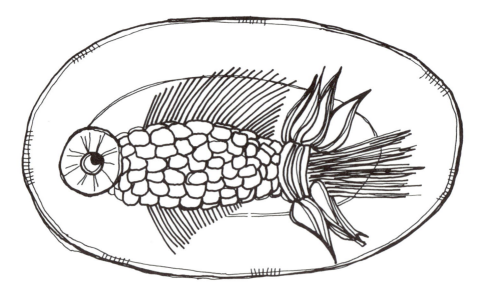

# HUNAN CHICKEN SALAD  *Miriam Steinberg*

**M**

For Marinated cucumbers:
2 medium cucumbers,
  peeled and seeded
4 Tbsps. vinegar
2 Tbsps. light soy sauce
⅛ tsp. sugar
⅛ tsp. sesame oil

For Chicken salad:
7 ounces noodles, extra
  thin, *or* vermicelli
Chicken stock
2 Tbsps. peanut butter
Hot water
4 Tbsps. dark soy sauce
Garlic
Chili paste*
2 whole chicken breasts,
  cooked and shredded
½ cup chopped peanuts
¼ cup sliced scallions
2 Tbsps. sesame seeds

1. Julienne cucumbers into large slices. Mix vinegar, light soy sauce, sugar, and sesame oil. Pour over cucumbers and marinate overnight.
2. Cover noodles with stock, bring to boil and turn heat off. Soak in stock until ready to assemble salad. (May be prepared several hours in advance.)
3. Mix peanut butter with enough hot water to make a thick sauce. Add dark soy sauce, sesame oil, garlic, and chili paste to taste. Stir well. (May be prepared several hours in advance; stir well before assembling salad.)
4. To assemble salad, drain noodles, toss with peanut butter sauce, and place on platter. Add in layers: drained cucumbers, chicken, peanuts, scallions, and sesame seeds.
Note: 1. Good with leftover soup or cooked chicken; may use dark meat.
2. To cook chicken: boil water, insert chicken and remove; bring water back to boil, add chicken, cover and remove from heat; let stand 2 hours.
3.*As a substitute for chili paste, cayenne or tabasco sauce both work well; or see p. 326.
Makes 6 to 8 servings.

# FRUIT "FISH"  *Miriam Steinberg*

1 pineapple, cored and
  sliced; reserve leaves
4 kiwi, peeled and sliced
1 can mandarin oranges,
  drained
1 can lichees, drained
1 papaya *or* cantaloupe,
  sliced
1 strip of red pepper
1 raisin *or* currant

1. For the head, form pineapple slices into circle.
2. For the upper body form kiwi slices into 3 overlapping rows. Form the middle body with 3 overlapping rows of oranges. Form the lower body with 3 rows of lichees.
3. Form the tail with papaya slices.
4. Decorate the fish using slender pineapple leaves for the fins, red pepper strip for the mouth, and a lichee with raisin for the eye. Serve on oval platter.
Makes 6 to 8 servings depending on the amount of fruit used; size may be easily adjusted.
*Please see the illustration on the opposite page; this makes a beautiful presentation.*

# ▣ TARRAGON BEEFSTEAK SALAD  *Karen Barron*

1 scant cup oil (part
olive oil)
⅓ cup red wine vinegar
1 Tbsp. dried tarragon
leaves
1 tsp. salt
¾ tsp. sugar
½ tsp. dry mustard
½ tsp. freshly ground
pepper
¼ tsp. garlic powder
1½ pounds leftover
roast beef cut into
2-inch thin strips
1 red onion, sliced thin
and separated into rings
½ pound fresh mushrooms,
sliced
Lettuce leaves
½ cup parsley, chopped
2 Tbsps. capers, chopped

1. Combine oil, vinegar, tarragon, salt, sugar, mustard, pepper, and garlic powder in large bowl.
2. Add beef, onion rings, and mushrooms, tossing lightly to combine.
3. Cover and refrigerate overnight (or minimum of 2 hours). Stir occasionally.
4. To serve, arrange lettuce leaves on platter. Place steak salad on leaves. Sprinkle with parsley and capers.
*Delicious disguise for leftover roast beef.*

# ▣ CHICKEN PASTA SALAD  *Sarita Blau*

⅓ to ½ pound dry pasta
Orange juice
1 bunch broccoli
2 to 4 chopped scallions,
or equivalent finely
chopped onion
1 carrot
1 sweet pepper
4 chicken quarters, cooked

Optional:
Celery, chopped
Zucchini, chopped
Water chestnuts, sliced or
chopped
Salami or other cold cuts,
julienned
Salad dressing

1. Cook pasta, drain, rinse with cold water and drain. Put in bowl and toss with a little orange juice to keep from sticking together.
2. Cut broccoli into flowerets. Peel stems, cut in quarters lengthwise, and into bite-sized pieces crosswise. Steam 5 to 6 minutes to desired doneness. Drain and cool.
3. Chop onion or scallion finely. Mix with pasta.
4. Shred raw carrot or cut up cooked carrot.
5. Julienne or chop sweet pepper. Cut up chicken into bite-sized boneless pieces. Add whatever optional ingredients you wish. Mix all together and chill. Serve with salad dressing if desired. (See recipes, pp. 90-92.)
Makes 6 servings.
*Good for using up leftovers. Any meat or fish can be used instead of chicken.*

# TUNA AND PASTA WHEEL SALAD  *Chana Kaufman*  **D**

2 cups pasta wheels
  (rotelle)
½ cup green onion,
  sliced
¼ cup green or red
  pepper, chopped
1 stalk celery, with
  leaves, chopped
1 small carrot, diced
2 Tbsps. chopped fresh
  chives
1 Tbsp. chopped parsley
1 13-ounce can water-packed
  tuna, drained

Dressing:
⅓ cup olive oil
1½ Tbsps. white wine
  vinegar
1 tsp. sugar
⅓ cup mayonnaise
⅓ cup sour cream
½ tsp. salt
Fresh ground black pepper

1. Cook pasta just until *al dente*. Drain, rinse with cold water, and drain again. Let cool to room temperature.
2. Transfer pasta to large bowl and add green onion, green or red pepper, celery, carrot, chives, parsley, and tuna.
3. Mix dressing ingredients together. Beat with whisk until very smooth and creamy. Pour over salad ingredients.
4. Mix everything together well and serve. Makes 4 to 6 servings.

# PASTA BROCCOLI  *Janet Resnick*  **D**

1 pound bow-tie or shell
  macaroni, cooked and
  drained
½ cup red peppers,
  roasted, slivered
1 bunch broccoli
  flowerets

Dressing:
½ cup olive oil
½ cup salad oil
½ cup white wine vinegar
2½ tsps. salt
1 tsp. Dijon style mustard
½ tsp. white pepper
1 cup Parmesan cheese,
  grated

1. Combine dressing ingredients in a container with tight-fitting lid. Cover and shake well. Set aside.
2. In large bowl, combine macaroni and peppers. Pour on some of the dressing and toss. Cover and let stand at least four hours.
3. Blanch broccoli in water for 1 minute. Cool. Add to pasta salad 30 minutes before serving and let stand at room temperature. Add more of the dressing if necessary.

Salad

# VEGETABLE PASTA SALAD WITH
**P** # MUSTARD TARRAGON DRESSING *Janet Resnick*

½ pound spinach
  fettucine
1 very large red pepper,
  sliced
6 cups total of
  following vegetables:
Broccoli flowerets
Sliced carrots
Pea pods
Zucchini, sliced
Cauliflower flowerets
Green beans
Black olives, pitted
Dressing:
1 egg
¼ cup Dijon mustard
½ cup tarragon vinegar
2 Tbsps. sugar
2 cloves garlic, minced
2 Tbsps. onion, minced
2 Tbsps. dried tarragon
1 Tbsp. grated fresh
  ginger (optional)
2 cups olive oil

1. Add spinach fettucine to boiling water and cook for 6 to 8 minutes until tender; rinse with cold water and drain.
2. Cook assorted vegetables in boiling salted water for 3 to 4 minutes. Remove with slotted spoon and rinse with cold water; toss to dry.
3. For dressing, in food processor with metal blade, combine egg, mustard, vinegar, sugar, garlic, onions, tarragon, and ginger (if using). Process until well mixed. With machine running, slowly add olive oil in a steady stream until mixture thickens.
4. Toss pasta with ½ of the dressing, slowly adding more to taste. Add vegetables and toss. Remaining dressing can be kept in refrigerator for about 2 weeks.
*This makes a delicious meat main dish if you add 3 cups of cooked, white meat of chicken cut into bite-sized pieces.*

# MUSHROOM & ONION SALAD *Jona Peretz* Ⓟ

1 pound mushrooms, sliced
2 medium onions, diced
2 Tbsps. oil
6 hard-boiled eggs, diced
   and cooled
½ cup mayonnaise
Salt, pepper, and dill,
   to taste

1. In ungreased skillet sauté the sliced mushrooms (no oil). Transfer to large bowl and cool. Drain out all liquid until thoroughly dry.
2. In skillet sauté the diced onions in the oil until brown. Let cool and keep in the oil. Do not drain.
3. Mix mushrooms, onions, and diced eggs in large bowl. Season to taste, add the mayonnaise, and mix again. Serve cold.

# MARINATED VEGETABLES DELUXE *Lois Wallace* Ⓟ

1 head cauliflower broken
   into flowerets
1 bunch broccoli tops
1 basket cherry tomatoes,
   halved
3 small zucchini, sliced,
   not peeled
8 green onions, sliced
   with tops
½ pound mushrooms,
   sliced
1 can green beans, drained
1 can garbanzo beans,
   drained
1 can kidney beans,
   drained
1 can artichoke hearts
   (not marinated), drained

Dressing:
2 large bottles Italian
   dressing
1 tsp. garlic salt
1 tsp. lemon pepper
1 tsp. salad herbs
½ tsp. oregano
Tabasco sauce, 3 dashes

1. Place vegetables in a jar or bowl.
2. Combine salad dressing and spices. Pour over vegetables.
3. Marinate vegetables at least 2 days. Serve with a slotted spoon. Can use any variety of vegetables.
Makes 12 servings.

# ⓟ SALMON MOLD  *Sarita Blau*

1-pound can salmon
1 Tbsp. gelatin (plus 1 tsp. boiling water)
⅓ cup green onion, chopped, or ½ medium sweet onion, finely chopped
½ green pepper (approximately ⅓ cup), chopped
½ cup dill weed, chopped
1 cup tomato sauce or crushed tomatoes with juice
1 cup pareve sour cream

1. Drain salmon, saving liquid. Sprinkle gelatin on reserved liquid and let sit for 5 minutes.
2. Discard skin of salmon. Break up bones and mash chunks of fish.
3. In large bowl, combine fish, onion, green pepper, and dill.
4. Pour boiling water over softened gelatin, to make 1 cup total liquid. Stir well.
5. Pour tomato sauce into dissolved gelatin. Pour with pareve sour cream over fish mixture. Stir until well blended.
6. Pour into mold rinsed with cold water. Refrigerate until firm and unmold.
Makes 6 servings.

# ⓟ LAYERED SALMON SALAD  *Helene Blivaiss*

4 cups lettuce, shredded
2 cups tomatoes, chopped
2 cups cucumbers, chopped
1 15½-ounce can salmon, drained and flaked
1 10-ounce package frozen peas, defrosted
1 cup mayonnaise
½ tsp. dill weed

1. In 2½-quart glass serving bowl, layer lettuce, tomatoes, cucumbers, salmon, and peas.
2. Combine mayonnaise and dill weed.
3. Spread mayonnaise mixture over salad.
4. Cover and refrigerate overnight.
Makes 4 to 6 servings.

# ⓓ SALMON SALAD WITH CELERY  *Chris Erenberg*

1 6-ounce can salmon
4 ribs celery, finely chopped
1 Tbsp. slivered almonds
Salt and pepper, to taste
¼ pint whipping cream
3 Tbsps. grapefruit juice

1. Drain salmon and flake with a fork.
2. Mix salmon, celery, and almonds. Season well with salt and pepper.
3. Mix cream and grapefruit juice. Combine with salmon mixture. Serve.

# SALMON MOUSSE RING *Chris Erenberg*

1 16-ounce can salmon,
  drained, removing skin
  and spine
1 packet gelatin,
  unflavored
1 cup boiling water
¼ cup lemon juice
1 cup mayonnaise
2 tsps. Dijon mustard
1 to 2 tsps. white or red
  horseradish
Dill weed, to taste
Salt and pepper, to taste

1. Put the gelatin powder in electric mixer bowl. Add boiling water and lemon juice. Mix on low speed until well blended.
2. Add mayonnaise, mustard, horseradish, dill, salt and pepper. Mix well.
3. Mix in salmon. Beat at medium speed about 3 to 4 minutes, or until creamy looking.
4. Put mixture into 4-cup ring or fish mold. Chill several hours until firm, or overnight.
5. Unmold and serve. Garnish with fresh parsley sprigs or other leafy vegetable, if desired.
*Tart and tasty. Very decorative when made in individual fish molds. Makes a lovely luncheon dish. Also wonderful appetizer served with crackers!*

# SALMON OR TUNA MOUSSE *Karen Sager*

2 envelopes plain gelatin
½ cup hot water
¼ cup tarragon vinegar
½ tsp. salt
1 tsp. dry mustard
1-pound can sockeye
  salmon or white tuna
2 Tbsps. parsley leaves
1 medium onion, cut in
  chunks
1 large rib celery, sliced
1 medium cucumber,
  peeled and sliced
1 cup cream, whipped

1. Place gelatin and hot water in blender container. Blend on low speed for 30 seconds.
2. Add vinegar, salt, and mustard. Blend for 10 seconds.
3. Clean salmon or tuna, cut into chunks, and add to blender. Add parsley and onion chunks. Blend on high speed for 30 seconds; stop to stir mixture down, if necessary. Be sure the onion is puréed.
4. Add celery and cucumber. Blend on high speed for 10 seconds.
5. Pour puréed mixture into a bowl. Fold in the whipped cream.
6. Grease a 1½-quart mold. Pour fish mixture into mold and refrigerate overnight.
Makes 10 servings.
*A fish shaped mold makes a festive presentation. Decorate with pimento olive slices and thinly sliced cucumbers. May be accompanied with crackers or cocktail rye.*
*See CUCUMBER-DILL SAUCE, p. 324.*

## ◆ CRUNCHY PEA POD SALAD  *Evelyn Garber*

2 or 3 6-ounce packages
   frozen pea pods, thawed
2 cans water chestnuts
   (sliced are preferable)
½ to ¾ bag frozen green
   peas, thawed
1 cup sliced ripe olives,
   or more, if desired
2 cups thinly sliced
   celery crescents
2 to 2½ cups carrots,
   thinly sliced
1 medium Bermuda onion,
   thinly sliced

Dressing:
½ cup powdered sugar
⅜ cup wine vinegar
⅜ cup salad oil
2 Tbsps. soy sauce
1 tsp. paprika

1. Drain, thaw, and slice vegetables and combine.
2. Mix ingredients for the dressing and pour over the vegetables. Cover and refrigerate.
3. Adjust seasoning before serving. You may want to add more vinegar or soy sauce.
*Vegetables may be prepared a day in advance and dressing put on 4 to 6 hours before serving.*

## ◆ SPINACH SALAD  *Gail Lifshitz*

1 pound fresh spinach
   (or 1 10-ounce bag)
2 hard-boiled eggs,
   chopped
"Baco's," handful
½ cup vegetable oil
¼ cup ketchup
½ tsp. salt
1 small onion, minced
¼ cup sugar
⅛ cup vinegar
½ tsp. Worcestershire
   sauce

1. Wash spinach and dry. Add eggs and "Baco's" (if desired).
2. Combine oil, ketchup, salt, onion, sugar, vinegar, and Worcestershire sauce in a jar. Shake to mix. Chill.
3. When you are ready to serve, toss salad with dressing.
Makes 4 servings.

# TOMATOES VINAIGRETTE *Judy Miller* ◆P

12 to 16 tomatoes, thickly
  sliced
1 cup olive oil
⅓ cup wine vinegar
2 tsps. crushed oregano
  leaves
1 tsp. salt
½ tsp. pepper
½ tsp. dry mustard
2 cloves garlic, crushed
6 to 8 cups lettuce
Green onion, minced
Parsley, minced

1. Arrange tomato slices in a 8 x 8 x 2 inch baking dish.
2. Combine oil, vinegar, oregano, salt, pepper, dry mustard, and garlic. Spoon over tomatoes. Cover and chill for 2 to 3 hours. Baste tomatoes occasionally.
3. To serve, put lettuce cups on individual plates and arrange tomato slices on top. Sprinkle with minced green onion and parsley. Drizzle a small amount of dressing on each salad.
Makes 6 to 8 servings.

# SPINACH FRUIT SALAD *Chana Kaufman* ◆P

1 10-ounce package fresh
  spinach, washed well
1 to 2 red apples, sliced
½ cup walnut pieces
Sesame seeds

Dressing:
⅓ cup salad oil
1 Tbsp. white vinegar
1 Tbsp. prepared chutney
½ tsp. curry powder
½ tsp. dry mustard
½ tsp. salt

1. Mix dressing ingredients together well.
2. Just before serving, toss dressing with spinach leaves, apple slices, and nut pieces; garnish with sesame seeds.

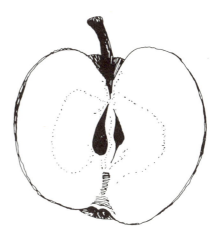

 SALADS

# ⓟ ISRAELI ARTICHOKE SALAD  *Sybil Zimmerman*

4 whole artichokes
  (bruised ones are good
  for this recipe)
1 garlic clove, sliced
¼ whole lemon
2 Tbsps. olive oil
¾ tsp. minced parsley
2¼ tsps. red wine vinegar
¼ tsp. Dijon mustard
⅛ tsp. garlic, minced
⅛ tsp. tarragon
Lettuce
Avocado
Cucumber
Red pepper
1 Tbsp. sesame seed
  kernels

1. Place artichokes in a pot of water with 1 sliced garlic clove and a piece of lemon. Bring to a boil. Cover and cook 45 minutes. Drain well. Remove hearts. Cut out thistle. Put in jar.
2. Add oil, parsley, vinegar, mustard, garlic, and tarragon to jar. Marinate overnight.
3. To serve: place artichoke hearts in a bowl. Add cut-up lettuce, avocado, cucumber, red pepper, and sesame seed kernels.
Makes 3 to 4 servings.
Double or triple recipe for more artichokes. For fast, easy preparation, use canned artichoke hearts.
*We lived in Israel for many years; I wrote cookbooks there as well as a cooking column and lectured on cooking. Here in the States, I am always on the lookout for new ideas to take back to Israel. Remembering the plentiful supply of artichokes we would get in the open market in Israel, I created this recipe one day when I found a large number of artichokes in the reduced section at the supermarket.*

# ⓟ TOMATO - ONION SALAD  *Goldie Langer*

3 medium tomatoes, sliced
1 onion, sliced
½ cup mushrooms, sliced
¼ cup black olives, sliced
Lo-cal dressing

Optional:
1 tsp. olive oil
Green olives

1. Combine vegetables and marinate in dressing at least 1 hour; better if marinated longer.
2. Arrange on bed of lettuce to serve.
Makes 4 to 5 servings.
*You can use any oil and vinegar dressing or make your own and include a sprinkle of basil.*

# ISRAELI EGGPLANT SALAD *Sheri Singer*

2 small to medium
  eggplants
Salt
Oil
2 sweet red peppers, diced
1 green pepper, diced
¼ cup vinegar
½ cup ketchup

1. Peel eggplants. Slice into thin strips. Place in colander. Dry with paper towel. Sprinkle on salt and leave for 20 minutes.
2. Heat oil in frying pan. Fry eggplant strips until browned on both sides. Drain on paper towels. Place in a bowl.
3. Add red and green peppers to eggplant.
4. Mix vinegar and ketchup in a bowl and pour over eggplant and peppers. Serve cold with crackers, as salad with main course, or as appetizer.

# FRAGRANT TABBOULEH *Miriam Steinberg*

2 tsps. powdered pareve
  "chicken" bouillon
2 cups water
1 cup bulghur wheat
½ cup zucchini, sliced
½ cup carrots, julienned
¼ cup raisins, plumped
¼ cup scallions, sliced
¼ cup almonds, slivered
¼ cup red peppers, diced

Dressing:
3 Tbsps. olive oil
2 Tbsps. vinegar
1 Tbsp. sugar
1 tsp. cinnamon
¼ tsp. fresh ginger, minced
¼ tsp. mustard
1 clove garlic, minced

1. Dissolve bouillon in hot water. Add bulghur wheat and soak 1½ hours.
2. Mix in all vegetables.
3. Whisk together dressing ingredients. Pour some of the dressing over the salad. Before serving, add salt and pepper, and adjust other seasonings to taste.
Makes 6 to 8 servings.
*May be made a day ahead. Do not add almonds or tomatoes until ready to serve.*

##  TRADITIONAL TABBOULEH  *Sarita Blau*

¾ cup bulghur wheat
¾ cup water
1 cup parsley, chopped
½ cup onion or scallion,
  minced
2 Tbsps. vinegar
4 Tbsps. oil
Allspice, dash

Optional:
½ to 1 cucumber, chopped
1 or 2 tomatoes, chopped
Garlic, finely minced or
  pressed
Mint, chopped

1. Soak bulghur wheat in water up to 1 hour or overnight.
2. Add parsley, onions, vinegar, oil, allspice, and any or all optional ingredients. Mix and chill to allow flavors to blend.
Makes 3 to 4 servings.

## TASTY TABBOULEH  *Sharlene Garfield*

¾ cup bulghur wheat
1 pareve bouillon cube
1 cup parsley leaves
½ cup fresh mint
  (or 1 Tbsp. dried mint)
2 celery ribs, chopped
8 green onions, chopped
3 medium tomatoes
½ cup toasted sunflower
  seeds
3 Tbsps. oil (olive oil
  is preferable)
2 Tbsps. fresh lemon juice
1 tsp. cumin
1 tsp. coriander
1½ tsps. salt
Black pepper, freshly
  ground
Spinach or lettuce leaves
  and cherry tomatoes
  for garnish

1. Put bulghur wheat in pot with bouillon cube, cover with water, bring to boil, then turn off fire. Let sit for 10 to 15 minutes.
2. Place parsley and mint in food processor and mince with steel knife. Put in large mixing bowl.
3. Place celery and green onions in food processor and chop coarsely with steel knife. Add to parsley and mint.
4. Place tomatoes in food processor and chop coarsely with steel knife. Add to mixture. Stir in bulghur wheat.
5. Put sunflower seeds, oil, lemon juice, cumin, coriander, salt, and pepper in mixing bowl. Taste and adjust seasonings. Stir into wheat mixture.
6. Serve mounded on leaves with cherry tomato garnish.
Makes 8 servings.
*Tabbouleh is a Middle Eastern dish. This adaptation to the food processor allows a quick preparation of many tasty ingredients.*

# COOL BARLEY SALAD
# WITH CRUNCHY VEGETABLES *Judy Wolkin*   M

1 10½-ounce can chicken soup
1⅔ cups water
1 tsp. salt, divided
1 cup medium pearled barley, rinsed
1 large clove garlic, flattened and peeled but left whole
¼ tsp. ground pepper
¼ cup oil
3 Tbsps. fresh lemon juice or red wine vinegar
1 cup diced sweet yellow or red onion
½ cup diced, seeded green pepper
½ cup diced, seeded red pepper
1 cup thinly sliced, peeled carrots
Dill weed, ¼ cup fresh, chopped, or 1 Tbsp. dried

1. In a heavy 2-quart saucepan bring soup, water, and ¼ tsp. of the salt to a boil over moderately high heat.
2. Add barley to pan. When liquid is boiling again, cover pan, reduce heat to low, and simmer 40 to 45 minutes, until barley is tender but still holds its shape. Check after 20 minutes and add a little more water if the barley seems dry.
3. Meanwhile put the garlic clove in a large bowl, and add remaining ¾ tsp. salt, pepper, oil, and lemon juice or vinegar; whisk with a fork to blend.
4. When barley is cooked, discard garlic, add barley to dressing, and toss gently to mix. Cover tightly and refrigerate at least 1 hour; longer is preferable.
5. Before serving, add onions, peppers, carrots, dill, and toss to mix.
Makes 6 servings.
*For a change, vegetables may be tossed with hot barley and the salad served warm. Can be pareve if the "chicken" soup used is pareve. Prepare a day in advance to enable flavors to blend.*

# MOM'S COLE SLAW AND DRESSING  *Anne Kahn*

Cole slaw:
1 medium-sized cabbage,
  shredded
1 green pepper, sliced
3 medium-sized carrots,
  grated

Dressing:
2 heaping Tbsps.
  mayonnaise
3 to 4 Tbsps. red wine
  vinegar
1½ to 2 ounces (3 to 4
  Tbsps.) lemon juice
1 Tbsp. sugar
Pepper, to taste

1. Toss cabbage, green pepper, and carrots together.
2. Put all dressing ingredients in jar and shake very well, or use blender and process until well blended.
3. Mix dressing and vegetables.
Makes 8 to 10 servings.

# MARINATED POTATO SALAD  *Ruth Taxy*

3 to 5 pounds of potatoes
¼ cup oil
¼ cup vinegar
Mustard, to taste
Salt and pepper, to taste
1 tsp. dill weed
6 hard-boiled eggs,
  chopped
2 dill pickles, diced
1 cup mayonnaise

Optional:
Celery, diced
Green onions, chopped

1. Boil potatoes until tender. Drain and immediately peel and cut up.
2. Mix together oil, vinegar, mustard, salt, pepper, and dill weed. Pour over hot potatoes.
3. Cover and let stand in refrigerator overnight or at least 4 hours.
4. Add chopped eggs, dill pickles, and any optional ingredients.
5. Mix in mayonnaise. Add additional seasoning if necessary.
Makes 10 to 16 servings.
*More flavorful if marinated 24 hours before serving.*

# CARROT SALAD *Arlene Levin*

P

1 10-ounce can tomato
soup
1 cup sugar
½ cup oil
½ cup vinegar
2 pounds frozen carrots,
defrosted
2 to 3 green peppers,
sliced
2 to 3 onions, sliced

1. Mix tomato soup, sugar, oil, and vinegar in large bowl.
2. Add carrots, peppers, and onions.
3. Refrigerate.
Makes 12 servings.
*Recipe can be made 2 days in advance. Use pareve tomato soup. Great for barbeque side dish.*

# GREEK SALAD *Jackie Siegel*

D

1 small head of lettuce
(or a mix of greens:
romaine, Boston, red
leaf, head lettuce)
2 celery ribs, chopped
1 medium-sized cucumber,
peeled and sliced
½ green pepper, chopped
2 medium tomatoes,
thinly sliced
1 small onion,
thinly sliced (optional)
⅓ cup pure olive oil
3 Tbsps. wine vinegar
(or juice from 2 lemons)
¼ tsp. garlic powder
(optional)
Salt and pepper, to taste
12 black olives
¼ to ½ pound feta or
goat cheese, crumbled
1 small container of
flat anchovies
6 to 8 green chili
peppers from jar
1 tsp. oregano

1. Wash and clean all vegetables. Cut lettuce into bite-sized pieces and place into a salad bowl. Add celery, cucumber, pepper, tomatoes, and onion.
2. Add olive oil, vinegar or lemon juice, garlic powder, salt, and pepper, and mix well with greens.
3. Arrange olives, crumbled cheese, anchovies, and peppers on top of greens. Sprinkle with oregano. May toss lightly just before serving. Makes 4 to 5 servings.

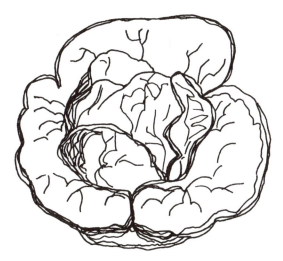

# Ⓓ BUTCHI'S 9 OR 10 LAYER SALAD  *Ruth Aberman*

1 head lettuce, shredded
1 16-ounce bag frozen peas
  (uncooked)
2 large green peppers,
  chopped
1 large cucumber, chopped
2 large tomatoes, chopped
1 16-ounce jar mayonnaise
3 Tbsps. lemon juice
1 tsp. black pepper
2 tsps. sugar
8 radishes, thinly sliced
3 hard-boiled eggs,
  chopped
1½ cups shredded Cheddar
  cheese, optional
5 green onions/scallions,
  chopped/sliced

1. Layer lettuce, peas, green peppers, cucumber, and tomatoes in large (preferably glass) bowl, in the order listed.
2. Combine mayonnaise, lemon juice, pepper, and sugar, and spread over tomatoes.
3. Layer radishes, eggs, cheese, and scallions in the order listed.
4. Cover bowl with plastic wrap and refrigerate overnight, up to 24 hours.

*For a pretty presentation, place bowl on table and then toss right before serving to blend dressing and all the vegetables. For a large crowd, buffet style, I've served it in my punch-bowl.*
◆ *This recipe is pareve if the cheese layer is omitted.*

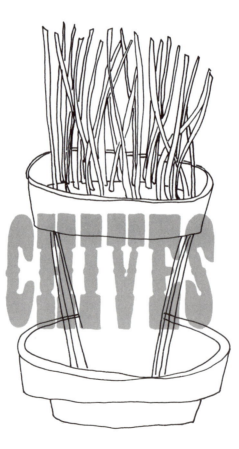

CHIVES

# SEVEN LAYER SALAD *Ava Burgher* Ⓓ

1 head lettuce, cut into bite-sized pieces
5 ribs celery, chopped
2 green peppers, chopped
1 10-ounce package frozen peas, uncooked, thawed
1 medium onion, thinly sliced
1 pint mayonnaise
2 Tbsps. sugar
2 Tbsps. Romano cheese
3 sliced hard-boiled eggs
2 large tomatoes, sliced

Day before serving:
1. Layer first 5 ingredients in order listed. Spread 1 pint mayonnaise on top.
2. Sprinkle sugar and cheese on top. Cover with plastic wrap and chill overnight.
Next day:
1. Layer sliced hard-boiled eggs and tomatoes on top.
Makes 8 servings.
*Excellent for parties. Doubles easily. Because it's made the night before, there's no bothering with cutting up vegetables on the party day. May also be served as a light meal.*
◆ *Omit cheese to make it pareve.*

# TAFFY APPLE SALAD *Elaine Semer & Dorene Benuck* Ⓓ

½ cup sugar
1 Tbsp. cornstarch
2 Tbsps. lemon juice
1 egg, beaten
1 2-ounce can pineapple chunks, drained reserving juice
1 8-ounce carton prepared whipped topping
3 medium Delicious apples, cored and chopped
2 cups miniature marshmallows
1½ cups salted peanuts

1. For dressing: in a saucepan, mix sugar, cornstarch, lemon juice, egg, and juice from pineapple. Cook over low heat, stirring constantly until mixture thickens, about 5 minutes.
2. Cool. Stir in whipped topping.
3. In large bowl, mix apples, pineapple chunks, marshmallows, and peanuts. Toss with dressing and refrigerate 2 to 3 hours before serving.
Makes 16 servings.
*Dorene uses 1 Tbsp. flour instead of the cornstarch and 1½ Tbsps. white vinegar instead of lemon juice.*

## Ⓓ STRAWBERRY MOLD  *Laura Wolf*

1 3-ounce package
  strawberry gelatin
1¼ cups boiling water
1 pint ice cream,
  slightly softened
1 to 1½ cups sliced
  fresh strawberries
Strawberries, to decorate

1. In bowl add boiling water to gelatin, stir until thoroughly mixed, then cool to lukewarm.
2. Cut ice cream into gelatin mixture. Beat by hand until completely mixed. Let stand out about 10 to 20 minutes or until slightly thickened. Fold in sliced fruit.
3. Pour into 6-cup mold. Refrigerate until hardened. Unmold and decorate with fresh strawberries.

*In individual molds, makes an elegant dessert, similar to strawberry mousse. Serve each topped with one beautiful strawberry!*

## MONKEY - IN - THE - MIDDLE<br>Ⓟ JELLO MOLD  *Bonny Barezky*

1 3-ounce package
  raspberry gelatin
1 cup boiling water
½ cup cold water
¾ cup crushed pineapple,
  drained
2 bananas
4 empty 6-ounce cans
  with one end removed
½ cup chopped pecans

1. Pour gelatin in boiling water to dissolve. Add cold water and chill until the consistency of egg whites.
2. Add crushed pineapple. Chill until thickened.
3. Place 1 Tbsp. of mixture in each can.
4. Cut bananas in half and center banana halves in the cans. Spoon the rest of the mixture around the bananas. Place in refrigerator until firm.
5. To unmold, dip rim of can in warm water for 1 second. Puncture the bottom of the can and turn out. Cut in 2-inch discs. Garnish with chopped pecans.
Makes 4 to 6 servings.
*Children enjoy this!*

## 4TH OF JULY MOLD *Arlene Levin* 🇵

2 cups boiling water
1 6-ounce package
   strawberry gelatin
1 10-ounce package frozen
   sweetened strawberries,
   thawed and drained,
   reserving juice
1 3-ounce package
   lemon gelatin
1½ pints pareve
   whipping cream
1 6-ounce package
   black cherry or
   raspberry gelatin
1 large can blueberries,
   drained; reserve juice

1. Dissolve strawberry gelatin in boiling water.
2. To reserved strawberry juice, add enough water to measure 1½ cups. Add to hot gelatin. Pour into a 12-cup mold. Chill until almost set.
3. Add strawberries.
4. Make lemon gelatin according to package directions except add ¾ cup cold water to hot gelatin mixture. Chill until almost set.
5. Whip whipping cream until stiff. Add 1 cup to almost set lemon gelatin and whip. Pour over strawberry gelatin. Chill until set.
6. Prepare black cherry gelatin like the strawberry gelatin, adding water to make 1½ cups with reserved juice. Add blueberries, then add to mold. Chill until set.
Makes 26 servings.

## PINEAPPLE - ORANGE MOLD *Nomi Erlich* 🄳

2 small cartons of small
   curd cottage cheese
2 large containers whipped
   topping
1 package orange or
   pineapple gelatin
1 small can pineapple
   cubes
1 small can mandarin
   oranges

1. Mix cottage cheese and whipped topping together.
2. Add gelatin.
3. Drain juice from pineapple and oranges. Add fruit to mixture.
4. Grease mold with vegetable oil or margarine.
5. When pouring mixture into mold, press down on mixture. Refrigerate 24 hours before serving.
Makes 4 to 6 servings.

# ❶ RUSSIAN CREAM MOLD  *Bonny Barezky*

¾ cup sugar
1 envelope unflavored
  gelatin
1½ cups water
1 cup sour cream
1 tsp. vanilla
1½ cups whipped topping

1. In a saucepan mix sugar, gelatin, and water. Set aside 10 minutes. Stir over low heat to dissolve sugar and gelatin.
2. Remove from heat. Blend in sour cream and vanilla. Chill until thickened to a "custard" texture.
3. Blend in whipped topping. Spray 6-cup mold with shortening and pour into mold. Refrigerate. Makes 8 servings.

*For a "jeweled" effect, double the recipe, mold in a bundt pan, and fill the center with berries. This is a very festive and dramatic looking white mold.*

# ❶ BAVARIAN CREAM MOLD  *Charlotte Cleeland*

½ cup sugar
1 cup sweet cream
1 Tbsp. gelatin
½ cup cold water
1 cup sour cream
1 tsp. vanilla

1. Add sugar to sweet cream and heat in saucepan to lukewarm.
2. Soften gelatin in cold water 5 minutes and add to warm cream. Stir until dissolved. When it begins to thicken, stir in sour cream. Beat until smooth. Add vanilla.
3. Pour into individual molds that have been rinsed in cold water and chill.

*A lovely light dessert. Delicious and elegant served with fresh berries. Doubles and triples well for a single, fancy shaped mold.*

# CREAM CHEESE MOLD *Debbie Stern*　Ⓓ

11 ounces cream cheese, softened
8 ounces sour cream
10 ounces frozen strawberries or fresh strawberries
3 3-ounce packages red raspberry gelatin
1½ cups boiling water
1¾ cups apricot nectar

1. Soften cream cheese with electric mixer. Add sour cream and thawed berries, and mix.
2. Add gelatin to boiling water and blend.
3. Add gelatin water to cream cheese mixture and mix. Add apricot nectar. Stir. Pour into 6- to 8-cup mold. Chill until set.
Makes 8 to 10 servings.

# BORSCHT MOLD *Arlene Levin*　Ⓓ

2 3-ounce packages lemon gelatin
1½ cups boiling water
1½ cups beet juice (from borscht)
Juice of 1 lemon
1 cup sour cream
1 quart bottle of borscht with beets
Beets from borscht, drained
Cucumber slices, optional

1. Dissolve gelatin in boiling water. Stir in beet juice and lemon juice.
2. Cool 20 minutes in refrigerator. Add sour cream; beat until blended.
3. Stir in beets. Pour into 6-cup mold. Chill overnight. Garnish with cucumber slices if desired.
Makes 10 to 12 servings.

# GAZPACHO MOLD *Chris Erenberg*　Ⓟ

3 cups vegetable or tomato juice
2 envelopes unflavored gelatin
1 cup mayonnaise
½ cup red wine vinegar
4 Tbsps. vegetable oil
½ tsp. hot pepper sauce (Tabasco)
2 cloves garlic, crushed
1 cup celery, chopped (about 3 ribs)
½ cup green pepper, diced
¾ cup onion, diced
1 can artichoke hearts (optional)

1. In saucepan, sprinkle gelatin over juice and heat, stirring constantly, until gelatin is dissolved.
2. In a large bowl, mix together mayonnaise, vinegar, oil, Tabasco, and garlic.
3. Add to gelatin. Chill until slightly thickened.
4. Cut artichoke hearts into quarters. Add all vegetables to gelatin mixture. Turn into 6-cup mold. Chill until set.
Makes 6 to 8 servings.

#  VINAIGRETTE SALAD DRESSING *Jackie Siegel*

3 cups olive oil
½ cup apple cider vinegar
½ cup lemon juice
3 medium garlic cloves, crushed
2 tsps. salt
2 tsps. pepper
1 Tbsp. dry mustard
4 pinches tarragon leaves
1 to 2 Tbsps. prepared Dijon mustard

1. Blend all ingredients.
2. Store in a bottle.
3. Refrigerate.
*Great over fresh spinach, cold asparagus, artichoke hearts, or hearts of palm.*

# RHONDA'S ROYAL
#  SALAD DRESSING *Gail Taxy*

2 tsps. Dijon mustard
1 tsp. salt
1 clove garlic, crushed
4 Tbsps. red wine vinegar
Fresh pepper
12 Tbsps. olive oil
1 Tbsp. chopped chives

1. Mix mustard, salt, garlic, vinegar, and pepper in blender.
2. Add 2 Tbsps. olive oil and beat. Continue adding oil 2 Tbsps. at a time until all is used. Add chives.
*Especially well suited for spinach, Romaine, or Bibb lettuce salads.*

# HOMEMADE
#  1000 ISLAND DRESSING *Gail Taxy*

16 ounces mayonnaise
1 bottle chili sauce
1 Tbsp. coarse stoneground mustard
1 tsp. hot picante sauce
1 tsp. horseradish
3 cloves fresh garlic, pressed
2 ounces water

1. Combine all ingredients except water in blender.
2. Add small amounts of water and blend until proper thickness.
Makes about 3½ cups.

## "VEGI" DRESSINGS *Barbara Ament*

Dressing I:
1 cup mayonnaise
Juice of 2 lemons
1 Tbsp. horseradish

Dressing II:
1 cup mayonnaise
Curry powder, to taste
Garlic, to taste
Dry mustard, dash

Salad:
Cauliflower flowerets
Broccoli flowerets
Cherry tomatoes
Pitted black olives
Diced zucchini

Mix either dressing and pour over salad of the raw vegetables.
*Better made the day of serving.*

## PERFECT VINEGAR AND OIL DRESSING *Bonny Barezky*

¼ cup apple cider vinegar
1 tsp. garlic powder
2 Tbsps. Dijon mustard
2 tsps. sugar
½ tsp. salt
½ tsp. pepper
1 cup olive oil

1. Place vinegar, garlic powder, mustard, sugar, salt, and pepper in food processor. Turn on.
2. While machine is running, slowly drizzle in olive oil. Refrigerate.
Makes 1½ cups.
*Fast, easy, and true to its name!*

## GREEN GODDESS DRESSING *Fran Hass*

1 bunch green onion,
   tops only
¼ cup vinegar
¼ cup white wine
1½ cups vegetable oil
1 tsp. salt
3 tsps. Dijon mustard
1 raw egg

· Put all of the ingredients in a blender. Blend thoroughly.
*Easy, delicious pareve dressing. For creamy dairy version, see next page.*

# GREEN GODDESS
 SALAD DRESSING *Bonny Barezky*

1 clove garlic, crushed
1 ounce anchovies,
  chopped well
¼ cup chopped chives or
  scallions
1 Tbsp. lemon juice
2 Tbsps. wine vinegar
1 cup mayonnaise
½ cup sour cream
2 Tbsps. chopped fresh
  parsley
Tabasco sauce, dash
¼ tsp. black pepper

Blend all ingredients, cover, and refrigerate overnight.
*Easy, rich, and tasty!*

#  HONEY-CURRY SALAD DRESSING *Chana Kaufman*

2 Tbsps. honey
2 Tbsps. white vinegar
1 Tbsp. Dijon mustard
½ tsp. salt
White pepper, dash
½ tsp. curry powder
¾ cup salad oil

1. Mix together honey, vinegar, mustard, salt, pepper and curry powder.
2. Gradually whisk in the oil.
*To make even easier, blend everything in food processor!*

# POPPY SEED DRESSING *Bonny Barezky*

1½ cups sugar
2 tsps. dry mustard
2 tsps. salt
⅔ cup vinegar
3 Tbsps. onion, chopped
  fine, or onion juice
2 cups vegetable oil
3 Tbsps. blue poppy seeds

1. In processor, place sugar, mustard, salt, vinegar, and onion. Process until smooth.
2. Drop by drop, add oil to the running processor.
3. When thickened, stop machine and add poppy seeds.
4. Pulse 3 times until well blended.
*This is great on green salad or fruit.*

# POULTRY

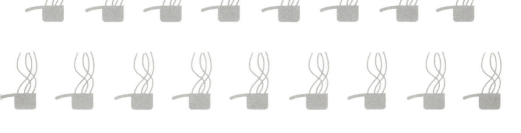

# DUCK BREAST
**M** ## IN LEEK AND MUSTARD SAUCE *Janet Resnick*

4 Tbsps. margarine
2 large leeks, white parts
  only, thinly sliced
4 boneless duck breasts,
  halved and cut into
  ¼ inch slices
½ cup dry vermouth
½ cup dry white wine
¾ cup non-dairy cream
  (may need arrowroot
  or cornstarch to thicken
  to consistency of
  whipping cream)
2 Tbsps. coarse grained
  mustard
Salt and pepper
Paprika and parsley

1. Melt 2 Tbsps. of the margarine in a skillet over medium heat. Sauté leeks for about 5 minutes. Season with a little pepper. Wrap in foil and set aside.
2. Melt remaining margarine, adding more if needed, in large skillet. Add duck breasts. Sauté about 2 to 3 minutes on one side. Sauté second side another minute. Transfer to foil with leeks.
3. Add vermouth to skillet, increase heat and bring to boil, scraping up any brown bits.
4. Add wine and boil until reduced by half, about 4 minutes.
5. Add non-dairy cream and boil until reduced by half, about 3 minutes.
6. Whisk in mustard. Season with salt and pepper.
7. Put a portion of leeks on each plate and several pieces of duck on top. Spoon sauce over duck, sprinkle with paprika, and garnish with parsley.
Makes 4 servings.

# ROAST DUCK A L'ORANGE *Fran Fogel* **M**

1 4- to 5-pound duckling,
  thawed
3 to 4 large garlic cloves
8 peppercorns
2 unpeeled oranges, cut
  into quarters

Orange sauce:
6 to 8 Tbsps. frozen orange
  juice concentrate
6 to 8 Tbsps. honey
6 to 8 Tbsps. lemon juice
1 tsp. ground ginger
1 tsp. whole allspice

1. Heat oven to 425 degrees. Spray roasting pan **KP** with non-stick spray, or cover with aluminum foil.
2. Remove giblets from cavity of duckling. Wash, drain, and pat dry.
3. Season cavity with very light sprinkling of salt. Place garlic, peppercorns, and oranges in cavity. Fasten neck skin to back with skewer. Close cavity with poultry pins or sew together. Bind wing tips under the duckling. Place duck breast side up on a rack in the roasting pan.
4. Mix the orange juice, honey, lemon juice, ginger, and allspice to make the sauce.
5. Pour some sauce over duck and roast for 45 minutes.
6. Reduce heat to 375 degrees. Continue roasting 2½ to 3 hours until fork tender. Every 15 minutes prick duck with fork to allow the fat to drain out, and baste with sauce after each poking. The duck should be very crisp. If the duck is not roasting as you would like, turn it over on the rack. Poke and baste this side too. *Crisp, moist, with no fat! Watch carefully, as skin may burn. Warm any extra sauce and serve on the side.*

# CHICKEN PICCATA *Karen Schur* **M**

2 chicken breasts
¼ tsp. paprika
¾ tsp. salt
2 Tbsps. flour
2 Tbsps. pareve margarine
2 Tbsps. vegetable oil
2 medium lemons,
  one for garnish, one for
  2 Tbsps. lemon juice and
  1 tsp. grated lemon peel
⅛ tsp. fresh black pepper
¼ tsp. salt
2 Tbsps. pareve margarine
Asparagus or broccoli

1. Pound chicken breasts until ¼ inch thick. Cut into 2-inch pieces.
2. Mix paprika, salt, and flour in a small bowl.
3. Coat chicken in flour mixture. Shake gently to remove excess.
4. In a 12-inch skillet, over medium-high heat, heat 2 Tbsps. each margarine and oil. Add chicken pieces; cook 3 to 4 minutes on each side. Remove to platter.
5. Make a sauce by adding to skillet lemon juice, peel, pepper, ¼ tsp. salt, and 2 Tbsps. margarine. Reduce heat to low, stir to loosen brown bits in skillet.
6. Arrange chicken on platter with steamed asparagus or broccoli. Pour lemon sauce over all. Garnish with remaining lemon.

POULTRY

## **M** CHICKEN DINNER  *Sarita Blau*

**KP**

1 3½- to 4-pound chicken,
 cleaned, rinsed, dried
4 to 6 carrots, peeled
1 small onion, peeled
 and sliced (optional)
Garlic powder
Paprika
Wine, soup stock, or water
4 potatoes, scrubbed
 and dried

1. Cut carrots across once and lengthwise in quarters. Put in bottom of small roasting pan. Add onion, if using.
2. Put rack in pan over carrots and onions. Put chicken on rack and sprinkle with garlic powder and paprika, if desired.
3. Pour about ¼ inch of liquid into bottom of pan to keep juices from burning.
4. Put potatoes into pan with chicken.
5. Place roasting pan in 350 degree oven and bake 1 to 1½ hours, depending on size of chicken.
Makes 4 servings.

## CHICKEN STARKAZIE
## **M** (STEWED CHICKEN)  *Anonymous*

**KP**

1 whole chicken, cut into
 8 pieces
1 garlic clove, minced
Pepper and paprika,
 to taste
1 large onion, sliced
1 Tbsp. cooking oil
2 tomatoes, cut into chunks
2 green peppers, cut into
 pieces
2 Tbsps. margarine

1. Put oil on bottom of 3-quart oven casserole. Add onions.
2. Place chicken in casserole and season with pepper, paprika, and garlic.
3. Scatter green peppers and tomatoes around chicken. Dot with margarine.
4. Cover casserole, place in 350 degree oven, and cook for 1 hour.
*Serving suggestion: Serve over very thin pasta.*
*Use juice from stew to season the pasta.*

## **M** HONEY BAKED CHICKEN  *Nancy Goldstein*

1 chicken, cut into pieces
Crisp rice cereal, crushed,
 or cornflake crumbs
Seasoned salt, to taste
Oil
Honey, approximately ½ cup

1. Put crushed rice cereal or cornflake crumbs in plastic bag; add seasoned salt.
2. Brush chicken with oil. Put in bag and shake.
3. Take chicken out of bag and place on greased and foil-lined pan.
4. Drizzle honey lightly over chicken.
5. Bake in 350 degree oven, uncovered, for 1 hour.
Makes 4 to 5 servings.

# POULTRY WITH FRESH FRUIT  *Scott Sandler*  **M**

4 chicken legs, or pieces
  of turkey leg
2 Tbsps. olive oil
1 large onion, sliced
Fresh cherries, peaches,
  or oranges, depending
  on the season
¼ cup fresh basil,
  or 1 Tbsp. dry basil
½ cup red wine, optional
Orange juice, optional

1. Preheat oven to 350 degrees. Oil an 8 x 10 **KP**
inch roasting pan.
2. Place sliced onion on bottom of pan.
3. Put sliced fruit in pan. Place chicken on top,
and sprinkle with the basil and garlic. Let
refrigerate for 2 hours.
4. Cook chicken, covered, for ½ hour in 350
degree oven.
5. Chicken may be basted with the orange juice
or wine.
6. Bake uncovered for ½ hour longer.
Makes 2 to 4 servings.
*The choice of fresh fruit in season makes this
an especially sweet Shabbat dish.*

# CHICKEN CURRY  *Susan Markowitz*  **M**

Vegetable oil for sautéing
1 medium onion, minced
Boned chicken, 6 to 8
  pieces per person
2 tsps. paprika
2 tsps. garlic powder
Salt and pepper, to taste
1 cup tomato sauce
2 to 3 cups chicken broth
2 to 5 tsps. curry powder
Choose from following,
  or use all:
2 to 3 carrots, peeled and
  cut into chunks
2 to 3 potatoes, peeled and
  cut into chunks
½ to ⅔ pound raw
  green beans
6 small flowerets, each,
  cauliflower and broccoli
½ cup frozen peas
½ cup frozen corn

1. Cover bottom of dutch oven or large soup
pot with oil. Heat and sauté onion lightly.
2. Add chicken pieces, sauté on all sides about
10 minutes. Add salt, pepper, paprika, and
garlic powder.
3. Combine in a bowl the broth, tomato sauce,
and curry powder. Add to pot. Make sure to
adjust amount of curry powder used to suit your
taste. If curry is too mild, then add more, 1 tsp.
at a time, and taste again.
4. Add vegetables in order listed. Simmer,
covered, for 1 hour.
5. Serve with boiled white rice, and chutney* of
your choice.
*This dish tastes better the second day when
warmed in the oven in a covered casserole.*
*\*See APPLE CHUTNEY, p. 317.*

 POULTRY

## Ⓜ GLAZED ROASTED CHICKEN *Irene Sufrin*

2 3-pound roasting chickens
1 orange, quartered
1 small onion, quartered
Salt and pepper
2 tsps. rosemary
½ cup water

Glaze:
3 Tbsps. margarine
3 Tbsps. Dijon mustard
3 Tbsps. honey
1 Tbsp. apricot preserves
3 Tbsps. orange liqueur

1. Prepare chickens by rinsing inside and out. Pat dry. Squeeze the juice of the orange pieces over the chickens, inside and out. Put the oranges and onions into the chickens.
2. Season chickens with salt, pepper, and rosemary. Place chickens in a roasting pan, and pour the water into the pan.
3. Roast the chickens in a pre-heated 400 degree oven for 20 minutes. Reduce heat to 350 degrees and roast for 1 hour longer.
4. Prepare the glaze by combining all the ingredients except the liqueur in a saucepan. Heat until smooth. Stir in the liqueur. Pour the glaze over the chickens and bake until the chickens are golden brown, about 20 minutes more.

## Ⓜ ISRAELI CHICKEN *Laurel Feldman*

1 large chicken, cut up
¼ cup margarine
3 Tbsps. brown sugar
1 4-ounce can frozen
   orange juice concentrate
1 onion, chopped
1 cup green olives
1 cup black olives

1. Place chicken in an ovenproof dish.
2. Melt margarine in a saucepan. Add brown sugar and orange juice concentrate; stir until well blended.
3. Add onion and olives; blend together.
4. Pour sauce over chicken. Cover with aluminum foil.
Bake in 325 degree oven for 2 hours total. Remove foil for last ½ hour.
*Great for company, especially for Shabbat dinner! You may wish to use a smaller amount of olives; adjust to taste. This recipe doubles easily.*

# MEXICAN ORANGE CHICKEN *Irene Sufrin* **M**

1 fryer, cut up
½ tsp. salt
¼ cup margarine
2 Tbsps. flour
2 Tbsps. sugar
½ tsp. cinnamon
⅛ tsp. ginger
3 ounces frozen orange
  juice concentrate
Water
½ cup raisins
½ cup coconut

*Prepare this recipe one day before serving.*

1. Salt chicken and brown in margarine in large skillet. Remove only chicken from the pan.

2. Add flour, sugar, cinnamon, and ginger to the drippings in the skillet. Stir to form a smooth paste *(roux)*.

3. Add enough water to the orange juice concentrate to make 1½ cups.

4. Gradually add this orange juice mixture to the *roux* in the skillet. Heat and stir continuously until the sauce comes to a boil.

5. Add the chicken and raisins. Cover skillet and simmer for 45 minutes.

6. Cool, and place in refrigerator overnight to mellow.

7. Reheat the next day. Sprinkle with coconut just before serving.

*The day-before preparation makes this a convenient company treat.*

 **POULTRY**

## M ONION SOUP CHICKEN  *Barbara Ament*

2 Tbsps. flour
1 large (14 x 20) inch
  oven cooking bag
1 envelope onion or
  mushroom soup mix
1 tsp. dry basil leaves
1 garlic clove, minced
1 14½-ounce can whole
  tomatoes
3 medium carrots, cut in
  2 x ¼ inch strips
3 medium zucchini, split
  lengthwise and cut in
  1-inch pieces
2 whole chicken breasts,
  split
Paprika

1. Preheat oven to 350 degrees. Shake flour in cooking bag. Place in 13 x 9 x 2 inch baking pan.
2. Add soup mix, basil, garlic, and tomatoes to bag. Squeeze gently to blend ingredients and break up tomatoes.
3. Add carrots and zucchini. Turn bag gently to coat vegetables with sauce.
4. Arrange vegetables in an even layer. Sprinkle chicken with paprika. Place in bag on top of vegetables. Close bag with nylon tie. Make 6 half-inch slits in top.
5. Cook in 350 degree oven for 50 minutes or until chicken is tender.
6. Remove chicken from bag, arrange on platter, and spoon vegetables and sauce on top.
Makes 4 servings.

## M STUFFED CHICKEN BREASTS  *Madeline Goldman*

6 boned chicken breasts
1 package long grain &
  wild rice mix
  (not quick cook)
1 pound fresh mushrooms,
  sliced
3 to 4 onions, chopped
Oil
1 cup water

1. Prepare rice according to package instructions.
2. In a frying pan, sauté onions and mushrooms in oil. Add to rice.
3. Place boned chicken breasts flat in a glass baking dish. Put a scoop of rice mixture in center of breast and fold over so that skin side is up.
4. Fill spaces between rolled breasts with the remaining rice mixture.
5. Put approximately 1 cup water over chicken, making sure that the water gets to the bottom of the pan.
6. Bake 1 hour in 400 degree oven.
Makes 4 servings.
*You can prepare everything, freeze, and then bake at a later date. Great company dish!*

# CHICKEN MASHEHU *Judith Taylor* M

2 chickens, cut into
serving pieces
2 onions, sliced
2 garlic cloves, minced
1 cup plain tomato sauce
¼ cup Marsala wine or
dry sherry
½ cup water
2 tsps. basil
2 tsps. oregano
2 tsps. parsley flakes
Small mushrooms, about 20
Salt and pepper, to taste

1. Sauté chicken pieces in oil until browned.
Place in large casserole.
2. Sauté onion and garlic until transparent. Do
not allow garlic to get dark.
3. Add tomato sauce, wine, water, and herbs to
skillet. Simmer 10 minutes.
4. Pour sauce over chicken.
5. Sauté mushrooms briefly. Scatter over
chicken and sauce.
6. Bake, covered, in a 350 degree oven for
1 hour.
7. Uncover and continue baking 15 minutes or
until top is glazed.
8. Serve with rice or pasta.
Makes 6 to 8 servings.
*"Mashehu" is Hebrew for "something special."*

# CHICKEN CHASSEUR *Arlene Levin* M

3 whole chicken breasts,
skinned, boned, and cut
in 1-inch pieces
⅓ cup cornstarch
1½ tsps. salt
¼ tsp. pepper
½ tsp. dried thyme
4 Tbsps. vegetable oil
6 green onions, sliced
¾ pound fresh mushrooms
½ cup dry sherry
1½ cups chicken broth
½ tsp. tarragon
3 fresh tomatoes, cut in
eighths, or a 1-pound
can whole tomatoes
Hot cooked rice

1. Mix cornstarch with salt, pepper, and thyme.
Dredge chicken pieces.
2. Heat the oil in a large skillet.
3. Add chicken and sauté until brown on all
sides.
4. Stir in onions and mushrooms; continue
cooking for 2 minutes.
5. Add sherry, broth, and tarragon. Cover skillet
and simmer 10 minutes.
6. Stir in tomatoes. Cover skillet and cook 5
minutes longer.
7. Serve spooned over hot rice.
Makes 6 servings.

## ☑ CHICKEN WITH CUMIN SAUCE Arlene Levin

3 whole chicken breasts,
  boned and skinned
½ tsp. salt, divided
¼ tsp. pepper, divided
2 Tbsps. salad oil
1 tsp. cumin
2 cloves garlic, crushed
1-pound can tomatoes
1 cup water
½ tsp. sugar
¼ cup green onions,
  chopped

1. Sprinkle chicken with ¼ tsp. salt and ⅛ tsp. pepper.
2. In a heavy skillet, heat oil over medium-high heat until hot. Add chicken breasts and cook 2 minutes on each side. Remove from skillet, cover, and set aside.
3. Sauté cumin and garlic in drippings in skillet for 30 seconds. Add tomatoes, water, sugar, and remaining salt and pepper. Cook over high heat 5 minutes, stirring occasionally.
4. Reduce heat and add chicken to sauce. Simmer 2 minutes, spooning sauce over cutlets. Garnish with green onions.
Makes 4 servings.

## ☑ CHICKEN A LA KEFAK Nomi Erlich

One 3-pound frying
  chicken, quartered
1 Tbsp. cooking oil
1 medium onion, cubed
¼ tsp. black pepper
2 tsps. sweet paprika
1 tsp. cumin seed,
  or to taste
Salt, to taste
1 green pepper, cut into
  strips
4 carrots, peeled and
  sliced ¼ inch thick
1 to 1½ cups water
¼ cup pitted black olives

1. Heat oil in a large pot. Fry onions until golden brown. Add green pepper.
2. Add chicken to pot. Sprinkle with black pepper, paprika, cumin, and salt. Cook over medium heat for about 10 minutes.
3. Add carrots to pot. Add more oil if needed. Cook 2 or 3 minutes longer.
4. Add water and stir. Cover pot and cook approximately 30 minutes.
5. Add olives and stir. Cover and cook another 20 minutes, or until chicken is tender.
6. Serve with rice, potatoes, or noodles.
Makes 4 servings.
*This is an Israeli recipe.*
*("A la kefak" is Arabic for "great" or "terrific.")*

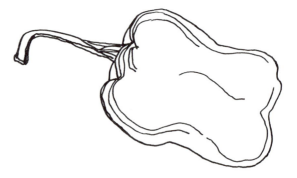

# EMPRESS CHICKEN *Irene Sufrin*  M

1 cup white meat of chicken,
  boned and cut in cubes
  (about 2 breasts)
2 green onions, cut in
  1 inch lengths
2 slices fresh ginger
2 tsps. sherry
3 Tbsps. soy sauce
½ cup water *or*
  chicken stock
1 can bamboo shoots
1 small jar chopped pimento
½ cup celery, sliced thin
½ cup mushroom slices
1 tsp. sugar
Peanut oil
1 package frozen peas,
  defrosted

1. Heat about 3 Tbsps. peanut oil in wok.
2. Stir fry onions, ginger, and chicken over high heat.
3. When chicken turns white, remove ginger slices and add sherry and soy sauce. Continue cooking over high heat for 5 minutes. Turn occasionally.
4. Add ½ cup water or chicken stock. Bring to a boil. Reduce heat and cook covered about 10 minutes.
5. Add bamboo shoots, celery, mushrooms, pimento, and sugar. Continue cooking until chicken is tender, about 10 to 15 minutes.
6. Add peas just before serving.
Makes 3 to 4 servings.
*Serve with cooked rice.*

# QUICK CHICKEN & VEGETABLE STIR FRY *Judy Miller*  M

2 pounds boneless chicken
  breast, cut into pieces
2 tsps. cornstarch
1 tsp. sugar
1 tsp. ground ginger
1½ tsps. salt (total)
2 Tbsps. dry sherry
3 Tbsps. soy sauce
¼ tsp. hot pepper sauce
½ cup vegetable oil
4 small zucchini, cut into
  bite-sized pieces
½ pound small mushrooms
½ pound fresh whole snow
  peas, string removed, or
  6 ounce package frozen
  Chinese pea pods, thawed

1. In medium-sized bowl, mix cornstarch, sugar, ginger, 1 tsp. salt, sherry, soy sauce, and hot pepper sauce. Add chicken pieces and toss. Set aside.
2. Heat oil in wok or large frying pan over medium-high flame. Add zucchini, mushrooms, and ½ tsp. salt, and stir over flame for 2 minutes. If using fresh snow peas, add to the mixture at this point and cook for another 3 minutes, stirring constantly. In either case, total cooking time for this step is 5 minutes.
3. Leaving oil in frying pan, remove vegetable mixture to a platter. If using frozen snow peas, add them to the rest of the vegetables.
4. In remaining oil, cook chicken mixture until tender, stirring frequently, about 10 minutes in all.
5. Add vegetable mixture, toss gently to mix. Heat thoroughly and serve immediately.
Makes 4 servings.
*Accompany with rice.*

## ORIENTAL CHICKEN
## Ⓜ & ASPARAGUS  *Laura Dudnik*

2 whole chicken breasts
2 Tbsps. oil
2 cloves garlic, minced
1 pound young asparagus
½ cup chicken broth
1 Tbsp. sherry
2 Tbsps. soy sauce
¼ tsp. sugar
Salt and pepper
2 tsps. cornstarch
2 tsps. cold water
2 Tbsps. toasted
    sesame seeds

1. Skin, bone and julienne chicken into 1 x 2 x ½ inch pieces. Slice asparagus diagonally, leaving tips whole.
2. Heat oil in skillet. Sauté garlic; sauté asparagus quickly. Remove with slotted spoon.
3. Add chicken to pan; sauté until firm and white.
4. Add broth, sherry, soy sauce, sugar, and seasonings. Mix thoroughly and simmer a short time. Add asparagus and heat through.
5. Blend cornstarch and water; add to sauce. Stir over moderately high heat until thick.
6. Sprinkle with sesame seeds. Serve immediately, while crunchy, over rice.
Makes approximately 4 servings.

## STIR-FRY SWEET & SOUR
## Ⓜ CHICKEN & VEGETABLES  *Hannah Engelman*

4 boneless chicken breasts,
    cut into strips or
    1 inch pieces
⅓ to ½ cup vegetable oil,
    for frying
½ cup flour
2 Tbsps. cornstarch
1 tsp. ground ginger
Salt and pepper
1 egg, beaten
1 8-ounce can tomato sauce
1 Tbsp. ketchup
¼ cup red wine vinegar
½ cup brown sugar,
    tightly packed
2 Tbsps. soy sauce
1 Tbsp. Worcestershire sauce
Choice of following
    vegetables, cut up:
    onions, mushrooms, green
    or red pepper, green beans,
    celery, carrots, bok choy,
    bean sprouts, or others of
    your choosing

1. Mix flour, cornstarch, ginger, salt, and pepper for coating in a bowl. Place beaten egg in a bowl next to it.
2. Dip chicken pieces in egg first, then dip in flour mixture. Leave pieces in flour.
3. Combine in a bowl the tomato sauce, ketchup, vinegar, brown sugar, soy sauce, and Worcestershire sauce. Set aside.
4. Heat oil in wok on high heat, drop all chicken pieces in, and fry, stirring constantly until golden brown, approximately 10 minutes. Remove and keep warm.
5. Prepare vegetables and stir fry together in remaining oil in wok for 5 minutes.
6. Add prepared sauce you have set aside. Cook for 3 minutes longer.
7. Add chicken and stir fry all together for 1 minute.
8. Serve immediately over rice or flat noodles.
❂ *Omit the meat and this is an equally delicious vegetarian meal.*

# CHICKEN WONTONS *Janet Resnick* 〔M〕

¾ pound skinned, boned, chopped chicken breast
1 Tbsp. each: sesame oil, soy sauce, sherry, cornstarch
1 tsp. each: sugar, minced, peeled ginger, minced garlic
2 Tbsps. oil
1 to 2 tsps. curry, or to taste
2 Tbsps. or less teriyaki sauce
1 tsp. sugar
2 Tbsps. sherry
1 Tbsp. cornstarch dissolved in ⅓ cup chicken stock
1 package wonton wrappers*
2 eggs beaten with 2 tsps. water for glaze
Approximately 1 cup vegetable oil

1. Toss chicken with sesame oil, soy sauce, sherry, cornstarch, sugar, ginger, and garlic. Let marinate several hours.
2. Heat wok or skillet. Add oil. Add chicken and stir until opaque. Stir in curry, teriyaki sauce, sugar, and sherry. Add dissolved cornstarch and bring to boil. This step can be done 1 day ahead.
3. Place wonton wrappers on work surface. Place 1 Tbsp. filling on one side of wrapper. Brush egg glaze on edge of wonton and fold over to form triangles; pinch sides together and brush with more glaze.
4. Heat oil in skillet. Fry until golden brown, turning once. Drain on a paper towel.
5. These can be made several hours ahead of time and reheated in low oven for 5 to 10 minutes.
6. Serve with black bean dipping sauce. (See following recipe.)
Makes 20 wontons.
*See EGGROLL OR WONTON SKINS, p. 328.*

# BLACK BEAN SAUCE *Janet Resnick* 〔M〕

2 Tbsps. fermented black beans, rinsed and drained
1 tsp. each: minced garlic, sugar, and fresh minced ginger
1 Tbsp. oil
1 cup chicken stock
2 Tbsps. soy sauce
1 Tbsp. sherry
1 Tbsp. cornstarch
Oriental type hot oil

1. Mash black beans, garlic, ginger, and sugar to make a smooth paste.
2. Heat oil in small skillet. Add bean mix and fry for about 30 seconds.
3. Stir in chicken stock, soy sauce, sherry, and cornstarch; add hot oil to taste.
4. Cook over medium high heat until slightly thickened.
5. Serve with CHICKEN WONTONS.

# ⓜ MOO SHU CHICKEN  *Janet Resnick*

12 ounces chicken,
  finely shredded
4 Tbsps. cooking oil
5 to 6 eggs, well beaten
1½ tsps. salt
2 Tbsps. dark soy sauce
4 to 5 ounces bamboo
  shoots, shredded
½ ounce dried lily
  flowers, soaked
¼ ounce dried cloud ears,
  soaked
½ tsp. sugar
½ tsp. m.s.g.
¼ tsp. black peppers
3 Tbsps. water
1 Tbsp. chili oil (optional)
2 Tbsps. Hoisin sauce*
1 Tbsp. sweet bean paste

1. Heat 2 Tbsps. of the oil in a wok on high heat. Add beaten eggs and scramble. Remove from wok and set aside.
2. Add remaining oil to wok. Add chicken and salt and stir fry for 2 minutes. Add dark soy sauce, then bamboo shoots, lily flowers, cloud ears, sugar, monosodium glutamate, black peppers, and water.
3. Cover to cook for 3 minutes, stirring occasionally. Add the cooked eggs and blend in with the other ingredients.
4. Remove and serve with Mandarin pancakes (see following recipe) and sauce made from 2 Tbsps. Hoisin sauce and 1 Tbsp. sweet bean paste.
*See HOISIN SAUCE, p. 327.

# ⓜ MANDARIN PANCAKES  *Janet Resnick*

3 cups flour
1 cup boiling water
⅓ cup cold water
4 Tbsps. vegetable
  shortening or oil

1. In a food processor put flour, hot water, cold water, and mix until a ball is formed.
2. Remove dough and divide in half. Roll each piece to about 12 inches long. Cut in 12 pieces (24 total).
3. Flatten each piece with the palm of your hand. With a rolling pin, work each piece into a thin pancake about 8 inches in diameter.
4. Brush one side of pancake with ½ tsp. of the shortening or oil. Place the pancakes together in pairs, back-to-back, greased sides out.
5. Fry each pair in an ungreased flat frying pan over a medium flame. It should be fried 30 to 45 seconds on each side until bubbles appear. Remove and separate pancakes quickly by pulling apart. Stack and cover with a moist towel.
6. Place 2 Tbsps. MOO SHU CHICKEN filling on each pancake. Fold edge to the center. Makes 24 pancakes.
*You may wish to spread each pancake with PLUM SAUCE (MOO SHU), p. 326, before adding the MOO SHU CHICKEN.*

# CHICKEN KABOBS *Sandi Dennis*  M

2 pounds boneless chicken,
  cut into large chunks
½ cup vegetable oil
¼ cup soy sauce
1 Tbsp. wine vinegar
½ tsp. garlic powder
½ tsp. ground ginger
1 large can pineapple
  chunks
1 green pepper,
  cut into chunks
15 to 20 fresh
  whole mushrooms
1 to 2 onions,
  cut into chunks

1. Mix oil, soy sauce, vinegar, garlic powder, and ginger together to make a marinade. Marinate the chicken overnight, if possible.
2. Before broiling, arrange chicken and pineapple, green pepper, mushrooms, and onion pieces alternately onto skewers.
3. Place on broiler pan. Broil 3 minutes on each side.
4. Serve with rice.
Makes 4 servings.

# CHICKEN CURRY WITH FRUIT *Naomi Pollak*  M

6 chicken breasts
¼ cup margarine
2 onions, chopped
2 apples, chopped and pared
1 Tbsp. curry
2 Tbsps. flour
1½ cups chicken broth

Optional additions:
Cooked diced potatoes
Green peas
Yellow raisins

Optional accompaniments:
Mandarin oranges
Coconut
Tomatoes
Peanut
Scallions
Bananas
Chutney*

1. Boil chicken in enough water to yield at least 1½ cups broth, about 30 to 40 minutes or until tender. Flake chicken. Set broth and chicken aside.
2. In a large frying pan, sauté onions and apples in margarine.
3. Sprinkle with flour and curry. Stir and cook for 2 to 3 minutes.
4. Add chicken broth. Bring to a boil. Add flaked chicken. Let simmer for 5 minutes while stirring.
5. Add any or all of the following: yellow raisins, green peas, diced, cooked potatoes. Mix well.
6. Place in a covered baking dish. Place in 300 degree oven for 10 minutes, or keep warm until ready to serve.
7. Serve with rice. Accompany with an assortment of Mandarin oranges, unsweetened coconut, diced tomatoes, peanuts, diced green onions, bananas, chutney, or other condiments of your choosing.
Makes 6 servings.
*This recipe is good to use for leftover chicken.*
*See APPLE CHUTNEY, P. 317.*

 **POULTRY**

## Ⓜ CHICKEN CACCIATORE  *Arlene Levin*

KP 2½ pound fryer chickens,
  cut in eighths
3 Tbsps. cooking oil
1 medium onion, coarsely
  chopped
1 medium green pepper,
  chopped
1 pound fresh mushrooms,
  sliced
1¼ tsps. salt
1 large clove garlic,
  minced
⅛ tsp. pepper
2 bay leaves
1 16-ounce can
  whole tomatoes
1 8-ounce can
  tomato sauce
¼ cup dry, white wine
2 Tbsps. parsley, chopped

1. Place large frying pan on heat. Allow to heat up before adding oil. Add chicken and cook until lightly browned, turning as needed. Remove from pan and set aside.
2. Add onion, green pepper, mushrooms, and garlic; cook about 3 minutes.
3. Add seasonings, tomatoes, tomato sauce, wine, and parsley. Return chicken to pan.
4. Cover, reduce heat to simmer, and cook 30 minutes or until chicken is tender. Turn chicken occasionally during cooking.
Makes 4 servings.
*Serve over hot white rice.*

## CHICKEN WITH GREEN BEANS
## Ⓜ IN TOMATO SAUCE  *Judie Zetouny*

1 2½-pound package
  frozen or fresh
  chicken breasts
1 large onion,
  peeled and sliced
4 cloves garlic, crushed
2 to 3 Tbsps. oil
1 large can green beans
1 large can tomato sauce
1 cube chicken bouillon
Salt and pepper

1. Heat oil in a pan. Sauté onion and garlic until soft.
2. Cut chicken into thin pieces, remove bones, if any, and braise with onion until golden.
3. Add drained beans, cook for 5 minutes.
4. Pour on tomato sauce, add bouillon cube and simmer 1½ hours. Add salt and pepper, if needed.
5. Serve with mashed potatoes. Garnish with 2 green onions chopped, or a sliced, hard-boiled egg.
Makes 6 servings.
*A nice treat for garlic lovers!*

# LO-CAL CHICKEN CACCIATORE *Rhonda Mlodinoff* **M**

1 cut-up frying chicken
1 10-ounce can tomato soup
¼ tsp. pepper
¼ cup water
2 cloves garlic, chopped
 (or more, if desired)
¼ tsp. salt (optional)
¼ cup red wine
½ medium green pepper,
 sliced
1 medium onion, sliced
1 Tbsp. white vinegar

1. Broil chicken slightly until just browned.
2. Mix soup, pepper, water, garlic, salt, wine, and vinegar together to make sauce.
3. Add chicken, green peppers, and onions to sauce in large sauté pan. Cover and cook over low heat approximately 45 minutes, or until chicken is tender. Stir often.
Makes 3 servings.

# BARBECUED CHICKEN WITH HONEY - MUSTARD GLAZE *Judy Wolkin* **M**

1 8-ounce can tomato sauce
½ cup oil
½ cup orange juice
¼ cup vinegar
1½ tsps. dried oregano,
 crushed
1 tsp. salt
6 peppercorns (leave whole)
1 clove garlic, minced
2 broiler/fryer chickens,
 quartered

For honey-mustard glaze:
¼ cup honey
1 tsp. Dijon mustard

1. In a large jar, combine tomato sauce, oil, orange juice, vinegar, oregano, salt, pepper, and garlic. Cover and shake well to blend.
2. Arrange chicken pieces in one layer in a shallow pan. Pour marinade over chicken; turn pieces to coat evenly on both sides.
3. Cover and marinate for 2 hours at room temperature or overnight in refrigerator, turning occasionally. Drain and reserve marinade.
4. Grill chicken over medium coals for 45 to 50 minutes, brushing with marinade and turning frequently.
5. Prepare glaze by mixing honey and mustard. Just before serving, brush chicken pieces with glaze, if desired.
Makes 8 servings.
*Chicken can also be broiled or baked using the same marinade.*

## ⓜ CHICKEN, POTATOES & PEAS *Jackie Siegel*

2 frying chickens, cut up
6 large baking potatoes,
  peeled, halved, and sliced
  lengthwise into wedges
Salt and pepper, to taste
½ cup olive oil
  (may use slightly less)
5 cloves garlic, crushed
1 tsp. oregano
½ large package frozen peas

1. Arrange chicken in an 11 x 14 inch baking dish.
2. Place potato wedges around the chicken. Season with salt and pepper. Mix olive oil, garlic, and oregano. Pour over chicken and potatoes, covering to coat. Add peas on top.
3. Bake at 350 degrees for 1 hour or until chicken is tender and potatoes are done. Baste chicken while baking.

## ⓜ TACO CHICKEN *Arlene Levin*

½ cup flour
1 1¼-ounce package taco
  seasoning mix
1 3-pound chicken,
  cut in eighths
½ cup margarine
1½ cups crushed corn chips

1. Combine flour and taco seasoning in a plastic or paper bag. Coat 2 to 3 pieces of chicken at a time by shaking them in the bag.
2. Melt margarine in a 15 x 10 inch baking dish.
3. Place coated chicken in dish, turning once to moisten surfaces with margarine. Roll in corn chips and return to baking dish.
4. Bake in 350 degree oven for 50 to 60 minutes. Makes 4 servings.

## ⓜ CHICKEN APRICOT *Helen Metnick*

1 chicken, cut into pieces
⅔ cup water
12 ounces apricot preserves
1 envelope onion soup mix
1 bottle Russian dressing

1. Put chicken pieces in shallow baking pan, skin side down.
2. Combine water, apricot preserves, onion soup mix, and Russian dressing. Spread half of the sauce onto the chicken.
3. Bake in 325 degree oven for 25 minutes.
4. Turn chicken over and add the rest of the sauce.
5. Continue baking for 50 to 60 minutes or until chicken is tender.
Makes 4 servings.
*Cranberry sauce may be used instead of the apricot preserves.*

# SHERRY AND CHERRY CHICKEN *Chris Erenberg* **M**

2 frying chickens, cut up
½ cup margarine, melted
Garlic salt, salt, and
    pepper, to taste

Sauce:
½ cup brown sugar,
    tightly packed
¾ cup sherry
2 large onions, sliced
    and sautéed brown
½ cup dark raisins
1 12-ounce bottle of
    chili sauce
1 cup water
1 large can Bing cherries,
    pitted and drained

1. Dip chicken pieces in melted margarine, season with garlic salt, salt, and pepper, and place in baking pan or roaster. Bake, uncovered, in 350 degree oven for 1 hour.
2. Prepare sauce. Slice and sauté onions in margarine until well browned. Remove from heat and combine with brown sugar, sherry, raisins, chili sauce, and water.
3. Remove chicken from oven, pour sauce evenly over it, and bake for 45 minutes longer at 325 degrees.
4. Add cherries and bake 15 minutes longer. Makes 4 to 5 servings.
*Easy and delicious Shabbat or company meal.*

## M CHICKEN-IN-THE-POT  *Bonny Barezky*

2 small fryers, cut up
2 quarts cold water
1 bay leaf
¼ cup celery leaves
2 Tbsps. onion, chopped
Salt and pepper, to taste
1 tsp. thyme
4 medium carrots,
  cut in halves
1 8-ounce package
  fine noodles, uncooked
1 12-ounce package
  frozen peas

1. Place washed and cut-up chicken in 5-quart saucepan or stock pot. Add water, bay leaf, celery leaves, and onions.
2. Cover and bring to a boil. Skim. Reduce heat and simmer uncovered for 30 minutes.
3. Add salt, pepper, thyme, and carrots. Cover and simmer for 15 minutes.
4. Add noodles and frozen peas. Cover and simmer for an additional 15 minutes.
5. Serve in a big soup tureen with crusty rolls. Makes 6 servings.
*This recipe takes only an hour to cook, but tastes as if you've spent all day in the kitchen! Good for Succot.*

## CHICKEN CUTLETS WITH
## M ORANGE-HONEY SAUCE  *Val Hakimi*

8 chicken cutlets
2 eggs, beaten with
  2 tsps. water
Bread crumbs
Salt and pepper
Oil for frying
1 cup orange juice
½ cup hot water
¼ cup honey
2 oranges, sliced

1. Place beaten eggs in one dish and bread crumbs in another. Coat chicken by dipping in eggs and crumbs.
2. Heat oil in a frying pan. Fry cutlets until lightly browned.
3. Arrange cutlets in a baking dish.
4. Combine orange juice, water, and honey. Mix and pour over cutlets. Top with sliced oranges.
5. Bake in 350 degree oven for 45 minutes. Cover and bake for 20 minutes; uncover and continue baking until chicken is tender.

# SESAME CHICKEN *Gail Taxy* **M**

6 chicken breasts or
  cutlets
4 cloves garlic, crushed
⅓ cup peanut oil
½ cup fresh parsley,
  chopped
½ cup fresh lemon juice
¼ cup sesame seeds,
  toasted

1. Clean, wash and pat dry chicken. Place **KP**
chicken in the bottom of a casserole.
2. Rub garlic into chicken.
3. Brush peanut oil on top of chicken. Sprinkle
with parsley.
4. Squeeze lemon juice over all.
5. Sprinkle with sesame seeds.
6. Bake uncovered in 350 degree oven for
35 to 45 minutes, or until chicken is tender.
Makes 4 to 6 servings.

# BREADED CHICKEN BREASTS IN GARLIC-WINE-TOMATO SAUCE *Judie Zetouny* **M**

4 boneless chicken breasts
1 egg, beaten
Bread crumbs
Oil for frying
1 cup white cooking wine
1 cup water
2 large tomatoes, chopped
1 garlic clove, crushed
1 chicken soup cube
Several fresh parsley
  sprigs, chopped
Salt and pepper, to taste

1. Flatten chicken breasts. Coat first with egg,
then bread crumbs.
2. Heat oil in a frying pan. Fry chicken until
golden brown on both sides. Remove from pan.
3. Pour water and wine into pan and bring to a
boil. Add tomatoes, garlic, soup cube, parsley,
salt, and pepper.
4. Simmer until tender, about 1 hour.
5. Serve with rice and tossed green salad.
Makes 4 servings.

# HONEY CHICKEN *Shirley Steinberg* **M**

1 chicken, cut into pieces
4 Tbsps. margarine
½ cup fresh chopped
  parsley or ¼ cup
  parsley flakes
¾ cup honey
1 tsp. salt

1. Melt margarine in a pan. **KP**
2. Add parsley, honey, and salt.
3. Add chicken, turning to coat.
4. Bake uncovered at 350 degrees for 1 hour or
until done, turning chicken pieces over once.
Makes 4 servings.

## M TURKEY CUTLET PICCATA  *Janet Resnick*

6 portions thinly sliced
   turkey fillets
   (approximately 6 to 7
   ounces per person)
¼ cup flour
1 cup seasoned bread crumbs
1 tsp. oregano, if desired
1 tsp. minced garlic
1 tsp. salt
½ tsp. pepper
2 eggs, beaten
1 Tbsp. lemon juice
1 Tbsp. honey
4 Tbsps. margarine
1 large lemon, sliced
Parsley

1. Pound turkey fillets until thin.
2. Place flour in one shallow dish; combine the crumbs, oregano, garlic, salt, and pepper in another.
3. Mix eggs, lemon juice, and honey in a small bowl.
4. Dredge turkey in flour; shake off excess. Dip in egg mixture, then coat with crumb mix. Place on a baking sheet and refrigerate at least ½ hour, or up to several hours.
5. Melt margarine in a large skillet over high heat. Sauté turkey slices about 2 minutes on each side or until golden brown. Remove to a platter.
6. Toss sliced lemon in pan juices and sauté about one minute. Spread lemon slices over turkey and serve with parsley garnish.
Makes 6 servings.
*If you prefer to bake the fillets, divide margarine into small pieces and spread over the meat. Bake at 375 degrees about 8 to 10 minutes or until golden brown. You do not need to turn these while baking. Place lemon slices on top during the last minute of cooking.*

# STUFFED TURKEY BREAST WITH DRIED MUSHROOM SAUCE  *Janet Resnick*

**M**

One 2- to 3-pound boneless turkey breast, cut in half
2 to 3 Tbsps. margarine
Salt and pepper, to taste
2 Tbsps. olive oil
2 large onions, finely chopped
2 Tbsps. garlic, minced
2 tsps. orange peel, minced
10 ounces fresh spinach, stems removed
Nutmeg, just a dash
½ cup pine nuts
½ cup currants

Sauce:
1 Tbsp. olive oil
2 ounces dried Shitake mushrooms, cut and soaked in hot water 30 minutes
1 Tbsp. parsley, minced
½ tsp. rosemary
1 tsp. garlic
½ cup Madeira or sherry

1. Have butcher butterfly turkey breast and pound it as thin as possible. Cut away skin. Sprinkle with salt and pepper, and spread with a little margarine. Place on a large sheet of heavy-duty foil.
2. Heat oil in skillet, add onions, and sauté about 8 minutes. Add garlic and orange peel and sauté another minute. Add spinach, cover and cook about 5 minutes. Uncover and increase heat to medium high. Cook until all liquid evaporates, pressing out as much liquid as you can. Season with salt, pepper, and nutmeg; add pine nuts and currants. This part can be done a day ahead.
3. Preheat oven to 325 degrees. Spread stuffing over turkey, leaving ½ inch border. Starting at shortest or uneven side, roll turkey jelly-roll-style, enclosing stuffing completely. Wrap turkey lightly in foil, folding foil along top and at ends. Transfer to roasting pan and cook about 1 hour.
4. Heat oil in skillet. Squeeze soaked mushrooms dry, and add to the skillet. Add Madeira. Bring to a boil over medium heat, scraping up the browned bits. Carefully open one end of the wrapped turkey, and let juices run into skillet. Boil for another 2 to 3 minutes. Return mushrooms to skillet.
5. Remove turkey from foil, slice in ⅜ inch pieces, and arrange on plate. Serve with sauce. Makes 6 servings.
*If your turkey is fresh, you can prepare the whole thing and freeze it before you bake it. Defrost in the refrigerator overnight.*

# VEGETABLE STUFFING
# FOR TURKEY *Karen Sager and Sharon Dorfman*

**KP**

1 pound fresh mushrooms
3 medium onions
1 pound carrots
3 garlic cloves
1 stalk celery (a complete stalk, not just 1 rib)
4 cups dry or toasted bread, cubed; or stuffing croutons*
3 to 4 cups boiling water
¼ cup peanut oil
3 eggs
Seasoned salt and pepper

1. Chop mushrooms, onions, carrots, celery, and garlic, either by hand, food processor, or food grinder.
2. Place bread or croutons in bowl. Pour boiling water over, to soften. Then drain, squeeze out excess moisture, and set aside.
3. Heat oil in large skillet or saucepan. Sauté chopped mushrooms, onions, carrots, celery, and garlic. Season with salt and pepper to taste.
4. Drain off approximately ½ liquid from vegetables. Add bread and mix well.
5. Beat eggs slightly. Add to vegetable mixture. Blend thoroughly.
6. Stuff turkey or capon with finished stuffing. Extra stuffing should be baked in a casserole, dotted with margarine, for 45 minutes in a 350 degree oven.

Makes enough stuffing for a 20 pound turkey.
*This is just as delicious for Pesach. Substitute 3 to 4 cups of Matzah farfel for the bread cubes.*

# mEAt

## **M** VEAL PICCATA *Arlene Levin*

1 small onion, chopped
2 cloves garlic, crushed
4 green onions, chopped
Oil for sautéing
1½ pound veal roast,
  sliced thin (easier to
  slice when partially
  frozen)
2 Tbsps. peanut oil
½ cup flour
½ tsp. salt
¼ tsp. pepper
2 Tbsps. dry sherry
2 Tbsps. fresh lemon juice
1 Tbsp. capers
8 thin lemon slices

1. Sauté onion, garlic, and green onions in oil just until tender. Remove from pan and set aside.
2. Mix flour, salt, and pepper together and place on a flat plate. Dip the veal slices in the flour mixture.
3. Lightly brown veal in 2 Tbsps. peanut oil for 3 minutes per side. Add sauteed onions and garlic.
4. Over high heat, add the sherry, lemon juice, and capers. Cook for 1 minute.
Garnish with lemon slices.
Makes 8 servings.

## **M** AUTHENTIC WIENER SCHNITZEL *Arlene Levin*

8 slices boneless veal
  (about 3½ ounces each)
2 tsps. salt
½ tsp. white pepper
1 cup flour
3 eggs plus 3 Tbsps. water,
  beaten together
2½ to 3 cups dry bread
  crumbs
1 cup peanut oil

1. Sprinkle veal with salt and pepper, and rub it in.
2. Let the veal stand at room temperature for 15 minutes.
3. Pound each slice, working from the middle to the edges.
4. First dip veal in flour, thoroughly coating it. Shake off excess flour. Then dip veal in egg wash, let excess drip off, and coat with bread crumbs. (You can do this procedure an hour before cooking.)
5. Cover veal with a towel and let stand at room temperature. (For perfect schnitzel, do not refrigerate.)
6. Heat a large frying pan. Add ¼ cup oil and add 2 schnitzels. Turn after 1½ minutes and cook for another 1½ minutes. Cook schnitzels 2 at a time, adding ¼ cup oil each time.
7. Remove to heated platter and serve immediately.
Makes 8 servings.

# FRENCH VEAL  *Jeanne Weinstein and Myra Dorf*  **M**

1½ pounds veal (4 slices, pounded)
1 egg, beaten
¼ cup bread crumbs
1 tsp. salt
2 Tbsps. oil
½ pound mushrooms, sliced
½ cup water
¼ cup sauterne
½ tsp. oregano
1 can of mushroom soup
1 can French fried onions

1. Pound veal until thin. Dip veal in egg, and then bread crumbs mixed with salt.
2. In a skillet, brown veal in oil. Place in baking dish.
3. Sauté mushrooms in the skillet. Add water and sauterne. Add oregano and mushroom soup. Try to scrape all breading off the pan. Pour over veal. Top with onion rings.
4. Bake in 350 degree oven for 1 hour.
*Quick and easy!*

# BLANQUETTE de VEAU (VEAL STEW)  *Chris Erenberg*  **M**

2½ pounds boneless veal stew (cut up)
4 ounces margarine
20 to 25 pearl onions, peeled, but left whole (about 1 package fresh)
4 carrots, cut into 1-inch pieces
1 *bouquet garni* (bay leaf, thyme, and celery flakes tied up in a square of cheese cloth)
2 Tbsps. flour
2 egg yolks
½ cup liquid non-dairy creamer
Juice of 1 lemon (or slightly less, depending on taste preference)
Salt and pepper, to taste

1. Over low heat, melt half the margarine in a Dutch oven. Keeping heat low, add the veal. Cook approximately 10 minutes until the meat gives off some juice, but do not brown meat.
2. Add enough water to barely cover the meat. Add onions, carrots, *bouquet garni*, and a little salt. Cover and simmer for 1½ hours.
3. Remove *bouquet garni*. After meat is cooked, make the sauce. Heat the rest of the margarine in a small saucepan. Stir in flour and add enough of the veal stock to make a thick sauce. Simmer for 5 minutes, stirring constantly.
4. Beat egg yolks, adding non-dairy creamer and lemon juice. Remove sauce from fire and stir in this egg mixture. Season to taste. Put sauce back on heat to warm, but do not let boil.
5. Drain any remaining stock from meat and vegetable mixture. Pour sauce over meat and vegetables. Serve with rice.
Makes 6 servings.
*Delicious kosher adaptation of traditional French provincial dish.*

# M VEAL STEW *Irene Sufrin*

1 pound veal for stew
1 green pepper, cut in
  1-inch squares
1 red pepper, cut in
  1-inch squares
Oil
4 potatoes, quartered
4 carrots, sliced
1 package peas, defrosted
2 cups chicken broth
Basil, to taste
Salt and pepper, to taste

1. Brown red and green peppers in oil in large Dutch oven or pot. Remove to platter.
2. Brown the veal pieces in same pot.
3. Add 2 cups of chicken broth. Simmer about 30 minutes.
4. Add potatoes and carrots. Simmer 30 minutes.
5. Add peas, salt, pepper, and basil. Simmer about 15 minutes.

# M VEAL STEW IN TOMATO MUSHROOM SAUCE *Fran Fogel*

1 to 1½ cups bouillon
  (beef or chicken)
1½ pounds cubed veal
4 to 5 cloves garlic,
  minced or pressed
½ tsp. fresh ground
  pepper
½ pound fresh mushrooms
  or more to taste, sliced
  thick (or 2 8-ounce cans)
1 8-ounce can tomato juice
Fresh tomato wedges
  (optional)
1 large onion, halved and
  sliced
3 bay leaves
1 Tbsp. oregano
2 tsps. basil
Salt, to taste (optional)

1. Heat ½ to ¾ cup bouillon in a pan. Add veal, garlic, and pepper. Add remaining bouillon, mushrooms, tomato juice, tomatoes, water, onion, bay leaves, oregano, and basil. Liquid should almost cover veal.
2. You may adjust recipe to taste at this point: more bouillon or more tomato juice.
3. Cover and cook over medium low heat until veal is done and sauce is thickened, approximately 25 to 35 minutes.
4. Serve over rice or noodles.
Makes 4 to 5 servings.

# ROLLED & STUFFED VEAL ROAST *Myra Dorf* **M**

5 pound veal breast for
   rolling, bones removed
   and saved
Garlic powder
Paprika
Pepper
Celery leaves

**Stuffing:**
2 Tbsps. oil
1 onion, chopped
2 celery ribs, chopped
1 garlic clove, minced
4 ounces mushrooms,
   chopped
½ tsp. salt
¼ cup parsley
2 cups stuffing croutons
1 cup boiling water with
   chicken bouillon cube
¼ cup pine nuts

**Stock:**
2 ribs celery
1 onion, sliced
1 bay leaf
1 cup veal stock *or*
1 cup chicken bouillon
½ cup Madeira or sherry
¼ tsp. rosemary

1. For stuffing, sauté chopped onions, celery, mushrooms, and garlic in oil. Season with salt. In large bowl, put stuffing croutons, sautéed mixture, parsley, boiling water with bouillon, and pine nuts. Mix and correct seasoning.
2. For stock, place veal rib bones in bottom of roasting pan. Add celery, sliced onion, bay leaf, veal stock or chicken bouillon, wine, and rosemary.
3. Season veal with garlic powder, pepper, and paprika. Place stuffing ½ inch from the end of roast. Roll and sew veal closed with white thread.
4. Place veal roast on bones in pan. Sprinkle paprika on top. Cover with celery leaves. Bake covered for 3 hours or until tender.
*Remove to platter and slice to serve. Stock from pot may be warmed and served as sauce. Elegant company fare.*

# LIVER FOR LOVERS *Bonny Barezky* **M**

12 ounces calves' liver
½ tsp. pepper
⅓ cup Dijon mustard
¼ cup sesame seeds
¼ cup mustard seeds
⅓ cup cooking oil

1. Dry liver with paper towels and broil quickly on both sides.
2. Sprinkle with pepper. Spread Dijon mustard on both sides.
3. Combine sesame seeds and mustard seeds on a dinner plate. Press liver onto seeds on both sides until most of the seeds are on the liver.
4. In a 10-inch skillet, fry the liver in the oil very quickly on high heat until brown on both sides.
Makes 2 servings.
*Salt-free, healthy, and tasty.*

## Ⓜ LOTUS BLOSSOM LAMB CHOPS *Judy Weiss*

6 lamb chops

Marinade:
½ cup soy sauce
¼ cup honey
2 Tbsps. vinegar
1 tsp. pepper

1. Combine soy sauce, honey, vinegar, and pepper. Marinate chops at least one hour (the longer the better).
2. Drain off marinade. May be baked or broiled in oven; however, these taste best when broiled on outdoor grill.

## LAMB WITH
## Ⓜ PRUNES, RAISINS AND WALNUTS *Chris Erenberg*

KP

2 pounds lamb, cut into
  bite-sized pieces
1 tsp. cinnamon
⅛ tsp. ground ginger
¼ tsp. nutmeg
¼ tsp. curry
¼ tsp. salt
¼ cup oil
8 medium onions, peeled
¼ pound medium-sized
  prunes
1 cup dark seedless raisins
1 Tbsp. sugar
1 cup walnuts, chopped,
  and lightly coated with
  sugar and cinnamon

1. Wash lamb and pat dry. Coat with mixture of cinnamon, ginger, nutmeg, curry, and salt.
2. Pour oil into 5-quart Dutch oven. Braise lamb at high temperature for 5 minutes, stirring occasionally.
3. Remove pot from heat. Add onions, prunes, raisins, and sugar. Put back on heat, bring to a boil. Reduce heat to simmer and let cook 2 to 3 hours, or until meat is tender.
4. The last 15 minutes of cooking, add the walnuts.
5. Arrange meat on a platter, garnish with the vegetables, fruit, and sauce.
Makes 5 to 6 servings.
*In Morocco, this dish is often served during Pesach, in commemoration of the paschal sacrifice.*

# SHISH KABOB *Irene Sufrin*

For 12 skewers:
3 thick tenderloins, cubed
Cherry tomatoes (whole)
Green peppers, cut
  in large pieces
Onions, quartered
Mushrooms, ends trimmed

Marinade:
½ cup oil
1⅓ cups soy sauce
4 Tbsps. molasses
4 tsps. dry mustard
4 tsps. powdered ginger
4 cloves garlic, minced

Day before serving:
1. Combine oil, soy sauce, molasses, dry mustard, ginger, and garlic for marinade in large bowl.
2. Add meat to marinade, and place bowl in refrigerator overnight.
Next day:
3. Place vegetables and meat cubes on skewers in unusual patterns (alternating attractively).
4. Brush marinade on the skewered vegetables and meat.
5. Place in baking pan for baking in 350 degree oven 45 minutes, or cook on a barbecue.

# CURRIED BEEF - RICE CASSEROLE *Harriet Chavis* M

1 pound ground beef
1 cup raw long grain rice
1 medium onion, chopped
6 Tbsps. oil
1 tsp. black pepper
1 Tbsp. Worcestershire
  sauce
¼ tsp. curry powder

1. Cook rice according to package directions. Set aside.
2. Heat oil, add onion, and sauté until brown.
3. In separate bowl mix together meat, pepper, Worcestershire sauce, curry powder, and rice. Pour into casserole. Stir well. Put in oven (middle rack).
4. Bake covered in 350 degree oven 30 minutes.
*Good with pita pocket bread.*

# MIDDLE - EASTERN RICE
# WITH BEEF *Susan Markowitz* M

½ to ¾ cup raw rice
½ cup margarine
½ cup blanched almonds
1 Tbsp. onion, chopped
½ pound lean ground beef
½ tsp. pepper
1 tsp. salt
½ tsp. cinnamon
½ tsp. nutmeg
2 cups water

1. Cook rice according to package directions.
2. Sauté almonds lightly in margarine. Remove almonds and sauté onions in same margarine.
3. Brown ground beef, add seasonings, and cook slowly for 5 minutes.
4. Add 2 cups water, an additional 1 tsp. of salt, drained rice, and almonds.
5. Simmer all together for 15 to 20 minutes.
*This rice dish may be used as a poultry stuffing or alone as a side dish. Sugar-free.*

MEAT

## M KUFTA *Naomi Levi*

1 cup water
1 mushroom soup cube
(½-ounce net weight)
or vegetable cube
1 pound lean ground beef
1 egg
Minced onion
¼ tsp. salt-free seasoning
Parsley flakes, pinch
1 4-ounce can mushroom
pieces
3 potatoes, cut into
pieces, *or,* sliced
carrots (optional)

1. Pour water into pan on top of stove.
2. Crumble mushroom soup cube, reserving ½ tsp. for use later. Add to water and bring to boil.
3. Meanwhile, add the ½ tsp. soup cube, egg, and spices to meat. Form into 4 loaves.
4. Lower heat under water to simmer.
5. Carefully place loaves into simmering water. (Optional: add potato or carrot pieces.) Cover and cook over low heat for 10 to 15 minutes.
6. Turn meat over, add mushroom pieces, and baste meat.
7. Cover and cook until meat is cooked through, about 5 minutes. Liquid will thicken.
8. Serve hot, pouring the sauce and the vegetables over the meat loaves.

## M ITALIAN BEEF BAKE *Debbie Nathan*

2 pounds boneless chuck,
cut into 1-inch thick
serving portions
(London broil cut is best.)
1 envelope onion soup mix
1 green pepper, in strips
¼ cup onion, chopped
1 16-ounce can tomatoes,
drained and chopped
(reserve liquid)
¾ tsp. salt
Pepper, to taste
1 Tbsp. steak sauce
1 Tbsp. cornstarch
2 Tbsps. parsley, chopped

1. Arrange meat slices, overlapping, on a 20-inch sheet of heavy-duty foil in a shallow baking dish. Sprinkle with soup mix, green pepper, and onion.
2. Add tomatoes, salt, and pepper over meat.
3. Combine reserved tomato liquid, steak sauce, and cornstarch, and pour over meat.
4. Bring foil up and fold and seal it over meat and vegetables.
5. Bake in 325 degree oven for 2 hours.
*Serve sprinkled with parsley over rice or noodles.*

# ITALIAN BEEF *Arlene Levin* M

5 to 7 pound roast
10 cups water
10 beef bouillon cubes
1 Tbsp. oregano
1 Tbsp. thyme
1 Tbsp. marjoram
½ tsp. Tabasco sauce
½ tsp. pepper
Salt, to taste
2 Tbsps. Worcestershire
  sauce
2 garlic cloves
1 green pepper, chopped

1. Roast the meat on a rack in an open roasting pan in a 325 degree oven for 30 minutes per pound. Roast will be rare. Cool and slice very thin.
2. To drippings in pan, add water and bouillon cubes. (Use the "Telma" small beef cubes that come 30 cubes to a container.) Add remaining ingredients. Simmer 15 minutes.
3. Add thinly-sliced beef and marinate overnight in refrigerator. To serve, heat only until hot. Do not boil.
Makes 10 servings.
*Delicious served sandwich-style on crusty Italian bread.*

# MEAT LASAGNE *Adele Cohen* M

8 lasagne noodles

Tomato sauce:
1 large onion, chopped
2 to 3 cloves garlic,
  minced
¼ cup oil
3½ cups tomatoes,
  peeled
1 small can tomato paste
2 bay leaves
1 tsp. salt
¼ tsp. pepper
½ cup water
1½ pounds ground chuck

Bechamel sauce:
1 medium onion, finely
  chopped
4 Tbsps. vegetable oil
3 Tbsps. flour
2 cups chicken broth
2 egg yolks

1. Boil noodles, drain, and set aside.
2. For tomato sauce place in pan: onion, garlic, ¼ cup oil, tomatoes, tomato paste, bay leaves, salt, pepper, and water. Mix well. Add ground chuck. Cover and simmer 45 minutes, stirring occasionally.
3. Prepare the Bechamel sauce: cook finely chopped onion in vegetable oil. Add flour and mix well. Stir in the chicken broth slowly, cooking over low heat until sauce is thick. Add slightly beaten egg yolks. Cook 10 minutes more.
4. In greased 12 x 7 inch baking dish, place layer of noodles, then tomato sauce, and then Bechamel sauce. Repeat.
5. Bake in 325 degree oven for 20 minutes.
Makes 6 servings.
*Kosher adaptation of traditional Italian favorite.*

## M EGGPLANT ITALIANO   Val Hakimi

2 Tbsps. salad oil
½ cup onion, chopped
1 clove garlic, crushed
½ pound ground chuck
1 3-ounce can Italian
 tomatoes, undrained
1 6-ounce can tomato paste
2 tsps. dried oregano
 leaves
1 tsp. basil leaves
Salt and pepper
1 Tbsp. brown sugar
1 large eggplant
2 eggs, slightly beaten
½ cup Italian-flavored
 bread crumbs

1. In 2 Tbsps. salad oil, sauté onion, garlic, and chuck in a large skillet, stirring occasionally until meat is browned.

2. Add tomatoes, tomato paste, oregano, basil, salt, pepper, and sugar. Bring to a boil, stirring with a wooden spoon.

3. Reduce heat, simmer, covered, stirring occasionally for 45 minutes.

4. Meanwhile preheat oven to 350 degrees. Lightly grease a 9 x 13 x 2 inch baking dish. Wash eggplant. Do not peel. Cut crosswise into slices ¼-inch thick.

5. In pie plate, combine eggs and 1 Tbsp. water. Mix well with fork. Place bread crumbs on wax paper. Dip eggplant slices into egg mixture, then dip into crumbs, coating evenly.

6. In 1 Tbsp. hot oil in skillet, sauté eggplant slices until golden brown and crisp on both sides. Add more oil if needed. Drain on paper towel.

7. Arrange half of eggplant slices in bottom of prepared baking dish. Cover with half of tomato-meat sauce. Arrange remaining eggplant over tomato sauce. Cover with rest of tomato sauce.

8. Bake uncovered in 350 degree oven 20 minutes.

Makes 8 servings.

*You may make ahead, bake, and freeze. Bake frozen in 350 degree oven, covered, 45 minutes, then uncover and bake 15 minutes longer.*

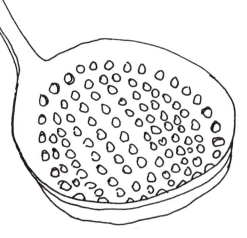

# GREEK MOUSSAKA *Judith Farah* M

KP

1 medium-sized eggplant
Oil
1 egg
1 cup tomato sauce,
  divided
1 pound ground meat
1 onion, finely chopped
½ cup water
1 tsp. sugar
Black pepper, dash
¼ tsp. cinnamon
1 bay leaf, halved

1. Peel eggplant and slice into ¼-inch slices. Brush both sides lightly with oil. Arrange slices in large baking pan. Broil on both sides until lightly browned.
2. In medium bowl, beat the egg with ½ cup tomato sauce.
3. Add ground meat and finely chopped onion. Thoroughly blend the egg mixture with ground meat.
4. Line an ungreased 7 x 11 inch baking dish with half of the slices. Spread meat mixture over eggplant. Top with remaining slices.
5. Mix remaining ½ cup of sauce with water, sugar, pepper, and cinnamon. Pour mixture over eggplant. Place ½ bay leaf in each end of the baking pan.
6. Bake uncovered in a 350 degree preheated oven approximately 1 hour until top is nicely browned and most of gravy has evaporated. Discard the bay leaf halves before serving. Makes 4 to 6 servings.

# HUNGARIAN GOULASH *Bess Sender* M

1 pound lean beef stew
  meat
1 tsp. salt
1 large onion, cut up
1 1-pound can tomatoes,
  strained
1 8-ounce can tomato sauce
1 6-ounce can tomato paste
1 bay leaf
1 pinch thyme
1 pinch marjoram
1 pinch salt
⅛ tsp. pepper

1. Sprinkle 1 tsp. salt on beef. Sauté beef with onion in a large covered pot until beef becomes very juicy.
2. Add tomatoes, tomato sauce, and tomato paste. Add 1 bay leaf, 1 pinch of thyme, and 1 pinch of marjoram to rest of ingredients. Salt and pepper to taste.
3. Simmer for 2 hours on top of stove, or until meat is done.
4. Serve goulash over broad noodles, or with noodles on the side.
Makes 4 servings.
*Easy and authentic!*

# MEAT LOAF & BARBECUE SAUCE *Myra Dorf*

2 pounds ground chuck
3 envelopes brown seasoning
1 small onion, grated
1 carrot, grated
2 eggs
½ cup bread crumbs
1 cup water

Barbecue sauce:
1 cup ketchup
½ cup barbecue sauce
½ cup water
3 Tbsps. brown sugar
2 tsps. lemon juice

1. Mix ground beef with seasoning.
2. Add grated onion, carrots, eggs, bread crumbs, and water.
3. Mix well.
4. Bake covered in 375 degree oven for 20 minutes.
5. Mix together barbecue sauce ingredients.
6. Pour out liquid from meatloaf. Add barbecue sauce to meatloaf. Bake in 325 degree oven for 1½ hours.
Makes 5 servings.

# MEAT LOAF *Sharon Dorfman*

1½ to 2 pounds ground beef
1 package onion soup mix
3 Tbsps. chili sauce
½ cup bread crumbs
3 Tbsps. water

1. Mix ingredients together.
2. Bake in a loaf pan at 350 degrees for approximately 1 hour.

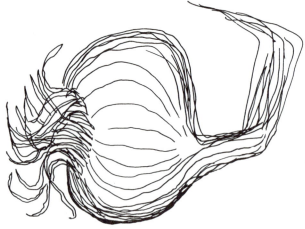

# 20 - MINUTE SPAGHETTI SAUCE  *Arlene Levin*  **M**

2 Tbsps. oil
½ cup onion, chopped
1 large clove garlic,
  minced
½ pound ground beef
1 12-ounce can tomato
  paste
1 1-pound can tomatoes
1 cup water
½ tsp. each basil, salt,
  and oregano
⅛ tsp. pepper

1. In heavy saucepan heat oil, and sauté onion, garlic, and ground beef.
2. Add tomato paste, tomatoes, water, basil, oregano, salt, and pepper.
3. Simmer, covered, 15 minutes, stirring occasionally.
4. Serve over favorite pasta.
Makes 1 quart sauce.

# SPAGHETTI SAUCE WITH GROUND BEEF  *Gayle Shapiro*  **M**

½ cup oil
2 medium onions, chopped
2 medium green peppers,
  chopped
½ pound mushrooms, sliced
2 pounds ground chuck
4 6-ounce cans tomato
  paste
2 8-ounce cans tomato
  sauce
1 28-ounce can tomatoes,
  cut up
1 6-ounce can water
1 bottle Carmel medium
  sweet wine
2 tsps. salt
½ tsp. pepper
2 tsps. oregano
1 tsp. basil
1 tsp. crushed red pepper
2 cloves garlic, minced

1. Sauté onions in ¼ cup oil until translucent. Transfer to saucepan.
2. Sauté green peppers until soft in remaining oil. Transfer to saucepan.
3. Sauté mushrooms until browned. Add to saucepan.
4. Brown meat, discard excess juices. Add to saucepan.
5. Add tomato paste, tomato sauce, tomatoes, water, wine, salt, pepper, oregano, basil, crushed red pepper, and garlic. Mix thoroughly.
6. Simmer on a very low heat for about 6 hours or overnight in a crockpot.
*Freezes beautifully and can be easily reheated in a microwave oven.*

# M SPAGHETTI ITALIENNE *Laura Wolf*

1 cup celery, diced
1 cup onion, diced
1 cup green pepper, diced
6 carrots, grated
2 to 3 cloves garlic, crushed
4 to 5 Tbsps. olive oil
2½ pounds ground chuck
4 tsps. salt
½ tsp. nutmeg
½ tsp. pepper
1 tsp. oregano
2 tsps. sugar
½ cup parsley, chopped
4 15-ounce cans tomato puree
2 6-ounce cans tomato paste
1 tsp. baking soda

1. In a heavy frying pan, sauté celery, onion, green pepper, carrots, and garlic in 2 Tbsps. oil until the onions are transparent. Set aside.
2. In another heavy frying pan, sauté chuck in 2 to 3 Tbsps. oil until brown. Drain fat and combine with sautéed vegetables in a large Dutch oven or soup pot.
3. Season with salt, nutmeg, pepper, oregano, sugar, and parsley.
4. Add tomato puree and tomato paste.
5. Simmer slowly for 2 hours or longer. Stir intermittently.
6. Add baking soda for the last 10 minutes of cooking.

*This is a very thick sauce. It may be thinned by adding an additional ½ can of tomato puree. This freezes very well. It's delicious with spaghetti, but more festive for company over spinach fettucini.*

# M SARAH'S FAVORITE MEATBALLS *Debbie Stern*

1½ pounds ground veal
2 Tbsps. margarine
¾ cup onion, finely chopped
1 tsp. garlic, minced
10 Tbsps. raw rice
1 tsp. mint, dried, crumbled
1 Tbsp. dill, finely chopped
4 eggs
Salt, to taste
Fresh pepper, to taste
3 cups chicken broth
1 Tbsp. cornstarch
¼ cup fresh lemon juice

1. Put the veal in a mixing bowl.
2. Melt margarine in a skillet; add onions and garlic. Cook, stirring until transparent. Scrape the mixture into the bowl.
3. Add the rice, mint, dill, 1 lightly-beaten egg, salt, and pepper. Blend well and shape into 24 balls.
4. Bring 2 cups of the broth to a boil, and add the meatballs. Partly cover, and let simmer 30 minutes. Drain the meatballs, but reserve the broth. Add additional broth to make 1½ cups. Bring to a simmer.
5. Beat remaining 3 eggs until light and lemon-colored. Beat in the cornstarch and lemon juice. Pour into the hot broth while beating vigorously. Bring to simmer while continuing to stir rapidly. Add meatballs and heat.

# QUICK AND EASY MEATBALLS *Eva Sideman* **M**

1 pound hamburger meat
Pepper
Paprika
Cracker meal
Chopped onions
1 egg

Sauce:
1 can tomato-mushroom
   sauce
⅔ cup water
⅓ cup sugar (or less)
1 Tbsp. lemon juice

1. Combine tomato-mushroom sauce, water, and sugar in a saucepan and heat.
2. Mix meat with pepper, paprika, cracker meal, chopped onions, and the egg. Shape into small balls.
3. Put meatballs into the hot sauce. Add lemon juice and, if desired, a pinch of ketchup. Cook for 1 hour.
Doubles or triples easily.

# MEATBALLS IN FRENCH BREAD BOWL *Chana Kaufman* **M**

1 pound ground beef
1 egg
½ cup dry bread crumbs
2 Tbsps. parsley, chopped
½ tsp. basil
½ tsp. oregano
Oil
1 15-ounce jar pareve
   marinara sauce
1 round (1 pound) loaf
   French bread (We prefer
   sour dough.)
Parsley for garnish

1. Combine beef, egg, bread crumbs, parsley, and herbs. Shape into 10 to 12 meatballs. Heat oil in wide frying pan and cook meatballs until brown on all sides.
2. Add marinara sauce. Cover and simmer for 20 to 25 minutes.
3. Cut off top third of bread, and scoop out insides (reserve for other uses), leaving a 1-inch thick shell. Heat, uncovered, in 350 degree oven for 10 minutes.
4. Transfer meatballs to warmed bread shell with slotted spoon. Garnish with parsley. Pour sauce into a bowl, and place at table to serve over meatballs and bread.
*Children's favorite—French bread makes an edible serving bowl.*

# ☒ MEXICAN HAMBURGER CASSEROLE *Harriet Chavis*

2 pounds ground beef
4 Tbsps. margarine
1 cup onions, chopped
4 cloves garlic, crushed
2 Tbsps. chili powder
2 tsps. paprika
1 tsp. salt
½ tsp. oregano
Pepper, generous dash
2 8-ounce cans tomato
  sauce
3 15-ounce cans kidney
  beans, undrained
1½ cups crushed corn
  chips

1. Melt margarine in large skillet. Brown beef, crumbling with fork as it cooks. Remove from skillet with slotted spoon. Set aside.
2. Add onion, garlic, chili powder, paprika, salt, oregano, and pepper. Sauté about 5 minutes.
3. Stir in tomato sauce, then mix thoroughly with beans, corn chips, and meat.
4. Turn into casserole dish and bake in 375 degree oven 1 hour or until edges are bubbly and brown.

# ☒ CHILI MACARONI *Helene Blivaiss*

½ pound ground beef
½ cup onion and celery,
  chopped
1 16-ounce can tomatoes,
  broken up
2 cups kidney beans,
  drained
1 cup elbow macaroni
1½ cups water
2 tsps. chili powder
¼ tsp. garlic powder

1. Cook beef, onion, and celery in large skillet.
2. Add tomatoes, kidney beans, macaroni, water, chili powder, and garlic powder to meat mixture.
3. Heat to boil. Reduce heat and cook uncovered until mixture thickens, about 20 minutes.
Makes 3 to 4 servings.

# BARBECUED BRISKET  *Joan Sohn*

**M**

4- to 5-pound beef brisket
Liquid hickory sauce
Barbecue sauce
Salt and pepper
Garlic powder, to taste
Onion powder, to taste
Paprika
Tenderizer

For paste:
2 Tbsps. brown sugar
1 Tbsp. mustard
2 tsps. vinegar

For gravy:
Pan drippings
½ cup ketchup
¼ cup barbecue sauce
1 cup water

1. Day before serving: Brush both sides of brisket with liquid hickory sauce and barbecue sauce. Let stand for ½ hour.
2. Put in large oven roasting pan, with the fat side down. Season with salt, pepper, garlic and onion powders, paprika, and tenderizer.
3. Roast the brisket uncovered at 300 degrees for 1 hour.
4. Take brisket out of oven, turn over on the other side. Season, as above, with salt, pepper, garlic and onion powders, paprika, and tenderizer, using somewhat less than on first side. Continue roasting, uncovered, for 1½ to 2 hours in a 300 degree oven.
5. Make a paste with the brown sugar, mustard, and vinegar. Brush this mixture on the fat side of the brisket. Roast ½ hour longer.
6. Remove from pan and refrigerate overnight. Put pan drippings in separate container and refrigerate also.
7. The next day, slice the brisket. Make gravy by heating the pan drippings with the ½ cup ketchup, ¼ cup barbecue sauce, and 1 cup water.
8. Heat sliced brisket. Serve with gravy.

# BREEZY BRISKET  *Robyn Turic*

**M**

7-pound brisket
1 can beer
3 onions, peeled in strips
4 potatoes, peeled and
    quartered
2 packages dry onion soup
Kishke (optional)

1. Wash brisket, pat dry, and place in roasting pan. Pour beer over brisket.
2. Lay strips of onions on and surrounding brisket. Arrange potatoes around brisket.
3. Shake the 2 packages of onion soup mix over meat. Add water (if needed), no more than 1 cup. Tightly cover and seal contents of pan.
4. Place in 300 degree oven, and cook slowly. Check once to maintain liquid level (do not let liquid cook away; add more water if necessary).
5. Place kishke around and uncover brisket ½ hour before finished. Replace in oven and cook until brown.
Makes 6 servings.

## M EASY BRISKET *Jackie Siegel*

4- to 6-pound first-cut, scored brisket
1 medium onion, chopped
½ cup ketchup
½ cup barbecue sauce
¼ cup wine
1 cup brewed coffee
Water
Salt and pepper

1. Season brisket with salt and pepper, to taste.
2. Place onion on bottom and top of brisket in roasting pan.
3. Combine ketchup, barbecue sauce, wine, and coffee. Pour mixture over brisket. Bake covered in 350 degree oven. Check in 1 hour to see if water is needed. Bake 2½ to 3 hours.

## M TZIMMIS WITH KNAIDLACH *Jennifer Gritton*

5-pound brisket
Pepper, to taste
Oil
Water
7 to 8 sweet potatoes, peeled and cut into large chunks
2 to 3 bunches carrots, peeled and cut into large chunks
1 or 2 packages frozen lima beans
1½ boxes prunes
½ to 1 cup brown sugar, to taste

For Knaidlach:
6 eggs*
3 Tbsps. sugar
3 Tbsps. oil
¾ to 1 cup flour

1. Season brisket with pepper. Sear with oil. Cover with water in pot and cook on stove 1 hour.
2. Add sweet potatoes, carrots, lima beans, prunes, brown sugar, and knaidlach, last.
3. For knaidlach: Combine eggs, sugar, and oil. Beat with spoon. Add enough flour to thicken to a rich consistency. (It will no longer look like eggs, but can still be poured.) Pour into the pot and cover. Cook everything until done and tasty, (at least 2 more hours).

*The amount of vegetables should be determined by personal preference; any quantities listed here are guidelines. *In our family, we usually double or triple the knaidlach, using 18 eggs, and it is still the first thing to disappear! My grandmother Edith made this dish every Rosh Hashanah, and we continue this tradition.*

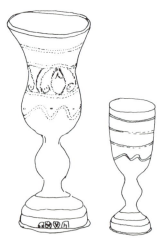

# FRIDAY NIGHT BRISKET  *Karen Sager*

4- to 5-pound brisket,
first cut
1 cup chili sauce
1 cup vinegar or old wine
3 Tbsps. brown sugar
2 tsps. seasoned salt
2 medium onions, sliced
very thin
1 to 2 cups bouillon

1. Marinate brisket in sauce made by mixing together the chili sauce, vinegar, brown sugar, and seasoned salt. Allow to marinate in refrigerator several hours or overnight.
2. Place brisket in a covered roasting pan. Arrange onion slices on top, and pour sauce over all.
3. Cover pan and roast in 325 degree oven for 3 to 4 hours.
4. Baste every 30 minutes. Add hot bouillon as necessary to replenish sauce and prevent burning. (May be made to this point the day before.)
5. Slice meat thin against the grain. Arrange slices carefully on ovenproof platter or in a large Pyrex. Pour approximately half the sauce over the meat, cover and keep warm, or reheat in very low oven or microwave.
6. Warm remaining sauce on stovetop and pass in gravyboat; it is also delicious over boiled or roasted potatoes.

*This is a mainstay of our Shabbat dinner table; it is adapted from my mother's recipe. Basting is the secret to successful brisket!*

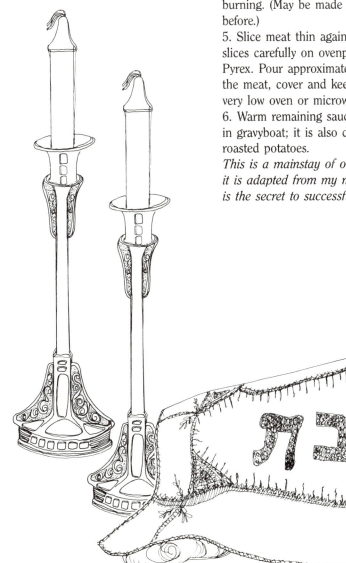

# M MONGOLIAN BEEF *Janet Resnick*

1 flank steak

Marinade mix:
1½ Tbsps. light soy
   sauce
1 large egg
2 Tbsps. cornstarch

1½ Tbsps. light soy sauce
1 tsp. salt
½ tsp. sugar
1 tsp. sesame oil
½ tsp. monosodium
   glutamate
2 to 3 cups vegetable or
   peanut oil
2 to 3 ounces "rice sticks"
3 to 4 dried red hot
   peppers (soak in water
   for 30 minutes)
10 green onions cut in
   ½-inch angled pieces

1. Place steak in freezer for 30 minutes; cut into thin slices ¹⁄₁₆ inch thick by 1½ inches long.
2. Marinate beef with the soy sauce, egg and cornstarch mixture for 15 to 30 minutes.
3. Mix together soy sauce, salt, sugar, sesame oil, and monosodium glutamate.
4. Heat 2 to 3 cups vegetable oil in a wok at 400 degrees. Loosen rice sticks. When the oil is hot, deep fry rice sticks for 3 seconds on each side. Remove to paper towel. Crush and put on a platter.
5. With the same oil, deep fry marinated beef at 375 degrees for 20 seconds and set aside.
6. Remove most of the oil from the wok, leaving 1½ Tbsps. of oil. Heat until smokey hot. Add red hot peppers and green onions. Stir well. Then add beef and seasoning sauce. Mix well. Place the mixture on top of the rice sticks.

# M CHIN CH'IEN NIU PAI *Irene Sufrin*

1 pound beef, sliced for
   cooking in wok
1 tsp. sugar
2 Tbsps. soy sauce
1 Tbsp. sherry
2 tsps. cornstarch
4 dried mushrooms, soaked
   for ½ hour in water
1 package frozen snow peas
1 can water chestnuts,
   sliced
½ tsp. salt
4 slices ginger root *or*
1 tsp. powdered ginger
Peanut oil

1. Combine sugar, soy sauce, sherry, and cornstarch.
2. Toss meat in the marinade.
3. Place 1 Tbsp. oil in wok. Heat. Add mushrooms, snow peas, water chestnuts, and salt.
4. Stir fry about 2 minutes and set aside.
5. Add ginger, 2 Tbsps. oil, and meat to wok. Brown meat.
6. Remove and discard ginger slices.
7. Return vegetables and heat for a few seconds until hot.
8. Serve over rice.

# PEKING NOODLES  *Miriam Steinberg*  **M**

1 pound vermicelli or
  thin spaghetti
¼ cup brown bean sauce
2 tsps. hoisin sauce*
2 scallions, chopped
½ cup chicken stock
¼ tsp. sugar
¼ tsp. chili oil or
  powder
1 Tbsp. peanut oil
½ tsp. salt
1 Tbsp. garlic, minced
1 pound ground beef

Garnishes:
Jullienned cucumber
Jullienned radishes
Bean sprouts
Water chestnuts, diced
Scallions, sliced

1. Cook noodles, al denté.
2. Combine bean sauce, hoisin sauce, scallions, stock, sugar, and chili oil or powder.
3. Heat oil in frying pan or wok. Add salt and garlic. Stir fry meat until just done. Add sauce. Stir, cover, and cook 5 minutes over medium heat. (May be done up to 2 days ahead; reheat in microwave or in wok.) Serve hot or tepid.
Serve noodles, sauce, and garnishes in separate bowls.
Makes 6 to 8 servings.
*The sauce is highly flavored so that each person uses only a small amount.*
*\*Hoisin sauce may be difficult to find with kosher certification; see HOISON SAUCE, p. 327. For a complete buffet including this recipe, see p. 68.)*

# TOMATO PEPPER BEEF  *Joyce Kamen*  **M**

1 pound beef (thin chuck)
¼ cup soy sauce
1 tsp. sugar
2 large, firm tomatoes,
  cut in wedges
1 green pepper, cut in
  strips
¼ cup vegetable oil
½ tsp. ground ginger
1 to 2 cloves garlic

1. Slice beef in narrow strips (it will slice easily if partially frozen).
2. Pour ¼ cup soy sauce and sugar over meat and marinate 1 hour. Cut up tomatoes and green pepper.
3. Heat oil in large skillet, and add garlic and ginger. Add meat and green pepper. Cover and cook 1½ hours.
4. At the last minute, add tomatoes. Cook a minute or two.
Serve over a bed of rice.
Makes 3 to 4 servings.
*Easy, yet elegant.*

MEAT

# M BEEF WELLINGTON *Myra Dorf*

Crust:
2 cups flour
6 Tbsps. margarine
6 Tbsps. Crisco
¾ tsp. salt
5 Tbsps. cold water
1 egg yolk (for glaze)

Marinade:
1½ Tbsps. soy sauce
1½ Tbsps. Worcestershire
sauce
1 Tbsp. Madeira
2 tsps. cognac

5 pound eye-of-the-rib
roast

Beef Wellington stuffing:
1½ Tbsps. margarine
3 large shallots, chopped
½ pound mushrooms,
chopped
1 Tbsp. flour
2½ Tbsps. non-dairy
cream
2½ Tbsps. Madeira
¼ tsp. salt
½ tsp. chervil
1 Tbsp. parsley
4 shakes pepper

Sauce Madere:
3 Tbsps. margarine
3 Tbsps. flour
1 cup beef bouillon
2 shallots, chopped
1 clove garlic, minced
1 small onion, chopped
3 sprigs parsley
¼ tsp. thyme
⅓ cup Madeira wine

The day before serving:
1. Mix crust by placing flour and salt in bowl. Cut in shortening and margarine. Add water 1 Tbsp. at a time until dough holds together in a ball. Refrigerate overnight.
2. Mix marinade ingredients and marinate the rib roast overnight.
The day of serving:
3. Melt margarine, sauté shallots and mushrooms. When soft and moisture is absorbed, add flour, stir, and lower flame. Add cream and other ingredients. Cook 5 minutes or until thick. Cool.
4. Preheat oven to 450 degrees. Rub rib roast with oil and roast for 10 minutes. Remove from oven and cool. Reserve juice in pan for sauce.
To assemble:
5. 2 hours before dinner, take crust dough from refrigerator. Divide dough into 2 main parts, reserving a little extra for decorations. Roll the bottom and put on cookie sheet. Place dried, cooled roast on dough.
6. Spread stuffing over meat. Cover carefully with other half of dough. Wet and seal the edges of the pastry.
7. Decorate the top of the pastry with extra dough forming flowers. Beat egg yolk, mix with a little water, and brush over pastry for a glaze. Refrigerate 10 minutes before cooking.
8. Preheat oven to 450 degrees. Insert meat thermometer in roast. Bake about 45 minutes or until thermometer reaches rare.
9. While meat is baking, prepare Sauce Madere. In a saucepan, prepare a *roux* by melting margarine and quickly stirring in flour. Add hot beef bouillon, stirring to blend. Add shallots, garlic, onion, parsley, and thyme. Simmer covered for 30 minutes. Strain, add Madeira, juice reserved from pre-cooking roast, and season to taste.
*Makes a beautiful presentation for company. Slice at the table, arrange meat and crust on individual plates, spoon sauce over meat.*

# FiSH

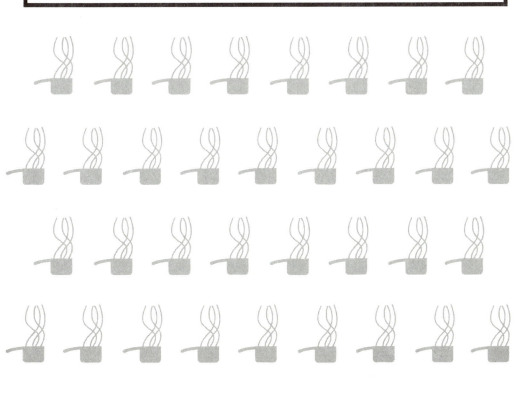

#  SPINACH STUFFED FISH *Joan Sohn*

5-pound trout or white-
fish, boned and split
6 Tbsps. butter, melted
1 cup dry wine

Stuffing:
4 Tbsps. butter
3 Tbsps. scallions or
shallots, finely chopped
1 10-ounce package chopped
frozen spinach, defrosted
and squeezed dry
1½ cups bread crumbs
2 to 4 Tbsps. heavy cream
¼ tsp. lemon juice
½ tsp. salt
Pepper to taste

1. Melt butter for stuffing in skillet. Cook
scallions or shallots for 2 minutes until soft.
2. Add spinach and cook over high heat,
stirring 2 to 3 minutes until moisture
evaporates. (Transfer to large bowl.)
3. Add crumbs, cream, lemon juice, salt and
pepper.
4. Preheat oven to 400 degrees.
5. Fill fish with stuffing. Brush 2 Tbsps. melted
butter on bottom of baking dish. Place fish in it
and put 2 Tbsps. melted butter on top.
6. Combine remaining 2 Tbsps. melted butter
with wine and pour over fish. Bring to simmer
on stove, then bake, uncovered, basting often
for 40 to 50 minutes. Add more wine if it
evaporates.
*Serve with hollandaise (for a recipe, see p. 325).*
*Beautiful and delicious company fare!*
*Recommended for Shavuot or other dairy holiday.*

# SALMON IN PUFF PASTRY *Janet Resnick*

12 ounces salmon, cubed
Margarine
3 onions, sliced
½ pound mushrooms,
sliced
¼ cup cooked rice
1 sheet puff pastry,
(frozen)
1-ounce slice nova lox
Chopped parsley
Pepper
Lemon juice
1 egg, slightly beaten

1. Heat margarine in a frying pan. Sauté onions
and mushrooms.
2. Cook rice in boiling water.
3. Wet baking tray. Defrost and place the sheet of
puff pastry on the baking tray.
4. Arrange salmon, onions, mushrooms, rice, nova,
parsley, salt, pepper, and lemon juice in center.
5. Fold over pastry and seal with water. Vent top.
Brush with water. Bake in 400 degree oven 15
minutes.
6. Glaze with egg. Bake in 425 degree oven 25 to
30 minutes and then glaze again.
Makes 8 servings.
*Serve with sour cream, melted butter, or dill sauce.*

# FISH IN PHYLLO *Evelyn Aronson*

¾ pound of sole in two
   pieces (sprinkled
   lightly with lemon juice)
½ pound fresh salmon
   (may use canned salmon)
2 egg whites
½ tsp. salt
½ tsp. dill
3 shakes cayenne pepper
1 cup whipping cream
8 phyllo leaves
2 sticks butter, melted
Bread crumbs

1. After removing skin, place salmon in bowl of food processor and chop with metal blade.
2. Add egg whites, salt, dill, and cayenne pepper. With food processor going, add cold whipping cream. Turn off when all cream is added. Set aside.
3. Butter and stack 8 sheets of phyllo, leaf by leaf, sprinkling bread crumbs between each layer.
4. Put sole (wiped dry) on top of buttered phyllo leaves, either on the length or width side, depending on size of fish.
5. Brush fish with melted butter, salt, and pepper. Sprinkle with dill.
6. Spoon prepared salmon mousse on top of fish. Butter second piece of fish, sprinkle with salt, pepper, and dill, and place on top of mousse.
(Note: Place fish about ½ of the way up from bottom of phyllo).
7. Carefully roll up phyllo; use wax paper and damp towel to help. Roll up loosely, leaving room for expansion. Shape one end into a head and pinch other end to resemble tail.
8. Very carefully place on cookie sheet. Try not to break. Brush with butter. Bake in preheated 375 degree oven for 40 minutes or until brown. During baking, brush with butter.
*Festive and delicious!*

141

# ⓓ BRIOCHE *Jennifer Gritton*

**Brioche dough:**
½ cup milk
½ cup butter
½ cup sugar
1 package active dry yeast
¼ cup lukewarm water
4 whole eggs, beaten
3¼ cups flour, sifted
1 egg, beaten, to brush top

**Filling:**
1 onion
½ pound mushrooms
Butter for sautéing
2 cans salmon
8 ounces sour cream
Fresh or dry dill
Salt and fresh ground
    pepper

**Creamy sweet and
    sour sauce:**
2 Tbsps. fancy prepared
    mustard
¼ cup sour cream
⅓ cup mayonnaise
1 Tbsp. lemon juice
1 Tbsp. sugar
1 tsp. honey (optional)
1 tsp. cider vinegar
    (optional)

To prepare brioche dough the day before:
1. Scald milk; cool to lukewarm. Set aside. Cream butter and sugar in bowl. Soften yeast in water in another bowl.
2. Blend milk, creamed butter mixture, and yeast. Add beaten eggs and flour and beat with a wooden spoon. Cover and let rise until doubled in bulk.
3. Stir down and beat thoroughly. (Don't be alarmed by gooey consistency.) Cover and refrigerate overnight.

To prepare filling the next day:
4. Sauté onion and mushrooms in butter. Mix in salmon, sour cream, dill, salt, and pepper.
5. Remove dough from refrigerator, stir down and turn out on floured pastry cloth or board. Roll out into rectangle 18 inches by 16 inches (approximately).
6. Take a square baking pan or 10 x 6 x 1¾ inch rectangle pan. Center cloth with dough-side up over pan. Pile salmon filling into dough.
7. Draw the long edges of the dough together over the filling and pinch to seal. Fold the ends like envelope flaps over filling. Cut off excess dough and save.
8. Flip over onto lightly greased and floured baking sheet, seam side down. Remove pan and cloth from top. Use excess dough to create decorations, such as flowers or a fish; place these on top of brioche.
9. Brush with beaten egg. Make 2 to 3 steam holes along side. Bake in 425 degree oven 10 minutes. Lower to 350 degrees, and bake for 10 to 15 minutes more.
10. Mix mustard, sour cream, mayonnaise, lemon juice, and sugar together. Add honey and vinegar, if using. Chill.
*Slice to serve and spoon sauce over individual servings. Gourmet fare to impress your guests!*

# BAKED SALMON *Gail Taxy*

Salmon fillets for 4
  (½ fish butterflied,
  not steaks)
½ lemon, for juice
Salt, to taste
Fresh ground pepper
Butter
1 Tbsp. mayonnaise
  (optional)
1 tsp. Dijon mustard
  (optional)*

KP

1. Rinse fish and pat dry. Spray baking dish with non-stick oil spray. Place fish in pan.
2. Squeeze ½ fresh lemon over fish. Season with salt and fresh ground pepper. Dot with thin pats of butter.
3. Bake in 350 degree oven 30 to 40 minutes.
4. Spread lightly with mixture of 1 Tbsp. mayonnaise and 1 tsp. Dijon mustard. Bake additional 10 minutes.
Makes 4 servings.
*Low calorie, especially if mayonnaise is omitted. Simple, yet tasty; even kids like it!*
*\*Omit mustard for Pesach recipe.*

# FRESH SALMON STEAKS BAKED
# IN RED WINE WITH GRAPES *Irene Sufrin*

4 salmon steaks
1 tsp. salt
¼ tsp. pepper
1 Tbsp. melted butter*
3 Tbsps. green onion,
  chopped
½ cup red wine
Juice of ½ lemon
½ tsp. cornstarch
1 Tbsp. cold water
2 cups seedless green
  grapes

1. Preheat oven to 400 degrees. Grease an ovenproof dish or casserole.
2. Season salmon with salt and pepper. Brush with melted butter. Place in oven for 5 minutes.
3. In a saucepan, combine the green onion, wine, and lemon juice. Bring to a boil and simmer for 5 minutes.
4. Dissolve cornstarch in water and stir into the sauce, to thicken.
5. Remove the salmon from oven and pour sauce over it. Return to oven for 5 minutes.
6. Add the grapes and bake 5 minutes more.
◆ *This recipe may be made pareve by substituting margarine for butter.*

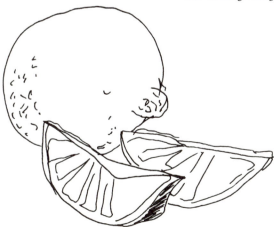

## ◆ₚ GRILLED SALMON  *Arlene Levin*

1½ to 2 pounds fish
  fillets (salmon, white
  fish, pike, snapper)
½ cup margarine, melted
¼ cup lemon juice
2 tsps. salt
½ tsp. Worcestershire
  sauce
¼ tsp. white pepper
Hot pepper sauce, dash

1. Place fillets on enclosed greased wire grill (or greased foil). Combine melted margarine, lemon juice, salt, Worcestershire sauce, pepper, and hot pepper sauce in a pan.
2. Baste fish with sauce. Cook fish about 6 to 8 minutes per side.
3. Baste often with sauce .
When serving leftovers, sauce can be added to fish if desired.
Makes 6 servings.
*Fast and easy.*

## ◆D SALMON PATTIES  *Nancy Goldstein*

1 15½-oz. can red salmon,
  flaked
2 eggs, beaten
Salt and pepper, to taste
½ cup milk
½ cup matzah meal
¼ cup baking soda
Oil for frying

White sauce:
1 cup hot milk
2 Tbsps. butter or
  margarine
2 Tbsps. flour
¼ tsp. salt
⅛ tsp. pepper
½ can small peas
  (optional)

1. Flake salmon, removing bones.
2. Add salt, pepper, and eggs. Mix.
3. Add milk, matzah meal, and baking soda. Mix well.
4. Spoon batter in "patty" shapes into hot oil. Fry until golden brown. Turn and repeat on other side.
5. Drain oil by putting patties on paper towel to absorb grease.
6. To make white sauce: Scald the milk. Set aside. Melt butter in second pan or microwave. Add flour, stirring constantly.
7. Stir in the hot milk gradually and cook, stirring constantly, until mixture thickens. Add peas, if desired.
8. Add seasonings. Serve hot.
Makes about 10 patties.
*Delicious and different family meal.*

# PECAN SCROD *Bonny Barezky* **D**

2 16-ounce scrod
(or other flat) fillets
3 Tbsps. sour cream
2 Tbsps. liquid margarine
3 tsps. cheddar cheese
spread
¼ cup pecans, chopped
½ tsp. garlic powder

1. Spray a broiling pan with non-stick cooking spray. Place fillets on pan.
2. Combine sour cream, margarine, cheese, pecans, and garlic powder. Spread on fillets.
3. Broil approximately 5 minutes or until brown spots appear. Reduce oven temperature to bake at 350 degrees and bake for 5 more minutes. Makes 2 servings.

# TWO EASY SCRODS *Fran Fogel* **D**

**SCROD I**
1 to 1½ pound fresh scrod
Favorite oil and vinegar
dressing
Seasoning, to taste

**SCROD II**
1 to 1½ pound fresh scrod
½ cup white wine, *or*
2 Tbsps. lemon juice mixed
with 2 Tbsps. water
½ to ¾ cup lightly
seasoned bread crumbs
Onion powder, *or*
Seasoning of choice
Fresh lemon, for juice
¼ cup butter

**SCROD I**
1. Pick your favorite oil and vinegar salad dressing. Brush a small amount on pan. Then brush 2 Tbsps. or more to taste on top of fish. Use any additional herbs or spices desired.
2. Bake in 350 degree oven 15 to 22 minutes until fish flakes (if necessary bake several minutes longer).
Can sprinkle with Parmesan cheese (optional).

**SCROD II**
1. Take the same scrod and put 2 Tbsps. to ½ cup white wine or lemon juice and water mixture in pan.
2. Place scrod in pan, sprinkle with bread crumbs lightly seasoned with onion powder, "Bon Appétit," or any other spices of your choice.
3. Squeeze lemon juice on top of crumbs and either dot with butter or pour melted butter or margarine over top and bake in 350 degree oven 15 to 22 minutes until fish is flaky.
**P** *This recipe may be made pareve by substituting margarine for butter.*

## ⒟ COCONUTTY SOLE *Bonny Barezky*

2 12-ounce sole
  (or other flat) fillets
⅓ cup sour cream
¼ cup brown sugar
¼ cup cream of coconut
2 Tbsps. ground almonds
2 Tbsps. liquid margarine
1 ripe banana, sliced in
  discs ¼-inch wide
  (optional)

1. Spray broiling pan with non-stick coating spray. Place fillets on broiler pan.
2. In a bowl, combine sour cream, brown sugar, cream of coconut, ground almonds, and liquid margarine.
3. Make a "stripe" with 1 Tbsp. of sour cream mixture down the center of each fillet.
4. Place banana discs on each fillet over the sour cream stripe. Spoon remaining mixture over fillets trying to completely cover bananas and fillet.
5. Broil until brown in spots, approximately 8 to 10 minutes.
Makes 2 servings.
*Easy and different!*

## ⒟ GRAPE SOLE *Bonny Barezky*

2 12-ounce sole
  (or other flat) fillets
⅓ cup sour cream
2 Tbsps. liquid margarine
⅓ cup fresh parsley
1 scallion, cut in
  1-inch pieces
½ tsp. curry powder
  (optional)
⅛ tsp. garlic powder
½ cup green seedless
  grapes

1. Spray broiling pan with non-stick cooking spray. Place fillets on broiler pan.
2. Place sour cream, liquid margarine, parsley, scallion, curry powder, and garlic powder in food processor.
3. Process until smooth, about 30 seconds, and pour into a bowl. Add grapes to bowl and stir.
4. Pour mixture over fillets and broil until brown spots appear, approximately 8 to 10 minutes.
Makes 2 servings.
*This is a "spring green" colored sauce and looks beautiful for company, especially with an orange or red vegetable on the plate (try carrots or broiled tomato). It is helpful to cook in the dish it will be served in for presentation purposes.*

# FISH IN PAPER *Joel Jacobs*

1 whole red snapper or
   sea bass (about 5 pounds)
   scaled and washed, boned
   and spine removed, but
   head left on
2 medium leeks
3 carrots, peeled, cut
   in julienne strips
1 green pepper, seeded and
   cut in julienne strips
1 red pepper, seeded and
   cut in julienne strips
Vegetable or olive oil
1 small, fresh chili or
   Jalepeño pepper
2 ripe tomatoes, peeled
   and sliced thin
¼ cup fresh ginger, cut
   in julienne strips
4 cloves garlic, trimmed,
   peeled, and sliced thin
Salt for seasoning
¼ cup fresh parsley
½ cup cider vinegar

1. Preheat oven to 400 degrees.
2. Cut leeks in half lengthwise; wash and soak for 5 minutes in cold water. Cut in julienne strips. Blanch separately in boiling water, the julienned leeks, carrots, green and red pepper, about 1 minute each.
3. Put a large piece of aluminum foil on a baking sheet. It should be large enough to wrap the entire fish. Line foil with parchment paper. Oil parchment so fish will not stick.
4. Mix all the blanched vegetables, chili pepper, tomatoes, ginger, and garlic together in a bowl.
5. Place fish on parchment, and sprinkle with salt. Place some of the vegetable mixture into cavity.
6. Place remaining vegetables on top of fish.
7. Chop parsley and sprinkle over fish.
8. Pour cider vinegar over fish.
9. Fold parchment over fish and wrap tightly with foil (see illustration). Before last fold, insert a straw and blow up paper to form a pocket. Remove straw before baking.
10. Bake for 20 to 30 minutes, or 10 minutes per inch of fish thickness.
Makes 4 to 5 servings, as a family dinner.
*Fish may also be cooked in an oven baking bag. Vegetables may be sautéed in olive oil instead of blanched. In addition to being a Schechter parent, Joel is a gourmet chef and caterer (The Kosher Gourmet).*

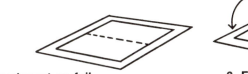

**1. Parchment on foil**

**2. Fold parchment over fish**

**3. Fold foil over straw
and parchment**

**4. Foil edges crimped
with straw in corner**

##  PEASANT'S FISH *Bonny Barezky*

1½ pounds flat fish
   fillets (such as sole
   or whitefish); fillets
   should be skinned
⅓ cup olive oil
⅓ cup melted margarine
4 Idaho potatoes, sliced
   thin with peel on
3 cloves garlic, minced
½ tsp. pepper
½ tsp. paprika
¼ cup parsley, chopped
1 tsp. basil or dill
Juice of 1 lemon
¼ cup margarine, melted

1. In a glass baking dish, pour oil and melted margarine. Layer potatoes.
2. Sprinkle on half of garlic, pepper, paprika, parsley, and dill.
3. Bake in 450 degree oven 20 minutes.
4. Layer fish fillets on potatoes. Sprinkle with remaining seasonings and the lemon juice. Drizzle on ¼ cup margarine. Bake in 400 degree oven 10 minutes.
Makes 4 servings.
*Easy and tasty!*

## BAKED TURBOT FILLETS *Sarita Blau*

1 pound turbot, thawed
Juice of ½ lemon
1 Tbsp. mustard

Optional Ingredients:
1 Tbsp. butter
¼ to 1 tsp. soy sauce
1 Tbsp. parsley, chopped
1 scallion, chopped
1 tsp. fresh dill, chopped

1. If using the butter, put it in the pan in the oven to melt (can be done while oven is preheating).
2. Rinse fish and place in pan, cutting if need be, to fit. If using butter, turn over to coat.
3. Squeeze lemon juice over fish. Spread mustard over fish. Sprinkle with any other desired optional ingredients. The butter does not have to be used with the herbs. All are independent.
4. Bake in 425 degree oven 10 to 15 minutes until fish flakes easily and is opaque.
Makes 3 to 4 servings.
*Low calorie if butter is eliminated. Handle fish carefully. Biscuits can be baked in the oven at the same time and temperature, and go well with it!*
◆ *Pareve when butter is omitted.*

# BLUEFISH *Sarita Blau* **D**

2 to 2½ pounds bluefish
  fillets
2 tsps. Dijon mustard
1 Tbsp. chopped fresh dill
1 tsp. onion powder
½ cup white wine
4 mushrooms, sliced
  (optional)
1 to 2 Tbsps. butter

1. Lightly grease flameproof pan.
2. Rinse off fish; drain and place in pan.
3. In small bowl or in cup, mix together mustard, dill, onion powder, and white wine. Pour over fish.
4. Sprinkle mushrooms over fish. Dot with butter. Broil 6 to 8 inches from flame or broiler element for 15 minutes or until done.
Can be prepared several hours ahead of time and kept in refrigerator until ready to cook.
Makes 6 servings.
*Easy and delicious!*
♦ *This recipe may be made pareve by substituting margarine for butter.*

# WHITEFISH PARMESAN *Bonny Barezky* **D**

2 12-ounce whitefish
  (or other flat) fillets
⅓ cup sour cream
3 Tbsps. liquid margarine
¼ cup Parmesan cheese,
  grated
¼ cup bread crumbs

1. Spray broiling pan with non-stick cooking spray.
2. In a bowl, combine sour cream, margarine, and Parmesan cheese to make a paste.
3. Place fillets on broiler pan. Spread sour cream paste on fillets. Sprinkle on bread crumbs, pressing crumbs into the paste.
4. Place under broiler until brown spots appear, approximately 8 minutes.
Makes 2 servings.

BASIL

## TEA SMOKED FISH *Miriam Steinberg*

1 to 1½ pounds fillets of
salmon or flounder
(butterflied)

Marinade:
3 Tbsps. soy sauce
1 Tbsp. dry sherry
2 slices ginger
1 Tbsp. sugar
1 small onion, sliced
2 scallions, cut in 2-inch
lengths

Smoking mixture:
⅓ cup dry, black tea leaves
⅓ cup raw rice
⅓ cup brown sugar, packed
1 tsp. Szechwan
peppercorns, crushed
1 cinnamon stick
Peel of ¼ of an orange or
tangerine
1 tsp. sesame oil (optional)

1. Wash and dry fish. Arrange fillets in shape of whole fish.
2. Combine marinade ingredients and pour over fish. Let stand 2 hours, basting fish frequently. (May be refrigerated, tightly covered, overnight; bring to room temperature before continuing.)
3. Place in baking dish and bake in preheated 400 degree oven for 15 minutes. (Or may be refrigerated at this point, tightly covered, overnight, once cooled; bring to room temperature before continuing.)
4. Line wok or large heavy pot, and cover with several layers of foil. Place smoking mixture inside. Place fish on 4 chopsticks, or oiled rack, in pot. Set pot over high heat until sugar begins to bubble and sends up several thick plumes of smoke, from 4 to 10 minutes. Cover tightly, crimping foil. Smoke fish for 10 minutes, turn off the heat and let rest 5 minutes.
5. Carefully uncrimp foil, near window or exhaust. Remove fish and immediately discard foil and contents. Place fish on platter and rub with sesame oil.
Makes 4 to 6 servings.
*Serve hot or at room temperature. Leftovers keep 3 to 4 days tightly covered in the refrigerator; serve cold with mayonnaise or mustard, or reheat in airtight foil package in 450 degree oven for 10 minutes. See ORIENTAL SALAD BUFFET, p. 68.*

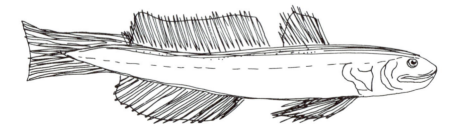

# GOLDEN BRAISED FISH Arlene Levin

1 to 2 pounds whole fish
(whitefish, snapper or
bass)
Salt
Flour for coating
2 Tbsps. peanut oil
6 dried Chinese mushrooms,
soaked for ½ hour,
drained, stemmed,
and shredded
4 green onions, cut into
½-inch pieces
1 tsp. ginger root, minced
1¼ cups fish stock or
water
2 Tbsps. light soy sauce
1 Tbsp. pale dry sherry
2 garlic cloves, minced
1 whole star anise
1 tsp. sugar

1. Clean the fish. Make 2 diagonal slits on each side, in the thickest part of the body. Sprinkle fish with salt, and coat with flour.
2. Heat a large frying pan. Add the oil. Add the fish and fry on both sides until golden.
3. Pour off excess oil. Add the mushrooms, onions, ginger, stock or water, soy sauce, sherry, salt, garlic, star anise, and sugar.
4. Bring to a boil; cover and simmer about 30 minutes.
5. Transfer fish to a large serving platter and pour sauce over fish.
Makes 3 servings.
*Delicious!*

# SESAME BAKED FISH Arlene Levin

2 Tbsps. peanut oil
1 clove garlic, minced
1 tsp. fresh ginger,
chopped
1 cup celery, sliced
1 cup red pepper,
julienned
3 Tbsps. soy sauce
4 tsps. honey
¼ cup grapefruit juice
1¼ to 2 pounds fish
fillets (whitefish, pike
or other flat fillets)
2 Tbsps. sesame seeds

1. Heat medium size skillet, add oil and heat. Add garlic and ginger. Cook 2 to 3 minutes.
2. Add celery and red pepper. Stir-fry 1 minute, just to coat with seasoned oil.
3. Add soy sauce, honey, and juice from grapefruit.
4. Place fish in a shallow baking pan. Spoon vegetable mixture over fish. Sprinkle with sesame seeds.
5. Bake in 350 degree oven 15 to 20 minutes.
Makes 4 servings.

# ⓟ BAKED FISH TERIYAKI *Fran Fogel*

¾ to 1 cup Teriyaki sauce
⅔ Tbsp. dehydrated onion
1 Tbsp. fresh lemon juice
2 to 4 garlic cloves,
crushed
1 to 1½ lbs. fresh trout
or halibut

1. Mix together Teriyaki sauce, onion, lemon juice, and garlic. Pour over the fish. Marinate at least 20 minutes before cooking.
2. When using trout, you may bake at 350 degrees for 20 minutes in marinade or broil it out of marinade.
3. When making halibut, only bake at 350 degrees for 20 to 25 minutes.
*Onions may brown, but don't worry. Enjoy eating them or brush them off. Easy, no-fuss recipe.*

# ⓓ DELICIOUS CHINESE TUNA *Berdie Held*

2 cans crispy chop suey
noodles
2 Tbsps. butter
2 onions, chopped
1 celery rib, chopped
2 6½-ounce cans tuna,
packed in water, flaked
2 cans cream of mushroom
soup, undiluted
2 cans fancy chop suey
vegetables, drained

1. Butter 9 x 13 inch casserole dish and cover bottom of dish with chop suey noodles.
2. Sauté onions and celery over low heat in butter until they are soft.
3. Place tuna in a large mixing bowl. Add cream of mushroom soup and chop suey vegetables.
4. Add the sautéed onion and celery to the other and mix well.
5. Put the mixture in the baking dish. Cover the mixture with remaining chop suey noodles and bake in 325 degree oven 45 minutes.
Makes 8 servings.

# ⓓ HOT TUNA SALAD *Judy Miller*

2 7-ounce cans tuna,
drained
2 cups celery, chopped
2 cups croutons, divided
1 cup mayonnaise
½ cup whole almonds
(or cashews)
1 Tbsp. onion, minced
1 Tbsp. lemon juice
½ tsp. salt
½ cup Cheddar *or* Swiss
cheese, shredded

1. In 2-quart casserole, mix together tuna, celery, 1 cup croutons, mayonnaise, almonds, onion, lemon juice, and salt. Cover. Microwave at medium high 9 to 11 minutes, stirring after 5 minutes, until hot.
2. Sprinkle with cheese and remaining 1 cup croutons.
3. Microwave at medium high 1 to 2 minutes until cheese is bubbly.
Makes 6 servings.

# TUNA LASAGNE *Adele Cohen* Ⓓ

6 ounces spinach noodles
1 medium onion, diced
Oil
2 6-ounce cans tuna,
 drained and flaked
1 can tomato soup
½ cup water
Salt, sugar, pepper to taste
8 ounces cream cheese
½ pint cream
1 cup Cheddar cheese,
 grated
¼ cup Parmesan cheese

1. Boil green spinach noodles; drain and set aside.
2. Brown diced onion in a little oil. Add tuna, tomato soup, and water. Stir in salt, pepper, and sugar to taste (can leave out salt and ½ tsp. pepper and 1 tsp. sugar). Simmer for about 7 minutes.
3. Beat cream cheese with cream.
4. Grease 9 x 9 inch glass baking dish.
5. Place one layer noodles, then tuna, then sauce. Repeat.
6. Sprinkle with Cheddar cheese and Parmesan.
7. Bake in 350 degree oven 45 minutes. Switch off oven until ready to eat.
Makes 4 to 6 servings.

# ITALIAN FISH *Helene Blivaiss* Ⓓ

1½ pounds fish fillets
 (turbot or scrod)
Salt and pepper, to taste
1 tsp. oregano
1 cup tomatoes, puréed
1 onion, thinly sliced
¼ cup olive oil
¼ cup cheese, grated
 (Mozzarella or Parmesan)

1. Place fillets on greased cookie sheet. Sprinkle salt, pepper, and oregano.
2. Add tomatoes and onions. Drizzle oil on top. Sprinkle with cheese.
3. Bake in 350 degree oven 30 minutes.
Makes 4 servings.
*Kids refer to this as "pizza" fish because the topping resembles pizza! Fast and tasty family fare!*

## ⓓ TUNA COTTAGE CHEESE CASSEROLE *Florence Sager*

1 7-ounce can tuna
1 carrot, sliced
1 celery rib, chopped
2 Tbsps. onion, chopped
2 Tbsps. margarine or
butter, melted
3 eggs, slightly beaten
¾ cup cottage cheese
½ cup dry bread crumbs
⅛ tsp. curry powder
¼ tsp. garlic or onion
powder (optional)
Salt and pepper, to taste

1. Wash tuna or use tuna packed in water.
2. Sauté carrot, celery, and onion in margarine (or steam in water).
3. Mix eggs, cottage cheese, sautéed vegetables, bread crumbs, and spices with tuna. Turn into oiled 1-quart casserole.
4. Bake in 350 degree oven 35 to 40 minutes. Makes 4 to 6 servings.
*Omit salt or margarine, and this makes a nice dish for restricted diets.*

## ⓟ LOX, EGGS AND ONIONS, NEW YORK STYLE *Judith Schuster*

Margarine
4 onions, sliced thin
Paprika
¾ pound lox
Green peppers, diced
(optional)
8 eggs
Garlic
Black pepper, to taste

1. Melt margarine in frying pan.
2. Sprinkle onions with paprika.
3. Sauté onions until golden brown.
4. Break lox into bite-sized pieces. Place in frying pan with onions. Add green pepper.
5. Sauté until desired consistency.
6. Beat eggs in a bowl. Sprinkle with garlic and black pepper. Pour eggs into frying pan. Stir well.
7. Stir often. Cook until desired consistency. Makes 8 servings.

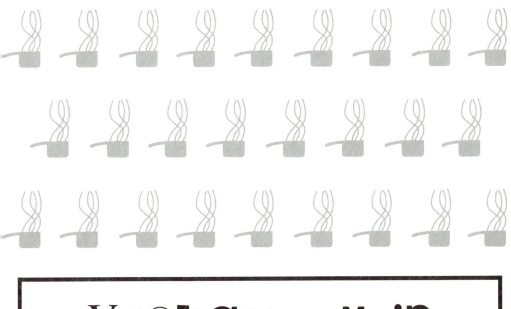

# VEGEtaRian MAiN
# DiSHeS

# ❶ LOWER EAST SIDE KOSHER PIZZA *Eugene Goldfarb*

2 pounds bread dough,
   fresh or frozen*
   (1 pound for each pizza)

Sauce: (for 2 pizzas)
1 28-ounce can of peeled,
   whole tomatoes, cut up
1 12-ounce can of tomato
   paste
⅓ cup of wine
Pepper, oregano, garlic, and
   hot pepper, to taste
Parmesan cheese, to taste

Toppings:
1 green pepper, chopped
½ pound mushrooms, sliced
1 zucchini, cut in rounds
12 to 16 ounces kosher
   mozzarella or muenster
   cheese, shredded

1. Place tomatoes in saucepan with tomato paste. Add wine and spices. Add vegetables. Add Parmesan cheese. Simmer for ½ to 1 hour.
2. Spread dough out on two 14-inch pizza pans (or cookie sheets). Let dough stand for 15 minutes, then do final spreading.
3. Spread 90% of cheese on dough. Spread sauce evenly over cheese. Add vegetable toppings of your choice. Add final 10% of the cheese on top.
4. Bake for 20 to 30 minutes until cheese starts to bubble and brown, but before bread dough burns.
Makes 2 pizzas.
*Tastes just like "stuffed pizza from a restaurant"! Kids love to roll the dough and sprinkle the ingredients. Family fun!*
*\*Frozen bread dough works well; allow 6 hours or overnight to defrost. Or, see PIZZA DOUGH, p. 49.*

# ❶ MARK'S EGGPLANT CASSEROLE *Mark & Sylvia Neil*

3 eggplants
2 large green peppers
2 very large onions
Margarine or butter
1 1-pound can whole
   tomatoes, strained,
   reserving juice
Bread crumbs
1 pound mozzarella
   cheese, shredded
Parmesan cheese

1. Chop eggplant, green peppers, and onions. Sauté in margarine or butter.
2. Strain tomatoes.
3. Layer in a large, covered casserole dish as follows: bread crumbs, sautéed vegetables, tomatoes, mozzarella cheese, and Parmesan cheese. Repeat layers at least once (cheese on top).
4. Cover and bake for 1 hour in 375 degree oven and serve.
Makes 6 to 8 servings.
*Two small casseroles may be used.*
*For a half-recipe, use 1 eggplant and ½ the other ingredients.*

# EGGPLANT PARMESAN  Rachel Engler  **D**

1½- to 2-pound eggplant, skinned and cut into ¼ inch slices
2 eggs, beaten
1 cup bread crumbs
¾ cup oil
½ cup Parmesan cheese, grated
2 tsps. dried oregano
2 cups tomato sauce
½ to 1 pound mozzarella cheese, sliced

1. Place eggs in one bowl, bread crumbs in a second bowl. Dip each slice of eggplant into eggs and then dip into bread crumbs.
2. Heat oil, and sauté each slice in oil until brown on both sides. Place one layer of eggplant in 2-quart casserole. Now layer on top a sprinkle of Parmesan cheese and oregano. Cover well with tomato sauce. Add a layer of mozzarella. Repeat until all ingredients are used up.
3. Bake in 350 degree oven for 30 minutes. Uncover last 15 minutes.
Makes 4 to 6 servings.
*Parmesan cheese may be omitted, if desired– still delicious!*

# TOFU SUKIYAKE  Marsha Arons  **P**

¼ cup tamari sauce
1 cup water
3 green onions, minced
1 large clove garlic, sliced
1½ tsps. fresh ginger, grated
1 Tbsp. cider vinegar
1 Tbsp. honey
1 to 2 Tbsps. dry sherry
1 rib celery
1 large carrot
1 large green bell pepper
⅓ pound green beans
1 pound tofu, cut into 1-inch cubes
½ pound fresh mung bean sprouts

1. In a large saucepan, combine the tamari sauce, water, green onions, garlic, ginger, vinegar, honey, and sherry.
2. Cut the celery, carrot, bell pepper, and fresh green beans into small chunks.
3. Add the tofu, the vegetable chunks, and the mung bean sprouts to the sauce.
4. Bring to a boil; cover and reduce heat to slow simmer. Cook until all vegetables are tender, about 10 to 15 minutes.
Makes 4 servings.
*Serve over steamed rice, with some sauce spooned over each serving.*

## Ⓓ BOREKAS  *Nancy Goldstein*

**Dough:**
1 cup oil
1 cup water
Salt, dash
½ tsp. baking powder
4 cups flour

**Filling:**
1 potato, cooked and mashed
2 packages farmer's cheese
½ package (large) cream
  cheese
3 to 4 slices American
  cheese, broken into pieces
1 to 2 eggs
Salt and pepper
Matzah meal

1. Mix oil, water, salt, and baking powder in a pot with a wooden spoon. Bring to a boil. Remove from heat. Add approximately 4 cups flour. Form into dough.
2. Peel potato. Place in pot with water. Cook 15 to 20 minutes. Drain. Mash.
3. For filling: Mix cheeses, eggs, mashed potato, salt and pepper. Use matzah meal to bind.
4. Roll out dough. Cut in circles. Spoon filling onto dough, fold over to make semi-circle shape, and crimp edges together.
5. Line baking sheet with foil. Spray with non-stick cooking spray. Place borekas on foil.
6. Beat egg yolks and brush on top of borekas.
7. Bake in 350 degree oven 15 to 20 minutes.
*Delicious Sephardi filled-pastry often served on Shavuot.*

## Ⓟ YATAKLETE ALECHA (ETHIOPIAN VEGETABLE DISH)  *Aviva Rodin*

KP

6 small boiling potatoes
  (about 2½ to 3 inches
  long each)
½ cup vegetable oil
2 medium onions, cut in
  thin slices
1 Tbsp. garlic, chopped fine
½ tsp. tumeric
2 Tbsps. ginger root,
  chopped fine
1 tsp. salt
½ pound fresh string beans,
  cut into 2-inch lengths
3 large carrots, cut
  lengthwise and crosswise
  into quarters 2 inches long
1 small hot green pepper,
  cut in thin strips
1 large green pepper, cut
  in thin strips
¼ cup water

1. Peel and trim potatoes to form oval shapes. Cut v-shaped wedges ¼ inch deep at ½-inch intervals all around to form flower shape.
2. In 4- to 5-quart heavy Dutch oven, heat oil and onion over moderate heat, stirring frequently until onion is soft, but not brown. Add garlic, tumeric, ginger, and salt and keep stirring for 3 to 5 minutes.
3. Add string beans and cook 3 minutes. Add carrots and peppers and cook another 2 to 4 minutes.
4. Add water and potatoes. Reduce heat to low and cook 5 to 8 minutes or until vegetables are tender, but still crisp.
Makes 6 servings.
*The source of this recipe was a Peace Corps volunteer who worked in Ethiopia. There, this delicious stew was served traditionally during Pesach with a flat bread similar to our crepes. For a regular meal, try serving with pita.*

# TIBETAN ROAST *Aviva Leberman*

1 tsp. oil
4 ounces barley
1 large onion, diced
8 ounces mushrooms
¼ pint pareve chicken stock
¼ pint red wine
8 ounces frozen spinach,
  chopped
4 ounces ground walnuts
1 tsp. dried rosemary
1 tsp. dried sage
1 egg, beaten
Salt and pepper, to taste

1. Preheat oven to 375 degrees.
2. Fry barley in oil for 2 to 3 minutes. Add onion and fry for 3 minutes longer.
3. Add mushrooms, cover saucepan, and cook on low to medium heat for 5 minutes.
4. Add wine and stock. Bring to a boil. Reduce heat and cook for about 50 minutes adding more stock if necessary.
5. Defrost and warm up spinach. Allow to cool and add ground walnuts, rosemary, and sage. Mix in egg. Add to barley mixture. Season well.
6. Grease 1-pound loaf pan and turn in mixture.
7. Bake 50 to 60 minutes until golden brown. Makes 4 to 6 servings.
*Serve hot with MUSHROOM AND WINE SAUCE (see below), or cold with salad.*

# MUSHROOM AND WINE SAUCE *Aviva Leberman* D

1 ounce butter
8 ounces mushrooms,
  quartered
1 Tbsp. wine
4 tsps. flour
1 pint pareve chicken stock,
  strong
Salt and pepper, to taste

1. Melt butter in saucepan. Add mushrooms and wine.
2. Cover saucepan. Cook for 3 minutes on high heat. Uncover and cook until liquid evaporates. Stir constantly.
3. Reduce heat and add flour. Stir for 5 to 6 minutes. Cook thoroughly.
4. Add stock slowly and simmer 3 to 5 minutes. Season.
5. Allow mixture to cook, then blend until smooth.
*Makes a very rich, vegetarian gravy, excellent on vegetarian roasts.*

## **P** LEMONY RICE STIR FRY  *Judy Miller*

1 cup raw brown rice
2 Tbsps. margarine
4 scallions, chopped
4 sprigs of parsley, chopped
1 10-ounce box frozen peas
½ lemon peel, grated
2 Tbsps. soy sauce
½ cup cashews or peanuts
Dash hot pepper sauce
  (optional)

1. Prepare brown rice according to package directions. Set aside.
2. Sauté scallions and parsley in margarine until tender (approximately 2 minutes).
3. Add frozen peas. Cover, lower heat, and cook for 5 minutes, stirring occasionally.
4. Add rice, lemon peel, soy sauce, cashews, and optional pepper sauce. Heat thoroughly and serve.
*Low cholesterol, health-food fare.*

## **D** MUSHROOM CUTLETS  *Judy Wolkin*

1 cup mushrooms, finely
  chopped
½ onion, finely chopped
2 eggs
Salt, to taste
Pepper, to taste
Garlic powder, to taste
½ cup bread crumbs
¾ cup cheddar cheese,
  grated
Butter, margarine, or oil
  for frying

1. Mix mushrooms, onion, eggs, salt, pepper, garlic powder, bread crumbs, and grated cheese. Blend well. (Mixture may be liquidy.)
2. Form into patties. Place on a plate and chill. Drain off liquid if it accumulates.
3. Melt butter or margarine in a frying pan. Fry patties in butter until nicely browned on each side.
*Fast and fabulous!*

## **D** NUT LOAF  *Aviva Leberman*

1½ cups brown rice,
  cooked
½ cup wheat germ
¾ cup chopped walnuts
¼ cup chopped sunflower
  seeds (use food processor)
1 large onion, chopped
½ pound kosher, shredded,
  sharp Cheddar cheese
Salt and pepper, to taste
1 tsp. yeast extract
4 eggs

1. Preheat oven to 350 degrees.
2. Combine all ingredients in greased 9-inch loaf pan.
3. Cook for approximately 50 minutes.
4. Allow to cool before turning out of pan.

# MEXICAN PLATTER  Nancy Goldstein  Ⓓ

1 can pink pinto beans
Salsa sauce, mild or
  medium spicy
Garlic salt
Avocado
Lemon juice
Sour cream
1 tomato, chopped
1 onion, chopped
Black or green olives,
  chopped
1 8-ounce package Cheddar
  cheese, grated

1. Put pinto beans into frying pan, and mash them as you cook over medium heat.
2. Add ½ jar or more salsa sauce as you mash. Add garlic salt. Pour mixture onto lipped platter.
3. Crush avocado and mix with lemon juice and garlic. Spoon on without evenly spreading.
4. Spoon or spread on sour cream. Sprinkle chopped tomato, chopped onion, chopped black or green olives. Top with grated Cheddar. Refrigerate until ready to serve.
Serve with chips.
*May be served as an appetizer, but our family likes it as a meal!*

# TORTILLA PIE  Karen Barron  Ⓓ

1 16-ounce can kidney
  beans, drained
1 4-ounce can chilis,
  drained and chopped
¼ cup onions, minced
1 Tbsp. chili powder
½ tsp. oregano
¼ tsp. salt
⅛ tsp. Tabasco sauce
Dash ground cumin
4 corn tortillas (6-inch
  size)
1 cup Cheddar cheese,
  shredded

1. In medium bowl, mash beans to a paste. Add chilis, onions, and seasonings. Mix well, set aside.
2. Cut each tortilla in half. On baking sheet or foil, bake halves in preheated 400 degree oven about 2 minutes or until crisp. Remove from oven. (Leave oven on.)
3. Arrange baked halves, curved side out and overlapping, around edge of 8-inch pie plate.
4. Spread bean mixture evenly over tortillas, leaving border of tortillas all the way around. Sprinkle with cheese.
5. Bake 10 to 15 minutes or until cheese melts and pie is hot.
*Easy, fast, delicious!*

# Ⓓ MEDITERRANEAN PLATTER *Miriam Steinberg*

3 green peppers
3 red peppers
½ tsp. salt
3 large cloves garlic
Oil
½ pound string cheese
½ tsp. pepper
3 hard boiled eggs
Black olives
1 can anchovies in oil
(optional)

1. Char peppers under broiler for 2 to 5 minutes per exposed side. Continue until puffed and blackened on all sides, including top and bottom.

2. While still warm, cut in half and remove seeds. If possible, collect juices. Pull off the skin, which will come off easily if really charred. Cut into strips and place into separate bowls with any accumulated juices.

3. Place ½ tsp. of salt in small mortar or bowl and puree it into the garlic. Whisk in several tablespoons of oil. Add to peppers with any collected juices.

4. If necessary, cut cheese into 8-inch lengths. Put into thin strands.

These steps may be done up to 2 days in advance; cover and refrigerate. (Bring to room temperature before assembling.)

5. To assemble the platter: Toss cheese with several drops of oil and several turns of fresh pepper. Place in center of platter. Lift peppers out of sauce. Place red peppers on one side of cheese and green peppers on the other side. Quarter eggs and place wedges on both sides. Place black olives at both sides. Arrange strips of anchovies over the peppers.

Platter may be assembled several hours in advance except for the anchovies. Cover loosely and refrigerate. Bring to room temperature before serving.

Makes 6 servings. May be doubled.
*Beautiful, easy, and delicious!*

# BROCCOLI QUICHE  *Eva Sideman*  Ⓓ

9-inch pastry-lined pan
  (pie crust)
5 eggs
½ cup Swiss cheese,
  shredded
1 10-ounce package frozen
  broccoli, well drained
1 can, or ½ pound
  fresh mushrooms, sliced
½ cup whipping cream
¾ tsp. salt
¼ tsp. sugar

1. Break 4 eggs into mixing bowl.
2. Separate 1 egg and put yolk with rest of eggs. Put white in another bowl.
3. Brush pastry dough with some egg white.
4. Arrange cheese on the bottom of the pie crust. Cover with vegetables.
5. Blend eggs with whipping cream, salt, and sugar. Pour over the vegetables. Bake in 350 degree oven on the lowest rack for 1 hour, or until the knife inserted in the quiche comes out clean. Let stand for 20 to 30 minutes before cutting.
Makes 8 to 10 servings.
*The recipe doubles well, and freezes well.*

# CRUSTLESS SPINACH QUICHE  *Goldie Langer*  Ⓓ

4 eggs
2 cups half & half cream
½ tsp. salt
1 to 1½ cups Swiss cheese,
  shredded
1 10-ounce package chopped
  spinach, squeezed very dry
1 Tbsp. flour*
Mushrooms (optional)
Oil
½ cup onion, chopped
¼ cup Parmesan cheese

KP

1. Beat eggs well in a bowl. Add half & half, salt, Swiss cheese, spinach, and flour. Add mushrooms if using.
2. Heat oil in a pan. Sauté onion. Add to main mixture. Grease 9-inch baking dish. Pour in spinach-cheese mixture. Sprinkle with Parmesan cheese.
3. Bake in 325 degree oven 40 to 45 minutes. If doubled, increase baking time.
*Can be used for Passover if the flour is replaced with potato starch.*

# 🅓 EGG AND CHEESE CASSEROLE  *Phyllis Cantor*

½ cup onions, chopped
¼ pound mushrooms, sliced
4 Tbsps. butter or margarine
16 to 18 eggs

Cheese sauce:
3 Tbsps. butter or margarine, melted
3 Tbsps. flour
¾ tsp. salt
⅛ tsp. pepper
3 cups milk
1½ cups or 6 ounces sharp Cheddar cheese, grated

Bread cubes:
2 Tbsps. butter, melted
3 cups bread cubes (4 to 5 slices bread)
⅛ tsp. paprika

1. Cook onions and mushrooms in butter until tender. Add eggs – scramble until set. Put in 13 x 9 inch pan.
2. For sauce: Melt butter or margarine in a saucepan. Stir in flour, salt, and pepper. Add milk and cook until bubbly.
3. Stir in grated sharp cheddar cheese.
4. Pour sauce over eggs and vegetables and mix lightly.
5. Melt butter in pan. Add bread cubes and paprika and brown. Mix as they cook. Top casserole with cooked bread cubes.
6. Chill. Remove 30 minutes before cooking. (May be prepared the night before, and baked in the morning.)
7. Bake in 350 degree oven about 30 to 45 minutes.
Makes 12 to 14 servings.
*Can be doubled and made in a foil roaster for a large crowd. Great for brunch.*

# 🅓 EVONNE'S CHEESE SOUFFLÉ  *Estelle Schnitzer*

8 slices white bread
6 eggs
1 tsp. salt
2 cups milk
½ pound sharp cheddar cheese
¼ cup butter, melted

1. The day before serving, remove crusts from bread and cut into 1-inch cubes. Butter a 9 x 14 inch casserole.
2. Mix eggs, salt, and milk.
3. Layer bread and cheese alternately with egg mixture. Cover with foil and refrigerate overnight.
4. Next day, bring to room temperature ½ hour before baking. Pour melted butter on top. Bake, uncovered, in 350 degree oven 1 hour.
5. Simple Method: Cube bread, leaving crust on. Butter casserole. Mix all ingredients, including melted butter, in large mixing bowl. Bake uncovered in 350 degree oven 1 hour or until browned.
Makes 10 to 12 servings
*Quick and easy!*

# CHEESE SPINACH BAKE *Lois Wallace*

**D**

½ pound fresh mushrooms, sliced

4 green onions, sliced with tops

3 Tbsps. butter

2 Tbsps. butter

2 Tbsps. flour

2 cups milk

½ tsp. salt

¼ tsp. basil

¼ tsp. pepper

Dash nutmeg

¼ cup Parmesan cheese, grated

8 ounces very thin spaghetti, cooked "al dente"

2 cups mozzarella or monterey jack cheese, shredded

1 package chopped spinach, thawed, drained dry, uncooked

1 package creamed spinach, thawed or 2 packages plain chopped spinach, thawed, drained dry, uncooked

1. Sauté mushrooms and onions in 3 Tbsps. butter for 1 minute. Set aside.
2. Melt 2 Tbsps. butter in a saucepan. Add flour and stir. Add milk and seasonings. Heat until smooth and thickened. Add ¼ cup Parmesan cheese. Remove from heat.
3. Put half cooked spaghetti, half of the cheese, half of the mushrooms and juice in layers in greased 9 x 13 inch dish.
4. Add all spinach in one layer. Add rest of spaghetti, cheese, and mushrooms in layers. Pour cream sauce over all. Sprinkle with additional Parmesan cheese.
5. Bake in 350 degree oven 20 to 30 minutes. Let stand 5 minutes before cutting.

Serves 5 to 6 as a main dish, 10 to 12 as a side dish.

*Freezes well.*

# Ⓓ SWISS CHEESE FONDUE  *Jay Leberman*

1 clove garlic
8 ounces "Emmenthaler" or Swiss cheese
8 ounces Gruyere or Cheddar cheese
¾ cup dry white wine
2 Tbsps. Kirschenwasser (cherry brandy)
2 tsps. cornstarch
Pepper, to taste
Nutmeg, to taste
1 loaf Italian style bread

1. Rub garlic around inside of fondue pot.
2. Cut cheeses in chunks. Place cheese and wine in fondue pot over double flame. Stir to mix and melt cheese.
3. Make a paste of cherry brandy and cornstarch. Add to fondue pot. Stir until even consistency.
4. Season with pepper and nutmeg, to taste.
5. Cut bread into large cubes and toast lightly in low oven.
6. To serve, place bread cubes in basket next to fondue pot. Each person takes a long fork, spears a bread cube, and swirls it in the fondue pot.
Makes 6 servings.

*Accompany with tossed salad for a delicious, easy vegetarian meal! Jay Leberman is the director of the Sager Solomon Schechter Day School. He learned to make fondue while studying abroad. His fondue dinner is always a welcome fund-raiser at the School Auction!*

# OVEN PANCAKE   *Nancy Goldstein*   **D**

½ cup butter
4 eggs
½ cup sugar
1 cup flour
2 cups milk
Salt, dash
Blueberries, *or*
Strawberries, sliced
Cinnamon, to taste
Sugar, to taste

1. Place ¼ cup butter in each of two 9-inch round layer cake pans. Melt butter in 425 degree oven.
2. Mix together eggs, sugar, flour, milk, and salt. Pour into pans.
3. Distribute berries evenly in pans.
4. Sprinkle with cinnamon and sugar.
5. Bake for ½ hour in 425 degree oven.
Makes 8 servings.
*If desired, heat berries in a pot, and serve warm with the pancakes. Or sprinkle pancakes with powdered sugar and serve with syrup.*

# PAN-FRIED APPLE RUM CAKE   *Eva Sideman*   **P**

¾ cup flour
2 large eggs, beaten
⅓ cup sugar
½ cup milk
2 Tbsps. dark rum
2 golden delicious apples, peeled and sliced thin
2 Tbsps. oil
Raisins (optional)
Confectioner's sugar

1. Put the flour in a large mixing bowl and make a well in the center. Add the eggs to it.
2. Blend the sugar with the milk, and add this to the flour mixture.
3. Add the rum, stirring, 1 Tbsp. at a time.
4. Add apples and oil to the batter. Add a handful of raisins. Place the batter in a large skillet. Cook over medium heat until the top of the pancake is almost set.
5. Slip the pancake onto a plate, and then invert it back into the skillet, so the other side can also brown. Continue cooking until brown on both sides, and set inside as well. Invert the pancake onto a platter.
Sprinkle with confectioner's sugar. Cut into wedges.
Makes 6 servings
*Great for a Sunday breakfast or brunch.*

## Ⓓ COTTAGE CHEESE PANCAKES *Sarita Blau*

2 Tbsps. butter or oil
1 cup flour
1 tsp. baking powder
¼ tsp. baking soda
1 to 2 Tbsps. sugar
4 eggs
1 pound cottage cheese
1 apple, chopped (optional)

1. Melt butter in frying pan.
2. Sift or stir together flour, baking powder, baking soda, and sugar in a medium bowl.
3. Put eggs and cottage cheese in blender and blend until smooth (with oil, if using it).
4. Put egg mixture into flour. Add melted butter, if using, and stir. Add chopped apple, if desired.
5. Drop batter by spoonfuls into hot frying pan. Flip when top has bubbles.
Serve plain or with cinnamon and sugar.

## Ⓓ EASY APPLE PANCAKE *Rochelle Marshak*

1 20-ounce can apple pie
  filling
1 Tbsp. butter
3 eggs
½ cup milk
½ cup flour

Topping:
5 Tbsps. butter
½ cup sugar
2 Tbsps. cinnamon

1. Melt 1 Tbsp. butter in frying pan. Add apple pie filling.
2. Beat eggs, milk, and flour with a wire whisk until smooth.
3. Pour mixture over apple pie filling. Bake in preheated 500 degree oven until it puffs and browns slightly at edges, about 10 minutes.
4. Meanwhile, melt 5 Tbsps. butter.
5. Mix sugar and cinnamon.
6. When pancake is browned remove from oven, pour butter over it, and sprinkle sugar mixture on top.
7. Return to oven for 5 minutes, until sugar carmelizes.

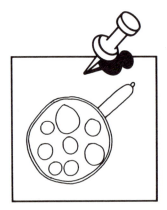

# APPLE CINNAMON PANCAKE  *Ruth Taxy*  **D**

2 large apples
5 Tbsps. butter
½ cup milk
½ cup flour
1 tsp. sugar
Dash salt
3 eggs
½ cup sugar
2 tsps. cinnamon
Lemon juice (optional)

1. Slice apples and sauté butter in large casserole with lid. When soft, remove from heat.
2. Combine milk, flour, 1 tsp. sugar, salt, and eggs. Pour over apples and cook 6 to 7 minutes on top of stove.
3. Mix remaining ½ cup sugar and cinnamon, and sprinkle over partially cooked pancake. Place in preheated 500 degree oven for 8 minutes.
Sprinkle with lemon juice, if desired.

# BREAKFAST APPLE PANCAKE  *Arlene Levin*  **D**

2 eggs
½ cup milk
⅛ tsp. salt
½ cup flour
2 medium apples, peeled, cored, and cut into thin slices
¼ cup sugar
1 tsp. cinnamon
1 Tbsp. margarine or butter, for greasing pan

1. Beat eggs, milk, salt, and flour until smooth with a wire whisk or rotary beater. Let batter rest.
2. Place apples in bowl. Combine sugar and cinnamon, sprinkle over apples, and toss to mix.
3. Grease a 9-inch pie pan. Place apples on bottom of pan.
4. Stir batter and pour over apples. Bake in preheated 350 degree oven for 30 minutes. Serve hot.
Recipe can be doubled and baked in two 9-inch pie pans.
*This makes a nice dessert as well as a main course.*

# BLINTZ CASSEROLE  *Nomi Erlich*  **D**

12 already-made blintzes
6 eggs, beaten
½ cup orange juice
2 tsps. sugar
1 tsp. vanilla
1½ cups sour cream
Oil or margarine

1. Grease baking or casserole pan with oil or margarine.
2. Put the blintzes in the pan.
3. Beat eggs well in a bowl. Add orange juice, sugar, vanilla, and sour cream. Mix very well.
4. Pour the mixture over the blintzes. Bake in 325 degree oven for 1 hour l5 minutes.
Serve with sour cream and cinnamon or apple yogurt.
*Try for Shavuot!*

## Ⓓ CHEESE BLINTZES *Goldie Langer*

Batter:
4 eggs
1 cup milk
¼ tsp. salt
1 cup flour

Filling:
1 pound dry cottage cheese,
   or baker's cheese
1 egg yolk
¼ cup sugar
½ tsp. cinnamon

Sour cream (optional)
Fresh strawberries or
   blueberries (optional)
Butter

1. Combine eggs, milk, salt, and flour in a bowl.
2. Use crepe maker, if possible. If not, use 6- to 7-inch frying pan. Brush with butter.
3. Pour in enough batter to make 1 thin crepe, tilting pan from side to side. Brown only on bottom.
4. Turn out onto a cloth. Stack crepes.
5. Blend cottage cheese, egg yolk, sugar, and cinnamon until smooth.
6. Put a spoonful of filling on one cooked side of crepe – not too close to edge. Fold over edge and sides and continue with first side until rolled up and neat.
7. Fry in a little butter and serve hot with sour cream, sugar, or fruit.
Makes 16 blintzes.
*If you use a crepe maker, the crepes will be much thinner and the batter will go farther. These can be frozen before fried.*

## Ⓓ FOOD PROCESSOR BLINTZES *Jennifer Gritton*

Batter:
2 eggs
1 cup milk
Dash of salt (optional)
1 cup flour (approx.)

Cheese Filling:
2 large packages cream
   cheese
1 egg
2 Tbsps. sugar

1. In food processor, blend eggs, milk, salt, and ½ the flour. Gradually add the rest of the flour. Batter should be smooth with no lumps.
2. Heat a small frying pan, grease lightly. Pour in small amount of batter, rotate pan to make a thin crepe. Cook only one side until lightly browned.
3. Turn out onto towel.
4. Combine cream cheese, egg, and sugar in food processor.
5. Put 1 Tbsp. of filling in center. Fold over to make an envelope.
6. Bake on a buttered cookie sheet in 425 degree oven approximately 10 minutes.
*These can be frozen and baked at a later time.*

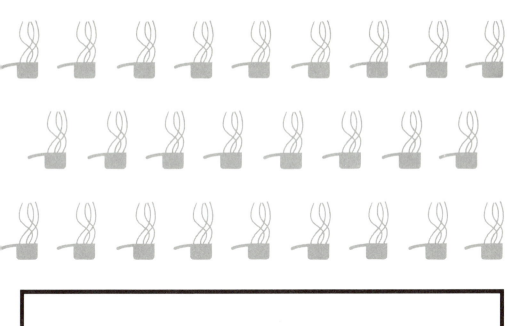

# Pasta & Rice

## ⓟ MOROCCAN COUSCOUS *Irene Sufrin*

Couscous (quick-cooking)
1 small zucchini
1 small red pepper
3 green onions
2 to 3 Tbsps. olive oil
½ cup pine nuts
1 cup currants
½ tsp. ground cumin

1. Prepare the couscous according to package directions. Make enough couscous for 6 to 8 servings.
2. Chop the zucchini, red pepper, and green onions into small pieces.
3. In a large sauté pan, heat the oil over medium-high heat. Add the pine nuts. Sauté until lightly toasted, then add the zucchini, onions, and red pepper. Sauté just until the vegetables soften. Add the currants and cook about 1 minute more.
4. Combine the couscous and the vegetables in a large bowl. Sprinkle with the cumin and stir thoroughly. Serve immediately.
Makes 6 to 8 servings.

## Ⓜ EASY COUSCOUS *Sybil Zimmerman*

2 cups stock, *or* beef broth, *or* water with 2 tsps. beef bouillon or powder
2 cups couscous
2 Tbsps. margarine

1. Bring liquid to boil with margarine. Add couscous, stir, cover, and let sit 5 minutes. Fluff with a fork.
Makes 4 servings.
*Serve with stew and HARISSA (see below.)*

## ⓟ HARISSA *Sybil Zimmerman*

¼ cup stock or water
¼ cup oil
1 garlic clove, crushed
⅛ tsp. cumin
2 Tbsps. lemon juice
⅛ tsp. cayenne pepper
2 tsps. red pepper flakes

1. Combine all ingredients in blender or food processor and blend well.
Serve with couscous and stew as side sauce.

# KASHA VARNISHKES *Jackie Siegel* **M**

1 cup medium-grain kasha
1 egg, beaten
2 cups boiling water, *or*
  1 cup chicken broth and
  1 cup water
2 Tbsps. chicken fat, nya
  fat, or margarine
1 tsp. salt
½ tsp. pepper
½ tsp. garlic powder
¼ tsp. paprika
1 medium onion, chopped
½ box bow tie shells
Water to boil pasta

1. Mix kasha with the beaten egg. Stir mixture in pan over low flame until the kasha grains are separated.
2. Add 2 cups boiling water (or water and chicken broth mixture), 1 Tbsp. chicken fat, salt, pepper, garlic powder, and paprika. Cover and simmer for 15 minutes or until moisture evaporates.
3. While kasha is cooking, sauté the chopped onion in 1 Tbsp. fat. Cook the shells in a medium saucepot until al dente. Drain.
4. Stir the sautéed onion and cooked shells into the kasha mixture. Adjust seasonings to taste.
*Great with brisket, or any meat with sauce.*
**℗** *Pareve when made with water and margarine.*

# FARFEL *Bonny Barezky* **M**

½ pound mushrooms,
  chopped
1 small onion, chopped
8 ounces egg barley
2 cups chicken or beef
  bouillon (or soup)
¼ cup chicken fat (or
  oil)

1. Sauté mushrooms and onion in chicken fat until soft.
2. Add barley. Brown slightly. Add bouillon or soup. Place in a covered casserole.
3. Bake in 350 degree oven for 20 minutes.
**℗** *Also delicious made with pareve bouillon.*

## ◆ FARFEL CASSEROLE *Susan Markowitz*

1 8-ounce package toasted
   farfel
4 large celery ribs, cut
   into small pieces
1 large onion, diced
1 pound fresh mushrooms,
   sliced
2 Tbsps. soy sauce
1 15-ounce can mushroom
   steak sauce

1. Cook farfel according to package directions.
Drain well.
2. Add celery and simmer with onions and
mushrooms, until very brown.
3. Combine vegetables with steak sauce, soy
sauce, and farfel in casserole.
4. Press top down and bake in 350 degree oven
45 to 60 minutes.

## ◆ AUNT FANNY'S FAMOUS FARFEL *Barbara Wohlstadter*

1 pound toasted farfel
1 pound fresh mushrooms,
   sliced
4 Tbsps. soy sauce
4 large onions, sliced
½ cup margarine

1. Cook farfel in 4 quarts boiling salted water
for 10 minutes. Drain.
2. Steam mushrooms in soy sauce for 10
minutes.
3. Sauté onions in margarine.
4. Mix all ingredients in 9 x 13 inch pan.
5. Bake covered in 350 degree oven 45 minutes.

## ◼ MULTI-GRAIN CASSEROLE *Marsha, Mel & Rachel Abrams*

Margarine, to taste
1 medium onion, chopped
½ pound fresh mushrooms,
   sliced
1 cup brown rice
½ cup barley
½ cup wheat berry
Beef or vegetable bouillon
   *or* water
¼ cup pine nuts, lightly
   toasted
Salt as desired

1. Sauté onion in margarine on medium-high
heat until golden brown. Set aside.
2. Sauté mushrooms. Set aside.
3. Cook rice, barley, and wheat berry in water
or bouillon separately, since cooking times vary.
Drain if necessary.
4. Add additional margarine, mushrooms,
onions, salt, and pine nuts. Toss all together
and put into a casserole.
Can be prepared up to this point and reheated
in microwave or oven before serving.
Makes 10 to 12 servings.
*Created and enjoyed by the whole family!*

# ORIENTAL FRIED RICE  *Sybil Zimmerman*  M

Oil, to taste
2 to 3 Tbsps. walnuts,
  broken in pieces
1 to 2 eggs
1 medium onion, chopped
1 to 2 cloves garlic,
  chopped
2 cups bean sprouts
1 scallion, chopped
½ pound pea pods
2 cups day-old rice
Salt and pepper, to taste
1 tsp. soy sauce
Sesame oil, dash
Left-over meat or chicken

1. Heat a wok or frying pan. Add oil and fry walnuts. Remove to a bowl.
2. Scramble eggs in pan. Remove. Add onions and garlic and stir-fry 1 to 2 minutes over high heat.
3. Add bean sprouts, scallion, pea pods, and stir-fry 2 to 3 minutes.
4. Add rice, salt and pepper, soy sauce, and sesame oil.
5. Add in meat, walnuts, and eggs. Stir-fry 3 minutes.
Serve immediately.
Makes 4 servings.

# MUSHROOMS & WILD RICE  *Janet Resnick*  M

1 cup wild rice
1 cup water
½ cup white rice
2 ounces dried mushrooms
3 shallots, sliced
4 Tbsps. margarine
½ pound small fresh
  mushrooms, sliced
¾ tsp. salt
Pepper, to taste
6 large green onions,
  sliced
½ cup chicken soup
  or stock

1. Cook wild rice in a pot full of water. Boil for 45 minutes and drain well.
2. Combine 1 cup of water and ½ cup of white rice. Cook for 20 minutes.
3. Soak mushrooms in hot water for 30 minutes. Drain, rinse well, and squeeze dry. Throw out any hard stems.
4. With 3 Tbsps. of margarine sauté shallots for 1 minute, then add all of the mushrooms. Cook for 4 minutes or until liquid begins to release.
5. Add all of the rices, salt, and pepper, and cook until almost dry. May be prepared ahead and set aside at this point.
6. Reheat, and add green onions, 1 Tbsp. of margarine, and chicken stock.

## **M** RICE PILAF  *Phyllis Rine*

½ cup pareve margarine
1 medium onion,
  finely chopped
1¼ cups uncooked rice
½ tsp. salt
¼ tsp. pepper
1 10¾-ounce can clear
  chicken soup
1 can water
¼ cup almond slivers

1. Melt margarine in 1-quart saucepan. Add onion and cook until softened.
2. Meanwhile put uncooked rice, salt, and pepper into casserole dish. Add melted margarine and onions.
3. Pour chicken soup into saucepan. Fill the can with cold water and add to saucepan. Bring to a boil.
4. Pour into casserole dish. Add almonds.
5. Bake in 350 to 375 degree oven ½ hour until the moisture is all absorbed into the rice. Serve hot.
Makes 8 servings.
*Delicious with meat.*

## **M** FABULOUS RICE  *Harriet Chavis*

1 Tbsp. margarine
1 onion, sliced
2 cups uncooked parboiled
  converted rice
2 10¾-ounce cans chicken
  broth, mixed with 2 cans
  water
½ cup light or dark
  raisins
½ cup flaked coconut
½ tsp. salt
2 tsps. curry powder
½ cup salted peanuts,
  chopped (chop in food
  processor—not too fine,
  just a few seconds)

1. In 3-quart saucepan, heat margarine and sauté onion until golden brown. Add raw rice and continue sautéing until rice is lightly brown (about 5 minutes).
2. Pour in chicken broth and water. Add raisins, coconut, salt, and curry powder.
3. Cover and simmer, stirring occasionally, 20 to 25 minutes or until rice is tender and liquid is evaporated.
4. Fluff rice with fork and spoon into serving dish. Sprinkle with peanuts.
Makes 8 to 10 servings.

# BLACK BEANS & RICE *Beverly Siegel*

4 cups water
1½ cups dried black beans
5 whole cloves
1 3-inch cinnamon stick
1 Tbsp. cumin seeds
6 cups cooked brown rice
1 cup minced onion
½ to 1 cup fresh cilantro,
  minced
7 Tbsps. orange juice
¼ cup olive oil
3 Tbsps. vinegar
1 Tbsp. grated orange peel
Salt and pepper, to taste
½ cup toasted pine nuts
  or slivered almonds
2 oranges, peeled, sliced,
  and cut into rounds
Fresh cilantro leaves,
  for garnish
Tabasco sauce (optional)
  for serving

1. Combine water, dried black beans, whole cloves, and cinnamon stick in medium saucepan. Cover and simmer for 1 hour and 40 minutes, or until beans are tender. Drain and discard spices.
2. Stir cumin seeds in skillet for 3 minutes over medium-low heat. Crush cumin.
3. Set aside 1 cup of beans. Mix remaining beans and rice in a bowl. Add crushed cumin, onion, minced cilantro, orange juice, olive oil, vinegar, and orange peel. Season with salt and pepper.
4. Mix in pine nuts. Press mixture into soufflé dish and invert onto platter. Surround with reserved beans and orange slices. Garnish with cilantro leaves.
Makes 10 to 12 servings.

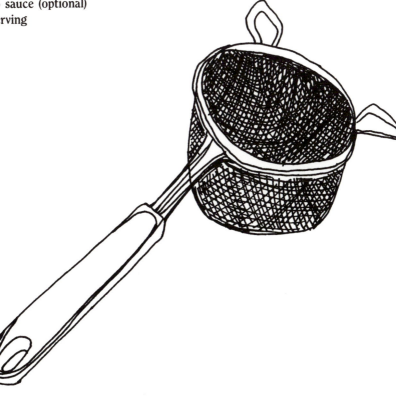

## Ⓜ BEEF FRIED RICE Arlene Levin

2 eggs, beaten
2 Tbsps. peanut oil
1 cup ground beef
6 green onions, thinly
sliced
4 cups cold cooked white
rice
2 Tbsps. dark soy sauce
½ tsp. sugar
Salt, to taste

1. Fry eggs, until firm, in the peanut oil in a large frying pan.
2. Dice the fried egg into ½-inch pieces.
3. Return the egg to the frying pan with the meat.
4. Add onions after cooking meat for 1 minute.
5. Cook over medium heat, stirring constantly for 3 to 4 minutes.
6. Mix the soy sauce and sugar into the cooked rice.
7. Add meat mixture and stir until blended.

## Ⓟ RICE RING SUPREME Faye Bright

2 large onions, chopped
4 ribs celery, chopped
½ cup margarine, melted
1½ pounds mushrooms,
sliced
2¼ cups hot cooked rice
1 8-ounce can water
chestnuts, sliced
1 Tbsp. seasoned salt

1. Sauté onions and celery in margarine. Add mushrooms. Sauté for 5 minutes longer. Mix with rice.
2. Stir in sliced water chestnuts and seasoned salt.
3. Spoon into well-greased 6-cup ring mold.
4. Bake in 350 degree oven for about 25 minutes.
Makes 12 servings.
*If you like, you can use fewer mushrooms. Easy, yet attractive, company dish.*

## Ⓟ PINEAPPLE RICE Nancy Goldstein

1 cup long grain rice
2 eggs
¼ cup margarine, melted
1 small can crushed
pineapple
¼ cup sugar
¾ tsp. salt

1. Cook rice according to package directions.
2. Add in eggs, margarine, crushed pineapple, sugar, and salt.
3. Pour into 1½-quart ovenproof baking dish. Bake in 350 degree oven 45 minutes.
Recipe doubles well.
*A sweet dish like rice pudding. Use less sugar if you prefer less sweet taste.*

# NOODLE RICE CASSEROLE *Bonnie Hemmati*  [M]

½ to 1 cup margarine
½ pound very fine noodles, uncooked
2 cups instant rice, uncooked
2 10-ounce cans onion soup
2 10-ounce cans chicken broth
1 tsp. soy sauce
1 cup water
1 can water chestnuts, drained and sliced

1. Melt margarine in large skillet. Add noodles and stir frequently until lightly browned.
2. Add rice, onion soup, chicken broth, soy sauce, water, and water chestnuts.
3. Turn into 3-quart casserole. Bake in 350 degree oven 45 minutes.

# SPINACH NOODLE KUGEL *Esther Moschel*

2 packages frozen spinach
12 ounces green noodles
¼ cup margarine, melted
3 eggs
1 package onion soup
1 cup non-dairy cream

1. Prepare noodles and spinach according to package directions. Drain.
2. Add margarine, eggs, spinach, onion soup, and non-dairy cream to the noodles.
3. Pour into greased 9 x 13 inch pan.
4. Bake in 350 degree oven over 1 hour or until brown.
*Easy and festive.*

# HEALTHFUL KUGEL *Sheila Meyer*  [P]

1 package whole wheat flat noodles
3 Tbsps. margarine, melted
1 carton egg beaters
1½ cup tofu, crushed
1 large can pineapple with juice (no sugar)
1 cup raisins
2 tsps. cinnamon

1. Cook noodles 15 minutes (*al dente*); rinse with cold water and drain.
2. Toss in melted margarine. Add egg beaters.
3. Mash tofu with fork to consistency similar to cottage cheese and add to noodles. Add pineapple with juice. Add cinnamon and raisins. Toss together as lightly as possible.
4. Pour into lightly oiled 9 x 13 inch pan. Bake in 350 degree oven 45 minutes.
*No cholesterol, high fiber, no sugar, no salt— healthful, but delicious. Those who like a sweeter taste can add more raisins or more drained pineapple.*

##  CINNAMON NOODLE KUGEL  *Cecelia Benensohn*

16 ounces broad noodles
½ cup margarine, melted
1 cup sugar
4 level tsps. cinnamon
(or to taste)
½ tsp. nutmeg
¼ tsp. salt
7 large eggs, separated
1½ cups dark and light
raisins

1. Cook noodles according to package directions. Drain very well.
2. Add melted margarine.
3. Mix sugar with the cinnamon, nutmeg, and salt. Add to noodles.
4. Add well-beaten eggs yolks. Add raisins.
5. Beat egg whites until they cling to beater.
6. Folding gently, add egg whites to noodles. Pour into a well-greased 9 x 13 inch Pyrex dish.
7. Bake in 350 degree oven 40 to 45 minutes. Makes 16 servings.
*A sneak-into-the-kitchen, can't-stop-eating recipe— for cinnamon lovers.*

## FRUIT AND NOODLE KUGEL  *Irene Sufrin*

1 8-ounce package noodles
4 eggs
½ cup sugar
1 tsp. cinnamon
1 small can crushed
pineapple, drained
1 small jar strawberry
preserves
½ cup margarine, melted
¾ cup pecans or walnuts,
chopped
1 cup raisins
2 apples, peeled and cut
into small pieces
10 pitted prunes, cut in
pieces

1. Cook noodles in boiling water. Drain and rinse.
2. Beat eggs.
3. Combine all ingredients in large bowl.
4. Grease a large rectangular pan about 11 x 7 x 2 inches. Pour in mixture. Sprinkle with additional nuts and cinnamon.
5. Bake in 350 degree oven 45 minutes.
*This is a delicious, sweet kugel that is especially nice for Rosh Hashanah. My mother has been preparing this kugel for almost 30 years.*

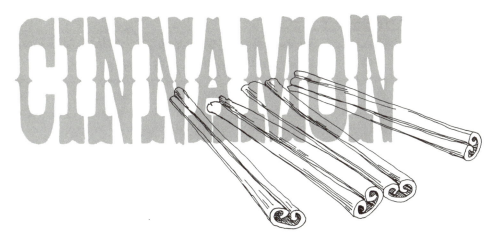

## JOAN'S NOODLE PUDDING  *Joan Sohn*  **D**

½ pound medium noodles
1 cup sour cream
¼ pound cottage cheese
½ cup butter, melted
2 eggs
½ cup sugar
Vanilla, to taste
Cinnamon, to taste

Topping:
¼ cup butter, melted
¼ cup sugar
1 to 2 tsps. cinnamon
1½ cups cornflake crumbs

1. Cook noodles in boiling water. Drain.
2. Add sour cream, cottage cheese, butter, eggs, sugar, vanilla, and cinnamon.
3. Combine topping ingredients. Sprinkle over noodle mixture.
4. Bake in 350 degree oven for 1 hour.
Can be made the night before, cooked ½ hour, and reheated for 45 minutes before serving. *Recipe can be doubled. Freezes well.*

## MAMA'S LUCHEN KUGEL  *Carmel Chiswick*  **D**

1 8-ounce package noodles
¼ cup butter or margarine
½ cup raisins
½ cup sugar
1 cup low-fat milk
4 eggs, beaten
¼ tsp. salt
¼ tsp. cinnamon

1. Cook noodles. Drain and mix in butter and raisins. Add rest of the ingredients.
2. Bake in 450 degree oven 20 minutes.
*"Mama" was Grandma Cynthia's mother, Mary Gerstin. Mama always made this kugel as a side dish, but the adults in the family usually saved it for dessert.*

## Ⓓ GOLDIE'S NOODLE KUGEL *Goldie Langer*

16 ounces broad noodles
4 eggs
1 small package cream
  cheese, diced
6 Tbsps. sour cream
4 slices American cheese,
  diced
1 cup sugar
4 Tbsps. butter, diced
1 cup milk
2 tsps. vanilla
1 tsp. lemon juice
Crushed cornflakes
  (optional)

1. Cook noodles and drain.
2. Mix together eggs, cream cheese, American cheese, sour cream, sugar, butter, and milk. Add to noodles.
3. Pour into greased 9 x 13 inch pan.
4. Add crushed cornflakes on top.
5. Bake in 350 degree oven 1 hour.
Makes about 10 to 12 servings.

## Ⓓ APPLE NOODLE KUGEL *Anne Lefkowitz*

16 ounces noodles
½ cup and 2⅔ Tbsps.
  butter or margarine, cut
  into chunks
1 cup brown sugar
3 tsps. cinnamon
3 eggs, slightly beaten
2 15-ounce cans
  unsweetened apples, sliced
1 cup yellow raisins

Topping:
Sugar
Cinnamon

1. Cook and drain noodles.
2. Stir butter or margarine into noodles. Mix in brown sugar, cinnamon, eggs, 1 can of apples, and the raisins.
3. Pour into greased oblong Pyrex baking pan.
4. Arrange the other can of apples symmetrically on top in rows. Sprinkle with sugar and cinnamon.
5. Bake in 325 degree oven 1 hour.

# JONA'S CUSTARD KUGEL *Jona Peretz* **D**

8 ounces broad noodles
8 ounces cream cheese, softened
1 cup sugar
8 eggs, separated
1 tsp. vanilla
1 stick butter, melted
1½ cups milk

1. Grease a 9 x 13 inch pan. Preheat oven to 350 degrees.
2. Cook and drain noodles, set aside in a large bowl.
3. In food processor, mix together cream cheese, sugar, egg yolks, vanilla, and melted butter. Add to noodles, mixing well.
4. Beat the egg whites until stiff but not dry.
5. Add milk to the noodle mixture; stir until well blended. Fold in egg whites.
6. Pour into pan and bake for 45 minutes.
*Best when made the day before and refrigerated. Cut into squares while cold and reheat at 350 degrees for 20 minutes.*

# APRICOT CUSTARD NOODLE KUGEL *Merle Cohen* **D**

2 3-ounce packages cream cheese, softened
1 cup sugar
6 to 8 eggs
2 cups milk
2 cups apricot nectar
1 pound medium noodles, cooked, rinsed, drained
8 Tbsps. butter, melted
1 cup golden raisins, optional

Topping:
½ cup sugar
2 tsps. cinnamon
2 cups cornflake crumbs
6 Tbsps. butter

1. Beat cream cheese until smooth with electric mixer.
2. Add sugar, eggs, milk, and nectar. Beat thoroughly.
3. Add noodles, melted butter, optional raisins, and mix well.
4. Pour into greased 9 x 13 x 2 inch Pyrex pan.
5. Combine topping sugar, cinnamon, and cornflake crumbs. Pour over noodles (the topping will absorb any excess liquid). Dot with butter.
6. Bake at 350 degrees for 1 hour.
Makes 16 servings.
*Freezes well; reheat and serve. Different, delicious kugel for easy entertaining.*

# Ⓓ LAZY KUGEL  *Marsha Emanuel*

2 cups milk
1 cup creamed cottage cheese
3 eggs
½ cup plain yogurt
¼ cup sugar
8 ounces medium yolkless noodles
Raisins, optional
Apple pieces, optional

1. Mix milk, cottage cheese, eggs, yogurt, and sugar together in blender on "blend" for 3 to 5 minutes.
2. Spray a medium-sized glass baking dish with non-stick cooking spray. Place yolkless noodles in pan. Pour mixture over noodles.
3. Place in 350 degree oven and bake 1 hour. Turn oven off and allow kugel to remain in oven for 10 to 15 minutes longer (if you have a gas oven).
Recipe can be doubled and baked 10 minutes longer. Raisins and/or apple pieces may be added.
*This kugel is great as a main dish with a tossed salad, side dish for a fish main course, or as an added attraction on a brunch buffet.*

# Ⓓ SHORT & SWEET NOODLE KUGEL  *Susan Rosenberg*

½ cup margarine or butter
1 8-ounce package medium noodles
3 eggs, slightly beaten
2 cups milk
½ cup sugar
1½ tsps. vanilla
1 8-ounce container small curd cottage cheese
1 2-ounce can crushed pineapple
Cornflake crumbs
Cinnamon

1. Preheat oven to 350 degrees.
2. Melt margarine or butter in a pan. In a large bowl, combine uncooked noodles, eggs, milk, sugar, vanilla, cottage cheese, and pineapple with a little liquid. Add melted butter or margarine.
3. Mix all ingredients together. Pour into a greased 9 x 13 x 2 inch pan. Make sure plenty of liquid is covering the noodles. Sprinkle top with cornflake crumbs and a dash of cinnamon.
4. Bake in 350 degree oven 1 hour.
Makes 10 to 12 servings.
*Quick and easy because you don't pre-cook the noodles.*

# KUGEL, JUST THE BEST *Joanne Kestnbaum*    **D**

1 16-ounce package broad noodles
6 eggs, well beaten
1 8-ounce container sour cream
2 to 5 apples, peeled and chopped
2 tsps. vanilla
½ cup sugar
1 cup butter or margarine
Cinnamon and sugar mixture
Salt and pepper, to taste

1. Boil noodles until soft. Drain and put back in pot.
2. Beat eggs very well (using an electric beater or food processor works well).
3. To the egg mixture add the peeled apples, sour cream, sugar, and vanilla, beating after each addition. Pour this mixture into the noodle pot and fold well. Add salt and pepper to taste.
4. Melt ½ cup butter or margarine and add to the noodles. Stir.
5. Melt the second ½ cup of butter or margarine and pour ½ of it onto the bottom of the pan. Pour the noodle mixture into an 8 x 11 inch rectangular or 10-inch square pan. Sprinkle with cinnamon and sugar mixture and remaining melted butter.
6. Bake in 325 degree oven for 1 hour.
*To lower cholesterol and calories, plain or vanilla yogurt or pureed cottage cheese will substitute nicely for sour cream.*
*This recipe can be made pareve if you change the sour cream to applesauce and use margarine instead of butter.*

# RUTH'S NOODLE KUGEL *Ruth Lipman*    **D**

½ pound broad noodles
3 eggs
1 pound small curd cottage cheese
½ tsp. vanilla
½ cup sugar
2 apples, cut into small pieces
1 20-ounce can crushed pineapple, drained, reserving ¼ cup juice
½ cup margarine

Topping:
⅔ cup cornflake crumbs
1 tsp. cinnamon

1. Cook and drain noodles.
2. Mix in eggs, cottage cheese, vanilla, sugar, apples, crushed pineapple, juice, and margarine.
3. Pour into a greased 13 x 9½ x 2 inch pan.
4. Mix cornflake crumbs and cinnamon together and sprinkle on top of kugel. Sprinkle additional cinnamon on top of mixture.
5. Bake in 350 degree oven 45 minutes. Cool and cut into squares.

# **D** DAIRY NOODLE KUGEL *Susan Markowitz*

1 pound extra broad
noodles
1 tsp. salt
1 Tbsp. vegetable oil
6 Tbsps. margarine or butter
4 large eggs
1 cup sugar
1 pint sour cream
6 ounces cream cheese
2 cups cottage cheese,
drained
1 15-ounce can fruit cocktail
or peaches (optional)
Cornflake crumbs
1 10-ounce package frozen
strawberries
Extra sour cream

1. Boil noodles with salt and oil, drain.
2. Measure margarine or butter into Pyrex or non-stick baking pan and mix together with noodles.
3. Using hand mixer or food processor, beat together eggs and sugar until creamy. Mix the sour cream and cream cheese into egg mixture until well blended.
4. Pour liquid mixture over noodles and mix well. Add cottage cheese to noodles and mix well (add fruit, if desired).
5. Sprinkle cornflake crumbs over top of noodle mixture to cover well.
6. Bake in 375 degree oven, uncovered, 25 minutes.
7. Cover with aluminum foil and continue baking another 15 to 20 minutes until all liquid is absorbed.
8. Serve with thawed and warmed frozen strawberries and sour cream.

*To bake ahead, remove from oven when a little liquid still rises to the top if you press down on the crust with your finger. When it is reheated, it will finish baking and not be too dry or burned on the edges.*

# AMERICAN "DAIRY" SPAGHETTI *Fran Fogel* **D**

3 ribs celery, sliced
2 to 4 onions, sliced
½ to 1 pound mushrooms, sliced
1 pound spaghetti (size of choice)
4 10-ounce cans tomato soup, undiluted
Optional: ½ pound cheese, 1 package mixed vegetables, or fresh vegetables of your choice

1. In a frying pan, sauté celery, onions, and mushrooms until tender, not well done or burned.
2. Cook pasta per package directions. Drain.
3. Toss spaghetti with cans of tomato soup and sautéed vegetables. Heat on stove and serve.
4. Optional: Dot casserole dish with butter. Pour spaghetti in and bake 45 minutes or so until crusty. Before baking, add cheese or vegetables of choice.
*This is truly '50's food! Kids love it!*

# SPAGHETTI SPINACH CHEESE CASSEROLE *Bonnie Hemmati* **D**

8 ounces spaghetti
2 10-ounce packages frozen chopped spinach, thawed and drained well
1 tsp. salt
¼ tsp. ground nutmeg
2 8-ounce cans tomato sauce
½ cup vegetable juice cocktail or tomato juice
1 Tbsp. sugar
Pepper, dash
8 ounces creamed cottage cheese
½ pound Cheddar cheese, shredded (2 cups)

1. Cook spaghetti according to package directions until just tender. Drain.
2. Combine thawed spinach, salt, and nutmeg. Set aside.
3. Stir together tomato sauce, juice, sugar, and pepper. Set aside.
4. Layer ½ spaghetti, ½ spinach mixture, ½ sauce mixture, ½ cottage cheese and ½ Cheddar cheese in 3-quart baking dish (in that order). Repeat layers.
5. Bake covered in 400 degree oven for 30 minutes.
6. Uncover, bake 10 minutes longer or until hot and bubbly.
*Quick, easy, healthful, and delicious!*

## **D** MACARONI FLORENTINE *Sybil Zimmerman*

2 Tbsps. butter or
  margarine
2 Tbsps. onion, chopped
½ cup celery, chopped
1 pound fresh or 10-ounce
  package frozen spinach,
  thawed
2 cups cottage cheese
1 egg
½ tsp. salt
Pepper, to taste
¼ tsp. nutmeg
2 cups shell macaroni

Sauce:
3 Tbsps. butter or
  margarine
2 Tbsps. onion, chopped
3 Tbsps. flour
Salt and pepper to taste
1½ cups milk
½ tsp. pareve chicken
  soup powder
½ cup hot water
½ cup Parmesan cheese,
  grated

1. Melt 2 Tbsps. butter or margarine in frying pan. Cook onion and celery 10 minutes. Pour into mixing bowl.
2. Add spinach, cottage cheese, egg, salt, pepper, and nutmeg and set aside.
3. Boil water, adding 1 tsp. salt. Add macaroni and cook 10 minutes. Drain.
4. Sauce: Melt butter or margarine in a saucepan. Sauté onion for sauce 15 minutes. Add flour, salt, and pepper. Stir in milk. Dissolve pareve chicken soup powder in hot water and add to sauce. Cook and stir until thick and smooth. Stir in cheese. Set aside.
5. Grease casserole. Pour in half the sauce. Add cooked macaroni. Add spinach mixture. Pour over rest of sauce. Bake in 375 degree oven 25 to 30 minutes.

## **D** LAZY MANICOTTI *Bonny Barezky*

1 box manicotti (12 pieces)
16 ounces spaghetti sauce
  (meatless)
1½ cups tomato juice
1 tsp. basil
1 tsp. oregano
Salt and pepper, to taste
1 pound drained ricotta
  cheese
3 ounces cream cheese
4 ounces mozzarella cheese,
  grated
½ cup Parmesan cheese

1. Combine spaghetti sauce, tomato juice, basil, oregano, and salt and pepper to taste.
2. Pour ⅓ of spaghetti sauce mixture into an oblong 3-quart casserole.
3. Mix together ricotta cheese, cream cheese, and mozzarella.
4. Stuff raw manicotti with cheese mixture and place in casserole. Cover with remaining spaghetti sauce.
5. Cover tightly with foil. Bake in 350 degree oven for 45 minutes.
6. Sprinkle Parmesan cheese over top before serving.

# SPINACH LASAGNE  *Goldie Langer*

1 box lasagne noodles
4 eggs
2 pounds ricotta (or use
half cottage cheese)
2 10-ounce packages
frozen, chopped spinach
2 15-ounce jars spaghetti
sauce
1 pound mozzarella,
sliced or shredded
Parmesan cheese, grated

1. Cook lasagne noodles according to package instructions.
2. Beat eggs in a bowl. Add ricotta. Drain spinach and add to eggs.
3. Layer in pan: sauce, noodles, spinach mixture, mozzarella, and Parmesan–repeating until used up.
4. Bake in 375 degree oven 30 to 45 minutes. Can be doubled.
Freezes well.

# EASY ONE-STEP SPINACH LASAGNE  *Barbara Glimer*

1 pound ricotta or
cottage cheese
½ cup mozzarella cheese
1 egg
Pepper, garlic, onion,
oregano, and salt, to taste
1 10-ounce package frozen,
chopped spinach, drained
19 ounces tomato sauce
Lasagne noodles
1 cup water

1. Mix together ricotta, mozzarella, egg, spices, and spinach.
2. In a 7 x 9 inch Pyrex pan, layer in order: tomato sauce, noodles, and cheese mixture. Continue alternating layers, ending with sauce.
3. Pour carefully 1 cup water around inside edge of pan (this cooks your noodles).
4. Cover tightly with aluminum foil. Bake in 350 degree oven 45 minutes to 1 hour.
*Fast and easy without pre-cooking the pasta!*

# GRANDMA DOT'S LINGUINE  *Gail Taxy*

3 to 4 cloves garlic,
crushed
½ cup fresh parsley,
chopped
¼ cup olive oil
1 6-ounce can tomato
paste
½ pound cooked linguine
⅛ tsp. cayenne
Black pepper, dash
Salt, to taste
Parmesan cheese,
grated (optional)

1. In a saucepan, sauté garlic and parsley in olive oil. Add tomato paste. Heat and stir for several minutes.
2. Cook linguine as directed. Drain. Toss linguine with sauce, cayenne, pepper, and salt.
3. Add grated Parmesan or Romano cheese.
*Pasta tastes even better cold the next day for lunch. To double recipe, double all ingredients except tomato paste; add 8-ounce can tomato sauce.*
◆ *Omit cheese for pareve recipe.*

## ❶ SPRING GARDEN PASTA *Judy Wolkin*

1 pound pasta (small mostaccioli works well)
3 Tbsps. butter or margarine
3 Tbsps. flour
1½ cups hot water
2 cups hot milk
Salt and pepper, to taste
8 ounces white cheese spread with garden vegetables (e.g. *Alouette*)
1 tsp. fresh parsley, chopped

1. Cook pasta. While pasta is cooking, prepare sauce.
2. Melt butter or margarine in saucepan over medium heat. Add flour gradually, stir with wooden spoon or whisk, and cook for 2 minutes.
3. Whisk in hot water and stir. Whisk in hot milk and continue stirring until sauce thickens. Season with salt and pepper.
4. Reduce heat and add cheese. Cook and stir until cheese melts and blends into sauce.
5. Drain pasta. Pour into serving bowl. Pour sauce over pasta; toss to blend. Sprinkle with parsley.
*You may substitute 8 ounces of herb-flavored cream cheese for vegetable cheese.*

## ❶ BUTCHI'S BAKED MOSTACCIOLI *Ruth Aberman*

1 pound mostaccioli
1 medium onion, chopped
2 cloves garlic, minced
1 small green pepper, chopped
Olive oil
1 48-ounce jar spaghetti sauce
½ tsp. Italian seasoning
1 10-ounce package frozen chopped spinach
1 16-ounce can zucchini
1 4-ounce jar sliced mushrooms
2 cups mozzarella cheese, shredded

1. Cook pasta *al dente* and drain. Reserve pot.
2. Sauté onion, garlic, and green pepper in small amount of olive oil.
3. Squeeze all moisture from spinach–do not cook.
4. In large pot that you just cooked the pasta in, combine sauce, Italian seasoning, spinach, zucchini (do not drain zucchini), mushrooms, and sautéed onion, garlic, and green pepper.
5. Mix pasta thoroughly with vegetable sauce.
6. Combine 1½ cups of mozzarella with the pasta.
7. Spoon into large casserole. Sprinkle with remaining ½ cup cheese.
8. Bake in oven at 350 degrees for 45 minutes.
*I have quadrupled this recipe and baked in large, disposable roasting pan to feed 40. You can cut recipe in half to accomodate the family. Serve with cheese and vegetable antipasto, tossed salad, and garlic bread.*
*Quicky and easy!*

# AUNT RONNIE'S FETTUCINE  *Gail Taxy*  Ⓓ

1 1-pound box fettucine
  noodles
4 cloves garlic, crushed
¼ cup parsley, chopped
¼ cup butter or margarine
⅛ tsp. white pepper
Salt, dash
2 cups heavy cream *or*
  half & half
½ cup Parmesan cheese,
  grated

1. Sauté garlic and parsley in butter or margarine in saucepan.
2. Add pepper, salt, cream, and Parmesan cheese. Stir thoroughly. Bring to a simmer. Turn off, cover, and let sit 15 to 20 minutes (except if it curdles or thickens).
3. Cook noodles as directed on package. Drain and put back into pot.
4. Reheat sauce just before tossing over noodles. Season more to taste.

# MIMI'S FAVORITE STUFFED SHELLS  *Karen Sager*  Ⓓ

1 box large pasta shells
  for stuffing

Filling:
3 pounds ricotta cheese
1 pound mozzarella cheese,
  shredded
1 10-ounce package frozen
  spinach, chopped (optional)
3 eggs
Salt, to taste
Pepper, to taste

Sauce:
2 29-ounce cans tomato
  puree
2 6-ounce cans tomato
  paste
2 Tbsps. olive oil
1 medium onion, chopped
¼ pound mushrooms, sliced
2 cloves garlic, minced
1 Tbsp. oregano
1 Tbsp. basil
½ tsp. pepper
*Or substitute:*
2 32-ounce jars
  prepared tomato sauce

1 cup Parmesan cheese,
  grated, for topping

1. Boil shells according to package directions. Do not over-cook. Drain and set aside.
2. Prepare sauce, if desired. Sauté onions, garlic, and mushrooms in oil in large saucepan. Drain liquid. Add tomato puree and paste, oregano, basil, and pepper; stir well, and simmer for 1 hour, while stuffing shells.
3. Mix together in a large bowl ricotta cheese, mozzarella cheese, and eggs. Add salt and pepper to taste.
4. Cook frozen spinach according to package directions, drain, and chop fine. Divide filling mixture in half. Add spinach to one half. (Optional: Recipe makes half with spinach filling, half without.)
5. Prepare two 9 x 13 inch Pyrex baking dishes by spreading a thin layer of tomato sauce over the bottom of each.
6. Stuff each shell with spinach or plain cheese filling. Place very close together on sauce in Pyrex pans.
7. Pour sauce over all shells. Top with Parmesan cheese. May be prepared to this point and refrigerated or frozen.
8. Bake at 325 degrees for 40 to 45 minutes. Serves 8 to 10.

## M HOT PASTA *Gail Taxy*

1 pound curled noodles
1 kosher sausage ring
3 Tbsps. vegetable oil
1 green pepper, chopped
1 quart fresh mushrooms
1 bunch green onions
½ carrot, grated
  (optional)
½ cup fresh broccoli
¼ cup black olives,
  chopped
1 small container pimento,
  chopped
Fresh pepper, to taste

1. Cook noodles. Drain off water. Peel off outer skin of sausage; cut into ¼-inch circles.
2. In large frying pan, sauté sausage pieces. Set aside in bowl.
3. Chop and then sauté green pepper, mushrooms, and onions in the same pan.
4. Toss sautéed vegetables with remaining oil and carrot, broccoli, olives, and pimento. Add sausage and noodles. Toss and season with fresh pepper.

*A hit, especially with men and kids. Great side dish with barbecued chicken or steak.*

## P EXOTICALLY DIFFERENT PASTA *Judy Schuster*

8 cups water
½ tsp. salt (optional)
1½ pounds thin spinach
  spaghetti
2 ounces olive oil
2 onions *or* 2 bunches
  scallions, sliced
2 cloves garlic, minced
½ pound Nova lox, cut
  into bite-sized pieces
1 3-ounce package sun-
  dried tomatoes
½ tsp. black pepper
1 tsp. basil
*Vegetables and herbs for
  vegetarian option

1. Bring water to a rolling boil; add optional salt. Drop in pasta a little at a time so that water remains close to a full boil. Stir often. Add a drop of oil. Cook to preferred consistency; drain in colander. Do not rinse.
2. While water is boiling, heat olive oil in a skillet over moderate heat. When the oil is hot, add onions or scallions and garlic. Fry approximately 5 minutes, stirring occasionally.
3. Add lox to onions and cook 5 more minutes. Add tomatoes and stir until thoroughly mixed.
4. Sprinkle with pepper and basil. Remove from heat and let stand a few minutes to blend flavors.
5. Transfer spaghetti to serving platter. Pour sautéed ingredients over pasta and toss lightly to coat all strands.
Makes 4 servings.

*Serve as a main course with salad and garlic bread, or as an accompaniment to broiled fish.*
*There are many interesting variations to this recipe. For a vegetarian meal, omit lox; slice into quarters two of the following: tomatoes, green peppers, onions; slice one large zucchini. Stir-fry the vegetables with basil, pepper, and garlic powder to taste. Stir ½ stick margarine into cooked pasta and sprinkle wih chopped parsley. Transfer pasta to platter, pour vegetable medley into center, and serve.*

# vEgEtɑBLEs

# THREE LAYER VEGETABLE TERRINE  *Myra Dorf*

KP

**Tomato layer:**
2 Tbsps. olive oil
1 pound very ripe tomatoes,
  peeled and seeded
2 tsps. mixed herbs
1 heaping Tbsp. tomato paste
2 eggs
2 Tbsps. non-dairy creamer
Salt and pepper, to taste

**Parsnip layer:**
1 pound parsnips, peeled
2 eggs
2 Tbsps. non-dairy creamer

**Spinach layer:**
1 to 2 bunches, *or*
  18 to 20 ounces frozen
  spinach
4 Tbsps. olive oil
1 tsp. minced garlic
1 tsp. minced onion
⅓ tsp. nutmeg
2 eggs
2 Tbsps. non-dairy creamer
Salt and pepper, to taste

1. Preheat oven to 350 degrees. Grease an
8 x 5 x 2 inch terrine or loaf pan; set aside.
Place a larger heat proof dish half filled with
water *(bain marie)* into the oven.

Prepare tomato layer:
2. Heat 2 Tbsps. oil in frying pan, add
tomatoes, and mash while cooking.
3. Add mixed herbs and tomato paste. Continue
cooking until moisture is absorbed (about 4 to
5 minutes).
4. Put tomato mixture in food processor; add 2
eggs and 2 Tbsps. non-dairy creamer; process
until smooth. Add salt and pepper to taste.
5. Pour into pan. Bake approximately 20
minutes in *bain marie* until set.

Prepare parsnip layer:
6. Boil parsnips in water until soft. Place in
food processor; add 2 eggs and 2 Tbsps. non-
dairy creamer; puree.
7. Pour on top of baked tomato layer in terrine.
Bake approximately 20 minutes in *bain marie*
until set.

Prepare spinach layer:
8. Carefully clean fresh spinach and discard
stems. Heat in 4 Tbsps. oil and sauté with
garlic. Add nutmeg, and cook until moisture is
absorbed.
9. Transfer to processor; add 2 Tbsps. non-dairy
creamer and 2 eggs, salt and pepper to taste;
puree.
10. Pour on top of baked parsnip layer in
terrine. Bake about 15 minutes until set.
May be served warm or cool. Cover and
refrigerate several hours or overnight. Unmold
before serving.
Makes 6 servings.
*Gourmet. Recipe may be doubled and baked in
two terrines for a larger dinner party.*

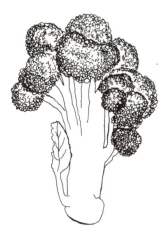

# BROCCOLI - CAULIFLOWER
# MARBLE "CAKE" *Bonny Barezky*

**D**

4 Tbsps. butter, melted
4 Tbsps. flour
1½ cups milk
2 pounds cauliflower
6 eggs
1 cup Cheddar cheese,
  grated (optional)
½ tsp. curry powder, for
  cauliflower
2 pounds broccoli
½ tsp. Tabasco sauce, for
  broccoli
Salt and pepper

1. Make a sauce by melting butter in saucepan. Add flour and cook 3 minutes on medium heat, stirring. Whisk in milk and cook 5 minutes or more, stirring constantly. Set aside.

2. Cook cauliflower (steam or microwave on high for 6 minutes). Cool. Place in bowl of food processor.

3. Add ½ of sauce, ½ cup cheese, and 3 eggs to cauliflower. Puree until smooth (in processor). Add curry, salt, and pepper. Set aside.

4. Repeat steps 2 and 3 for broccoli, but add the Tabasco sauce, salt, and pepper.

5. Alternate spoonfuls of each mixture in a greased 9 x 13 inch pan (Pyrex suggested). With the tip of a knife, marbelize the mixture. Mold can be refrigerated at this point, for one day. Cover with plastic wrap.

6. To bake, cover "cake" with buttered wax paper. Place in a large pan filled half way with boiling water. Bake in 375 degree oven for 45 minutes.

Cut into squares or diamonds to serve.

*This "marble cake" vegetable dazzles the eyes and cuts well into squares. It can be made a day ahead and refrigerated before baking.*

**P** *Converts into delicious pareve recipe by omitting cheese and substituting margarine and non-dairy creamer for butter and milk.*

# ◆ NO CRUST BROCCOLI QUICHE *Susan Markowitz*

Cornflake crumbs
2 packages frozen chopped
  broccoli
1½ Tbsps. pareve margarine*
1½ Tbsps. flour
½ cup non-dairy cream*
½ cup mayonnaise
1 Tbsp. onion, chopped
3 eggs, beaten
Dash garlic
Salt and pepper to taste

1. Preheat oven to 350 degrees. Lightly grease 8 x 10 inch or 9-inch round pan and coat with cornflake crumbs on the bottom and sides.
2. Cook frozen broccoli, according to package directions and drain.
3. Melt margarine in saucepan. Add flour and blend. Add non-dairy cream and stir until smooth. Add mayonnaise, onions, eggs, and seasonings to broccoli and mix well.
5. Pour into baking pan and bake for 35 minutes.
Makes 4 to 6 servings.
*You may substitute frozen chopped spinach, French-style green beans, or any combination of these. You may also add ¼ cup grated carrots for extra flavor and color.*
*\*Recipe may be prepared dairy using milk and butter instead of margarine and pareve cream.*

# BROCCOLI AND CAULIFLOWER
# ⒟ IN CREAMY PESTO SAUCE *Jennifer Gritton*

[KP]
1 bunch fresh broccoli,
  cut in chunks
½ head cauliflower,
  cut in chunks
1 to 1½ cups (packed)
  fresh basil leaves
½ cup fresh parsley
¼ cup almonds (to taste)
¼ cup olive oil
3 Tbsps. butter or margarine
½ cup Parmesan cheese
1 cup heavy cream or milk
  (to richness desired)

1. Lightly steam fresh broccoli and cauliflower, 10 minutes or so. Cool and put in buttered casserole dish.
2. Put basil leaves, parsley, almonds, and olive oil in food processor. Process to smooth paste.
3. In a saucepan, melt butter or margarine. Mix in Parmesan cheese. Then slowly pour in cream or milk.
4. Add mixture from food processor to saucepan. Stir constantly until sauce thickens.
5. Pour over vegetables in casserole.
6. Bake in 350 degree oven for 20 minutes. Stir slightly if sauce separates.
*Delicious, easy, and festive.*

# BROCCOLI - CAULIFLOWER BEEHIVE   Helene Bonner   Ⓓ

1 large head cauliflower,
  broken into flowerets
2 bunches broccoli,
  broken into flowerets

Cheese sauce:
½ cup mayonnaise
2 Tbsps. Dijon mustard
½ cup Cheddar cheese,
  shredded
2 Tbsps. onion, chopped

Microwave instructions:
1. Use any microwave-safe mold, bowl, or flower
pot which is beehive or slightly cone shaped.
The best thing is a 2-quart batter bowl, but
anything can be used. Line the bottom of the
mold with cauliflower.
2. Make a ring of broccoli, placing the stems to
the inside. Repeat alternate layers until all the
vegetables are used.
3. Cover tightly with plastic wrap and microwave
for 10 minutes on high. Test for doneness by
sticking with a knife tip or skewer.
4. When done, compress the cooked vegetables
with a saucer. Let cool about 5 minutes. Pour
off accumulated liquid. Place a serving plate
over the bottom and invert.
5. Combine ingredients for sauce and microwave
on high for about 1 minute. Stir well. Spoon
over warm beehive.

# BROCCOLI SOUFFLÉ   Irit Jacobson   Ⓓ

1½ Tbsps. butter
1½ Tbsps. flour
½ cup milk
¾ cup mayonnaise
3 eggs, beaten
2 packages frozen broccoli,
  cooked and drained
Salt, to taste
Pepper, to taste
Garlic, to taste
Bread crumbs (optional)

1. Melt butter in saucepan. Add flour and cook
over low heat several minutes.
2. Slowly add milk, stirring constantly until
smooth and thick. Remove from heat.
3. Stir in mayonnaise, eggs, broccoli, salt,
pepper, and garlic.
4. Put in a greased soufflé dish. You may
sprinkle with bread crumbs. Bake in 350 degree
oven for 45 minutes or until golden.
Makes 8 servings.
◆ *May be made pareve by substituting
margarine for butter and non-dairy creamer for
milk.*

# Ⓓ BROCCOLI & CORN CASSEROLE *Charlotte Cleeland*

1 package frozen chopped
  broccoli
1 can cream style corn
1 egg, beaten
1 tsp. salt
1 Tbsp. onion, minced
½ cup coarse cracker crumbs
1 Tbsp. butter or
  margarine, melted
Butter pieces
½ cup fine cracker crumbs

1. Cook broccoli slightly, add corn, beaten egg, salt, onion, coarse cracker crumbs, and butter. Mix carefully with fork.
2. Place in greased baking dish, cover with fine cracker crumbs. Dot with butter on top.
3. Bake in 350 degree oven 35 minutes. Makes 6 servings.
◆ *Equally delicious with margarine. A filling addition to a meal, or may be served as a meat substitute. Fast and easy.*

# Ⓓ BROCCOLI & RED PEPPERS *Janet Resnick*

4 bunches broccoli,
  blanched and chilled
6 red peppers,
  sliced into slivers
1 pint sour cream
¼ cup Dijon mustard
½ cup vinegar
1¼ cups olive oil
1 small tarragon,
  washed and minced
Salt and pepper, to taste

1. Cut broccoli into large pieces.
2. Combine sour cream, mustard, vinegar, oil, tarragon, salt, and pepper. Pour over broccoli and red pepper slivers and toss well.
Makes 10 servings.
*Great hot weather accompaniment to fish.*

# Ⓟ EGGPLANT CASSEROLE *Barbara Ament*

4 cups eggplant,
  pared and diced
1½ cups celery, diced
3 Tbsps. onions, minced
¾ cup stuffed olives,
  chopped
2 cups raw spaghetti,
  finely broken
1 cup condensed tomato
  soup, undiluted
2 Tbsps. salad oil
¾ cup water
2 tsps. Worcestershire sauce
1½ tsps. salt

1. Arrange eggplant, celery, onion, olives, and spaghetti in alternate layers in greased 2-quart casserole.
2. Mix together soup, oil, water, Worcestershire sauce, and salt. Pour over vegetables and spaghetti. Cover.
3. Bake in 325 degree oven 1½ hours or until eggplant is tender.
*Tasty accompaniment to fish or easy vegetarian main course. Fast, because there is no pre-cooking.*

# EGGPLANT KUGEL  *Sybil Zimmerman*  Ⓓ

1 pound eggplant,
  peeled and cut into cubes
Butter or margarine
1 small onion, chopped
1 egg
Cracker crumbs
Salt and pepper, to taste

1. Heat water in a saucepan with a little salt. Add eggplant and cook until soft. Drain well, then place in a bowl and mash.
2. Melt butter or margarine in a saucepan. Sauté onion. Add to eggplant. Add egg and cracker crumbs. Mix. Pour into a greased casserole.
3. Bake in 350 degree oven 30 minutes.
Makes 4 servings.
*The creator of this recipe is my late grandmother, Sade Lyon.*
◆ *Equally delicious with butter or margarine.*

# EASY EGGPLANT  *Arlene Demb*  Ⓟ

2 ripe eggplants
1 cup flour
2 eggs, beaten
Paprika
Salt and pepper, to taste
Oil, enough for frying
1 can tomato-mushroom
  sauce

1. Peel eggplant. Slice in vertical strips about ½ inch thick. Place eggs in one dish and flour in another. Add salt, pepper, and paprika to flour.
2. Dip eggplant slices first in egg, then in flour.
3. Heat oil in a frying pan. Fry eggplant until brown on both sides. Drain eggplant slices on paper towels.
4. Arrange layers of eggplant in casserole. Next, layer of tomato-mushroom sauce; continue alternating layers .
5. Bake in 350 degree oven for about ½ hour.
Freezes well.
Makes 8 servings.

##  EGGPLANT AND TOMATOES  *Jackie Siegal*

KP

1 large eggplant, sliced
Salt
1 onion, sliced
½ cup olive oil
2 green peppers, seeded, cored, and sliced
4 tomatoes, skinned, sliced
Salt and pepper, to taste

1. Sprinkle the eggplant slices with salt and let them drain in a collander for ½ hour. Wash and dry the slices.
2. Fry onion in olive oil until pale yellow in color. Add the sliced pepper and eggplant and fry for 10 minutes.
3. Add the tomatoes and season to taste with salt and pepper. Simmer for 30 minutes or until the liquid in the pan is reduced. Cool in pan.
*Great with saffron rice or, for a dairy meal, with yogurt seasoned with garlic and mint.*

##  FRIED GREEN PEPPERS  *Dolores Dimpfl*

KP

4 to 5 green peppers
1 small to medium onion
Oil
Garlic cloves (optional)
Salt and pepper

1. Cut green peppers from core down, making each slice about 1 inch to ½ inch wide. Cut onions in same manner, only thinner, about ⅛ inch wide.
2. Put oil in pan, enough to heavily coat the pan. Heat for about 1 minute. Season green peppers and onions with salt and pepper.
3. Then place peppers, onions, and garlic into oil and cook until soft (20 to 25 minutes) on low to medium heat. Turn occasionally. Cook, uncovered, 5 to 10 minutes. Cover and cook for another 15 to 20 minutes.
*Great as a side dish; fabulous on kosher Italian sausage or with Italian beef.*

## RATATOUILLE  *Chris Erenberg*

KP

2 onions, halved and cut into wedges
2 garlic cloves, minced
Oil for sautéeing
1 medium eggplant, peeled and cut into bite-sized pieces
1 green pepper, sliced
2 medium zucchini, cut julienne
2 large tomatoes, seeded and cut into wedges
1 tsp. thyme
Salt and pepper, to taste

1. In a large skillet, sauté the onions and garlic in about 3 Tbsps. oil over medium heat for 10 to 15 minutes, or until lightly browned.
2. Add cut-up eggplant and green pepper. More oil may be needed as vegetables are added. Sauté several minutes longer, until eggplant softens. Add zucchini, tomatoes, and spices. Mix all ingredients well. Continue cooking until zucchini and tomatoes are slightly soft.
Makes 6 to 8 servings.
*Just as good cold as it is hot!*

# DAVIDA'S ZUCCHINI  *Barbara Lavin*  **P**

**KP**

4 zucchini, sliced in half
lengthwise
1 large onion, diced
1 clove garlic, minced
½ green pepper, diced
½ tomato, chopped with
seeds removed
Oil, scant for sautéeing
1 tsp. salt
½ tsp. pepper
¼ tsp. oregano (scant)

1. Scoop out zucchini halves, leaving shells.
2. Sauté onion, garlic, green pepper, and zucchini insides in oil.
3. After a few minutes, add tomato and seasonings. Sauté a few more minutes.
4. Scoop mixture back into zucchini shells. (May be prepared ahead to this point.)
5. Bake on a cookie sheet in 350 degree oven for 1 hour.
*Festive and beautiful presentation for company, yet easy and fast to prepare!*

# ZUCCHINI CARROT PUDDING  *Barbara Ament*  **D**

4 eggs, beaten
6 large zucchini, peeled
3 large carrots, peeled
1 large Idaho potato, peeled
1 large onion, peeled
½ cup matzah meal
¾ cup bread crumbs
½ cup butter or margarine,
melted
Garlic powder, to taste
Salt and pepper, to taste

1. Place eggs in large bowl.
2. Grate zucchini, carrots, potato, and onion into bowl. Add eggs.
3. Stir in matzah meal, bread crumbs, and melted butter. Season with salt, pepper, and garlic powder to taste.
4. Turn mixture into an oiled 11 x 7½ inch glass baking dish. Bake in 350 degree oven 1 hour or until brown.
◆ *Equally delicious with margarine.*

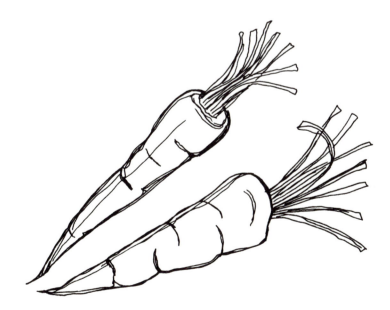

# ⓟ MOCK KISHKE  *Bonny Barezky*

| | |
|---|---|
| 1 box hexagonal crackers | 1. In food processor, combine crackers, carrots, |
| 2 large carrots, cut into | celery, onion, and margarine. Process until fine. |
| 1-inch pieces | 2. Spray foil with nonstick cooking spray. |
| 2 small ribs celery, cut | 3. Shape "dough" into a roll, like kishke, and |
| into 1-inch pieces | place on foil. Seal tightly. Freeze. |
| 1 small onion, chopped | 4. Place frozen on a cookie sheet and bake in |
| ½ cup margarine, melted | 350 degree oven for 1 hour. |

# FRESH VEGETABLES WITH
# ⓓ FROZEN SOUFFLÉS  *Charlotte Cleeland*

| | |
|---|---|
| Tomatoes, sliced | 1. Arrange tomato slices for corn on buttered |
| Corn soufflé, defrosted | baking dish. Spoon defrosted corn soufflé on |
| Onion salt | top. Add onion salt and crumbs. Dot with |
| Bread crumbs | butter. Bake in 350 degree oven for ½ hour. |
| Large mushrooms | 2. Arrange mushrooms upside down on buttered |
| Spinach soufflé, defrosted | baking dish. Stuff with defrosted spinach soufflé. |
| Bread crumbs | Apply Parmesan and crumbs. Bake in 350 |
| Parmesan cheese | degree oven for ½ hour. |
| Butter | *Quick, easy to prepare, and attractive.* |

# ⓓ CORN SOUFFLÉ  *Bonny Barezky*

| | |
|---|---|
| 1 17-ounce can corn | 1. Place all ingredients in food processor. |
| kernels, drained (2 cups) | Process until smooth. |
| ½ pound Muenster cheese, | 2. Pour into a well-buttered 1½ quart soufflé |
| grated | dish. |
| ¼ cup butter, in chunks | 3. Place dish in a pan of hot tap water. |
| 5 eggs | 4. Bake in 350 degree oven for 1 hour. |
| 1 tsp. curry powder | Makes 4 to 6 servings. |
| 1 tsp. sugar | *Fast and easy.* |

# REFRIED BEANS  *Sarah Hoffman*  **P**

1 pound black beans
  (if not available, use red
  beans)
1 head garlic (remove
  loose skins)
1 onion, cut in half
Salt
1 to 2 cups chopped onions
¼ to ½ cup oil

1. Remove any stones from beans, then wash the beans.
2. Place in pressure cooker with garlic, onion cut in half, salt, and enough water so that the cooker is about ½ to ⅔ full.
3. Cook beans for 1 to 1½ hours on low pressure. Reduce pressure, drain, and let beans cool.
4. Remove garlic and throw away. Mash beans in a food processor with some of the water.
5. Sauté the chopped onions in generous amount of oil in large frying pan. Add beans and keep frying until they are of desired consistency, stirring occasionally. You will need to fry the beans in two batches or in a very large fry pan.
*Serve with sour cream, for a dairy meal, rice and shredded lettuce and tomato salad for a "Tex-Mex" treat.*

# GREEN BEAN -TOMATO AMANDINE  *Sybil Zimmerman*  **P**

1 pound flat green beans
  (or string beans)
2 Tbsps. margarine
1 clove garlic, crushed
2 tsps. lemon juice
2 Tbsps. almonds, slivered
1 Tbsp. margarine
1 garlic clove, crushed
1 tsp. lemon juice
19 cherry tomatoes, halved
  (optional)

1. Place beans in a pan of water about 1 inch deep. Bring to a boil. Cook 4 minutes. Drain.
2. Melt 2 Tbsps. margarine in a saucepan or frying pan. Add 1 crushed garlic clove, 2 tsps. lemon juice, and almonds. Return green beans to pan and toss. Set aside.
3. Melt 1 Tbsp. margarine in a second pan. Add 1 crushed garlic clove, 1 tsp. lemon juice, and tomatoes. Sauté 5 minutes. Add to green beans. Heat before serving.
Makes 4 to 6 servings.
*Tomatoes add more color than taste, so they can be omitted if you like.*

## Ⓓ GREEN BEANS WITH CELERY  *Eva Sideman*

2 pounds fresh green beans
  or wax beans
½ cup celery, finely
  chopped
1 tsp. salt (or less)
¾ cup boiling water
2 Tbsps. lemon juice
2 Tbsps. butter melted
Pepper, freshly ground

1. Combine beans with celery, salt, and pepper in a saucepan.
2. Add the boiling water, cover, and simmer until tender (about 10 minutes).
3. Drain beans. Combine lemon juice and butter or margarine. Add to beans.
Makes 8 servings.
*Easy and quick!*
Ⓟ *Equally delicious prepared with margarine.*

## Ⓟ PEAS AND BLACK OLIVES  *Barbara Lavin*

2 Tbsps. margarine, melted
1 Tbsp. dry onions, minced
¼ tsp. oregano
Dash pepper
3 Tbsps. pimentos,
  chopped
¼ cup ripe black olives,
  chopped
1-pound package
  frozen peas

1. Melt margarine in saucepan. Add minced dry onions, oregano, pepper, pimento, and olives. Mix together and place in a bowl.
2. Refrigerate until ready to serve.
3. Before serving, cook frozen peas. Reheat refrigerated mixture.
4. Drain peas and add to reheated mixture.
*Elegant, yet easy.*

# ARTICHOKE & SPINACH CASSEROLE  *Irene Sufrin*  Ⓓ

1 package frozen artichoke
  hearts, defrosted
2 packages frozen spinach,
  defrosted
1 can cream of mushroom
  soup
¼ pint sour cream
¼ cup butter, melted
Salt and pepper, to taste
Cheddar cheese, grated

1. Combine artichoke hearts, spinach, mushroom soup, sour cream, butter, salt, and pepper in bowl. Pour into a greased casserole. Top with cheese.
2. Bake uncovered in 350 degree oven for 30 minutes.
Makes 4 to 6 servings.
*An easy but "fancy" recipe. It is delicious served with fish.*

# SPINACH-MUSHROOMS IN TOMATO SHELLS  *Marla Dorf*  Ⓓ

2 tomatoes
1 10-ounce package
  frozen spinach, chopped
4 Tbsps. butter
5 large mushrooms,
  chopped
2 Tbsps. onions, chopped
1 tsp. tarragon
½ tsp. salt
¹⁄₁₆ tsp. cayenne pepper
1 tsp. flour
4 Tbsps. cream

KP

1. Slice tomatoes in half, remove pulp. Salt cavity. Place tomatoes upside down on paper towel to drain.
2. Cook spinach according to package directions, drain very well.
3. Melt 2 Tbsps. butter, sauté mushrooms, then remove from pan.
4. Sauté onions, adding additional butter as needed. Add spinach, sautéeing 1 or 2 minutes.
5. Add tarragon, salt, cayenne pepper, and mushrooms. Sprinkle flour over all. Mix well, and add cream. Mix and remove from heat.
6. Fill tomato halves with spinach mixture. (May be prepared ahead to this point. Refrigerate.)
7. Bake in preheated 350 degree oven for 15 to 20 minutes. Serve hot.
Makes 4 servings.
*Easy, delicious, and beautiful company fare. Doubles easily.*
◆ *May be made pareve by substituting margarine and non-dairy creamer for butter and cream.*

##  BAKED MUSHROOMS AND BARLEY  *Arlene Levin*

½ cup margarine
1 pound fresh mushrooms,
  sliced
1 cup onion, coarsely
  chopped
1½ cups medium size
  pearl barley
¼ cup chopped parsley
2 cups chicken broth
½ tsp. salt
⅛ tsp. pepper

1. Melt ¼ cup margarine in large skillet. Add mushrooms and onions and sauté for 5 minutes. Remove from pan and place in a 1½-quart casserole.
2. Melt remaining ¼ cup margarine in skillet, add barley. Cook and stir until golden.
3. Add barley to casserole along with parsley, chicken broth, salt, and pepper. Stir gently.
4. Cover and bake in a preheated 350 degree oven 50 to 60 minutes or until barley is tender and liquid is absorbed.
If barley appears dry during baking, add more chicken broth or water.

## ◆ BAKED CARROT MOLD  *Eileen Brusso*

1 cup margarine
1 cup brown sugar
2 eggs
2½ cups all purpose flour,
  sifted
¾ tsp. baking powder
1 tsp. baking soda
1 tsp. salt
2 Tbsps. water
2 Tbsps. lemon juice
3 cups carrots, grated and
  loosely packed

1. Cream margarine well in mixer. Add brown sugar and beat 1 minute. Add 2 eggs and beat 3 minutes until batter is light.
2. Sift together flour, baking powder, baking soda, and salt.
3. Combine water and lemon juice. Alternate adding flour and lemon juice mixtures to batter, mixing well. Mix in grated carrots.
4. Spoon heavy batter into a well greased and floured 6-cup ring mold and spread evenly. Bake in 350 degree oven about 45 minutes or until firm to touch.
5. Unmold while still hot.
Makes 8 to 10 servings.
*For a festive touch, surround mold with a cooked vegetable, e.g., peas, corn, beets.*
*An excellent alternative to potatoes, rice, or pasta—and kids like it!*

# SWEET POTATO CASSEROLE  *Nancy Goldstein*  **P**

2 40-ounce cans yams,
   drained
½ cup margarine
¼ to ½ cup maple syrup
1 small can mandarin
   oranges
1 small can crushed
   pineapple in heavy syrup
1 tsp. cinnamon
Nutmeg (optional)

1. Drain fruits, reserving juices.
2. Mix yams, margarine, maple syrup, oranges, pineapple, cinnamon, and nutmeg. If needed, add some reserved juices.
2. Put into 2-quart casserole.
3. Bake in 350 degree oven 30 minutes.
Makes 4 to 8 servings.

# HONEY - THYME CARROTS  *Barbara Ament*  **M**

1 pound fresh carrots,
   cut julienne
2 to 3 cups warm
   chicken soup
½ cup margarine
½ tsp. thyme
Salt
Fresh pepper
Honey to taste

**KP**

1. Soak carrots in warm chicken soup for 30 to 45 minutes. Drain well.
2. Sauté carrots in margarine, thyme, and honey. Season to taste. Cook until crispy tender.

THYME

## ◆P◆ SWEET POTATO PUFF *Debbie Nathan*

6 large sweet potatoes
¼ cup margarine
3 eggs, separated (or 4,
  if using small eggs)
1 tsp. salt
⅛ tsp. pepper
¼ cup non-dairy creamer
  *or* orange juice
Marshmallows, cut in
  quarters, or miniature

1. Cook potatoes in salted water until tender (about 20 minutes).
2. Drain, cool, and peel. Mash or whip with a hand mixer.
3. Blend ½ cup of the margarine, the egg yolks, salt, and pepper. Add non-dairy creamer, or orange juice to the potatoes.
4. Beat egg whites until stiff. Fold into sweet potato mixture.
5. Turn into casserole. Melt remaining margarine and drizzle over the top.
6. Bake in 425 degree oven 15 to 20 minutes. (May be made ahead to this point and frozen.)
7. Just prior to serving, sprinkle marshmallows on top of casserole. Broil for about 3 minutes so marshmallows melt and brown. Be careful not to burn. Serve immediately.
Makes 10 to 12 servings.

## ◆P◆ CANDIED SWEET POTATOES *Cele Benensohn*

[KP]

4 to 5 pounds sweet
  potatoes
2 Tbsps. margarine
1 cup brown sugar
½ cup orange juice
2 heaping tsps. cornstarch,
  *or* potato starch
1 to 2 tsps. orange rind,
  grated
1 orange, sliced

1. Leave skins on washed sweet potatoes, place in Dutch oven or large saucepot, and cover with water. Boil until fork inserts easily into potatoes.
2. Cool and remove skins. Slice into halves or thirds. Place in well greased 9 x 13 inch Pyrex baking dish.
3. While potatoes are boiling, melt 2 Tbsps. margarine in pan, and remove from heat. Stir in brown sugar.
4. Dissolve cornstarch in orange juice. Add to brown sugar mixture. Stir well. Add grated orange rind.
5. Arrange orange slices in a line down middle of potatoes.
6. Pour brown sugar mixture over all.
7. Bake for 30 minutes in an oven preheated to 350 degrees, basting every 10 minutes.
Makes 8 to 12 servings.
*May be baked ahead, day or morning before. Reheat carefully to serve. For Pesach, substitute potato starch for cornstarch.*

# CREOLE STUFFED POTATOES *Arlene Levin* ◆ **P**

6 large Idaho potatoes,
washed and dried
4 Tbsps. margarine
1 cup onion, chopped
½ cup green pepper,
chopped
1 cup tomatoes, diced
2 Tbsps. non-dairy creamer
2 tsps. salt
¼ tsp. pepper
Paprika

**KP**

1. Bake potatoes in a preheated 400 degree oven for 1 hour.
2. Melt half the margarine in a saucepan. Sauté onion and green pepper until onion is transparent. Add tomatoes and cook 2 minutes.
3. When potatoes are baked, cut lengthwise in halves. Scoop out center to a bowl, leaving shells intact. Add non-dairy creamer and seasonings to potatoes. Mix well.
4. Add sautéed vegetables. Blend. Fill shells with mixture. Dot with remaining margarine. Garnish with paprika.
5. Bake in 400 degree preheated oven for 20 minutes.

*These may be made dairy with milk and/or butter, but it is rare to find a pareve recipe for twice-baked potatoes as delicious as this!*

# POTATO PUFF *Roberta Bell* **D**

2 pounds potatoes,
(approximately 5 medium)
peeled and quartered
2 Tbsps. butter,
at room temperature
4 ounces cream cheese,
at room temperature
4 to 6 Tbsps. milk
Salt and pepper, to taste

**KP**

1. In a saucepan cover potatoes with water and boil covered until tender (approximately 20 minutes). Drain well.
2. Put through ricer until smooth. Beat in butter, cream cheese, milk, salt, and pepper.
3. Turn into a 1¼-quart round casserole (about 8 x 2 inches). Bake in a preheated 350 degree oven until puffed and top is slightly golden (approximately 30 minutes).
4. Serve at once, while puffed.

*(If ricer is too much trouble, potatoes may be mashed.)*

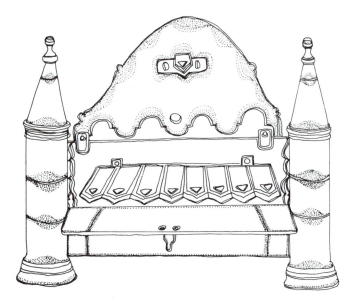

 # POTATO LATKES  *Bess Gold*

KP

| 4 pounds red potatoes, peeled | 1. Grate potatoes on hand grater. Remove approximately 1 cup liquid with a big spoon. |

4 pounds red potatoes, peeled
1 large yellow onion, peeled
3 eggs, beaten
1 tsp. salt
¼ tsp. pepper
½ cup matzah meal
Oil for frying

1. Grate potatoes on hand grater. Remove approximately 1 cup liquid with a big spoon.
2. Grate onion into small bowl with potatoes.
3. Add eggs. Add salt and pepper. Add matzah meal.
4. Heat oil in frying pan. Spoon batter around pan. Fry until edges start to brown. Fry on other side. At this point they may be drained and placed in foil to freeze. Can be frozen as long as 2 months.
5. To reheat, place a single layer on cookie sheet and place under broiler. Brown on each side until brown and crispy.
Serve while hot with applesauce.
(For a dairy variation, serve with sour cream.)
*These are the traditional Chanukah Latkes; however, the matzah meal makes them kosher for Pesach as well. Flour may be substituted for Chanukah, but we think the matzah meal lends a certain crispness. Grating potatoes in blenders and food processors saves a lot of work and wear and tear on the hands and elbows; but the latkes don't have the just right texture—and they don't taste as good!*

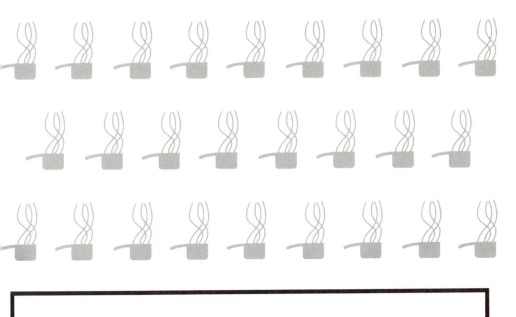

# DESSERTS

# ⓓ FRAN'S CHOCOLATE MOUSSE *Fran Abramson*

1 6-ounce package semi-
sweet chocolate bits
6 egg yolks, lightly beaten
2 Tbsps. cognac
6 egg whites, beaten
Salt, dash
Whipped cream garnish

1. Melt chocolate bits in double boiler over hot water.
2. Beat egg yolks in a bowl. Add cognac. Add chocolate, a little at a time, to egg yolks mixture and blend well.
3. Beat egg whites until stiff and fold into chocolate custard. Add salt.
4. Pour into glass dish or sherbet dishes and chill overnight.
Garnish with whipped cream.

# ⓓ MOUSSE ANISETTE AU CHOCOLAT *Miriam Lobstein*

½ pound chocolate bits or
other semi-sweet
chocolate
¼ cup anisette-flavored
coffee
10 eggs, separated
¼ cup anisette liqueur
Chocolate shavings
Slivered almonds
Whipped cream

1. Melt chocolate and flavored coffee in double boiler; cool.
2. Beat yolks, add liqueur, and mix in chocolate.
3. Beat egg whites until stiff and add to chocolate.
4. Pour into bowl and chill for one day.
5. Sprinkle with chocolate shavings and slivered almonds.
Serve with whipped cream.
*People will steal it off your plate. For adults only!*

# ⓓ CHOCOLATE WALNUT MOUSSE *Judith Taylor*

6 ounces semi-sweet
chocolate chips
¾ cup scalded milk
2 eggs
3 Tbsps. hot coffee
2 Tbsps. dark rum or
suitable liqueur
⅔ cup walnuts, chopped

1. Blend chocolate, milk, eggs, coffee, and rum in blender for 1½ minutes.
2. Add walnuts. Blend 30 seconds longer.
3. Pour into 6 small (or 4 large) ramekins. Chill for 2 hours. Serve plain or garnished with whipped cream.
Makes 6 servings.
*This is a rich, thick dessert and requires no garnish. Delicious!*

# CHOCOLATE MOUSSE
# IN CRINKLE CUPS *Arlene Levin* **D**

Dessert cups or muffin cups
12 ounces semi-sweet
  chocolate chips
2 Tbsps. margarine or oil

Mousse:
6 ounces semi-sweet
  chocolate chips
3 eggs, separated
1 cup whipped cream

1. Line muffin cups with paper liners.
2. In a small saucepan, over low heat, melt 12 ounces chocolate chips with margarine or oil. (Oil may be easier to work with; margarine causes chocolate to harden faster.)
3. Stir until smooth; remove from heat.
4. Using a small pastry brush, coat bottom and sides of liners with chocolate to about ¼ inch thickness.
5. Refrigerate until firm.
6. In a large saucepan, over low heat, melt 6 ounces chocolate chips.
7. Remove from heat, add 1 egg and 2 egg yolks, and mix well.
8. Cool.
9. In large bowl, beat remaining 2 egg whites and whipped cream, and fold into chocolate mixture. Chill.
10. To serve, peel liners from chilled cups.
11. Spoon mousse into prepared cups.
12. Garnish with whipped cream in center, if desired.
Makes 10 servings.
*Chocolate lovers and kids go crazy over this!*
◆ *An equally fancy pareve dessert may be made by substituting non-dairy whip for cream.*

# ⓓ CHOCOLATE ALMOND MOUSSE *Irit Jacobson*

8 ounces semi-sweet
chocolate
2 Tbsps. Amaretto liqueur
2 Tbsps. strong coffee
4 eggs, separated
¼ tsp. cream of tartar
2 Tbsps. sugar
2 cups whipping cream
Almonds, whole or sliced

1. Melt chocolate, liqueur, and coffee in double boiler over low heat.
2. When smooth, whisk in egg yolks. Remove from heat. Allow to cool.
3. Beat egg whites with cream of tartar until whites hold soft peaks.
4. Sprinkle in sugar. Beat until stiff. Fold ⅓ of the beaten egg whites into chocolate mixture, then pour all remaining whites on top of chocolate.
5. Set aside long enough to whip cream until it holds its shape.
6. Pour all whipped cream on top of egg whites and chocolate. Fold together well. Pour into serving dish. Garnish with whole or sliced almonds.
Makes 8 servings.
*Lovely company dessert.*

# ⓟ LAUREL'S CHOCOLATE MOUSSE *Laurel Feldman*

4 squares unsweetened
chocolate
¾ cup sugar
¼ cup water
5 eggs, separated
2 Tbsps. sherry

1. Combine chocolate, sugar, and water in top of double boiler. Stir occasionally until chocolate melts.
2. Add egg yolks, one at a time, beating vigorously (keep mixture over heat).
3. Remove mixture from heat and from water in double boiler. Cool.
4. Beat egg whites until stiff.
5. Fold egg whites into cooled chocolate mixture. Add sherry.
6. Turn into dessert bowls and refrigerate at least overnight.
*Serve with whipped cream for dairy variation. Easy, elegant.*

# CHOCOLATE ANGEL PIE *Phyllis Neiman*

Crust:
2 egg whites
⅛ tsp. salt
⅛ tsp. cream of tartar
½ cup sugar
½ cup pecans,
  finely chopped
½ tsp. vanilla

Filling:
1 package sweet chocolate
3 Tbsps. water
1 tsp. vanilla
1 cup whipping cream
Chocolate shavings

1. For crust, beat whites with salt and cream of tartar until foamy.
2. Gradually add sugar, beating until stiff. Fold in nuts and ½ tsp. vanilla. Spread in well greased 8-inch pie pan. Bake in 300 degree oven 50 to 55 minutes. Cool.
3. For filling: melt chocolate with water over low heat, stirring constantly. Cool until thickened. Add 1 tsp. vanilla.
4. Whip cream. Fold chocolate mixture into whipped cream.
5. Pile filling into cooled meringue pie shell. Smooth with knife or spoon. Chill for at least 2 hours.
Makes 8 servings, as small portions are suggested.
*Shave chocolate swirls for decorating on top. Additional whipped cream at side of portion is nice, but not necessary. Beautiful and rich!*

# TRIFLE *Hannah Engelman*

1 medium-sized sponge cake
  or angel food cake
1 package instant vanilla
  pudding or custard
1 tsp. any liqueur
1 pint whipping cream
Fruit to decorate: peaches,
  strawberries

1. Bake or buy sponge or angel food cake; cut cake into squares to fit base of your dish. Improvise in placing pieces to shape of bowl.
2. Sprinkle liqueur over cake. (If serving to children, omit liqueur.)
3. Make vanilla pudding or custard according to directions on package and pour on top of cake. Refrigerate until set.
4. Whip cream until stiff.
Decorate with whipped cream and garnish with fruit and/or sprinkles.
Makes 8 to 10 servings.
*Easy version of traditional English dessert.*

## DESSERTS

**Ⓓ PAVLOVA** *Hannah Engelman*

KP

6 egg whites
Salt, pinch
2 cups sugar
1½ tsps. vinegar
1½ tsps. vanilla
Fruit for decorating
1 to 2 cups whipped cream

NOTE: If you have a gas oven, preheat to 450 degrees before starting to beat egg whites. Just before you put the Pavlova in the oven, reduce temperature to 300 degrees. If oven is electric, preheat to 300 degrees from beginning to bake at 300 degrees.

1. Beat egg whites with salt at highest speed. When soft peaks form, add sugar, 1 Tbsp. at a time.
2. When whites are very stiff, and all sugar has been added, blend in the vinegar and vanilla gently, with a spoon.
3. Use a flat, round pizza tin and cover with foil. Heap the pavlova mixture in a pile in middle and using a fork, scoop up sides so that it is flat on top and high around sides and there are ridges left on sides from the fork. The pile will be about 3 to 4 inches high.
4. Bake in oven, preheated as indicated above, 40 to 50 minutes. Turn off oven, and leave Pavlova there until cold. The meringue will be hard, crisp and yellowish outside (knock with your knuckles for a hollow sound,) and soft marshmallow texture inside.
5. Decorate with whipped cream before serving, and garnish with strawberries, kiwi fruit, pineapple, or peaches.
Makes 8 to 10 servings.
◆ *Substitute non-dairy topping for pareve dessert. Very successful Australian dessert. Light and beautiful—easy to eat!*

# RICE PUDDING *Sarita Blau* Ⓓ

2 cups cooked rice
2 cups milk
⅓ cup sugar
2 eggs, beaten
1 tsp. vanilla
1 or 2 apples, chopped, *or*
¼ cup raisins (optional)

1. Butter 8 x 8 inch baking dish or 1-quart casserole.
2. In large bowl, mix together well rice, milk, sugar, eggs, vanilla, and apples or raisins. Pour into buttered baking pan. Bake in 350 degree oven 20 to 30 minutes.
Makes 12 servings.
*Fast and tasty.*

# BANANA SPLIT TOFUTTI *Renee Goldfarb* ◆P

1 cup flour
½ cup pecans, chopped
¼ cup brown sugar
¾ cup margarine, melted
2 to 3 bananas
4 pints "tofutti," chocolate chip (or preferred flavor)
1 cup pareve chocolate chips
2 cups powdered sugar
1½ cups non-dairy creamer
1 tsp. vanilla
1 pint non-dairy whipping cream
1 cup walnuts, chopped

1. Mix flour, chopped pecans, brown sugar, and ¼ cup melted margarine.
2. Spread in 11 x 15 inch foil-lined pan, and bake in 350 degree oven 10 to 20 minutes, stirring often until light brown in color.
3. Place these "crumbs" in the bottom of each of two 9-inch pie dishes.
4. Slice bananas and layer over crumbs.
5. Remove tofutti from containers and slice in ½ inch layers on top of bananas, forming a solid top.
6. Cover with waxed paper and freeze until firm.
7. Melt chocolate chips and ½ cup margarine. Add powdered sugar and non-dairy creamer.
8. Cook until well blended, stirring constantly. Add vanilla and cool.
9. Pour cooled mixture over the tofutti, cover with waxed paper, and refreeze.
10. Whip the pareve whipping cream and place on top with chopped walnuts when serving.
Makes 16 to 20 servings.
*A pareve dessert kids love!*

# ⓓ CHOCOLATE BANANA CHEESECAKE  Arlene Levin

**Crust:**
6 Tbsps. butter or
   margarine, melted
2 Tbsps. sugar
1¼ cups graham cracker
   crumbs

**Filling:**
24 ounces cream cheese,
   softened
4 squares unsweetened
   chocolate, melted & cooled
2 cups sugar
3 Tbsps. creme de cacao
5 bananas
½ pint whipping cream

1. Melt butter in a small pan. Blend in 2 Tbsps. sugar until dissolved. Stir in crumbs.
2. Pat over bottom and halfway up sides of a 9-inch springform pan.
3. Beat cheese until soft and fluffy.
4. Gradually beat in melted and cooled chocolate, 2 cups sugar, and creme de cacoa.
5. Mash enough bananas to make 1 cup (about 3), and fold into cheese mixture.
6. Whip cream until stiff, and fold into cheese mixture.
7. Turn into prepared springform pan.
8. Chill 8 hours or overnight.
9. Slice remaining 2 bananas and arrange over top before serving.

# ⓓ VAL'S CHEESECAKE  Val Hakimi

**Filling:**
16 ounces cream cheese,
   room temperature
1 cup sugar
2 envelopes whipped
   topping mix
2 tsps. vanilla
1 cup cold milk

**Crust:**
2 cups graham cracker
   crumbs
½ cup butter, melted
2 Tbsps. sugar

1. Mix cream cheese with sugar.
2. Beat whipped topping mix not too stiffly as per directions with milk and vanilla.
3. Add to cream cheese mixture.
4. Mix graham cracker crumbs, butter, and sugar. Press in bottom of a casserole or pie plate. Put filling into crust and chill 3 hours.

# PRAELINE CHEESECAKE *Phyllis Neiman* Ⓓ

Crust:
1 cup pecans, chopped
3 Tbsps. sugar
3 Tbsps. butter, melted

Filling:
24 ounces cream cheese
1¼ cups dark brown sugar, packed
3 eggs
2 Tbsps. flour
1 cup pecans, chopped
1½ tsps. vanilla

Garnish:
Maple Syrup
½ cup pecans, chopped or halved

1. Mix together pecans, sugar, and melted butter.
2. Lightly grease an 8 or 9-inch springform pan. With the back of a spoon, press crust mixture into the bottom of the pan. Bake in 350 degree oven for 10 minutes. Cool.
3. Cream brown sugar and cream cheese until fluffy. Add eggs, one at a time.
4. Sift in flour. Add nuts and vanilla. Pour into cooled, prepared crust. Bake in 350 degree oven for 55 to 65 minutes or until firm. Allow to cool in pan.
5. Brush top with maple syrup. Put pecans on top. Chill in pan for at least 3 hours. Remove side, but not the bottom, and serve.
*Elegant, special cheesecake.*

# CHEESECAKE "EL MOLINO" *Mitchell Taxy* Ⓓ

Crust:
1½ cups graham crackers, crushed
½ cup sugar
½ cup butter (soft)

Filling:
24 ounces cream cheese
4 eggs
1½ cups sugar
1 tsp. vanilla

Topping:
2 cups sour cream
2 tsps. vanilla
½ cup sugar

1. For crust: combine graham crackers, sugar, and butter. Thinly pat into bottom and sides of 9-inch springform pan. Chill crust while making filling.
2. Beat cream cheese until smooth. Add eggs one at a time. Add sugar and vanilla.
3. Pour filling into crust and bake in 350 degree oven for approximately 1 hour or until firm. Remove from oven and cool 15 minutes.
4. Blend sour cream, vanilla, and sugar for topping. Pour over top of cake. Bake an additional 10 minutes.
5. Cool and chill. May be served with blueberries, sliced strawberries, or pineapple.
*This recipe came from restaurant owners in Guadelajara, Mexico. Excellent and different!*

# COOKIES & CREAM CHEESECAKE Miriam Steinberg

**Crust:**
1¼ cups graham cracker crumbs
⅓ cup sweet butter, melted (5⅓ Tbsps.)
¼ cup brown sugar, firmly packed
1 tsp. cinammon

**Filling:**
2 pounds cream cheese, room temperature
1¼ cups sugar
2 Tbsps. flour
4 whole eggs (extra large)
2 egg yolks (extra large)
⅓ cup heavy cream
1 tsp. vanilla
1½ cups round filled cookies, coarsely chopped
2 cups sour cream
¼ cup sugar
1 tsp. vanilla

**Glaze:**
1 cup heavy cream
8 ounces semi-sweet chocolate, chopped
1 tsp. vanilla
6 round filled cookies, halved

1. For crust: Blend all ingredients in bottom of 9 or 10-inch springform pan; press into bottom and sides. Refrigerate 30 minutes.
2. For filling: preheat oven to 425 degrees. Beat cream cheese in large bowl on low speed until smooth. Beat in sugar and flour until well blended. Beat in eggs and yolks until smooth. Stir in cream and vanilla.
3. Pour half of batter into prepared pan. Sprinkle with chopped cookies and pour in remaining batter. Bake in 425 degree oven 15 minutes. Lower temperature to 225 degrees and bake 50 minutes.
4. Increase temperature to 350 degrees. Blend sour cream, sugar, and vanilla. Spread over cake. Bake 7 minutes. Cover with plastic wrap, refrigerate immediately, and chill overnight.
5. For glaze: scald cream. Add chocolate and vanilla, and stir 1 minute. Remove from heat, and stir until smooth.
6. Refrigerate, stirring occasionally, until thickened, 10 to 20 minutes.
7. Pour glaze over cake, smoothing sides. Decorate with cookie halves. Refrigerate until serving.
Makes 10 to 12 servings.
*May be frozen, before or after glazing, although cookies will soften. May omit crushed cookies or substitute mini-chips, changing decoration also. Spectacular! And kids always love cookies and cream!*

# GERRY'S CHEESECAKE Gerry Kaplan

**Crust:**
16 graham crackers
½ cup sugar
⅓ cup melted butter

**Filling:**
8 ounces cream cheese
½ cup sugar
2 eggs
1 can pie filling

1. Crush graham crackers. Add sugar and butter and mix well. Pat firmly into bottom of 8-inch pan.
2. Combine cream cheese and sugar. Add eggs one at a time. Beat well after each addition.
3. Pour on top of crust. Bake in 350 degree oven for 25 to 30 minutes. Cool.
Top with any pie filling.
*Quick and easy.*

# SOUR CREAM CHEESECAKE *Ethel Addison* Ⓓ

Crust:
1¼ cups graham cracker
  crumbs
2 Tbsps. butter, melted
2 Tbsps. sugar

Filling:
16 ounces cream cheese
1 cup sugar
3 eggs
1 tsp. vanilla
1 pint sour cream

1. Mix graham cracker crumbs, butter, and sugar together and press onto bottom and sides of buttered 9-inch springform pan.
2. Beat together cream cheese, sugar, eggs, and vanilla until thoroughly mixed. Fold in sour cream.
3. Bake in 375 degree preheated oven 30 minutes. Turn off oven and leave cake in oven for 1 hour. Chill before serving.
*Optional fruit toppings of strawberries or blueberries may be added before serving.*

# MARBLE CHEESECAKE *Faye Newman* Ⓓ

Crust:
1¼ cups chocolate cookie
  crumbs
½ tsp. cinnamon
¼ cup butter, melted

Filling:
12 ounces cream cheese,
  softened
½ cup sugar
1 tsp. lemon rind,
  grated
2 eggs
1½ cups sour cream
1⅓ cups semi-sweet
  chocolate bits, melted

1. For crust, combine chocolate cookie crumbs, cinnamon, and melted butter. Place in 9-inch springform pan and chill.
2. Combine cream cheese, sugar, and lemon rind. Beat until blended.
3. Add eggs and sour cream, and beat until smooth.
4. Add melted chocolate and stir with fork to marbelize.
5. Pour into crust. Bake in 350 degree oven 40 to 50 minutes. Let stand in oven for one hour with door open.
Chill two hours.
*Beautiful, creamy, and delicious.*

# ⬦ MARBLE CHIFFON CAKE *Naomi Futorian*

¼ cup cocoa
¼ cup sugar
¼ cup boiling water
2¼ cups cake flour
1½ cups sugar
3 tsps. baking powder
1 tsp. salt (optional)
5 egg yolks, unbeaten
½ cup salad oil
¾ cup cold water
2 tsps. vanilla
8 egg whites
½ tsp. cream of tartar

1. Mix together cocoa, sugar, and boiling water. Set aside to cool.
2. Sift together 3 times flour, sugar, baking powder, and salt. Place in a bowl.
3. Make a well in the center of the dry ingredients. Add egg yolks, oil, water, and vanilla. Mix well.
4. Beat 8 egg whites and ½ tsp. cream of tartar until stiff.
5. Pour yellow batter carefully into egg whites (by hand) and mix well. Divide into 2 parts (one slightly smaller). Fold chocolate mixture into smaller part.
6. Alternate pouring white and chocolate batters into ungreased angel food cake pan. With a thin spatula or knife, cut into batter and swirl to marbelize.
7. Bake in 325 degree oven for 50 minutes. Increase to 350 degrees for 10 more minutes. Turn upside down on bottle until cake is cold. Makes 10 servings.

*A light, beautiful, and delicious cake.*

# CHOCOLATE CHIFFON CAKE  *Sarita Blau*

½ cup cocoa, strained
1 Tbsp. instant coffee
¾ cup boiling water
1¾ cups cake flour,
   sifted
1 Tbsp baking powder
½ tsp. salt
1¾ cups sugar
7 large eggs, separated
1 egg white
½ cup oil
1 tsp. vanilla
½ tsp. cream of tartar

1. Put cocoa and coffee in small bowl; stir in boiling water and let cool.
2. Sift together into large bowl the flour, baking powder, salt, and sugar. Make well in center.
3. Pour in egg yolks, oil, vanilla, and cooled chocolate mixture. Stir until smooth.
4. Add cream of tartar to 8 egg whites, and beat until firm, but not dry.
5. Add whites to batter and fold in.
6. Turn into 10 x 4 inch angel food springform tube pan.
7. Bake in 325 degree oven 55 minutes; then increase oven to 350 degrees and bake 10 to 15 minutes until top springs back when lightly pressed.
8. Cool upside down in pan.
9. When cool, cut between cake and outer side of pan, remove side and then cut around tube and bottom.

# CHOCOLATE CHIP CAKE  *Arlene Levin*

1 cup margarine or
   shortening
½ cup sugar
½ cup brown sugar
3 egg yolks
2 Tbsps. water
1 tsp. vanilla
2 cups flour
1 tsp. baking powder
¼ tsp. baking soda
¼ tsp. salt
12 ounces chocolate chips

Topping:
1 cup brown sugar
3 egg whites

1. Mix all ingredients except chips and topping in a large mixing bowl or food processor.
2. Pat dough evenly in a greased 9 x 13 inch pan.
3. Sprinkle the chips over the dough.
4. Beat the egg whites with 1 cup brown sugar and spread on top of the chips.
5. Bake in 350 degree oven for 40 minutes.
Makes 12 servings.

## ⓓ CHOCOLATE LAYER CAKE *Sharon Dorfman*

¼ cup butter
1½ cups sugar
2 eggs
2 ounces chocolate, melted
2 cups cake flour, sifted
1 cup sour milk
1 tsp. baking soda
1 tsp. vinegar

1. Cream butter and sugar together.
2. Add eggs and chocolate, beating thoroughly.
3. Add flour and milk alternately, a little at a time.
5. Mix baking soda and vinegar together; add last.
6. Divide into 3 8-inch or 2 9-inch greased and floured layer cake pans. Bake at 350 degrees for 1 hour.
*Also makes 24 cupcakes; bake 35 minutes. Great for kid's birthday parties. Frost with CHOCOLATE FROSTING, below.*

## ⓓ CHOCOLATE CHIP DATE CAKE *Barbara Ament*

¾ cup dates, chopped
1 cup tap water, hot
1¾ cups flour
3 Tbsps. cocoa
1 tsp. baking soda
1 cup butter, softened
1 cup sugar
2 tsps. vanilla
2 large eggs
¾ cup semi-sweet
   chocolate chips

1. Put dates in small bowl and cover with hot water.
2. Mix flour, cocoa, and baking soda.
3. In large bowl, beat butter, sugar, and vanilla until fluffy. Beat in eggs, one at a time until well blended. Stir in flour mixture alternately with dates and water until well blended. Fold in chocolate chips.
4. Spread batter evenly in 2 8-inch layer pans lined with greased wax paper. Bake in 350 degree oven 35 to 40 minutes until toothpick comes out clean. Cool in pans on rack 5 minutes. Invert on rack and peel off paper. Cool completely.
❖ *Substitute margarine for butter.*
*If desired, frost with CHOCOLATE FROSTING, below.*

## ⓟ CHOCOLATE FROSTING *Eva Sideman*

2 eggs, separated
1 cup powdered sugar
1 stick margarine
1½ tsps. vanilla
3 ounces chocolate, melted

1. Beat egg whites.
2. Mix powdered sugar with margarine. Add one yolk at a time and vanilla. Add the melted chocolate.
3. Fold in the stiffly beaten egg whites.
*Easy and outstanding!*

# CHOCOLATE NUT ZUCCHINI CAKE *Irene Sufrin* Ⓟ

3 squares unsweetened
  chocolate
3 cups flour
1½ tsps. baking powder
1 tsp. baking soda
1 tsp. salt
4 eggs
3 cups sugar
1½ cups vegetable oil
3 cups zucchini, grated
1 cup walnuts or pecans,
  finely chopped

1. Melt chocolate over very hot water. Cool.
2. Preheat oven. Grease and flour 10-inch tube pan.
3. Mix flour with baking powder, baking soda, and salt. Set aside.
4. In large bowl of electric mixer beat eggs at high speed until thick and light.
5. Gradually add sugar ¼ cup at a time, beating well after each addition.
6. Add oil and cooled chocolate. Beat until well blended.
7. At low speed add combined dry ingredients, mixing until smooth.
8. Add grated zucchini and nuts. Stir with wooden spoon until blended.
9. Turn batter into prepared pan. Bake in 350 degree oven for 1 hour and 15 minutes or until surface springs back when touched lightly. Cool in pan on wire rack 15 minutes. Remove from pan and cool thoroughly on wire rack. If desired, sprinkle top with powdered sugar.
Makes 12 servings.
*Delicious cake for company. Nice for Sukkot or when you have an abundance of fresh zucchini from a garden!*

# ⒟ BLACK BOTTOM CUPCAKES  *Barbara Ament*

8 ounces cream cheese,
   softened
1 egg
⅓ cup sugar
Salt, pinch
1 cup chocolate chips
1½ cups flour
1 cup sugar
¼ cup cocoa
¼ tsp. salt
1 tsp. baking soda
1 cup water
⅓ cup oil
1 Tbsp. vinegar
1 tsp. vanilla

1. In a small bowl, beat cream cheese with electric mixer. Add egg, ⅓ cup sugar, and salt.
2. Stir in chocolate chips with spoon.
3. In a larger bowl, mix flour, sugar, cocoa, salt, and baking soda. Add water, oil, vinegar, and vanilla and beat well.
4. Fill muffin tins ½ full of chocolate mixture from larger bowl. Top with cheese mixture.
5. Bake in 350 degree oven 15 to 20 minutes.
*Kids love these, and they look festive!*

# ⒟ JANET'S FLOURLESS CHOCOLATE CAKE  *Janet Resnick*

9 ounces dark chocolate,
   melted
9 Tbsps. butter, melted
6 eggs, separated
½ cup sugar
6 Tbsps. cornstarch
Flour
Powdered sugar

1. Melt chocolate and butter. Cool and whisk together.
2. Beat egg whites until soft peaks have formed. Add the sugar, tablespoon by tablespoon.
3. Beat egg yolks with a fork. Add to egg white mixture. After they have been completely incorporated, beat three minutes longer.
4. Sift half the cornstarch through a strainer into egg mixture. Add half the melted chocolate/butter mixture on top and fold in. Add the remaining half of the ingredients in the same way, and fold them in. Be careful to reach all the way to the bottom of the mixing bowl, since the chocolate will sink to bottom.
5. Butter and flour a 9 x 2 inch round, false-bottomed cake pan. Pour in the batter.
6. Bake in a 350 degree oven for 30 minutes. Cool 10 minutes in the pan. Loosen the sides and let cool completely. Put on plate and dust with powdered sugar.
*Rich and elegant.*
❖ *Substitute margarine for butter for a fabulous pareve dessert.*

# CHOCOLATE SACHER TORTE *Fran Fogel* Ⓓ

1¼ cups semi-sweet
  chocolate chips, melted
1 cup butter, melted
8 eggs, separated
1 cup sugar
1½ cups almonds, ground
2 Tbsps. flour
6 to 9 ounces preserves,
  apricot or raspberry

Icing:
1 cup semi-sweet chocolate
  chips, melted
½ cup butter, melted
Powdered sugar

1. Combine melted 1¼ cups chocolate chips and butter. Set aside.
2. Beat egg yolks and sugar in mixer on medium or high speed for 3 to 5 minutes until light and fluffy.
3. Add melted chocolate chips and butter, almonds, and flour. Mix until blended. Set aside.
4. Beat egg whites until stiff. Fold whites into batter. Grease a 10-inch springform pan. Pour batter into pan. Bake in 350 degree oven for 60 minutes.
5. Test with toothpick to be certain cake is done. Remove and cool on a wire rack.
6. When the cake is cool, brush the top with the preserves. Let set for an hour or more.
7. Melt together and combine 1 cup chocolate chips and ½ cup butter. Allow to cool 10 minutes. Slowly sift in powdered sugar until the proper consistency is obtained.
8. Cover torte with icing. Decorate with slivered almonds.

*To serve, cut in wedges. May be served with whipping cream on the side.*
*Outstanding for entertaining.*
◆ *Substitute margarine for butter to make an elegant and delicious pareve dessert.*

# MARBLE BUNDT CAKE *Eva Sideman* Ⓓ

1 cup shortening
2 cups sugar
3 eggs
1 tsp. vanilla
¼ tsp. baking soda
2 tsps. baking powder
Salt, dash
2½ cups flour
1 cup milk
6 tsps. cocoa

1. Mix shortening with sugar. Add one egg at a time.
2. Add vanilla, baking powder, baking soda, and salt. Mix well.
3. Alternate adding flour and milk, and mix well. Pour ⅔ of the batter into a well-greased bundt pan.
4. Add cocoa to the remaining batter. Pour it on top of the batter in the bundt pan, and with a wooden spoon, swirl to marbelize.
5. Bake in 350 degree oven for 50 to 60 minutes. Put on a plate as soon as you take it out of the oven.

*Easy and attractive. Sugar may be reduced by ½ cup if a less sweet cake is preferred.*

## ◆ⓟ SPONGE CAKE *Goldie Langer*

10 eggs, separated
1½ cups sugar
Salt, pinch
½ orange, grated peel
and juice
½ lemon, grated peel
and juice
1 cup flour

1. Beat egg whites with ¾ cup sugar and pinch of salt until stiff. Set aside in refrigerator.
2. Beat yolks with remainder of sugar until thick and ribbons form on batter when stirred.
3. Add peel and juice of fruit to yolks.
4. Add yolk mixture to whites, folding gently with whisk. Sprinkle flour over egg mixture and continue folding gently.
5. Pour into 10-inch springform tube pan sprayed lightly with no-stick cooking spray.
6. Bake in preheated 325 degree oven for 60 to 70 minutes until done.
7. Invert when removed from oven. Remove carefully from pan when cool.

*A light cake that is often served sprinkled with confectioner's sugar and accompanied with fruit.*

## ◆ⓟ SUNSHINE CAKE (SWEDISH SPONGE CAKE) *Charlotte S. Cleeland*

5 large eggs, separated
½ cup cold water
1½ cups sugar
½ tsp. vanilla
½ tsp. almond extract
¼ tsp. salt
1½ cups flour, sifted
(5 times in old recipe)
1 tsp. cream of tartar

1. Beat yolks until thick and lemon-colored (use electric beater—do not underbeat).
2. Add water to yolks and beat again until very light and thick. Add sugar slowly, beating hard; then add vanilla, almond extract, and salt.
3. Add flour gradually, continuing to beat.
4. In a separate bowl, beat whites with wire whisk. When frothy, add cream of tartar to finish. Fold into cake mixture. Pour into angel food pan.
5. Bake in 325 degree oven for nearly one hour.
6. Invert and cool on rack.

*This can be frosted with a white boiled frosting and was a traditional birthday cake in our family. It's also delicious with fruit and ice cream.*

# PRIZED BUNDT CAKE *Irene Sufrin*

**Cake:**
2 cups flour
1 cup graham cracker crumbs
1 cup brown sugar
½ cup sugar
1 tsp. salt
1 tsp. baking powder
1 tsp. baking soda
½ tsp. cinnamon
1 Tbsp. orange rind, grated
1 cup margarine, softened
1 cup orange juice
3 eggs

**Topping:**
1 Tbsp. margarine, melted
2 Tbsps. brown sugar
5 Tbsps. pareve cream
Confectioner's sugar
1 cup nuts, finely chopped

1. Combine all cake ingredients in order listed in bowl or mixer.
2. Beat for 3 minutes at medium speed.
3. Butter and flour 10-inch bundt pan.
4. Pour batter into pan.
5. Bake in 350 degree oven for 45 to 50 minutes. Remove from oven to cool.
6. After 15 minutes, remove cake from pan and cool on rack.
**Topping:**
1. Mix margarine, brown sugar, and pareve cream.
2. Add enough confectioner's sugar to reach a glaze consistency. Dribble glaze over cake.
3. Sprinkle with nuts.
*This cake is equally delicious with dairy ingredients: use butter for margarine, and milk for pareve cream.*

# HONEY CAKE *Ruth Levenson*

3 eggs
1 cup sugar
3 cups flour
1 tsp. baking soda
3 tsps. baking powder
1 tsp. cinnamon
¼ tsp. ginger
½ tsp. salt
½ tsp. cloves
½ tsp. allspice
1 cup coffee (can be instant)
1 cup honey
½ cup raisins, floured
½ cup slivered almonds

1. Beat together sugar and eggs in a large bowl.
2. Combine flour, baking soda, baking powder, cinnamon, ginger, salt, cloves, and allspice.
3. Add dry ingredients to egg mixture alternately with coffee and then honey. Beat 2 minutes.
4. Fold in floured raisins.
5. Put batter in greased 9 x 13 inch pan. Place slivered almonds on top.
6. Bake in 375 degree oven 40 minutes, then test, baking more only if necessary.
*A great family recipe originated by Grandmother Dora Cohen Dunn. Honey cake is traditionally served at Rosh Hashanah.*

# ⬥ CARROT CAKE *Joyce Kamen*

1 cup shortening
⅔ cup brown sugar
2 eggs, beaten
1⅔ cups flour
⅔ tsp. baking soda
1½ tsps. baking powder
2 cups carrots, grated
2 Tbsps. lemon juice

1. Cream shortening and sugar.
2. Add eggs, flour, baking soda, baking powder, carrots, and lemon juice. Mix well. Pour into greased ring mold, pan or individual dishes.
3. Bake in 300 degree oven one hour.
*If using cupcake tins, adjust baking time to 30 minutes, or until done.*

# ⬥ PROCESSOR CARROT CAKE *Susan Markowitz*

3 carrots, peeled
1 apple, peeled and cored
3 eggs
1¼ cups sugar
1 cup vegetable oil
2 cups flour
2 tsps. baking soda
1 tsp. baking powder
2 tsps. cinnamon
1 cup raisins

1. Cut carrots to fit feed tube of food processor. Grate, using firm pressure. Cut apple to fit feed tube. Grate, using medium pressure. Measure carrots and apple to equal 2 cups lightly packed.
2. Remove grater from processor and insert steel blade. Process eggs with sugar for 1 minute. While machine is running, add oil through feed tube. Process 45 seconds longer.
3. Add carrots and apple and process 8 to 10 seconds until blended.
4. Add flour, baking soda, baking powder, and cinnamon. Pulse 3 to 4 quick on/off turns, just until the flour disappears.
5. Sprinkle raisins over batter. Pulse 1 to 2 more times to blend. Scrape down bowl as necessary.
6. Pour batter into a well-greased pan: 12-cup bundt pan, 10-cup tube pan, or 9 x 13 inch baking pan.
7. Bake in 350 degree oven for 40 to 50 minutes until cake tests done.
*Quick and easy! Freezes well.*

# FESTIVE CARROT CAKE *Karen Sager*

**Cake:**
3 cups raw carrots, grated
   (approximately 1 pound)
1 cup pecans, chopped
4 eggs
2 cups sugar
1¼ cups vegetable oil
2 cups flour
1 tsp. baking soda
2 tsps. baking powder
2 tsps. to 1 Tbsp. cinnamon
1 tsp. salt

**Frosting:**
8 ounces cream cheese
⅔ stick of butter or
   margarine (or ⅓ stick
   of each)
1 pound powdered sugar
½ tsp. vanilla
1 cup flaked coconut
Pecan halves (optional
   decoration)

1. Grease and flour 3 9-inch cake pans. Preheat oven to 325 degrees
2. Wash and peel carrots. Cut to fit feed tube of food processor. Grate carrots with grating disk. Remove and measure.
3. Place steel blade in food processor. Chop pecans. Remove and measure.
4. Leaving steel blade in place, beat eggs, sugar, and oil until light. Stir down when necessary. Add next five (dry) ingredients and pulse until well blended.
5. Add carrots and pulse until blended. Be careful not to purée the carrots.
6. Add pecans last and pulse 2 to 3 times until blended.
7. Divide batter among three pans. Bake 60 to 70 minutes until toothpick inserted in middle comes out clean.
8. Cool in pans 10 to 15 minutes, then carefully remove to racks.
9. Frosting: make sure cream cheese and butter or margarine are soft at room temperature. With steel blade, whip in food processor until blended.
10. Add powdered sugar and vanilla. Blend until spreading consistency, scraping sides with spatula.
11. Add coconut last. Pulse 1 to 2 times or blend in with rubber scraper.
12. Spread between layers, frost top and sides. Decorate with pecan halves if desired. Refrigerate until ½ hour before serving.
*I adapted this recipe to the food processor, but it may be grated and mixed by hand as well. Although the frosting is a cream cheese base, it is so rich that it is often mistaken for white chocolate!*

# ◆ BANANA CAKE *Goldie Langer*

½ cup margarine
1 to 1½ cups sugar
2 eggs
2¼ cups flour
½ tsp. baking powder
¾ tsp. baking soda
1 cup bananas, mashed
¼ cup orange juice
1 tsp. vanilla
1 cup nuts, chopped
(optional)
1 cup chocolate chips
(optional)

1. Cream margarine and sugar well.
2. Add eggs. Beat until light and fluffy.
3. Add other ingredients in order given. Do not overbeat.
4. Stir in nuts and chocolate chips.
5. Pour into greased 9 x 5 inch loaf pan. Bake in 350 degree oven for one hour. Let cool 15 minutes and then remove from pan to cool completely.

For food processors:
1. Mash bananas then remove.
2. Cream sugar and margarine. Add eggs, vanilla, and orange juice and mix.
3. Add dry ingredients. Stir in chips and nuts. Pour into greased 9 x 5 inch loaf pan. Bake as above.

*If bananas are very ripe, use less sugar.*
*This recipe also makes 20 cupcakes. Increase oven temperature to 375 degrees and bake 25 to 30 minutes or until done.*

# "FAMILY FAVORITE"
# ◐ BANANA CAKE *Marsha Arons*

3 ripe bananas
½ cup margarine
2 eggs
½ cup vanilla yogurt
1½ cups flour
1 cup sugar
1 tsp. baking powder
1 tsp. baking soda
1 tsp. vanilla
½ tsp. cinammon

1. Mash bananas and margarine together.
2. Beat eggs. Add to banana mixture.
3. Combine all other ingredients and mix well. Pour into greased loaf pan. Bake in 325 degree oven for 1 hour and 15 minutes.

*Gets better after 2 days in the refrigerator. (But it never lasts that long!)*

# BANANA CHOCOLATE CHIP CAKE *Ruth Taxy* **D**

1 package banana cake mix
1 package vanilla
 pudding mix
¾ cup water
¾ cup oil
4 eggs
6 ounces chocolate chips
4 ounces German sweet
 chocolate bar, shredded
Powdered sugar

1. Mix package of cake mix and pudding mix with oil and water in large bowl.
2. Add eggs one at a time.
3. Fold in chocolate chips and shredded German sweet chocolate.
4. Liberally grease a bundt pan and pour in batter.
5. Bake in 350 degree oven for 50 to 60 minutes.
6. Remove from pan after 15 minutes and continue to cool.
7. Dust with powdered sugar.
*For quick dessert or unexpected company.*

# BANANA CHOCOLATE LOAF *Gerry Kaplan* **D**

½ cup butter or
 margarine
1⅔ cups sugar
2 eggs, slightly beaten
¼ tsp. salt
1½ tsps. baking powder
½ tsp. baking soda
4 Tbsps. sour cream *or*
 4 Tbsps. orange juice
1 cup bananas, mashed
 (5 to 6 bananas)
2 cups flour, sifted
¼ tsp. vanilla
2 cups chocolate chips
 (large package)

1. Cream margarine and sugar. Add beaten eggs and salt. Mix well.
2. Dissolve baking powder and baking soda in orange juice or sour cream. Add to first mixture.
3. Stir in bananas. Add flour, gradually.
4. Add vanilla and chocolate bits. Pour into loaf pan.
5. Bake in 350 degree oven for 90 minutes.
◆ *Becomes pareve cake when made with margarine and orange juice. Freezes well.*

# APPLE CAKE *Nancy Goldstein and Debbie Stern*

3 cups apples, peeled, cored, and sliced (about 6 apples)
5 Tbsps. sugar
5 tsps. cinnamon
3 cups flour
3 tsps. baking powder
1 tsp. salt
2 cups sugar
1 cup oil (scant)
4 eggs
¼ cup orange juice*
1 Tbsp. vanilla

1. Cover apple slices with cinnamon and 5 Tbsps. sugar. Set aside.
2. Combine flour, baking powder, salt, and 2 cups sugar. Stir a bit.
3. Make a well in the center of the dry ingredients. Into the well add the oil, eggs, orange juice, and vanilla. Mix well.
4. Grease tube pan. Spoon alternate layers batter and apples in pan, starting with batter and finishing with apples. Bake in 375 degree oven one hour or until done.

*Easy, great pareve cake!*

*May be made dairy with milk instead of orange juice. Nancy's recipe, called AUNT CISSY'S APPLE CAKE, is almost identical to Debbie's (printed above). Nancy uses 4 tsps. cinnamon and ½ cup orange juice; bake at 350 degrees for 90 minutes.*

# "GATEAU AUX POMMES" (APPLE CAKE) *Claire Stern*

2 cups flour
4 tsps. baking powder
¾ cup oil
3 eggs
⅔ cup orange juice
1 tsp. orange peel, grated
¾ cup sugar
6 large apples, peeled
1½ tsps. cinnamon
⅓ cup brown sugar
½ cup nuts, chopped

1. In a small bowl, mix flour and baking powder; set aside.
2. In a large bowl, mix oil, eggs, orange juice, orange peel, and ½ cup of the sugar.
3. Slice apples thin, and cut each slice into 3 pieces. Add apples and 1 tsp. cinnamon to egg mixture. Add flour mixture, and combine well.
4. Pour into oiled 8 x 10 inch Pyrex pan.
5. Combine brown sugar, remaining ¼ cup of sugar, ½ tsp. cinnamon, and nuts. Sprinkle over top.
6. Bake in 350 degree oven for about 45 to 50 minutes. Test with a knife. For best results, bake the same day that you are going to serve.

*Claire is French, grew up in Morocco, and has taught French cooking classes to children and adults.*

# LUSCIOUS APPLE CAKE  *Susan Markowitz*  ⬦ⓟ

**Filling:**
9 large apples, peeled
  and cored
½ cup brown sugar, packed
1 Tbsp. cinnamon
½ cup raisins, optional
2 Tbsps. flour

**Batter:**
1 cup margarine, in chunks
4 eggs
1¾ cups sugar
1 tsp. vanilla
½ cup apple juice
  or whiskey
2¾ cups flour
4 tsps. baking powder

1. Slice apples very thinly by hand or in processor. Transfer to large bowl and mix with brown sugar, cinnamon, raisins, and flour for filling.
2. Beat together margarine and eggs, then add sugar and vanilla until well blended. Add apple juice or whiskey and blend through.
3. Mix together flour and baking powder.
4. Gradually add flour mixture to the liquid and mix well, scraping sides of bowl as necessary.
5. Spread ⅓ of batter in a greased and floured 12-cup bundt or 10-cup tube pan.
6. Arrange ½ of apple filling over batter. Do not allow filling to touch sides of pan.
7. Repeat until all ingredients are used, ending with the batter.
8. Bake in 350 degree oven 70 to 75 minutes, or until cake tests done.
9. Cool for 20 minutes before removing from pan.
*Dust with powdered sugar when done. Freezes well. A Canadian recipe; if you eat the whiskey version—don't plan to drive!*

# JOAN'S APPLE CAKE  *Joan Sohn*  ⬦ⓟ

4 cups tart apples, chopped
  (Jonathan or McIntosh)
2 cups sugar
2 eggs
½ cup vegetable oil
2 tsps. vanilla
2 cups flour, sifted
2 tsps. baking soda
2 tsps. cinnamon
1 tsp. salt
1 cup walnuts, chopped

1. Combine apples and sugar; let stand.
2. Beat eggs slightly; beat in oil and vanilla.
3. Mix and sift flour, baking soda, cinnamon, and salt.
4. Stir dry ingredients into egg mixture alternately with apple mixture. Stir in chopped walnuts.
5. Pour into greased and floured 13 x 9 x 2 inch pan. Bake in 350 degree oven one hour.
*Makes the house smell delicious!*

## ⓓ EASY APPLESAUCE CAKE *Debbie Stern*

1 cup raisins
1 cup nuts, chopped
(optional)
½ cup butter
2 eggs
2 cups sugar
2 cups applesauce
(sweetened)
4 cups flour
2 tsps. baking soda
1 tsp. cinnamon
1 tsp. nutmeg (scant)

1. Combine all ingredients.
2. Stir well.
3. Grease and line 2 loaf pans with waxed paper. Pour in batter. Bake in 350 degree oven for one hour.
◆ *Equally good with margarine or butter. Freezes well.*

## ⓟ APPLE STRUDEL *Jackie Siegel*

3 cups Granny Smith apples, peeled, cored, sliced thin
½ cup frozen unsweetened apple juice concentrate (1 small can)
½ cup dark raisins
1½ Tbsps. brown sugar
½ tsp. lemon peel, grated
1 tsp. cinnamon
½ tsp. nutmeg
3 sheets phyllo-pastry, defrosted per package directions
2 Tbsps. margarine, melted
2 Tbsps. bread crumbs, unseasoned
Confectioner's sugar

1. Heat apple juice concentrate in medium saucepot over low flame. Add sliced apples and cook for 10 minutes.
2. Add raisins, brown sugar, lemon peel, cinnamon, and nutmeg; stir together, and remove from heat to cool.
3. Brush top of each sheet of phyllo-pastry carefully with cooled, melted margarine. Stack the three sheets carefully on waxed paper. Sprinkle the top with bread crumbs.
4. Spoon the cooled apple filling along the width of the phyllo-pastry rectangle. Roll up carefully.
5. Transfer to cookie sheet sprayed with vegetable oil. Brush top of strudel roll lightly with melted margarine. (Score the top diagonally to mark the seven places where you will cut into servings, if desired.)
6. Bake in preheated 400 degree oven for 15 to 20 minutes until a golden color. Dust with confectioner's sugar before serving.
Makes 8 servings.
*May be served cooled or warm. Delicious with pareve ice cream or whipping cream.*

# STRUDEL *Shoshanah Winer*

**Dough:**
1 cup margarine
1 cup sour cream
2 cups flour
1 tsp. salt

**Filling:**
Cornflake crumbs
Apricot jam
Cinnamon and sugar
Raisins, optional
Nuts, ground, optional

1. The day before baking, mix the dough ingredients together thoroughly. Press together into ball of dough. Refrigerate overnight. (Dough may be divided and frozen for later use at this point.)
2. To form strudels, divide dough into four equal parts. Roll out each part, one at a time. Sprinkle with cornflake crumbs. (Cookie crumbs may be substituted.)
3. Spread apricot jam over dough. On top, sprinkle cinnamon and sugar and/or any other filling desired, such as ground nuts or raisins.
4. Roll up jelly-roll fashion. Score diagonally on upper crust; do not cut all the way through! Place on ungreased cookie sheets.
5. Bake in preheated 400 degree oven for 15 minutes; reduce heat to 350 degrees and continue baking 15 minutes until golden.
Makes 4 dozen servings.
*Slice each strudel roll into approximately 12 pieces. Dust with powdered sugar. Delicious for dessert or brunch!*

# "SPOON" CAKE *Karen Sager*

3 cups all-purpose flour
2 cups sugar
1 tsp. baking soda
1 tsp. salt
1 tsp. cinnamon
1 cup almonds, ground
3 eggs
1½ cups vegetable oil
1 tsp. almond extract
1 8-ounce can pineapple, crushed
2 cups firm bananas, chopped, *not* mashed

1. In a large bowl, with a wooden spoon, mix together flour, sugar, baking soda, salt, and cinnamon. Add ground almonds.
2. Continue using spoon to beat in eggs, oil, flavoring, and pineapple. Add bananas last, stirring lightly; bananas should remain in small chunks.
3. Spoon batter into greased and floured 10-inch tube pan. Bake in preheated oven at 325 degrees for 1 hour and 20 minutes. Test.
4. Remove from oven; let stand 10 to 15 minutes; invert on wire rack; remove from pan to cool. Sprinkle with powdered sugar.
Makes 12 to 14 servings.
*Moist and simple pareve cake.*

## Ⓓ APPLE CREAM TORTE *Judy Wolkin*

14 golden delicious apples
½ cup water
2 cups sugar
2 Tbsps. butter
1 box vanilla wafers
3 Tbsps. butter, melted
8 eggs
1 pint heavy cream or half
   and half
Salt, pinch
1½ tsps. vanilla

Rum sauce: (optional)
1 pint sour cream
8 Tbsps. confectioner's sugar
6 Tbsps. rum
½ tsp. vanilla
Salt, pinch

1. Peel and slice apples into a large pot or Dutch oven. Add ½ cup water, 2 cups sugar and 2 Tbsps. butter to apples. Cook apples slowly until they are tender, but hold their shape, 20 to 25 minutes. Drain ½ cup of the liquid and cool.
2. While apples are cooking, crumb the vanilla wafers and combine them with the 3 Tbsps. melted butter.
3. Grease a 10-inch springform pan. Pack the crumb mixture along bottom and 1½ to 2 inches up side of pan.
4. Combine eggs, cream, salt, and vanilla in bowl. Mix well. Pour over the cooled, cooked apples.
5. With a large spoon, gently place apple-cream mixture into springform pan.
6. Bake in a preheated 325 degree oven for 60 to 70 minutes or until nicely browned and a knife inserted comes out clean.
7. For rum sauce: Combine all of the sauce ingredients. Serve with the apple cream torte, if desired. Can be prepared in advance and refrigerated until serving time.
*This is a beautiful dessert that looks like a crown. Serve on a footed cake plate for a dramatic presentation. Best served warm or on day prepared. Lovely for Shavuot.*

## Ⓟ CHERRY TORTE *Bev Fox*

½ pound sweet margarine
1 cup sugar
4 egg yolks
1⅔ cups flour
Salt, pinch
½ lemon rind, grated or
   1 tsp. lemon juice
4 egg whites, beaten
1 can pitted cherries,
   drained
Powdered sugar

1. Cream margarine and sugar. Add yolks, flour, salt, and lemon rind.
2. Fold in beaten egg whites.
3. Line 10½ x 15½ inch jelly roll pan with waxed paper. Spread batter evenly in pan.
4. Drop drained cherries evenly across batter.
5. Bake in 350 degree oven for 30 minutes.
6. After cooling, sprinkle with powdered sugar. Cut into squares or diamonds.
*A real Viennese pastry!*

# LINZER TORTE *Fran Fogel*

2 cups almonds, ground
1 cup margarine, room
   temperature
4 egg yolks
½ cup sugar
1¼ cups flour
2 Tbsps. cinnamon
½ cup raspberry jam

1. Preheat oven to 350 degrees.
2. If you grind almonds in food processor, you may leave in bowl. Add margarine, egg yolks, sugar, flour, and cinnamon. Process until a ball forms.
3. Pat ⅔ of dough into bottom of 9-inch springform pan. Spread with jam.
4. Place remaining dough on a lightly floured board. Dust surface with flour; add enough flour to dough so it is not too sticky.
Cover with plastic wrap or waxed paper. Roll dough ⅛ inch thick.
5. Cut into ½-inch strips with a plain or fluted pastry wheel. Arrange strips in a lattice pattern on top of torte. Press gently around rim to attach strips to dough bottom, then trim excess.
6. Bake until lattice is golden (about 50 minutes). Remove from oven to wire rack to cool.
Dust with confectioner's sugar and serve.
*Elegant Viennese pastry.*

DESSERTS

# ◆ⓟ VIENNESE PANCAKE *Eva Sideman*

2 Tbsps. raisins
¼ cup dark rum
4 egg yolks
3 Tbsps. sugar
2 cups non-dairy cream
1 cup all-purpose flour
1 tsp. vanilla
1 tsp. lemon peel, grated
4 egg whites,
   room temperature
2 Tbsps. margarine
Powdered sugar
Preserves, warmed

1. Soak raisins in rum in a small bowl for half an hour or overnight. Drain rum from raisins. Reserve rum for another use.
2. Heat oven to 400 degrees. Beat egg yolks and granulated sugar in medium-sized bowl until thick and lemon colored. Beat in non-dairy cream. Add flour ½ cup at a time. Add the vanilla and lemon peel.
3. Beat egg whites in a small bowl. Fold into egg mixture.
4. Melt butter or margarine in a 10-inch ovenproof skillet. Pour the batter into the pan, and sprinkle with raisins.
5. Bake until the top is puffed and golden, about 15 minutes. Invert pancake onto a serving platter. Tear into 2-inch pieces with a fork. Dust with powdered sugar. Serve immediately with warm preserves.

# ◆ⓟ LEMON ALMOND TART *Janet Resnick*

Crust:
1¼ cups flour
¼ pound margarine
¼ cup sugar
1 egg
1 tsp. vanilla extract

Filling:
3 eggs
¾ cup sugar
1½ tsps. lemon peel, grated
½ cup lemon juice
½ tsp. almond extract
¼ cup blanched almonds,
   finely chopped

Garnish:
2 cups almonds, sliced
1 cup apricot preserves

1. In bowl of food processor using metal blade, mix flour and margarine until crumbly.
2. Add sugar, egg, and vanilla. Mix. (Dough may be refrigerated or frozen at this point.)
3. Press dough into bottom and sides of a 9-inch removable-bottom quiche pan. Set aside.
4. In bowl of food processor with metal blade, beat eggs until frothy. Blend in remaining filling ingredients. Pour into prepared crust.
5. Bake in 350 degree oven 15 to 18 minutes. The top will form somewhat of a crust. Do not overbrown. Cool.
6. Decoratively arrange sliced almonds on top of filling.
7. Melt preserves; add a little water (or fruit liqueur), if necessary, and spoon over almonds. Garnish with a strawberry or mint leaf.

# PEAR TART *Janet Resnick*

**P**

**Dough:**
1¼ cups flour
6 Tbsps. cold margarine
2 Tbsps. shortening
2 to 3 Tbsps. ice water

**Filling:**
½ cup margarine
½ cup sugar
1 egg
1 cup almonds, finely ground
1 Tbsp. Amaretto
1½ tsps. almond extract
1 Tbsp. flour
4 pears, poached* (See the following recipe.)

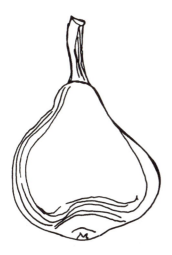

1. Preheat oven to 425 degrees.
2. In food processor with metal blade, mix flour, margarine, and shortening until crumbly. With machine running, pour ice water through feed tube and continue to process until dough forms a ball.
3. Remove dough from machine and knead by hand briefly. Roll out on a lightly floured board, and fit into a 9- to 10-inch removable bottom quiche pan. Place foil on top of dough and cover with baking weights or beans.
4. Bake for 10 minutes. Remove crust from oven and set aside, but do not turn oven off!
5. Cream margarine and sugar together until light and fluffy. Add egg, ground almonds, liqueur, almond extract, and flour. Beat until smooth. Spread the mixture evenly into the pastry shell.
6. Remove the cooled poached pears from the liquid. Cut in half lengthwise, removing core and stem. Place each half, cut side down, on a cutting board and cut crosswise into thin slices. Arrange sliced pears around the edge of the tart with narrow part facing in toward the center. If the pears are small enough, place an additional half in the center of the tart.
7. Bake for 40 to 45 minutes or until the tart shell is golden brown.
8. Bring ½ cup poaching liquid to a boil and reduce. Use this to glaze the tart when it has finished baking. Serve at room temperature.

# POACHED PEARS FOR TART *Janet Resnick*

**P**

4 to 6 pears
½ bottle dry white wine
2 Tbsps. lemon juice
½ cup sugar
1 cinnamon stick
1 tsp. vanilla

**KP**

1. Combine wine, lemon juice, sugar, cinnamon stick, and vanilla in saucepan. Bring to a boil and simmer for 5 minutes.
2. Peel pears, add to saucepan, and simmer for 30 minutes (covered). Turn several times while cooking.
3. Refrigerate at least 6 hours in liquid. Makes 2 cups.
*Pears may be prepared several days in advance.*
*Also good with apples or oranges.*

# Ⓓ RASPBERRY CHOCOLATE TART *Janet Resnick*

Chocolate crust:
6 ounces semi-sweet
  chocolate chips
¼ cup unsalted butter
1 cup graham cracker
  crumbs
2 Tbsps. sugar

Berry filling:
10 ounces frozen raspberries
  in syrup, thawed
2 Tbsps. plus 1½ tsps.
  lemon juice
2 Tbsps. cornstarch
6 Tbsps. sugar
1½ pints fresh raspberries
  or strawberries

1. For crust (may be prepared a day ahead): preheat oven to 400 degrees.
2. Melt chocolate and butter in top of double boiler slowly. Stir until smooth.
3. Combine crumbs and sugar in large bowl and stir in chocolate gently.
4. Pat mixture in bottom of a 9-inch tart pan with removable bottom.
5. Freeze 5 minutes.
6. Bake about 8 minutes until crust is firm. Cool or refrigerate until ready to use.
7. For filling: purée frozen raspberries in food processor. Strain through a sieve into a saucepan.
8. Mix lemon juice and cornstarch and whisk into purée. Add sugar.
9. Stir over medium heat until very thick. Cool slightly.
10. Add fresh raspberries or strawberries and stir until well coated. Transfer to crust and arrange decoratively. (If using strawberries, each may be coated separately and arranged on top of crust.) Whipped cream may be piped around border of tart.

◆ *May be made pareve by substituting margarine for butter.*
*An elegant, beautiful dessert either way.*

# Ⓓ FRENCH TARTS *Eva Sideman*

⅔ cup butter
⅓ cup sugar
1 egg yolk
⅓ blanched almonds, grated
1½ cups flour

1. Cream butter and sugar until fluffy.
2. Add egg yolk, almonds, and flour and mix. Chill.
3. Grease small tins and, with floured thumbs, coat inside with dough.
4. Bake in a 325 degree oven until the tarts are light brown (about 10 minutes). Allow to cool in tins, then unmold. Serve filled with fruit, jam, or whipped cream.

◆ *These pastry shells may be made pareve by substituting margarine for butter.*

# RASPBERRY CAKE *Marcy Rotenberg*

1½ pound pareve
French bread (day old)
½ pound unsalted
margarine, softened
3 10-ounce boxes frozen
raspberries with juice
(may use canned)
¾ cup sugar
½ pint pareve whipped
cream, sweetened with
2 Tbsps. powdered sugar

1. Grease a mold 10 inches round by 3 inches deep; dust with sugar.
2. Slice bread ½ inch thick. Spread margarine on both sides of every slice and remove crusts.
3. Line mold with a layer of bread.
4. Sprinkle with ⅛ cup sugar.
5. Cover with ⅓ of the raspberries and juice.
6. Sprinkle again with ⅛ cup sugar.
7. Add another layer of bread and repeat sugar, raspberries and juice, sugar sequence.
8. Add another layer bread and again repeat sugar, raspberries, juice, and sugar.
9. Cover with plastic wrap. Weight with small juice or small tomato paste cans. Cover tightly with foil. Chill for a minimum of 6 hours. Can be made up to 2 days in advance.
10. Unmold and "ice" with sweetened pareve whipping cream.
Makes 10 servings.
*This is also a delicious dairy recipe with butter and real cream.*

## ◆ WALNUT - APPLE PIE  *Janet Resnick*

1½ cups sugar
3 Tbsps. flour
1½ tsps. cinnamon
¼ tsp. nutmeg
¼ tsp. salt
10 cups tart apples,
　thinly sliced
1 Tbsp. lemon juice
1½ cups walnuts,
　coarsley chopped
12 phyllo-pastry leaves
½ cup margarine, melted

1. In a large bowl, toss sugar, flour, cinnamon, nutmeg, and salt; mix well.
2. Sprinkle apples with lemon juice. Add apples and nuts to sugar mixture.
3. In a 10-inch pie plate, layer eight phyllo leaves, brushing the top of each lightly with margarine.
4. Turn apple filling into pastry-lined pie plate.
5. Layer on top four more phyllo leaves, brushing each with margarine.
6. With scissors, cut a 3-inch wide circle from center of top crust. Trim edge all around, leaving a 2-inch overhang. Fold overhang under; form into edge all around.
6. Bake in 375 degree oven 50 to 60 minutes until apples are tender and crust is golden.
*Time-consuming, but worth the effort. Looks and tastes "divine"!*

## ◆ LEVIN'S FAVORITE
## FRESH BLUEBERRY PIE  *Arlene Levin*

Crust:
1¼ cups graham cracker
　crumbs
¼ cup sugar
⅓ cup margarine, melted

Filling:
1 quart fresh blueberries
1 cup sugar
3 Tbsps. cornstarch
⅛ tsp. salt
1 cup water
1 Tbsp. margarine
1 cup pareve whipped cream*

1. Wash and drain berries thoroughly. Mix together in a saucepan the sugar, cornstarch, salt, water, and 1 cup of the blueberries. Cook and stir over low heat until thick (about 8 minutes).
2. Add the rest of the berries and add 1 Tbsp. margarine. Mix well and cool about 15 minutes in pan.
3. To prepare crust, combine graham cracker crumbs, sugar, and melted margarine. Press mixture firmly into bottom and sides of 9-inch pie pan.
4. Pour fruit mixture into prepared crust and chill.
Makes 6 servings.
*For dairy variations, add whipped cream, if desired, or serve "a la mode" with vanilla ice cream for a refreshing summer dessert.*

# CRANBERRY PIE *Irene Sufrin*

2 or more cups cranberries,
washed
1½ cups sugar
¾ cup margarine, melted
1 cup nuts, chopped
2 eggs, beaten
1 cup flour

1. Grease pie pan. Spread berries in pan.
2. Cover with only ½ cup sugar. Cover with nuts.
3. Mix melted margarine with remaining 1 cup sugar in a bowl.
4. Add eggs and flour to butter and sugar mixture. Pour over pie. Bake in 325 degree oven for 1 hour.

*This colonial American dessert is easy to prepare and great to serve for Sukkot, Thanksgiving, or Shabbat dinner.*
*For a dairy dessert, serve "a la mode" with vanilla ice cream.*

# CRANBERRY APPLE CRISP *Bonny Barezky*

3 cups apples (peeled and
cored), chopped
2 cups fresh cranberries
2 tsps. lemon juice
1½ cups white sugar
1⅓ cups quick-cooking
oatmeal
1 cup walnuts, chopped
⅓ cup brown sugar
½ cup margarine, melted

1. Spray a two-quart casserole with no-stick coating spray.
2. Combine apples, cranberries, lemon juice, and sugar. Place in casserole.
3. In a bowl combine oatmeal, walnuts, brown sugar, and melted margarine.
4. Pour crumbs over fruit.
5. Bake uncovered in 325 degree oven for 1 hour and 15 minutes.
*Easy, fast, fabulous!*

# MILNOT GRAHAM CRACKER PIE *Eva Sideman*

1 lemon, juice and grated
peel
½ cup water
1 box lemon gelatin
¾ cup sugar
2 cups graham crackers
½ cup butter
1 12-ounce can "Milnot,"
chilled for 24 hours

1. Combine juice and pulp of lemon and heat with ½ cup water. In the mixture, melt the gelatin, add the sugar and let cool.
2. For crust, mix the graham cracker crumbs with the butter, and line the pan. Leave half the mixture for the top of the cake.
3. Whip Milnot as you would whip heavy cream. Add the gelatin mixture and beat a little longer.
4. Pour into lined pan, cover the cake with the remaining graham cracker mixture, and refrigerate. Pie may be made ahead and frozen.

# ◆ⓟ RHUBARB NO-CAL DELIGHT *Laura Rushakoff*

1 cup fresh (or frozen)
   rhubarb
⅛ to ¼ cup water
Sugar-free gelatin
   (strawberry or orange)

1. Boil rhubarb (low temperature) in ⅛ to ¼ cup water (very little) until rhubarb is stringy.
2. Dissolve gelatin in 1 cup boiling water.
3. Add rhubarb.
4. Refrigerate until solid.

*No-sugar, calorie trimmed, great for diabetic diets!*

# ◆ⓟ NAOMI'S APPLE PIE *Shira Birnbaum*

1 6-ounce can frozen apple
   juice concentrate, thawed
2 Tbsps. cornstarch
1 Tbsp. margarine*
1 tsp. cinnamon
5 large apples (red
   delicious), peeled and
   sliced thin
1 prepared double crust
   (9-inch pastry shell)
Margarine, melted

1. Preheat oven to 400 degrees. Mix 2 Tbsps. thawed concentrate with cornstarch.
2. In a small saucepan, heat remaining concentrate. Blend in cornstarch mixture, stirring constantly until the mixture thickens and is smooth. Stir in margarine and cinnamon.
4. Pour mixture over sliced apples and toss to coat. Pour mixture into bottom pie crust.
5. Cover with top crust. Cut vents to allow steam to escape. Brush crust with melted margarine.
6. Bake 50 minutes.

*Good dessert for diabetics. One slice equals 1 bread exchange, 1 fruit exchange and 1 fat exchange.*
*\*For dairy: substitute butter for margarine. Add milk to melted margarine.*

# ALL NATURAL SUGAR-FREE
# ◆ⓟ APPLE PIE *Susan Holtzman*

2 Tbsps. cornstarch
1 tsp. cinnamon
½ cup defrosted apple
   juice concentrate
5 to 6 large apples
   (Granny Smith)
2 frozen pie crusts

1. Mix cornstarch, cinnamon and defrosted apple juice together.
2. Add peeled and sliced apples to above mixture.
3. Place mixture into frozen pie crust and put second crust on top.
4. Slit top to allow steam to escape. Place on a cookie sheet because it tends to overflow.
5. Bake in 425 degree oven for 45 minutes or until golden brown.

*Dietetic (no sugar). Excellent for sugar restricted diets—delicious enough for anyone!*

# cOoKieS

**Chocolate Chip Cookie**

##  DOUBLE CHOCOLATE COOKIES *Miriam Steinberg*

5 ounces semi-sweet
  chocolate, broken in
  pieces
½ cup dark brown sugar,
  firmly packed
½ cup white sugar
½ cup unsalted margarine,
  softened, cut in pieces
1 egg
1 tsp. vanilla
1 cup minus 2 Tbsps. flour
½ tsp. baking soda
Salt, pinch
1 cup chocolate chips
½ cup pecan pieces

1. Preheat oven to 350 degrees.
2. Combine chocolate and sugar in work bowl of processor fitted with steel blade. Pulse 6 times to chop chocolate, then process until chocolate is as fine as sugar (approximately 1 minute).
3. Add margarine, process 30 seconds to blend, scraping down sides of bowl as necessary.
4. Add egg and vanilla, process to blend.
5. Add flour, baking soda, and salt; pulse twice to blend.
6. Add chocolate chips and nuts; pulse 4 times. Scrape down sides of bowl and mix by hand to evenly distribute chips and nuts. (May be refrigerated overnight at this point, if desired; bring to room temperature to proceed.)
7. Drop by slightly rounded Tbsps. onto ungreased cookie sheets, spacing 1½ inches apart.
8. Bake 10 minutes, cool 3 minutes on cookie sheet, then finish cooling on rack.
Makes approximately 3 dozen cookies.
*Freezes well. Recipe can be doubled in large capacity processor. Delicious and different! (For dairy version, try white chocolate chips.)*

# "MRS. FIELD'S" COOKIES  Danit Jacobson & Barbara Ament  D

2½ cups oatmeal
2 cups flour
½ tsp. salt
1 tsp. baking powder
1 tsp. baking soda
1 cup butter or margarine
1 cup sugar
1 cup brown sugar
2 eggs
1 tsp. vanilla
12 ounces semi-sweet
  chocolate chips
4 ounces chocolate, grated
1½ cups nuts, chopped
  (optional)

1. Pulverize oatmeal in food processor or blender until it is a consistency like powder. (If using processor, continue mixing in processor bowl. Otherwise, place oatmeal powder in mixing bowl.)
2. Add flour, salt, baking powder, and soda; mix well. Set aside.
3. Cream together butter, sugar, and brown sugar. Add eggs and vanilla; mix well.
4. Combine flour mixture with butter mixture; blend well.
5. Add the chocolate chips, grated chocolate, and chopped nuts.
6. Make golf-ball size cookies. Place on an ungreased cookie sheet about 2 inches apart. Bake for 6 minutes at 350 degrees.
*This delicious recipe was submitted by two different cooks; we have consolidated their two methods. Try an ice-cream scoop to form consistent-size cookies. Kids love them—enjoy!*
**P** *For pareve cookies, use margarine for butter, pareve chocolate and chips.*

# ONE BOWL COOKIES  Lois Berkson  P

1⅛ cups flour, sifted
½ tsp. baking soda
½ tsp. salt
½ cup sugar
¼ cup brown sugar
1 egg
1 tsp. vanilla
½ cup shortening
½ cup walnuts, chopped
1 cup semi-sweet
  chocolate bits

1. Sift together flour, soda, and salt. Add and blend together both sugars, egg, vanilla, and shortening. Add nuts and chocolate chips and blend.
2. Drop dough by teaspoonfuls onto ungreased cookie sheet. Bake in 375 degree oven 10 to 12 minutes.
Recipe doubles easily. Dough may be turned into a brownie pan (9 x 13 inch) if doubled. For chocolate chip brownies, adjust baking time; lower the heat by 25 degrees for Pyrex pan.

## ◆ⓟ CRISPY NUT BALLS *Rochelle Jacob*

1 cup margarine
2 cups flour
1 cup walnuts, chopped
1 tsp. vanilla
1 Tbsp. sugar
Powdered sugar

1. Mix margarine, flour, nuts, vanilla, and sugar together.
2. Roll into small balls and bake in 325 degree oven 20 minutes or until golden brown.
3. Remove from oven and while hot, roll in powdered sugar.
Makes approximately 50 cookies.
*Easy to make; fabulous to eat; everyone's favorite!*

## ◆ⓟ OATMEAL CHOCOLATE CHIP COOKIES *Aviva Rodin*

¾ cup shortening
1 cup brown sugar
½ cup sugar
1 egg
¼ cup water
1 tsp. vanilla
3 cups oatmeal
1 cup flour
1 tsp. salt
½ tsp. baking soda
12 ounces semi-sweet
  chocolate chips

1. Beat together all ingredients in food processor or mixing bowl.
2. Grease cookie sheets. Drop the dough by the teaspoonful on the sheets.
3. Bake in 350 degree oven 15 minutes.
Let stand on cookie sheet for a few minutes before removing to cool.
*Delicious and fast. Mixes quickly and well in the food processor.*

## ◆ⓟ OATMEAL COOKIES *Sarita Blau*

½ cup margarine
¾ cup brown sugar
1 egg
1 tsp. vanilla
1 cup flour
½ tsp. baking soda
1 cup oatmeal

1. Cream margarine and sugar. Beat in egg and vanilla.
2. Sift or stir together flour and baking soda. Add to egg mixture. Stir in oatmeal.
3. Form into roll on plastic wrap. Freeze.
4. Preheat oven to 350 degrees. When frozen, slice ⅛ to ¼ inch thick. Place on ungreased cookie sheets.
5. Bake in 350 degree oven 5 to 10 minutes. Cool on racks or flat on waxed paper. Store in jars.
*Must be frozen to slice well.*

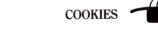

# PECAN DAINTIES  *Bonnie Hemmati*

**Dough:**
½ pound butter or
  margarine
8 ounces cream cheese
3 cups flour

**Filling:**
1 stick butter or margarine
1½ cups brown sugar
1 tsp. vanilla
2 eggs
4 ounces ground pecans or
  walnuts

1. Preheat oven to 350 degrees. Very small, 1½ inch diameter, muffin tins are required.
2. Mix together ½ pound butter, cream cheese, and flour, and refrigerate.
3. In small saucepan, prepare filling. Melt butter or margarine, sugar, and vanilla. Remove from heat and let cool.
4. Add eggs to saucepan ingredients. Stir well. This will make a thick sauce. Set aside filling.
5. Place a piece of dough (about the size of a walnut) in each muffin pan. Press down with thumb in center of dough ball and smooth up sides of cup to make shell. Refrigerate.
6. Place small amount of ground nuts in each dough cup. Place spoonful of filling in each cup over the nuts. Fill almost to the top. Sprinkle each dainty with more nuts.
7. Bake in 350 degree oven ½ hour or less until dough is lightly browned.
Makes 4 dozen.
*These freeze well. Dough may be made a day ahead and refrigerated.*

# NUT COOKIES  *Sarita Blau*

¼ pound margarine, room
  temperature
5 Tbsps. confectioner's
  sugar
1 cup flour
2 tsps. vanilla
1 tsp. water or coffee
1 cup almonds or pecans,
  ground
Additional confectioner's
  sugar

1. Cream margarine and sugar.
2. Stir in flour. Add vanilla and coffee or water; then work in the ground nuts.
3. Preheat oven. Roll dough into balls using about one Tbsp. of dough.
4. Place on cookie sheet. Bake in 350 degree oven 20 to 25 minutes or until set and bottoms are lightly browned.
5. Cool on racks or sheet of waxed paper. Store in additional confectioner's sugar in a cookie jar.
*Dough may be crumbly and require some kneading to roll into balls. These cookies can be stored in the freezer, then rolled in confectioner's sugar just prior to serving.*

# SPRITZ COOKIES *Charlotte Cleeland*

1 cup butter
⅔ cup sugar
3 egg yolks
2½ cups flour
1 tsp. almond extract
Colored candies,
   for decoration

1. Cream butter and sugar. Add egg yolks and almond extract. Stir in flour, a tablespoon at a time.
2. Let dough stand in a cool place from 4 to 24 hours. Put in cookie press. Make various shapes. Form cookies right on greased cookie sheet, as they tend to break if moved.
3. Decorate with colored candies.
4. Bake in 400 degree oven on cookie sheet approximately 8 minutes.
*Dip in melted chocolate and nuts or sprinkles for a variety of fancy cookies.*

#  EGG YOLK COOKIES *Barbara Ament*

2 sticks margarine,
   softened
½ cup sugar
5 eggs yolks, hard boiled
   and mashed
2 cups flour
½ tsp. baking powder

1. Cream margarine and sugar. Add mashed egg yolks.
2. Add flour and baking powder. Roll into balls.
3. Place balls on a lightly greased cookie sheet. Bake in 350 degree oven 7 to 10 minutes.
*These may be topped with sugar, cherries, chocolate kisses, jelly, nuts, or whatever!*

# CHOCOLATE SHORTBREAD *Sarita Blau*

½ pound sweet butter
1 tsp. vanilla extract
1 cup confectioner's sugar
   (or ½ cup granulated
   sugar)
2 cups flour
½ cup cocoa

1. Cream butter. Add vanilla and sugar and mix well.
2. Add flour and cocoa. Mix until dough holds together.
3. Roll out on lightly floured surface to ½-inch thickness.
4. Cut into 1½ inch rounds or 1½ x 1½ inch rectangles. Reroll scraps and cut.
5. Place cookies 1 inch apart on ungreased cookie sheets. Pierce each cookie with fork several times.
6. Bake in 300 degree oven 25 to 30 minutes or until firm.
7. Cool and keep in cookie jar.
*For plain shortbread, leave out cocoa and use only butter for proper consistency.*
◆ *The chocolate shortbread may be made pareve with margarine instead of butter.*

252

# POWDERED SUGAR COOKIES *Rebecca Eisenberg* **P**

1 cup margarine
4 Tbsps. powdered sugar
2 cups flour
1 tsp. baking powder
Chocolate chips or nuts
Extra powdered sugar

1. Mix together margarine, powdered sugar, flour and baking powder.
2. Make into balls, adding more sugar, if necessary. Press each ball flat by hand.
3. Place a few chocolate chips or nuts in the middle of each. Reform ball.
4. Place on cookie sheet. Bake in 350 degree oven for 10 minutes.
5. Roll in powdered sugar while still warm.
*Kids enjoy making and eating these.*

# POTATO CHIP BUTTER COOKIES *Laura Wolf* **D**

1 pound (4 sticks) lightly salted butter, softened
1 cup sugar
2 tsps. vanilla
3½ cups flour
1 cup potato chips, crushed

1. Mix sugar and vanilla with softened butter.
2. Add crushed potato chips and flour alternately to butter mixture.
3. Place small teaspoons of mixture on ungreased cookie sheets.
4. Bake in 350 degree oven 15 to 20 minutes.
*Try these baked to a light brown color; they taste more buttery and crisper. These are bite-sized, melt-in-your-mouth butter cookies. Fast and easy if made in a food processor.*

# BUTTER COOKIES *Sarita Blau* **D**

½ pound butter
1½ cups sugar
2 tsps. vanilla
2 eggs
1 Tbsp. coffee creamer
3½ cups flour, unsifted

1. Cream butter. Beat in sugar, then add vanilla.
2. Beat in eggs, one at a time, then coffee creamer.
3. Stir in flour gradually until dough is no longer sticky if lightly touched. Wrap dough in waxed paper and refrigerate overnight.
4. Next Day: Roll out to ⅛-inch on lightly floured surface and cut into shapes.
5. Place on ungreased cookie sheets and bake in preheated 350 degree oven 8 to 12 minutes.
6. Remove from cookie sheets and cool on racks or on waxed paper.

## Ⓓ CHEESE TARTS *Helen Metnick*

Crust:
1¼ cups graham crackers
  or vanilla wafers
3 Tbsps. butter, melted
1½ Tbsps. sugar

Filling:
8 ounces cream cheese
¼ cup sugar
1 egg
1 tsp. vanilla
21 ounces cherry (or other)
  pastry or pie filling

1. Arrange 24 cupcake papers in muffin pans.
2. Combine crust ingredients, mix thoroughly. Spread 1 Tbsp. into each cup and press down.
3. Beat together cream cheese, sugar, egg, and vanilla until smooth.
4. Spoon a scant tablespoon of filling over crumbs. Bake in 375 degree oven for 10 minutes.
When cool, spoon cherry or other filling over each tart.
*To add to the already great eye appeal of this dessert, use two kinds of pie fillings, such as cherry and blueberry.*

## ⒫ SPICE COOKIES *Sarita Blau*

¼ pound margarine
¾ cup sugar
1 Tbsp. molasses
1 egg
1½ cups unsifted flour
⅛ to ¼ tsp. ground cloves
½ tsp. ginger
1 tsp. cinnamon
1 Tbsp. cocoa

1. Cream margarine and sugar. Beat in molasses and egg.
2. Stir or sift flour, cloves, ginger, cinnamon, and cocoa together. Stir into molasses mixture.
3. Add more flour if needed to make a dough that does not stick to fingers if lightly touched.
4. Wrap well in plastic and refrigerate.
5. When chilled, roll out on lightly floured board or waxed paper to ⅛-inch thickness.
6. Cut into desired shapes. Place on ungreased cookie pan and bake 8 to 12 minutes.
7. Remove from cookie sheets and cool on rack or waxed paper on flat surface.

# BOURBON - RUM BALLS *Shirley Steinberg*

6 ounces semi-sweet
   chocolate chips
3 Tbsps. corn syrup
½ cup bourbon or rum
2½ cups vanilla wafer
   cookie crumbs
½ cup powdered sugar
1 cup nuts, finely chopped
Granulated sugar or
   sprinkles

1. Melt chocolate in saucepan. Remove from heat and add corn syrup and liquor.
2. In a large bowl, combine crumbs, sugar, and nuts. Add chocolate mixture and form into a large ball. (This should be moist). Let stand for 30 minutes.
3. Shape balls using 1 tsp. dough. Roll in granulated sugar or sprinkles. Store in air-tight container.
*Easy, fast and fun! Sprinkles may not stick as well as sugar.*

# BUTTER FUDGE FINGERS *Roberta Bell*

Cake (brownie):
2 1-ounce squares
   unsweetened chocolate
⅓ cup butter
1 cup sugar
2 eggs
½ tsp. salt
½ tsp. baking powder
¾ cup flour, sifted
½ cup broken walnuts

Butter icing topping:
2 cups confectioner's sugar,
   sifted
3 Tbsps. soft butter
1½ Tbsps. cream
½ tsp. vanilla extract

Glaze:
2 1-ounce squares
   semi-sweet chocolate
2 Tbsps. butter

1. Heat oven to 350 degrees. Melt chocolate and butter over hot water in double boiler. Beat in sugar and eggs. Sift salt, baking powder, and flour together and stir into chocolate mixture.
2. Add nuts. Spread in greased 8-inch square pan.
3. Bake in 350 degree oven 30 to 35 minutes until top has dull crust. Cool slightly, until not warm to the touch.
4. Butter icing topping: Blend sifted confectioner's sugar and butter. Stir in about 1½ Tbsps. cream and ½ tsp. vanilla until smooth. Spread on brownies.
5. Glaze: Melt chocolate and butter over low heat. Apply over cooled icing. When glaze is set, cut in 2 x 1 inch "fingers."
Makes 32 fabulous "fingers."

## **D POPPY SEED COOKIES** *Florence Sager*

½ cup butter or margarine
¼ cup oil
1 cup sugar
1 egg
½ tsp. fresh lemon juice
1 tsp. vanilla
2¾ to 3 cups flour
½ tsp. baking soda
½ tsp, salt
Cream of tartar, pinch
4 Tbsps. poppy seeds

1. Cream butter or margarine and oil with sugar.
2. Add egg, lemon juice, and vanilla; beat well.
3. Mix baking soda, cream of tartar, and salt with flour, and sift two times.
4. Mix all together well, either in a food processor or with hand mixer. Add poppy seeds.
5. Make four rolls; place each in waxed paper and chill from 1 hour to overnight.
6. After refrigeration, slice into ¼-inch slices.
7. Bake in 375 degree oven 10 minutes.

**●** *For pareve, substitute margarine for butter.*

## **"KORASHKAS"**
## **D (POPPY SEED COOKIE STICKS)** *Harriet Chavis*

1 cup sugar
½ cup butter, softened
1 egg
2½ cups flour
1 tsp. baking soda
½ tsp. salt
5 Tbsps. sour cream
1 small bottle poppy seeds
½ cup butter or margarine, melted
1 cup cinnamon and sugar

1. Combine butter and sugar until creamy. Beat in egg.
2. Mix the soda and salt into flour and then alternate flour mixture and sour cream into egg and butter mixture until well blended.
3. Stir in bottle of poppy seeds, or more if desired.
4. Refrigerate for several hours, overnight, or several days.
5. Take very small amount of dough in floured hands and roll out into cigarette length. Dough may get stringy at ends, so snap off.
6. Drop several at a time into melted butter (using a fork). Carefully pick them up and roll into cinnamon and sugar mixture. Place on a greased cookie sheet.
7. Bake in 375 degree oven 10 minutes.

*Don't be surprised if they spread and assume unusual shapes. These crispy, melt-in-your-mouth treats are time-consuming to make, but easy to eat!*

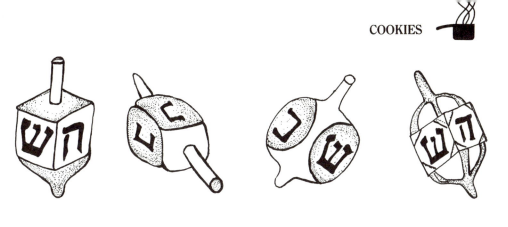

# HOLIDAY COOKIES

*Special cookies are traditionally prepared for two Jewish holidays, Chanukah and Purim. For Chanukah, it is traditional to serve foods fried in oil, including doughnuts and jelly rolls. The SUFGANIYOT and MOGEN DAVIDS which follow are special examples of these. Making cookies cut in favorite shapes of the holiday, such as dreidels or menorahs, is a popular activity children love. For Purim, it is traditional to bake a triangular shaped cookie, HAMANTASCHEN, which is in the shape of the three-cornered hat attributed to the infamous villain of the Book of Esther, Haman. Children customarily deliver Mishloach Manot (baskets full of baked cookies and HAMANTASCHEN) to friends and neighbors. For more ideas and recipes, see KIDS pp. 280-282; pp. 302-303, and HOLIDAYS pp. 373-374; pp. 376-377.*

## SUFGANIYOT *Chana Kaufman*  Ⓓ

1 envelope dry yeast
3 Tbsps. warm water
¾ cup milk
¼ cup margarine or butter
¼ cup sugar
1 tsp. salt
1 egg
½ tsp. lemon rind, grated
3½ to 4 cups flour
Vegetable oil for frying
Jelly for filling
Powdered sugar

1. Dissolve yeast in water. Set aside.
2. Heat milk with margarine or butter until milk is scalded. Add sugar and salt and stir to dissolve. Cool to lukewarm.
3. Beat egg slightly and add to lukewarm milk with lemon rind and yeast mixture. Gradually add flour, beating until smooth. Knead until smooth and elastic. (Or start with flour in food processor and add liquids, mixing and kneading in processor.)
4. Let dough rise until double, about 1 hour. Shape into small, walnut-sized balls. Cover and let rise another 30 minutes.
5. Heat oil to 375 degrees. Fry balls, a few at a time, turning once, until brown all over. Drain on paper towels.
6. Fill each with jelly using pastry tube (or make slit with knife). Sprinkle with powdered sugar.
Makes 3 dozen.
*A traditional Chanukah delicacy!*

 COOKIES

## ◆ HOLIDAY COOKIE DOUGH *Goldie Langer*

2 eggs
½ cup oil
1 tsp. vanilla
½ cup sugar
¼ tsp. salt
1 tsp. baking powder
Flour, enough to make
  a stiff dough

1. Mix together eggs, oil, vanilla, sugar, salt, and baking powder.
2. Add flour gradually until a stiff dough is formed. Refrigerate one hour.
3. Roll out and cut into shapes. For hamantaschen, cut circles, put favorite filling in center, and pinch closed in triangular shape.
4. Bake in 375 degree oven until lightly browned.

*This is my mother's recipe. It is a wonderful dough for making holiday cookies.*

## ◐ SUGAR COOKIES *Sharon Dorfman*

3½ cups butter
¾ cup sugar
2 eggs
1 tsp. baking powder
1 Tbsp. half & half cream
1 tsp. almond extract
2½ cups flour

Decorations:
1 egg white
Sugar
Sprinkles

1. Cream butter and sugar. Add eggs.
2. Add baking powder, then cream, then almond extract. Add flour, 1 cup at a time. Blend together.
3. Refrigerate dough for at least 1 to 2 hours.
4. Roll out on floured board. Cut in shapes or circles.
5. To decorate: Whip egg white until frothy. Brush on cookies. Sprinkle sugar or sprinkles, or both. Transfer to cookie sheets.
6. Bake in 325 degree oven 8 to 10 minutes. Watch them carefully since they cook quickly; don't over-brown.

*Fun for a kid's party!*

*For Chanukah cookies: Use star, dreidle and menorah-shaped cutters. Sprinkle with blue sugar and/or silver ball decors.*

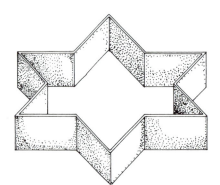
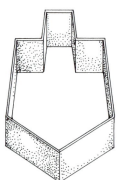
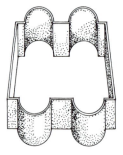

# MOGEN DAVIDS  *Bonny Barezky*

**D**

2 eggs
1 egg yolk
⅔ cup whipping cream
1 cup flour
⅓ cup sugar
2 tsps. vanilla
2 Tbsps. orange liqueur
  (optional)
Oil for frying
Powdered sugar to garnish

1. Beat eggs, egg yolk and whipping cream together. Add flour, sugar, vanilla, and orange liqueur. Stir until well blended. Let stand 2 hours. Stir again.

2. Fill pot with oil (deep). Put rosette iron in enough cold oil to cover in a deep frying pan. Heat to 375 degrees. Remove iron, and wipe off the bottom of the iron with a cloth.

3. Dip the iron into the batter, never allowing the batter to run over the top of the iron. The batter will immediately adhere to the iron. Return iron to hot oil. After 10 seconds, use fork to push rosette off of the iron. Fry for about 1 minute until rosette turns golden brown. Remove to paper towels to drain.

4. Heat iron again and repeat wiping off the bottom of the iron with a cloth each time before dipping in the batter.

5. If you wish to rewarm the rosettes, put them in a warm oven.

6. Before serving, sprinkle liberally with powdered sugar.

Makes 50 rosettes.

*This is a rosette recipe which I have developed. It is a fried dough recipe which is loved by adults and children at Chanukah. This may be made 1 day in advance. Cover loosely with foil. Do not sprinkle powdered sugar on until before serving. Keep at room temperature. My mother says: "Rosettes are like children. You make all your mistakes on the first one."*

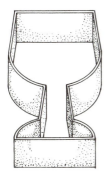
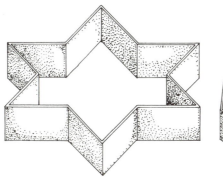
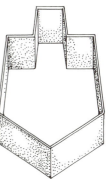

# P FAMOUS HAMANTASCHEN *Isabel Kogan & Arlene Levin*

1 stick margarine
1 egg
1 cup sugar
1 tsp. vanilla
2 Tbsps. orange juice
2 cups flour
2 tsps. baking powder
Salt, pinch
Any flavor pastry or pie
   filling

1. Mix together margarine, egg, sugar, vanilla, and orange juice.
2. Add the flour, baking powder, and salt. Mix well.
3. Roll out the dough on a floured board to about ¼-inch thickness. Cut into circles. Fill the circles with the pastry filling and pinch dough into triangles around the filling. Place in jelly roll pan or on cookie sheets.
4. Bake in 375 degree oven for 15 to 20 minutes until lightly browned.

*Isabel's version of this recipe allows lemon juice as an alternative to the orange juice.*
*Arlene is a professional baker. Customers like her hamantaschen so much, that she has difficulty filling the orders for hundreds of dozens at Purim time!*

# D HAMANTASCHEN - CHEESE DOUGH *Karen Barron*

8 ounces cream cheese,
   softened
1 cup butter, softened
2 cups flour
¼ cup powdered sugar

1. Cream together cream cheese and butter.
2. Add flour and powdered sugar.
3. Wrap and refrigerate 4 hours or overnight.
4. Roll, cut, and fill with your favorite filling.
5. Bake in 400 degree oven 12 to 15 minutes on greased cookie sheet.

*Different and delicious dairy dough!*

# YEAST - DOUGH HAMANTASCHEN *Anonymous* Ⓓ

**Dough:**
1 package dry yeast
½ cup warm water at
about 105 to 115 degrees
1 cup butter or margarine
½ cup sugar
2 egg yolks
2¾ cups flour

**Filling:**
1 cup prunes
½ cup water
½ tsp. cinnamon
½ tsp. lemon rind, grated

1. Dissolve yeast in warm water.
2. In large bowl, beat butter or margarine with sugar and egg yolks until fluffy. Stir in yeast mixture.
3. Gradually add flour, blending well. Chill dough several hours or overnight.
4. Turn onto floured board and roll to ⅛-inch thickness. Cut into 3-to 4-inch rounds.
5. Fill and fold. Place on greased cookie sheet and let rise in warm place, about one hour.
6. Bake in 350 degree oven 15 to 20 minutes.
7. Filling: Cook prunes with water until tender. Add cinnamon and lemon rind and mash or process to filling consistency.

❶ *Becomes pareve when you substitute margarine for butter. We never discovered the donor of this welcome, traditional, yeast-dough Hamantaschen!*

# CREAM CHEESE HAMANTASCHEN *Susie Weiss* Ⓓ

2 cups flour
2 sticks margarine (room temperature)
2 Tbsps. sugar
8 ounces cream cheese (room temperature)
Jelly

1. Mix flour, margarine, sugar, and cream cheese together by hand.
2. Knead until it is the consistency of dough and form into a large ball. Divide into 24 pieces.
3. Chill overnight or several hours.
4. Pat each piece flat. Put 1 teaspoon of jelly in center and pinch up on 3 sides.
5. Bake in 350 degree oven for 25 minutes or until golden brown.
*Easy, tasty refrigerator dough!*

## ⓟ IRIT'S HAMANTASCHEN  *Irit Jacobson*

1 cup sugar
1 cup oil
2 eggs
2 tsps. honey
3¾ cups flour
2 tsps. baking powder
Favorite jam

1. Using a fork or a mixer, mix oil with sugar. Add the eggs one a time and mix well.
2. Add honey. Slowly add flour and baking powder, and mix. Dough will begin to be difficult to mix, so use your hands.
3. Taking a handful of dough, roll it out between 2 sheets of waxed paper until it is about ¼-inch thick. Dip a wide mouth jar into flour and press it on the dough to make a circle shape.
4. Put a small amount of jam in the center of the circle. Bring the sides together to form a triangle. Pinch sides together to form a seam. Repeat process until all the dough has been formed into hamantaschen.
5. Bake in 350 degree oven for 20 minutes or until golden.
*Dough sometimes gets a little hard to work with, but these are delicious!*

## ⓟ SARAH'S HAMANTASCHEN  *Sarah Hoffman*

1 cup shortening
1¼ cups sugar
6 eggs
1 tsp. vanilla
1 tsp. almond extract
1 tsp. lemon juice
5 cups flour
4 tsps. baking powder
Jelly or pie filling

1. Cream shortening and add sugar. Beat in eggs, one at a time. Add vanilla, almond extract, and lemon juice. Combine flour and baking powder and fold into mixture. Refrigerate dough overnight.
2. Pat out dough with hands or use floured rolling pin. Cut into circles with a cup.
3. Put jelly or pie filling in center of each circle. Pull up sides to shape triangles and pinch top (sides) together.
4. Bake in 350 degree oven for 20 minutes on greased cookie sheets.
*Very good for a large batch. Not a sweet dough, but tasty and easy to work with.*

# HONEY HAMANTASCHEN *Susan Markowitz*

4 cups flour, sifted
½ tsp. salt
1 tsp. baking powder
½ cup shortening
4 eggs
1 cup honey
Blueberry, cherry, apple, apricot, raspberry, almond, or prune pie filling

1. In a large bowl, sift together flour, salt, and baking powder.
2. Make a well in the center of the flour, and add the shortening, eggs, and honey. Work together with a wooden spoon until dough is formed. You may also use your hands.
3. Roll out on a floured board. Cut into 2½ to 3-inch circles. Fill each circle with 1 tsp. of your favorite filling. Pinch and seal edges together, forming a triangular shape.
4. Bake on a greased cookie sheet in 350 degree oven for 20 minutes until lightly browned.

*This dough has a lovely texture and holds the triangle shape very well. Delicious with "QUICK AND FANCY POPPY SEED FILLING" (see below).*

# QUICK & FANCY
# POPPY SEED FILLING *Karen Sager*

1 can Solo poppy seed filling
¼ cup raisins, dark or light
½ cup dried apricots, chopped
¼ to ½ cup ground pecans, optional

1. Mix poppy seed filling, raisins, apricots, and pecans together.

*Use to fill hamantaschen. Adults like this filling – kids prefer jam!*

# MANDELBROT (ALMOND BREAD)

*"Mandelbrot" is an Ashkenazi pastry which is still popular in American Jewish kitchens, as the large number of versions which follow will testify. Its name is usually translated, "Almond Bread"; it is, strictly speaking, a kind of rusk or twice-baked bread. It stores well in covered jars, and can be freshened up in a low oven. We find it interesting that, despite its name, only one of the recipes submitted calls for any almond flavoring at all, and none call specifically for ground almonds. We also find the variety of spellings charming, and have therefore not standardized them.*

## ⓟ MAXINE'S MANDEL BREAD  Maxine Szmulewitz

3 eggs
1 cup sugar
⅓ cup oil
1 tsp. vanilla
2½ cups flour
2 tsps. baking powder
One or all of the following:
  chopped nuts, chocolate
  chips, raisins (¼ cup
  each)

Topping:
2 Tbsps. sugar
¼ tsp. cinnamon

1. Mix eggs, sugar, oil, vanilla, flour, and baking powder together.
2. Form dough into three balls. If dough is too wet, add flour; if too crumbly, add oil. Dough should be of such consistency that balls may be formed without much trouble.
3. Add chopped nuts to one ball, raisins to one and chocolate chips to another (you can make any variety). Form each ball into a long log. It should be about 2 inches wide and the length of a cookie sheet.
4. Bake in 350 degree oven for 30 minutes. Remove from oven, loosen logs from pan, and slice each into ½-inch diagonals.
5. Turn pieces on their sides and sprinkle with cinnamon/sugar topping. Put under the broiler until light brown. Remove, flip pieces over and repeat.
*Be careful pieces don't burn under the broiler. Easy and yummy!*

# SHOSHANAH'S MANDEL BROIHT  *Shoshanah Winer*  **P**

3 eggs, room temperature
1 cup sugar
½ cup oil or margarine
1 tsp. vanilla
3 cups flour
3 tsps. baking powder
1 tsp. cinnamon
1 cup nuts, chopped, or
  1 cup chocolate chips,
  or 1 cup raisins

1. Beat eggs. Add sugar, oil or margarine, and vanilla. Beat well.
2. Mix together flour, baking powder, and cinnamon. Add to egg mixture. Mix well.
3. Add nuts or chocolate chips or raisins.
4. Divide dough into thirds. Make three rolls. Place on greased cookie sheet.
5. Bake in 350 degree oven until brown. Remove from pan. Cut into slices and place slices back on cookie sheet.
6. Return to oven. Turn off heat. Leave in oven several minutes.

*The mandel broiht will come out crispy. And tasty!*

# TANTE SHERI'S MONDEL BREAD  *Sharon Dorfman*  **P**

4 eggs
½ cup oil
1 cup sugar
½ cup shortening
Rind of 1 orange, grated
1 tsp. baking powder
¼ tsp. baking soda
1 tsp. vanilla
4 cups flour (or less)
Cinnamon
Sugar

Optional:
Chocolate chips
Chopped nuts
Raisins

1. Mix eggs, oil, sugar, and shortening together.
2. Add orange rind, baking powder, baking soda, and vanilla. Add enough flour until firm.
3. Add chopped nuts, chocolate chips, or raisins – all or none.
4. Roll into two or three long ropes. Grease cookie sheets.
5. Sprinkle top with cinnamon and sugar.
6. Bake in 350 degree oven until light brown. Remove from oven and cut into ½ to 1-inch pieces.
7. Place back in oven and bake at 200 degrees until hard.

*Rave reviews! A Shabbat and holiday dessert tradition.*

#  AVIVA'S MANDLE BREAD  *Aviva Rodin*

3½ cups flour
2 heaping tsps. baking
   powder
1 cup shortening
1 cup sugar
4 eggs
½ cup walnuts, chopped
6-ounces chocolate chips
Cinnamon-sugar

1. Sift flour and baking powder. Set aside.
2. Cream shortening and sugar until light and fluffy. Add eggs and flour mixture. Beat well.
3. Blend in nuts and chocolate chips.
4. Grease two cookie sheets.
5. Divide dough into four parts and place two long strips on each greased cookie sheet. Bake in 350 degree oven 15 minutes or until bottom is brown.
5. Cut and lay slices on side. Sprinkle with cinnamon-sugar. Return to oven. Bake in 300 degree oven for additional 15 minutes.
Makes about 60 pieces.
*Everyone likes this version!*

# CHOCOLATE CHIP MANDEL BREAD  *Barbara Ament*

3 cups flour
Salt, pinch
3 tsps. baking powder
1 cup sugar
4 eggs
¾ cup oil
1½ tsps. vanilla
6-ounces chocolate chips

Topping:
¼ tsp. cinnamon
½ cup sugar

1. Mix flour, salt, baking powder, and sugar.
2. Make a well and add eggs, oil, and vanilla. Mix until smooth.
3. Add chocolate chips. Spread in large, greased jelly roll pan.
4. Combine cinnamon and sugar for topping. Sprinkle on top.
5. Bake in 325 to 350 degree oven for 30 minutes or until lightly browned. Slice when cool.
*Especially good when warmed in the oven for about 10 minutes before serving.*

# AUNT SONIA'S MANDLE BREAD  *Lorraine Horwitz*  P

4 eggs
1½ cups sugar
5 cups flour
2 tsps. baking powder
½ tsp. salt
1 tsp. almond extract
1 tsp. vanilla extract
1½ cups oil
½ cup nuts
½ cup chocolate chips

1. Beat eggs with sugar.
2. Mix together flour, baking powder, and salt.
3. Add extracts, oil, flour mixture, nuts, and chocolate chips to egg and sugar mixture.
4. Shape dough into long strips. Sprinkle cinnamon and sugar on top.
5. Place in 350 degree oven for 30 minutes. Remove from oven and slice. Return to oven for 10 minutes on each side.
*Great texture; cuts well; easy and delicious! The almond extract makes this version true to its name!*

# GRANDMA'S "AIR" KICHELS  *Bonny Barezky*  P

3 large eggs
3 level Tbsps. sugar
½ cup oil
1 cup flour
Sugar for sprinkling
Oil for greasing

1. Preheat oven to 325 degrees. Place eggs and sugar in mixer. Blend. Add oil and beat on high for 20 minutes.
2. Add 1 cup flour and beat 10 minutes.
3. Grease a cookie sheet with oil. Drop spoonfuls of batter onto sheet. Sprinkle with the sugar.
4. Reduce temperature to 300 degrees and bake for 25 minutes.

# TOFFEE SQUARES  *Janet Resnick*  D

½ pound butter
1 cup brown sugar
1 egg
1 tsp. vanilla
2 cups flour
6 ounces semi-sweet chocolate chips
1 cup walnuts, finely chopped (optional)

1. Mix butter, sugar, egg, vanilla, and flour.
2. Spread in ungreased baking pan.
3. Bake in 350 degree oven 25 minutes.
4. Remove from oven, put chocolate chips on top. Return to oven for a minute. Spread chocolate, then sprinkle on the nuts. Cut while warm.
P *Substitute margarine for butter for pareve cookies.*

##  CONGO BARS  *Karen Barron*

1¾ sticks butter
1 pound dark brown sugar
3 eggs
2¾ cups flour
2½ tsps. baking powder
½ tsp. salt
6 ounces chocolate bits
6 ounces butterscotch
    bits
½ cup nuts (pecans),
    chopped (optional)

1. Melt butter in saucepan. Add brown sugar. Blend and gently cook together until melted. Set aside to cool.
2. Beat in 3 eggs, one at a time.
3. Sift together flour, baking powder, and salt.
4. Combine all ingredients. Add chocolate bits and butterscotch bits. Add nuts if desired.
5. Spread in greased 10½ x 15½ inch pan. Bake in 350 degree oven for 25 to 30 minutes.
6. Cut into bars when cool.

## PEANUT BUTTER - CHOCOLATE SQUARES  *Fran Fogel*

Crust:
2 cups powdered sugar
1½ cups graham cracker
    crumbs
1 cup creamy peanut
    butter
1 stick margarine, softened

Topping:
12-ounce bag chocolate
    chips, melted
1 cup creamy peanut butter

1. Combine powdered sugar, graham cracker crumbs, peanut butter, and margarine for crust. Press into bottom of 9 x 13 inch pan.
2. Melt chocolate chips and stir in 1 cup creamy peanut butter.
3. Pour on top of crust and refrigerate. Cut into squares when hardened. Soften to room temperature to serve.
*Freezes well. Easy cookie for kids!*

##  FUDGY BROWNIES  *Goldie Langer*

4 eggs
2 cups sugar
1 cup flour
4 squares chocolate
1½ sticks margarine
2 tsps. vanilla
1 cup nuts

1. Beat eggs with sugar until thick (about 10 minutes). Add flour.
2. Melt chocolate with margarine in saucepan. Cool. Add chocolate to egg mixture. Add vanilla. Stir in nuts.
3. Pour into greased 9 x 13 inch pan.
4. Bake in 325 degree oven 30 minutes.

# DEBBIE'S BROWNIES *Debbie Stern*

4 ounces chocolate
⅔ cup margarine
2 cups sugar
4 eggs
1 tsp. vanilla
1¼ cups flour
1 tsp. baking powder
1 tsp. salt
Nuts (optional)

1. Melt margarine and chocolate in double boiler. Add sugar, eggs, vanilla, flour, baking powder, salt, and nuts, if using. Mix well.
2. Spread in 9 x 13 inch pan. Bake in 350 degree oven 30 minutes.
*Rich! Delicious! Quick and easy!*

# STOVE TOP BROWNIES *Jacqueline Siegel*

½ pound butter (2 sticks)
4 squares unsweetened
   chocolate squares
1½ cups sugar
4 eggs
4 tsp. vanilla
¼ tsp. salt
1 cup flour
Powdered sugar

1. Combine butter and chocolate in a saucepan. Add sugar, eggs, vanilla, salt, and flour. Stir and blend until smooth.
2. Flour and oil an 8 x 10 inch baking pan. Pour batter into pan.
3. Bake in 350 degree oven 12 to 15 minutes. The top of the brownies should bubble. Cool on a rack.
4. Dust powdered sugar on top of the brownies. Slice and serve.

# RUTH'S BROWNIES *Janet Resnick*

½ cup semi-sweet
   chocolate chips, melted
½ cup butter, melted
1 cup sugar
1 tsp. vanilla
2 eggs
½ cup flour
½ cup milk chocolate chips
1 cup nuts, chopped
1 cup small marshmallows

1. Mix by hand melted semi-sweet chocolate chips and butter. Add sugar, vanilla, eggs, and flour.
2. Mix in milk chocolate chips, chopped nuts, and marshmallows.
3. Spread dough in 9 x 9 inch pan.
4. Bake in 350 degree oven 25 minutes.

# NORWEGIAN ALMOND BARS   *Charlotte Cleeland*

2 cups sifted flour
1 tsp. double-acting
  baking powder
1 tsp. salt
¾ cup sugar
¾ cup butter
½ cup mashed potatoes
¼ cup confectioner's
  sugar, sifted
½ cup ground almonds
1 tsp. cinnamon
½ tsp. cardamon
1 Tbsp. water
1 egg white
1 egg yolk

1. Sift together flour, baking powder, salt, and sugar. Cut in the butter until particles are size of small peas.
2. Press ¾ of mixture into ungreased 13 x 9 x 2 inch pan. Reserve remainder for topping.
3. Bake in 375 degree oven 10 minutes.
4. Blend mashed potatoes, confectioner's sugar, almonds, cinnamon, cardamon, water, and egg white. Mix thoroughly and spread over partially baked dough.
5. Combine remaining ¼ flour mixture with egg yolk. Press together for topping dough.
6. Roll dough on floured pastry cloth or board to 10 x 6 inch rectangle. Cut in ½-inch strips. Place across filling, criss-cross fashion.
7. Bake in 375 degree oven 20 to 25 minutes. Cut into bars while warm.
*Rich and delicious and worth all the trouble.*

# CRUNCHIES   *Hannah Engelman*

1 cup margarine
1 tsp. baking soda
2 Tbsps. light or dark
  corn syrup
2 cups quick-cooking
  oats
1 cup sugar
1 cup flour
1 cup coconut flakes

1. Melt margarine over low heat. Add baking soda and syrup. When this begins to bubble, remove from heat.
2. One by one, swiftly add quick-cooking oats, sugar, flour, and coconut. Stir firmly and press into pan approximately 10 x 12 inches in size.
3. Bake in 350 degree oven 25 to 30 minutes, until golden brown. Cut into squares while warm.
*These South African cookies are like granola bars. Kids love them! They may seem greasy; adjust amount of margarine to taste, if necessary.*

# SCOTCH BARS *Eva Sideman*

⅓ cup margarine
1 cup brown sugar
1 egg
½ to 1 tsp. vanilla
1 cup flour
½ tsp. baking powder
½ tsp. salt
½ tsp. baking soda
Nuts, chopped
6 ounces chocolate chips

1. Melt the margarine. Stir in sugar, egg, and vanilla.
2. Add flour, baking powder, salt, baking soda, and chopped nuts.
3. Spread in an 8 x 8 inch greased pan. Sprinkle with chocolate chips.
4. Bake in 350 degree oven 20 minutes.

# SWISS CHOCOLATE BARS *Irit Jacobson*

1 cup water
½ cup margarine
1½ squares unsweeted chocolate (can use 1 ounce semi-sweet chocolate chips)
2 cups flour
2 cups sugar
2 eggs
½ cup sour cream
1 tsp. baking soda
½ tsp. salt

Frosting:
½ cup margarine
6 Tbsps. milk
1 ounce semi-sweet chocolate chips
4½ cups confectioner's sugar
1 tsp. vanilla
½ cup nuts

1. Combine water, margarine, and chocolate in saucepan. Bring to boil. Remove from heat.
2. Combine flour and sugar. Add chocolate mixture, eggs, sour cream, baking soda, and salt. Mix well.
3. Pour into greased and floured jelly roll pan.
4. Bake in 375 degree oven 20 to 25 minutes.
5. Frost cake while warm. Prepare frosting by combining margarine, milk, and chocolate in saucepan. Bring to boil. Remove from heat. Add sugar. Beat until smooth. Add vanilla.
6. Sprinkle with nuts. Cut into squares when cool.

## ⓓ CARAMEL BROWNIES  *Dorene Benuck & Barbara Ament*

14-ounce bag caramels
½ cup evaporated milk
1 package chocolate cake
  mix
¾ cup butter, melted
⅓ cup evaporated milk
1 cup nuts, chopped
1½ cups chocolate chips

1. In a saucepan, combine caramels and ½ cup evaporated milk. Over low heat, stir until smooth. Set aside.
2. In large bowl, mix dry cake mix, melted butter, ⅓ cup evaporated milk, and nuts. By hand, stir until dough holds together.
3. Press ½ dough into greased 9 x 13 inch pan. Bake in 350 degree oven 10 minutes.
4. Sprinkle chocolate chips over top. Return to oven for a couple of minutes.
5. Spread caramel on top of chocolate chips. Cover with remaining dough. Bake 15 to 18 minutes. Cool.
6. Refrigerate 1 hour or longer, but serve at room temperature.
*Remember to divide dough in half. Kids love this! Barbara's version calls for German chocolate cake mix and 1 cup chocolate chips.*

## COUSIN BEV'S TRIPLE FUDGE
## ⓓ CHOCOLATE BROWNIES  *Arlene Demb*

8 2-ounce squares
  unsweetened chocolate
½ pound butter
5 large eggs
3¾ cups sugar
1 Tbsp. vanilla
½ tsp. salt
1⅔ cups flour
2 cups pecan chips
12 ounces chocolate chips

1. Combine unsweetened chocolate and butter in a saucepan and melt over low heat. Cool chocolate and add to eggs, sugar, salt, and vanilla in mixer bowl.
2. Beat at high speed in mixer to blend. Then lower speed and slowly add flour and pecan chips.
3. Line a 9 x 13 inch pan with foil and melted butter. Pour in batter.
4. Place chocolate chips over batter.
5. Bake in preheated 375 degree oven 30 to 40 minutes.
Brownies must sit for a few hours before cutting.
Makes about 40 pieces.

# COCOA BROWNIES  *Naomi Strauss*

4 eggs
1¾ cups sugar
1 tsp. salt
1 tsp. vanilla
1 cup margarine, melted
1½ cups flour
½ cup cocoa
9 ounces chocolate chips
1 cup nuts, chopped

1. Combine eggs, sugar, salt, and vanilla. Mix 2 minutes at low speed with mixer. Add margarine.
2. Sift together flour and cocoa and pour into mixture at low speed.
3. Add chocolate chips and nuts at low speed and mix briefly until blended. Spread into greased 13 x 9 x 2 inch pan.
4. Bake in 350 degree oven 20 to 25 minutes until an inserted toothpick comes out somewhat dry.

# WHITE CHOCOLATE BROWNIES WITH CHOCOLATE CHUNKS  *Susan Margolis*

7 Tbsps. sweet butter
8 ounces high-quality white chocolate, finely shredded
2 eggs, room temperature
Salt, pinch
½ cup sugar
1½ tsps. vanilla extract
1 cup flour
4 ounces bittersweet chocolate, cut into chunks

1. Preheat oven to 350 degrees. Lightly grease 8-inch square baking pan. Line the bottom and two sides with aluminum foil that extends two inches over each side and lightly grease foil.
2. In a small pan over low heat, melt the butter. When butter is melted, remove from heat and add half of white chocolate; do not stir. Let mixture sit until needed.
3. In a large mixing bowl, combine eggs and salt. Beat with an electric mixer at high speed for about 30 seconds until frothy. Gradually add sugar and continue to beat for 2 to 3 minutes until light in color.
4. Add the white chocolate and butter mixture, vanilla and flour. Quickly beat until smooth. Stir in remaining white chocolate and the bittersweet chocolate chunks.
5. Scrape the batter into the prepared pan, smoothing the top with a spatula.
6. Bake exactly 35 minutes. Leave brownies in pan until cooled completely.
7. Run a sharp knife around the brownies to loosen them, and using the extended foil, pull them out of the pan. Peel off the foil and cut into 16 squares.
*A food processor can be used to grate or chop the white chocolate. The baking rack should be placed in the middle of the oven.*

# ⓟ 3 LAYER COOKIE BROWNIES  *Barbara Ament*

Layer 1:
1 cup margarine, softened
4 ounces unsweetened
   chocolate
4 eggs
2¼ cups sugar
2 tsps. vanilla
1 cup flour
12 ounces chocolate chips

Layer 2:
1 to 2 cups miniature
   marshmallows, and/or
1 cup nuts, chopped

Layer 3:
2¼ cups flour
1 tsp. baking soda
1 tsp. salt
1 cup margarine, softened
¾ cup sugar
¾ cup brown sugar,
   firmly packed
1 tsp. vanilla extract
2 eggs
12 ounces chocolate chips

1. To prepare layer 1: Melt margarine and chocolate in saucepan. Cool; set aside.
2. Beat eggs. Add sugar and continue beating until light and fluffy. Add vanilla.
3. Add flour gradually and continue beating.
4. Add melted chocolate mixture; beat just until blended. Stir in chocolate chips.
5. Pour into greased 9 x 13 or 11 x 13 inch pan. Bake in 325 degree oven for 25 to 30 minutes.
6. While layer 1 bakes, prepare layer 3: Combine flour, baking soda, and salt; set aside.
7. In a large bowl, beat together the margarine, sugar, brown sugar, and vanilla. Add eggs; beat well.
8. Gradually add flour mixture to batter.
9. Stir in chocolate chips. Set aside.
10. When the baking of layer 1 is complete, remove from oven. Cover with marshmallows and/or nuts. Top with layer 3 cookie dough.
11. Bake an additional 45 to 50 minutes.
*Time-consuming, but worth the effort. A good, "noshy" pareve dessert!*

# ⓓ CHOCOLATE MINI - CHIP BROWNIES  *Bonny Barezky*

1 cup butter
4 ounces unsweetened
   chocolate
4 eggs
2 cups sugar
2 tsps. vanilla
1 cup flour
12 ounces chocolate
   mini-chips

1. Melt butter in saucepan with chocolate. Set aside.
2. In food processor, place eggs, sugar, and vanilla, and pulse 3 times. Add flour and melted chocolate mixture. Process until smooth.
3. Spray a 9 x 13-inch pan with non-stick cooking spray. Pour in batter. Sprinkle mini-chips on top.
4. Bake in 325 degree oven for 40 minutes. Cool, refrigerate, then cut.
You may halve the recipe. Use an 8 x 9-inch pan.
*These taste great partially frozen. Defrost only 10 minutes before eating.*

kids

## ALPHABET SOUP
*Karen Sager*

Are your children finicky eaters?
Do they whine at dinner time?
Do they hate the foods their parents like?
In short—are they like mine?

Do they defy your expectations
And exhaust your will to cook?
Do they pass up even chicken soup
With a sour and naughty look?

Then let me share with you a charm
Your mother probably once knew—
It's a civilized alternative
To throwing kids into the stew:

Add alphabet noodles to the soup
Just before you pour—
They'll forget it's good for them,
And they'll come back for more!

What is more—they'll learn to spell,
And to turn meals into play,
Which is what we all could use—
At least three times a day!

# ALPHABET SOUP (Vegetable Beef) *Karen Sager* **M**

2 pounds short ribs
(approximately)
1 onion bouillon cube
2 Tbsps. salt
Water
2 medium onions, peeled
2 tsps. seasoned salt
6 peppercorns
2 cups baby lima beans,
rinsed
2 38-ounce cans tomatoes
4 large carrots, sliced
4 ribs celery, sliced
1 pound mushrooms, sliced
1 package frozen peas
1 cup alphabet macaroni

1. Place meat, bouillon cube, and 1 Tbsp. salt in 5-quart Dutch oven or stock pot; cover with water; place on stove at high flame. Bring to a boil, uncovered.
2. Strain scum from top as it rises, and reduce heat to simmer.
3. Add onions, seasoned salt, and peppercorns. Simmer, covered, 1 hour.
4. Add lima beans, canned tomatoes, carrots, celery, and mushrooms. Simmer, covered, 2 hours.
5. Remove meat. Add peas, if desired. Taste and adjust seasoning, adding more salt if necessary.
6. Cook alphabets in water according to package directions. Strain. Add to soup.*
7. Place piece of meat in each bowl and ladle hot soup over it.

*Alphabets may be kept separate and served individually, like the meat. You may want to try making your own, larger-sized alphabets from the recipe below.*

►►►(See KEY TO KIDS' RECIPES, p. 278.)

# HOMEMADE NOODLES *Irene Sufrin* **P**

⅔ cup flour
1 egg
1 Tbsp. water
½ tsp. salt
1 tsp. oil

1. Put flour on a large pastry board or table top, or in a bowl. Make a well in the center.
2. In a bowl, lightly combine egg, water, salt, and oil. Pour into well in center of flour.
3. Work the mixture with your hands until the dough can be rolled into a ball.
4. Knead the dough as you would for bread for about 10 minutes.
5. On a floured surface, roll the dough with a rolling pin. Sprinkle the dough with flour to keep it from sticking to the rolling pin.
6. Roll dough until it is paper thin.
7. Cut dough with cookie cutters or knives.
8. Boil about 2 quarts water with 1 Tbsp. salt in a large pot. Cook pasta dough for 10 minutes in the boiling water. Drain.

*Eat with margarine. This recipe was adapted for use in classrooms. The dough may be divided and refrigerated or frozen; roll, cut, and cook as needed.*

►►(See KEY TO KIDS' RECIPES, p. 278.)

**KIDS**

# KEY TO KIDS' RECIPES

We hope this section will encourage kids to cook, but we are concerned about their safety. This key is a guideline to safety for kids in the kitchen. Kids, please use common sense, and follow your parents' safety rules! And don't forget: cleaning up will make you welcome back in the kitchen!

▶ ▶ ▶

An adult must be present to oversee or assist in the preparation of this recipe.

▶ ▶

Middle School aged children (approximately 11 years or older) may attempt this on their own, with parental permission; younger children require adult supervision.

▶

Most school aged children (6 years or older) may attempt this on their own, with parental permission.

## Ⓓ DUMP SALAD *Sheila Patt*

2 large containers whipped topping
2 cans cherry pie filling
1 large can crushed pineapple, drained
1 small can evaporated milk
1 cup walnuts, chopped

1. Take all ingredients and "dump" in a bowl.
2. Stir well.
3. Refrigerate overnight.
Makes 10 to 20 servings.
*This is a recipe for a crowd. Once they taste it, they'll want more. Easy enough for kids to make.*
▶

# BUNNY ANIMAL SALAD *Adam Nemirow* Ⓓ

Pear half: for body
Raisins: for eyes and nose
Apple slices: for ears
Coconut: for back
Cream cheese: for tail
2 carrots

1. Take the pear half and put in the middle of a plate.
2. Take a very small amount of cream cheese and a raisin, and put the cream cheese on the raisin.
3. Put the raisin for a nose. Do the same for the eyes.
4. Take a knife and put a slit on each side of the top, big enough for the apple slices to fit in for ears. Take some coconut and sprinkle it on the top.
5. Take a chunk of cream cheese and shape it for a tail. Then put it on the back for a tail. Then put the two carrots on the side of the plate.
*Please see Adam's illustration above.*
►►

# KIDS & HOLIDAYS

*Kids love to help in holiday preparations. We have included on the next 3 pages a few special holiday recipes kids will enjoy. We also refer you to the holiday recipes in COOKIES, pp. 257-263, as well as the many ideas in HOLIDAYS.*

## Ⓟ CHALLAH *Sager School Kindergarten*

2 packages yeast
½ cup hot water
1 tsp. sugar
5 eggs
¾ cup sugar
½ cup oil
1½ cups water
1 tsp. salt
10 cups flour (minimum)
Egg yolks
Water
Poppy seeds

Shabbat

1. Dissolve yeast in hot water from the tap, and 1 tsp. sugar. Let it rise 10 minutes.
2. Beat eggs with sugar. Add oil, water, and salt.
3. Mix yeast mixture into egg mixture, using beater. Add 1 cup of flour at a time until mixture starts to run up beater.
4. Begin using spoon. Turn onto floured board, add flour when it gets sticky. Knead until smooth.
5. Place in large bowl. Cover loosely with towel.
6. After dough doubles in size, punch down.
7. Divide dough into 3 to 6 pieces. (Recipe will yield 3 large or 4 to 6 small breads.)
8. Divide each piece into 3 strips. Roll the strips between your hands as though you were making clay "snakes." Pinch the three strips together at one end. Braid the dough just like you braid hair.
9. Place on ungreased cookie sheets. Cover loosely with a towel. Let rise about 1½ hours.
10. Combine egg yolks and water. Brush on breads. Sprinkle with poppy seeds.
11. Preheat oven to 225 degrees. Place challot in oven; turn up heat to 325 degrees. Bake large breads 30 minutes, smaller ones 20 to 25 minutes.

Before eating, reheat at 200 degrees for 5 minutes.

*Kindergarteners and children of all ages enjoy kneading challah dough!*

►►

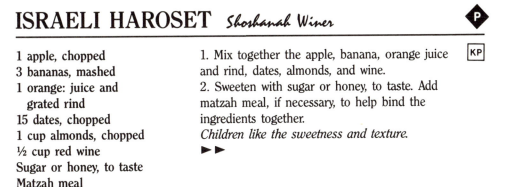

# ISRAELI HAROSET *Shoshanah Winer*

**P**

**KP**

1 apple, chopped
3 bananas, mashed
1 orange: juice and
   grated rind
15 dates, chopped
1 cup almonds, chopped
½ cup red wine
Sugar or honey, to taste
Matzah meal

1. Mix together the apple, banana, orange juice and rind, dates, almonds, and wine.
2. Sweeten with sugar or honey, to taste. Add matzah meal, if necessary, to help bind the ingredients together.
*Children like the sweetness and texture.*
►►

# MATZAH PIZZA *Danny Siegel*

**P**

**KP**

1 matzah square
Tomato sauce, with
   Pesach seasoning
Mozzarella cheese, shredded
Parmesan cheese, grated
Oregano, optional

1. Preheat oven to 400 degrees.
2. Place matzah on foil or baking sheet.
3. With a spoon, spread enough tomato sauce to cover the matzah evenly.
4. Sprinkle a generous layer of shredded mozzarella to cover the sauce.
5. Sprinkle with grated Parmesan and optional oregano.
6. Bake in the oven for 3 to 5 minutes, until cheese is melted. Watch carefully!
*Doubles, triples and quadruples easily.*
►►

# STRAWBERRIES AND RHUBARB *Harriet Berman*

**P**

**KP**

2 cups rhubarb, washed and
   cut into ½ inch pieces
1 cup sugar
3 cups hulled strawberries

1. The day before serving, place rhubarb in bowl. Sprinkle 1 cup sugar over the rhubarb.
2. Let these ingredients stand overnight.
3. Next day, add strawberries.
4. Place in 6-quart pot. Cook over medium heat until the fruit is tender.
May be served as a side dish or dessert (over ice cream for dairy option).
*This recipe comes from Camp Beber, the B'nai Brith Camp in Wisconsin. In 1984, the Beber campers prepared and ate this yummy dish when they studied early Americana.*
►►

# THANKSGIVING
# PUMPKIN BREAD  *Sager School Kindergarten*

3⅓ cups flour
2 tsps. baking soda
1½ tsp. salt
1 tsp. cinnamon
1 tsp. nutmeg
3 cups sugar
1 cup vegetable oil
4 eggs, beaten
⅔ cup water
2 cups (1 pound) pumpkin

1. Preheat oven to 350 degrees. Grease and flour 2 or 3 loaf pans or several cans.
2. Mix flour, baking soda, salt, cinnamon, nutmeg, and sugar in a large bowl.
3. Mix oil, eggs, water, and pumpkin in a bowl.
4. Make a "well" in the center of the dry ingredients. Pour the wet ingredients into the well, and mix everything together until smooth.
5. Fill pans or cans half full with the batter.
6. Bake for 1 hour. Cool and remove from pans.
*Kindergarteners enjoy making and eating this.*
►►

# GRANDMOTHER'S FAMOUS CRANBERRY
# BREAD  *Skokie School First Grade*

2 cups all-purpose flour, sifted
1 cup sugar
1½ tsps. baking powder
1 tsp. salt
½ tsp. baking soda
¼ cup margarine
1 egg, beaten
2 tsps. orange peel, grated
¾ cup orange juice
1½ cups fresh or frozen cranberries, chopped
1½ cups light raisins, optional; however, if omitting raisins, double amount of cranberries to 3 cups

1. Sift flour, sugar, baking powder, salt, and baking soda into a large bowl.
2. Cut in until mixture is crumbly.
3. Add egg, orange peel, and orange juice all at once. Stir just until mixture is evenly moist.
4. Fold in raisins and cranberries.
5. Spoon into a greased 9 x 5 x 3 inch loaf pan. Bake in 350 degree oven for 1 hour and 10 minutes, or until a toothpick inserted in center comes out clean. Remove from pan; cool on a wire rack.
*This bread is baked by the first grade of the Skokie School for their Thanksgiving feast.*
►►

thanksgiving

# SUPER EGGS *Leah Gritton* Ⓓ

6 eggs
¼ cup milk
Dill, to taste
Basil, to taste
2 to 3 slices American
   cheese
2 Tbsps. butter

1. In a bowl, mix eggs, milk, dill, and basil.
2. Tear cheese into smaller pieces.
3. In a frying pan, melt butter on medium heat.
Pour in eggs.
4. With a spatula, scrape down sides of pan.
Mix in the cheese. Turn and scrape eggs to melt
cheese. Then you're done. That's all!
Makes 3 to 4 servings.
►►

# FAVORITE FAMILY PANCAKES *David Sager* Ⓓ

1½ cups all-purpose flour
1½ tsps. baking soda
¾ tsp. salt
1½ Tbsps. sugar
½ cup sour cream
½ cup plain yogurt
½ cup milk
(or 1½ cups buttermilk
   to substitute for last
   3 ingredients)
3 eggs
3 Tbsps. butter, melted

Options:
1 cup chocolate chips, or
1½ cups apples, chopped,
   with 1 tsp. cinnamon, or
1 cup banana, mashed

1. Mix flour, baking soda, salt, and sugar in a
large bowl. Add sour cream, yogurt, and milk,
eggs, butter, and optional items. Batter will be
lumpy.
2. Lightly grease griddle or large frying pan.
(Wipe off excess grease with paper towel.)
3. Fry, flip, and serve.
Makes enough for a family of 5. Doubles easily.
*Delicious plain or with options. Batter may be*
*divided and different options added to suit*
*different tastes. Serve chocolate chip pancakes*
*with whipped cream. Serve plain, apple, or*
*banana pancakes with maple syrup, cinnamon-*
*sugar, or jam. A Sunday morning family*
*tradition. Extra batter may be stored in*
*refrigerator for a quick Monday morning*
*breakfast!*
►►

# ORANGE CREAM CHEESE *Sarita Blau* Ⓓ

8 ounces cream cheese,
   room temperature
1 large orange
2 Tbsps. vanilla
Sugar, to taste

1. Wash orange with soap and water. Dry.
2. Grate rind (colored part only).
3. Beat cream cheese to soften. Beat in grated
rind, adding more if necessary.
4. Beat in vanilla.
5. Beat in sugar, gradually, to desired sweetness.
*Good on sliced banana bread.*
►►

## ❶ CHEESE BAGEL *David Weiss*

Bagel
Cheese

1. Toast ½ bagel one time in the toaster-oven.
2. Then put 1 or 2 pieces of cheese on the half of a bagel.
3. Put in the toaster oven again and watch it. Then you have a cheese bagel.
▶

## ❶ PIZZA MUFFINS OR BAGELS *Robby Siegel*

English muffins or bagels,
  sliced in half
Seasoned tomato sauce
Mozzarella cheese, shredded
Oregano, optional

1. If using a microwave oven, place muffins or bagels on a paper plate. If using a toaster-oven, place them on foil.
2. With a spoon, spread enough tomato sauce to cover the muffin or bagel evenly.
3. Sprinkle a thick layer of shredded mozzarella to cover the sauce.
4. Sprinkle with oregano, if desired.
5. Place muffins or bagels in microwave oven or toaster-oven on high heat for 1 to 1½ minutes. The cheese should be melted and bubbly when done. Remove and serve immediately.
*Great after-school snack or lunch!*
▶▶

## Ⓜ SWEET LITTLE HOT DOGS *Nathaniel Sager*

2 packages (24) miniature
  hot dogs
½ cup ketchup
2 Tbsps. grape jelly
1 tsp. mustard
2 Tbsps. barbecue sauce,
  optional

1. In a frying pan, mix together ketchup, jelly, mustard, and optional barbecue sauce.
2. Add hot dogs. Heat over medium flame. Stir to coat hot dogs. When sauce starts to bubble, turn off heat. Serve, or cover to keep warm.
*Makes a great appetizer! Serve with chips or crackers.*
▶▶

# SLOPPY JOES *Michael & Danny Siegel* **M**

2 pounds lean, ground beef
1 cup ketchup
¼ cup barbecue sauce
1 Tbsp. mustard
1 to 2 Tbsps. brown sugar
¼ cup water
Hamburger buns

1. In a medium skillet, brown meat over low heat. Beef is done when it is brown and no longer red.
2. Take the pan from the stove with pot holders. Drain off the liquid fat at the sink. Use a lid to keep the beef from falling out.
3. Add ketchup, barbecue sauce, mustard, brown sugar, and water. Stir.
4. Return to the stove and cook over low heat 15 to 30 minutes. Stir occasionally. Add water if sauce is too thick.
5. Serve on hamburger buns.
Makes 6 to 8 servings.
►►

# TUNA FISH TACOS *Mimi Sager* **D**

1 13-ounce can tuna
2 ribs celery, minced
1 green pepper, minced
2 Tbsps. mayonnaise
Garlic salt, dash
1 package taco shells
8 ounces cheese, grated
1 wedge iceberg lettuce
1 medium tomato
¼ cup black olives, chopped (small can)
1 jar mild taco sauce

Optional ingredients:
1 avocado, chopped
1 small onion, chopped
Sour cream

1. Open can of tuna and drain juice. Place tuna in medium-sized bowl, and mash it with a fork. Add chopped celery, green pepper, mayonnaise, and garlic salt. You may want to add a little more mayonnaise. Put tuna in a serving dish.
2. Open taco shells; warm them in a low oven or toaster-oven, if the package directions say to.
3. Place grated cheese in a serving bowl. (I prefer Cheddar, but any favorite is fine.)
4. Wash, dry, and cut up lettuce.
5. Wash, dry, and chop tomato.
6. Place lettuce, tomato, olives, taco sauce, and any optional ingredients you choose into separate, small serving bowls. A divided platter or serving dish is very nice for this. Put taco shells in napkin in a bread basket to keep warm.
7. Each person makes his/her own taco by putting some tuna salad in the taco shell, then adding whichever other ingredients he/she wishes.
Makes 6 servings.
*This makes a great buffet for a kid's party.*
►►

## **Ⓟ KINDERGARTEN PRETZELS** *The Kindergarten Staffs*

1 package dry yeast
1½ cups warm water
1 tsp. sugar
1 tsp. salt
4 cups flour (use more
   if sticky)
1 egg, beaten
Coarse kosher salt

1. Combine yeast with a little warm water. Let sit 5 minutes.
2. Add rest of water, sugar, salt, and flour.
3. Press dough into shapes. Put on greased cookie sheet. Brush with beaten egg. Sprinkle on coarse salt. Bake in 425 degree oven 12 to 15 minutes.

Eat while warm.

*One of the Kindergarten's special cooking projects! The shapes they make vary from year to year and class to class. Pretzel dough may be rolled between the hands, just like challah dough (see p. 280). These strips may be arranged in "twists" like the familiar pretzel, or they may be shaped into letters or numbers. Kids like to make their initials or spell their names. Pretzel strips may also be arranged in holiday shapes. Alphabet Pretzels, Animal Pretzels, and Mogen Davids are favorites. See illustrations on these two pages.*
►►

 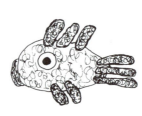 

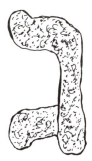

# PLAYDOUGH
## (NON-EDIBLE) *Nancy Goldstein & Judith Taylor*

2 cups flour
1 cup salt
2 cups water
1 Tbsp. oil
2 Tbsps. cream of tartar
2 Tbsps. vanilla, optional
Food coloring, optional

1. Mix all ingredients in large pot.
2. Cook over medium heat, stirring until mixture is shiny and holds together. Allow to cool just until mixture can be handled.
3. Knead for about 5 minutes.
4. Divide into portions.
*This is for children's playing, not for eating! Store in refrigerator, wrapped in plastic wrap or in covered container.*
►►

*Use this easy chart to scale the recipe to different amounts:*

| Flour | Salt | Water | Oil | Tartar |
|---|---|---|---|---|
| 1 cup | ½ cup | 1 cup | 1 Tbsp. | 1 tsp. |
| 2 cups | 1 cup | 2 cups | 2 Tbsps. | 2 tsps. |
| 3 cups | 1½ cups | 3 cups | 3 Tbsps. | 3 tsps. |

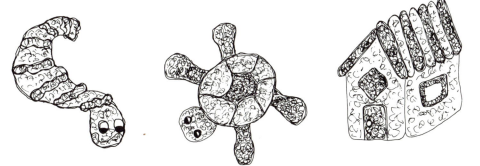

## ◆ BEN'S BAR  *Ben Taxy*

6 ounces peanut butter chips
6 ounces chocolate chips

1. Melt peanut butter chips in pan. Pour into loaf pan. Let cool in freezer for 5 minutes.
2. Do the same for chocolate chips. Pour on top of peanut butter.
Makes 12 big chunks.
► ►

## PEANUT BUTTER - ◆ BANANA POPSICLES  *Susan Zamarripa*

2 bananas
5 Tbsps. unsweetened peanut butter
1 Tbsp. maple syrup or honey

1. Peel bananas. Mash the bananas with a fork on a large plate, one at a time.
2. In a large bowl, mix the peanut butter and maple syrup together.
3. Add the bananas and mix well.
4. Scoop the peanut butter and banana mixture into popsicle containers. Put in freezer.
Makes 6 popsicles.
►

## ◆ PEANUT BUTTER CANDIES  *Hannah & Nathaniel Sufrin*

4 Tbsps. honey
½ cup peanut butter
1 tsp. lemon extract
½ cup sesame seeds, toasted
¼ cup raisins
¼ cup peanuts, shelled
¼ cup wheat germ, toasted
¼ cup almonds or walnuts, ground fine

1. In a large mixing bowl, cream together honey and peanut butter until they are smooth.
2. Add lemon extract and beat until well blended.
3. Add sesame seed, raisins, peanuts, and wheat germ. Mix thoroughly until all are coated with peanut butter mixture.
4. With your hands, form the candy mixture into 12 to 15 balls.
5. Place the ground nuts on a piece of waxed paper or a plate. Roll each ball in the nuts.
6. Wrap each piece in cellophane wrap or waxed paper.
*These healthful candies do not have to be refrigerated. If you have untoasted sesame seeds and/or wheat germ, you may bake each in a small baking pan for 10 to 15 minutes at 350 degrees before you begin the recipe. Otherwise, this is an easy, no-bake recipe even the smallest children will enjoy.*
►

# FRUIT ROLL  *Amy Simon*  P

Fruit (apples, peaches,
  or apricots)
Honey

1. Peel and core fruit, blend in blender.
2. Cook 5 minutes over moderate heat, adding
1 tsp. honey for each piece of fruit.
3. Place plastic wrap on cookie sheet.
4. Spread fruit on plastic, as thin as possible.
5. At night, put cookie sheet in oven, at lowest
possible temperature.
6. In the morning, remove from cookie sheet
and roll with plastic, as for jelly roll.
►►

# APPLE SMILE  *Shalisha Erenberg*  P

1 red apple
1 Tbsp. peanut butter
  (about)
7 marshmallows, miniature

1. Cut apple in 2 halves. Pick the reddest part
of the apple. Cut the reddest half of the apple
again into halves. Take paper towel and dry as
much as you can.
2. Put peanut butter on the white part of the
apple slice (not the red part). Then put
marshmallows on the front of the apple on the
peanut butter.
3. Put peanut butter on other half (the white
part) and put it on the marshmallows, and there
are your lips!
*Please see Shalisha's illustration to the left.*
►►

### KEY TO KIDS' RECIPES:

►►►     Adult supervision required.
►►     Adult supervision thru age 10.
►     Adult supervision thru age 5.

#  GRANOLA  *Chana Kaufman*

1 cup unblanched sesame
seeds
1 cup raw sunflower seeds
6 cups old-fashioned
oatmeal*
2 cups wheat germ
1 cup unsweetened, dried
coconut
1 cup walnuts, almonds, or
cashews, chopped
⅓ cup honey
⅓ cup vegetable oil
1 cup raisins (or other
chopped dry fruit)
*Rolled wheat, barley, or
rye may be substituted
for part of oats*

1. Toast sesame and sunflower seeds on a
cookie sheet, or any rimmed baking pan, until
they start to turn brown (15 to 20 minutes).
Grind all of sesame seeds and half of sunflower
seeds to a powder. Set aside.
2. Stir together oatmeal, wheat germ, coconut,
and nuts. Warm honey and oil in saucepan, and
pour into oat mixture, stirring constantly.
3. Spread out on one or more baking sheets
and bake in 300 degree oven for 30 to 35
minutes, stirring occasionally, until toasty.
4. Add raisins (or other dried fruit), plus ground
and whole sesame and sunflower seeds, to the
oat mixture. Let cool, pack in air-tight
containers, and store in refrigerator.
Makes 12 cups of granola.
*Chana teaches this recipe in her "Eating for
Better Health" class. It's delicious as a cereal
with milk, or as a between-meal snack. For
more healthful ideas, see Chana's nutrition
article, pp. 400-401.*
► ►

# ◆ ZACH'S CRACKER JACKS  *Zachary Sufrin*

¼ cup margarine
¼ cup honey
1½ quarts popcorn,
popped
¾ cup peanuts, shelled

1. Preheat oven to 350 degrees.
2. In a small saucepan, mix together the honey
and margarine. Heat over low heat until it is
blended together. Stir occasionally.
3. Place the popcorn and peanuts in a large
bowl. Mix together.
4. Slowly pour the honey mixture over the
popcorn mixture, stirring as you pour. Mix very
well, making sure all the popcorn and nuts are
covered with the honey mixture.
5. Spread the mixture in a single layer on a
cookie sheet or in a large baking pan. You will
have to make several batches unless you have
several cookie sheets or pans.
6. Bake for 10 to 15 minutes at 350 degrees or
until the "Cracker Jacks" are crisp.
7. Cool in large bowl. Store in covered
container.
► ►

# QUICKIE BROWNIES  *Charlotte Glass*

4 eggs
½ cup oil
1 cup sugar
1 tsp. vanilla
1 can chocolate syrup
½ tsp. salt
1 cup flour

1. Preheat oven to 350 degrees. Grease a 9 x 11 inch pan.
2. Beat eggs well.
3. Add oil, sugar, vanilla, and chocolate syrup. Mix well.
4. Add salt and flour. Mix well.
5. Pour into pan. Bake at 350 degrees for 30 minutes.
6. Cool and cut into squares.

*This quick and easy recipe comes from the busy director of the Solomon Schechter Day School in Skokie. Kids will enjoy making and eating them!*
►►

# CRANBERRY - RASPBERRY
# SORBET  *Joshana Erenberg*  P

12 ounces cranberry-raspberry juice concentrate, partially thawed
12 ounces frozen red raspberries, partially thawed
1½ cups cold water

1. Put cranberry-raspberry juice concentrate in blender. Blend on low speed.
2. Add raspberries and cold water. Continue blending until thoroughly mixed.
3. Pour into ½ gallon plastic container with tight-fitting lid. Freeze.

*Scoop into glass dessert dishes for a refreshing and beautiful snack or dessert.*
►►

## ⒹCARAMEL COOKIES *Debbie Azar & Monica Hakimi*

2 cups flour
2 eggs
1¾ cup white sugar
¼ tsp. baking soda
1 tsp. vanilla
½ cup butter
Non-stick cooking spray
5 caramels

1. Preheat oven to 350 degrees.
2. Put in a bowl flour, eggs, sugar, baking soda, and vanilla.
3. Put the butter into a small pot and put the pot on the stove. Heat it for 7 minutes or until it looks ready.
4. Mix all the ingredients that are in the bowl, and add the softened butter.
5. Spray the cookie sheets and place round cookies onto the sheet. Put in the oven and bake for 9 to 11 minutes.
6. Put the caramels into a small pot. Put on stove and heat until melted and creamy.
7. Take the cookies out and spread the nice caramel over the cookies. Cool for 5 minutes unless you want the caramel to harden onto the cookies. If you want to do that, place it in the refrigerator for 1 hour.
►►

## ⒹBUTTERSCOTCH COOKIES *Sarita Blau*

½ cup butter or margarine, softened
¾ cup brown sugar
1 egg
1 tsp. vanilla
½ tsp. baking soda
1¾ cups flour

1. Cream butter or margarine and brown sugar. Add egg and vanilla. Mix well.
2. Sift or stir baking soda with flour. Add to egg mixture. Blend well.
3. Form into roll on plastic wrap. Chill dough in refrigerator overnight, or freeze dough roll until ready to bake.
4. Slice dough into ⅛-inch slices with sharp knife for crisp cookies, or ¼ inch slices for soft cookies. On ungreased cookie sheets, leave 1 to 1½ inches between cookies, as they spread in oven.
5. Bake in preheated 350 to 375 degree oven for 5 to 12 minutes, depending on thickness.
6. Cool on rack or wax paper. Store in jars.
◆*Must be frozen to slice well if made with margarine.*
►►

# EASY CHEESE TARTS *Helene Blivaiss* **D**

24 to 30 foil cupcake liners
16 ounces cream cheese (two 8-ounce packages)
24 to 30 vanilla wafers
¾ cup sugar
2 eggs
1 tsp. vanilla
1 large can cherry pie filling

1. Cream sugar, eggs, cheese, and vanilla together until smooth.
2. Place 1 vanilla wafer in each cupcake liner flat side down.
3. Spoon cheese mixture into each liner.
4. Bake in 350 degree oven 15 to 20 minutes. Cool 1 hour. Top with pie filling.

*A quick recipe easy enough for kids to enjoy making.*

►►

# QUICK AND EASY CHOCOLATE CHIP COOKIES *Miriam Sager* **D**

1½ cups graham cracker crumbs (11 crackers, crushed)
1 15-ounce can sweetened condensed milk
1 (or 2) 6-ounce package(s) chocolate chips
½ cup nuts (optional)

1. Grease 9 x 11 inch Pyrex baking dish generously. Preheat oven to 350 degrees.
2. Place graham cracker crumbs in bowl. Add condensed milk. Stir with wooden spoon. (Batter is very sticky.)
3. Add chocolate chips. Add optional nuts. If you do not like nuts, or like more chocolate, add ½ package more chocolate chips (about 1 cup total chips).
4. Spread sticky dough as best as you can in pan.
5. Bake in preheated oven for 25 minutes until top starts to brown.
6. Cool only a few minutes in pan. While still warm, cut into squares and remove carefully from pan. Cool on wax paper.

*My Mom started making these when she was in 5th grade, and now so do I!*

►►

# COCOA KRISPIE TREATS *Ronnie Levin*

¼ cup margarine
4 cups miniature
  marshmallows
6 cups Cocoa Krispies

1. Melt margarine in large saucepan over low heat. Add marshmallows and stir until completely melted. Remove from heat.
2. Add Cocoa Krispies. Stir until well coated.
3. Grease a 13 x 9 x 2 inch pan. Using wax paper, press mixture evenly into pan. Cut into squares when cool.
Makes 24 squares.
*These tend to be sticky, so work quickly with the dough.*
►►

# NO-FAIL FUDGE *Mrs. Samuel Schwied & Ashley Rossman*

1½ cups sugar
¼ cup butter or margarine
5 ounces evaporated milk
Salt, pinch
20 marshmallows
12-ounces semi-sweet
  chocolate chips
1 tsp. vanilla
1 cup nuts, chopped

1. In saucepan combine sugar, margarine, and evaporated milk; cook over low heat, stirring well, about 10 minutes.
2. Add marshmallows, heating well to melt. Add chocolate chips, vanilla, and nuts. Stir until chocolate and marshmallows are melted and thoroughly blended.
3. Pour into well greased 9 x 9 inch Pyrex. Refrigerate until cool (at least 2 hours). Cut into squares and serve.
►►

# FUDGE ICICLE SQUARES *Bonny Barezky*

1 quart butter pecan ice
  cream, softened
1 9-ounce carton whipped
  topping
1 pound cream filled
  cookies, chopped coarsely
1 8-ounce can of fudge
  sauce

1. Spray 8 x 11 inch (2 quart) Pyrex with non-stick cooking oil.
2. Mix together ice cream, whipped topping and ⅔ of the chopped cookies. Pour into pan.
3. Drop several teaspoons of fudge onto ice cream and "marble" through with the tip of a knife. Pour remaining cookies over the top.
4. Cover with plastic wrap and freeze.
5. Cut in squares with a warm knife.
*This is well-liked by everyone—even those who don't like desserts! An easy make-ahead dessert that is ready whenever you are!*
►►

# "THURSDAY" SPECIAL  *Samuel Caplan*  **D**

Ice cream, any flavor
Chocolate sauce
Whipped cream
Cherries or strawberries

1. Have Mom scoop one large ice cream ball for each person to be served.
2. Spoon chocolate sauce over each ice cream ball, to taste. Top with a little whipped cream. Add one cherry or strawberry on top.
*Have the napkins available!*
►

# COLOSSAL CARAMEL PUDDING  *Rebecca Gritton*  **D**

1 can sweetened condensed milk
Water
Regular milk

1. Do not open can yet! Put can in pot.
2. Cover can with water.
3. Turn heat to high. Boil water.
4. Turn heat to low. Boil can in water for 3 hours.
5. Put can in refrigerator for 1 hour or more.
6. Take out the can. Open the can. Scoop the caramel into bowls.
7. Pour a little bit of cold milk on each one.
*Then, enjoy your colossal caramel pudding!*
►►

# ◆Ⓟ MY FAVORITE BREAD PUDDING  *Dawn Sideman*

Stale bread (use dark and
  white)
Milk (to soak the bread)
1 Tbsp. brown sugar
1 Tbsp. white sugar
¼ cup nuts
½ cup raisins
½ cup matzah meal
Apricot jam
1 banana (optional)
½ cup butter, melted
⅛ tsp. vanilla
¼ tsp. baking soda
¼ cup red, sweet wine
3 eggs, separated
½ tsp. cinnamon,
  both for the mixture,
  and to sprinkle on top

1. Break up the bread and soak it in milk until
it softens.
2. Add sugars, nuts, raisins, matzah meal,
banana, jam, butter, vanilla, baking soda,
cinnamon, and wine. If the mixture looks thin,
add some more matzah meal until the
consistency is on the thick side.
3. Take 3 eggs and ask your mother to separate
them for you—or go ahead and do it yourself if
you are the adventurous type. Mix up the yolks
with the rest of the mixture.
4. Beat the egg whites until they are stiff—
again, maybe you need some help from your
mother with this. Fold the stiff egg whites into
the mix gently.
5. Grease one of your favorite pans (a square
8 x 8 or 9 x 9 inch will do nicely, but any other
shape which will hold your mixture will be just
great also.) Pour everything into your pan and
then sprinkle some cinnamon on top. Since you
already have some inside the mixture, don't get
too carried away with the cinnamon this time.
6. Bake in 350 degree oven for about 45
minutes. Check it after about ½ hour and bake
until you think it's done.
*Serve hot with milk poured over it, or serve it
cold. Yummy either way!*
►►

# Ⓓ NOT - QUITE BANANAS FOSTER  *Karen Sager*

2 bananas or
  4 peaches
¼ cup butter
¼ cup brown sugar
Cinnamon, dash
Ice cream, or yogurt,
  or whipped cream

1. Peel and slice the bananas or peaches.
2. Melt the butter in a small frying pan over
low heat.
3. Add the brown sugar and cinnamon. Stir
continuously until sugar is melted and well
blended.
4. Add the fruit. Stir until all the fruit is well
coated. Remove from heat.
5. Serve warm over ice cream. Or place in
individual bowls and top with whipped cream or
yogurt.
Makes 4 servings.
►►

# PUFF PASTRY *Karen Sager*

1 cup hot water
7 Tbsps. margarine*
½ tsp. salt
1 tsp. sugar
1 cup flour
1 cup eggs (4 jumbo, or
   5 small)

Filling suggestions:
Tuna, egg, or chicken salad
Tofutti
Pareve whipped topping
Pareve ice "cream"

Dairy filling
  suggestions:
Pudding, any flavor
Whipped cream
Ice cream
*Butter may be used in puff
  for dairy version

Topping suggestions:
Chocolate sauce
Caramel sauce
Any sundae topping
Chocolate icing (p. 297)

1. Preheat oven to 425 degrees. Lightly grease two cookie sheets.
2. Place water, margarine, salt and sugar in heavy 2-quart saucepan. Bring to a boil on the stove over high heat. Remove from heat as soon as mixture boils; turn heat to low.
3. Quickly add flour. Return to low heat. Stir hard with a wooden spoon for 2 to 3 minutes until dough is a smooth ball in center of pan.
4. Remove from stove. Turn off heat. Put dough in a medium-sized bowl. Beat in eggs one at a time with wooden spoon or electric mixer. Make sure each egg is beaten in well before adding the next. (If electric mixer is used, dough may have to be chilled in refrigerator a few minutes before baking.)
5. Drop 12 large or 24 small spoonfuls onto greased cookie sheets. Leave 2 inches between spoonfuls.
6. For 12 large puffs, bake 15 minutes at 425 degrees; turn oven temperature down to 325 degrees, and bake 45 more minutes.
7. For 24 small puffs, bake 15 minutes at 425 degrees; turn oven temperature down to 325 degrees, and bake 30 more minutes.
8. Cool on a rack. Split carefully with a knife; fill with your favorite filling; top with your favorite topping.
*Thanks to an old friend, Sari Bahl, who amazed me years ago, first, by making her own eclairs, second by having her children help her, and third, by showing me how easy it can be.*
▶▶▶

# CHOCOLATE ICING *Karen Sager*

4 squares chocolate,
  unsweetened
2 Tbsps. water
6 Tbsps. margarine
2 eggs
1 cup confectioner's sugar

1. In a medium saucepan, melt chocolate with water and margarine. Remove from heat.
2. Beat in eggs and confectioner's sugar with a wooden spoon or an electric mixer.
*Spoon over cream puffs to make eclairs. Also good on unfrosted cakes; let it run down the sides.*
▶▶

# Ⓟ FRIED BOW-TIES *Jackie Siegel*

½ package wonton
  wrappers*
Vegetable oil (for frying)
Powdered sugar
*or see p. 328.

1. Heat 1 to 2 inches oil in deep fryer or saucepan.
2. While oil is heating, cut each wonton sheet into thirds with a knife. You can cut a stack of several at a time.
3. Cut a slit into the center of each piece. (You can also stack them to cut the slits.)
4. Fold one end of each piece through its own slit. Pull through for the bow-tie shape.
5. With adult supervision, drop 5 to 6 bows into the hot oil. Fry until golden color. (Frying will take 1 or 2 or 3 minutes, depending on the temperature of the oil.)
6. Remove bows with tongs. Drain on paper towels. Continue frying a few at a time.
7. Sift powdered sugar onto the drained bow-ties. Turn them carefully to cover both sides witht the sugar.

*Adult supervision is always necessary for frying, as hot oil can splatter and cause bad burns. However, even the smallest children enjoy forming the dough sheets into bow-ties and sifting the powdered sugar. Easy, yummy, and impressive looking!*

►►►

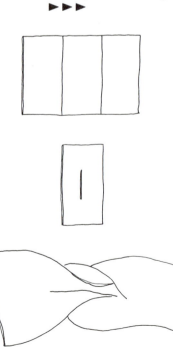

# ONE POT CHOCOLATE CAKE *Karen Sager*

1 cup water
4 squares chocolate,
  unsweetened
½ cup butter or margarine
½ cup buttermilk, or
  sour cream, or yogurt
2 eggs
2 cups flour
2 cups sugar
1½ tsps. baking soda
1 tsp. vanilla

1. Preheat oven to 375 degrees. Grease and flour an 8 x 13 inch baking pan.
2. Bring water to a boil in a large saucepot. Turn off heat.
3. Add chocolate and butter, stirring with a large wooden spoon until melted.
4. Stir in buttermilk.
5. Add eggs, one at a time, stirring well.
6. Add flour, sugar, and baking soda; stir until everything is well blended.
7. Add vanilla; beat well with spoon.
8. Pour into pan. Bake 30 to 35 minutes, or until cake tests done with a toothpick.
9. Cool in pan. Frost cake or sprinkle with powdered sugar, cut and serve from the pan. Or, cool cake only about 10 minutes in pan, cut around edges with knife and turn cake out of pan.
*This is a good recipe for the PARTY PICTURE CAKES, pp. 302-303. May also be baked in two 9-inch layer pans. Or, makes 24 cupcakes; bake in paper-lined muffin tins for 20 minutes.*
►►

# APPLESAUCE CAKE *Hope Sheppard*

⅔ cup margarine, melted
1½ cups unsweetened
  applesauce
1 cup sugar
2 cups flour (½ white,
  ½ whole wheat)
2 tsps. baking soda
1 heaping tsp. cinammon
1 cup raisins
1 cup nuts (optional)
2 Tbsps. wheat germ
  (optional)

1. Grease two 8-inch square or one 9 x 13 inch cake pan(s). Preheat oven to 375 degrees.
2. Heat applesauce in saucepan.
3. Pour melted margarine into hot applesauce. Add sugar.
4. Sift in flour, baking soda, and cinnamon. Add raisins, nuts, and wheat germ.
5. Pour into pan(s). If using 9 x 13 inch pan, bake in oven for 1 hour. If using two 8-inch pans, bake for 25 minutes. (You may want to serve one and freeze the other.)
*Good while still warm topped with powdered sugar or whipped cream. Healthful, yet tastes like gingerbread.*
► ► ►

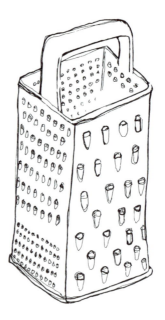

# ❶ PIZZA CAKE  *Barry Levin*

1 package cake mix
 (any flavor)
1 cup strawberry preserves
 ("pizza sauce")
1 16-ounce can vanilla
 frosting ("cheese")
Assorted M & M candies
 ("pizza toppings")
½ cup 2-ounce white
 chocolate, grated
Green sprinkles (optional)
 ("oregano")

1. Preheat oven to 350 degrees. Grease and flour a 14-inch deep dish pizza pan.
2. Prepare cake as directed on package. Turn batter into pan and spread evenly.
3. Bake for 25 to 30 minutes; cake is done if toothpick inserted in center comes out clean. Cool completely in pan on rack.
4. Spread frosting over top of cake, leaving ½ inch edge of unfrosted cake.
5. Spread preserves over frosting leaving ½ inch edge of white frosting showing.
6. Decorate with colored candies to resemble pizza topping. Sprinkle grated white chocolate and green sprinkles over all.
Makes 12 to 16 servings.
*Fun for kids to make and eat at a party!*
►►

**KEY TO KIDS RECIPIES:**

►►►   Adult supervision required.
►►    Adult supervision thru age 10.
►     Adult supervision thru age 5.

# 1-2-3-4 CUPCAKES *Karen Sager* Ⓓ

1 cup butter, softened
2 cups sugar
4 large eggs
3 cups flour
3 tsps. baking powder
3 pinches salt
1 cup milk
1 tsp. vanilla

1. Line 24 muffin tins with paper liners.
2. Preheat oven to 350 degrees.
3. Cream together butter and sugar with electric mixer or in a food processor.
4. Beat in eggs, 1 at a time with mixer; all together with processor.
5. Mix or sift together the flour, baking powder, and salt.
6. Add flour mixture to batter alternately with the milk. (First some flour, then some milk.) Begin and end with flour.
7. Last, add vanilla. Beat well.
8. Spoon into muffin tins. Fill each about ⅔ to ¾ full.
9. Bake 20 to 25 minutes. Test with toothpick to see if cakes are done.
Makes 24 cupcakes.

*These are ideal for little children's birthday parties. Kids like to frost and decorate them with sprinkles, M & M's, chocolate chips, cinnamon candies, etc. Decorating cupcakes, which Mom or Dad and the birthday child have already baked and frosted together, makes a fun activity at the party. (This recipe may also be baked as a sheet cake for the PARTY PICTURE CAKES, pp. 302-303.)*
▶▶

# BUTTERCREAM FROSTING *Karen Sager* Ⓓ

1 pound confectioner's sugar
½ cup butter, softened
1 tsp. vanilla
2 to 4 Tbsps. milk
Food coloring, optional

1. Cream together butter and 1 cup of the sugar with electric mixer or in food processor. Add vanilla. [KP]
2. Add remaining sugar alternately with milk, 1 Tbsp. at a time. Use as much milk as necessary to make a nice, spreading consistency.
3. If desired, add a few drops of food coloring to make your favorite color icing.

*Easy, no-bake frosting. Great for cupcakes!*
▶▶

# Ⓓ PARTY PICTURE CAKES

Have on hand any of
the following:
Chocolate sprinkles
Colored sprinkles
M & M's or similar candies
Red licorice strings
Cinnamon drops
Gumdrops
Chocolate chips
Marshmallows
Mint patties
Wafer cookies
Food coloring

Clown, for example:
Cookie ears
Cookie & gumdrop eyes
Marshmallow nose
Red licorice string hair

PARTY PICTURE CAKES are a fun and festive treat kids love to help make. Any cake baked in the appropriate sized pan(s) will do. Several cake recipes appear in this book (see pp. 224, 299, or 301); however, a cake mix is also adequate, and may make it easier for an older child to make an entire picture cake by himself. The frosting and decorations are the most important elements. (For frosting recipes, see p. 224 and p. 301.) A toothpick works well to draw the design in the frosting. Kids enjoy coloring white frosting with food coloring. All kinds of candy and sprinkles make great decorations. The following PARTY PICTURE CAKES were inspired by "Baker's Cut-Up Cake Party Book." They are only meant to serve as sources of ideas. Half the fun is thinking of your own different ways to represent design with edible confections, so be imaginative!

►►

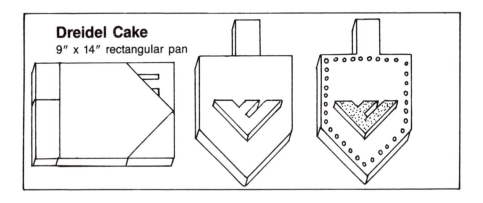

**Dreidel Cake**
9″ x 14″ rectangular pan

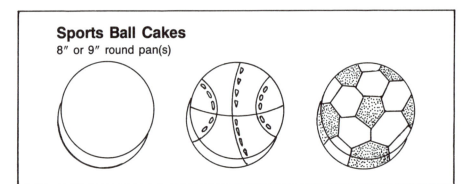

**Sports Ball Cakes**
8″ or 9″ round pan(s)

## Tulip Cake
### 9″ round pan

## Clown Cake
### 8″ or 9″ round and square pans

# Ⓓ ICE CREAM FANTASY *Irene Sufrin & Jackie Siegel*

1 half-gallon brick ice
  cream, any flavor,
  frozen very firm
2 round quarts ice cream,
  any flavor, frozen
  very firm
2 ice-cream cones
12 lollipops
24 flat gumdrop squares
24 jellybeans
1 flat chocolate bar
Licorice string
1 tray or cookie sheet
Blue cellophane, optional

1. Cover a tray or cookie sheet with blue cellophane to look like water. Assemble all decorations; you will have to work quickly so ice cream does not melt!
2. Place ½ gallon brick ice cream in center of tray. Place round quarts of ice cream on either side of brick.
3. Place ice cream cones upside down on each round quart for turrets.
4. Stick jelly beans around cones to form a parapet at the edge of the ice cream towers.
5. Stick square gumdrops along top edge of ice cream brick for battlements.
6. Cut some square gumdrops in half. Stick on sides of towers for windows.
7. Make a door and drawbridge from flat chocolate bar. Use licorice strings for drawbridge chains.
8. Place lollipops on either side of door and around base of towers to stand guard.
9. Return to freezer.
*Add flags at the top of each turret. These decorating ideas are only suggestions. Kids love this at birthday parties (see DO-IT-YOURSELF SUNDAES p. 311).*
▶ ▶

# LO - CAL MILKSHAKE  *Ben & Cara Taxy*  **D**

2% milk
Ice cubes, 1 tray
2 to 3 Tbsps. chocolate
  syrup
1 to 2 tsps. decaffinated
  coffee
1 to 2 Tbsps. smooth
  peanut butter (optional)

1. Place 7 to 9 ice cubes per person in blender.
Pour milk to reach ½ to ⅔ ice cube level. Add
flavorings.
2. Blend on "chop mode" until smooth.
►►

# EGG NOG SUPREME  *Joey Sager*  **D**

1 egg
1 cup milk
1 Tbsp. sugar or honey
1 tsp. vanilla
1 small banana, optional

1. Place all ingredients into a blender.
2. Cover. Blend on high speed for 30 seconds
without banana, 60 to 90 seconds with banana.
Pour into a glass.
Makes 1 large or 2 small servings.
*May be doubled if blender is big enough.*
*1 Tbsp. chocolate syrup may be substituted for*
*vanilla.*
►►

# FRUIT SLUSH  *Rachel Dorfman*  **P**

1 banana, or
1 cup strawberries
1 cup ice cubes
½ cup orange juice

1. Place all ingredients in a blender.
2. Blend at high speed for 1 minute, or until
ice is crushed and ingredients blended.
3. Pour into glasses.
Makes 2 servings.
*Healthful and delicious!*
►►

# ◉ IRENE'S DO-IT-YOURSELF DAIRY  *Irene Sufrin*

*Several years ago, Irene Sufrin taught kosher food and cooking as an extra-curricular class at the Solomon Schechter Middle School. Among the activites were making homemade yogurt, cottage cheese, and cream cheese. The methods, along with several of her recipes using the homemade yogurt, follow, pp. 306-309.*

# ◉ YOGURT

1 quart milk (whole or
   lowfat)
⅓ cup instant, nonfat
   dry milk
2 Tbsps. plain, lowfat
   yogurt, room temperature

Equipment:
2-quart double-boiler
Candy thermometer
7 8-ounce plastic or glass
   containers with lids
Electric yogurt maker, *or*
1 large foam picnic chest,
   insulated, *or*
1 large pot & a blanket

Flavorings (optional):
½ tsp. vanilla
Fresh fruit: Apples,
   bananas, strawberries,
   blueberries, or peaches
Wheat germ
Granola

1. Wash all equipment in hot sudsy water, and rinse with hot water.
2. Fill bottom of double boiler with water. Place on heat on stove. Dissolve the nonfat dry milk in the liquid milk in top of double boiler.
3. Stir until the mixture reaches 180 degrees. Hold that temperature for a minute; then allow it to drop down to 115 to 120 degrees.
4. Remove ⅓ of milk from the double boiler. Add to it 2 level Tbsps. of yogurt. Mix well.
5. Add the yogurt mixture to the milk remaining in the double boiler. Blend well.
6. Pour the mixture into 6 jars. Place these in an electric yogurt maker, or devise your own yogurt maker as follows:
7. Fill the 7th jar with boiling water. Place this jar in the insulated foam picnic chest. Put the 6 jars of yogurt mixture around the jar of water. Cover the chest. Set aside for 4 to 5 hours.
8. If you do not have a foam picnic chest, use a large pot. Wrap it in a blanket or tablecloth for insulation, and place it in a warm place for the 4 to 5 hours.
9. Any flavoring may be added to the jars after the yogurt process is completed.

*Yogurt is a very nourishing food. It has all the nutrients of milk plus special bacteria that are terrific for the digestive processes. Yogurt is low in calories and can be prepared in many ways. The following recipes show a variety of delicious uses for yogurt which kids will enjoy preparing and eating.*

►►►

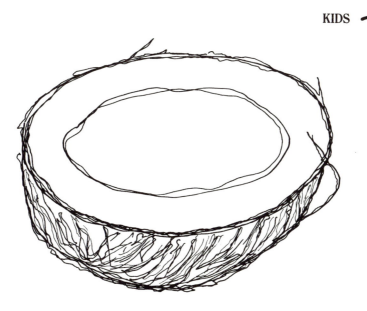

# BAKED BANANA  ⓓ

1 banana
1 tsp. honey or molasses
1 Tbsp. yogurt
1 tsp. coconut, shredded

1. Cut the banana in half, lengthwise.
2. Spread it with honey. Spoon yogurt on the honey. Top with coconut.
3. Bake in a 350 degree oven for 15 to 20 minutes. Serve hot.
Makes 1 to 2 servings.
►►

# RAISIN - COCONUT - YOGURT SANDWICH  ⓓ

½ cup plain yogurt
½ cup coconut, shredded
½ cup raisins

1. Mix the 3 ingredients in a bowl.
2. Spread on toast, bread, or crackers.
*Ideal lunch or snack.*
►

# VANILLA YOGURT MILKSHAKE  ⓓ

1 cup milk
½ cup yogurt
1 to 2 tsps. sugar
⅛ tsp. vanilla
½ to ¾ cup vanilla
   ice cream

1. Mix all the ingredients in a blender or shake up in a large jar.
Makes 2 servings.
►

# ❶ LEMON YOGURT PIE

1¼ cups graham cracker
  crumbs
¼ cup sugar
¼ cup butter
8-ounces cream cheese,
  room temperature
1 cup plain yogurt
4 Tbsps. honey
Juice of 1 lemon

1. The day before you wish to serve the pie, preheat oven to 375 degrees.
2. Mix the crumbs and sugar in an 8-inch pie pan.
3. Melt the butter. Add it to the pie pan slowly, blending it into the crumbs with a fork. Press the mixture against the bottom and sides of the pie pan.
4. Bake the crust 8 minutes. Let cool.
5. Place softened cream cheese in a bowl. Add a few tsps. of yogurt and beat until smooth.
6. Stir in the rest of the yogurt, honey, and lemon juice. Pour into the cooled crumb crust. Refrigerate overnight.
►►

# ❶ BANANA SPLIT SALAD

1 cup yogurt
½ cup crushed pineapple,
  drained
1 Tbsp. honey
4 bananas, peeled
4 large lettuce leaves
¼ cup nuts, chopped
½ cup strawberries, sliced

1. Mix the yogurt, pineapple, and honey.
2. Cut bananas in half, lengthwise.
3. For each serving, place a lettuce leaf on a salad plate. Put 2 banana halves on top. Spoon ¼ cup yogurt mixture over the banana.
4. Sprinkle with chopped nuts. Top with strawberries.
Makes 4 servings.
►►

# ❶ YOGURT POPS

Yogurt
Wooden sticks

Flavoring options:
Chocolate syrup
Vanilla
Honey
Concentrated lemonade or
  orange juice

1. Mix yogurt with your favorite flavoring. Taste to adjust amount.
2. Pour into an ice-cube tray ⅔ full.
3. Insert a wooden stick into the middle of the yogurt in each ice-cube cup.
4. Freeze until firm.
►

# HOMEMADE COTTAGE CHEESE    Ⓓ

1 quart milk (whole
  or skim)
2 Tbsps. buttermilk, or
  lemon juice, or vinegar
¼ tsp. salt

1. In a large pottery, glass, or porcelain bowl, combine the milk and buttermilk (or lemon juice, or vinegar). Mix thoroughly.
2. Cover with a clean cloth. Allow to stand for 18 to 24 hours in a warm place. Or place in a gas oven with only the pilot light burning.
3. When the milk has "clabbered" or thickened, place over low heat just until the curds separate from the whey. (This only takes a few minutes.)
4. Line a strainer with cheesecloth, and place it over a bowl. Pour curds and whey into the strainer and allow to drain.
5. When curds have drained, remove them from the cheesecloth into a container or bowl. Add the salt. Enjoy your cottage cheese!

*The liquid that has drained into the bowl is whey. It can be added to a dairy soup or drink, such as the yogurt milkshake. Or whip it with strawberries in the blender!*
►►

# HOMEMADE CREAM CHEESE    Ⓓ

2 cups yogurt
Seasonings (optional):
Chives, chopped
Salt, pinch
Fruit, chopped fine

1. Line a strainer with cheesecloth, and place it over a bowl.
2. Pour the yogurt into the strainer.
3. Place in the refrigerator. Allow to drain 8 hours, or until the yogurt has turned the consistency of cream cheese. Do not stir or press the yogurt through the sieve.
4. Remove cheese from cloth to a bowl. Leave plain, or add optional seasonings, as desired.

*The liquid in the bowl is whey, which may be added to dairy soups or drinks, as in HOMEMADE COTTAGE CHEESE, above.*
►

# CLAIRE'S COOKING BIRTHDAY BASH

*Claire Sufrin*

*For my 10th birthday, I invited my girlfriends to a cooking party.*
*We had as much fun making lunch as eating it!*

MENU

EASY SPINACH DIP

HOMEMADE POTATO CHIPS

SUPER HERO SANDWICH

DO-IT-YOURSELF SUNDAES

## **D** EASY SPINACH DIP

1 10-ounce package frozen chopped spinach
1 cup mayonnaise
1 cup sour cream
1 small onion, finely chopped
¼ cup green onion, chopped (include greens)
1 pinch garlic powder

1. Defrost spinach.
2. Squeeze spinach to remove all the moisture.
3. Mix the spinach together with all the other ingredients.
4. Serve with fesh raw vegetables or chips.
*Munch on this with raw veggies while you make the rest of the lunch.*
▶

310

# HOMEMADE POTATO CHIPS ⓟ

8 baking potatoes, peeled
Salt, pinch

1. Preheat oven to 400 degrees.
2. Slice potatoes into thin "chips" in a food processor. Keep chips in cold water to prevent browning.
3. Place chips in one layer on a well-greased cookie sheet.
4. Bake them in oven until lightly brown.
5. Turn the chips. Bake until other side is lightly brown.
Sprinkle with a pinch of salt.
*Enjoy!*
►►

# SUPER HERO SANDWICH ⓓ

1 loaf Italian bread
1 7-ounce can tuna
2 Tbsps. mayonnaise
6 slices cheese (Cheddar or Swiss)
1 cup lettuce
1 cup sliced tomato
1 cup sliced green pepper
½ cup sprouts*
2 tsps. vinegar
2 tsps. oil
1 pinch basil
1 pinch oregano

1. Put tuna and mayonnaise in a bowl. Mix well with a fork.
2. Carefully slice open loaf of bread, lengthwise.
3. Spread tuna mixture on bottom half.
4. Cover with cheese slices.
5. Add lettuce, then tomato slices, pepper slices, and sprouts.
6. Sprinkle oil, vinegar, basil, and oregano on top.
7. Place top of bread over all. Cut into as many slices as you want.
*For an interesting project kids will enjoy, see GROW YOUR OWN SPROUTS, p. 401.*
►►

# DO - IT - YOURSELF SUNDAES ⓓ

Ice cream, any flavor*
Chocolate sauce
Caramel sauce
Strawberry sauce
Whipped cream
Nuts, chopped
Sprinkles
M & M's
Maraschino cherries

1. Put the sauces and toppings out in bowls.
2. Kids like the whipped cream that you spray in a can.
3. Give everyone a bowl. Let each kid help her (him)self to whatever ice cream and toppings she/he wants.
*For an extra-special party, my Mom and I made the ICE CREAM FANTASY, p. 304; my friends scooped the ice cream for their sundaes, from the ice cream castle!*
►►

# ANNIVERSARY DINNER FOR MOM AND DAD
### *Caryn & Elan Peretz*

*We decided to do something special for our parents on their wedding anniversary. We cooked them dinner! You might enjoy doing the same.*

## MENU

HOT ORIENTAL CHESTNUTS

STEAMED ARTICHOKES WITH SALAD DRESSING

CHICKEN À LA CARYN & ELAN

BAKED POTATOES

FUDGE SQUARES

# HOT ORIENTAL CHESTNUTS

½ cup soy sauce
½ tsp. ground ginger
½ 8-ounce can water chestnuts, halved
6 slices beef fry
Sugar
Toothpicks

1. Combine soy sauce and ginger in 2 cup glass measure. Add water chestnuts. Stir and marinate for 3 to 4 hours.
2. Cut slices of beef fry into thirds.
3. Roll a water chestnut half in a beef fry piece. Push a toothpick through the wrapped chestnut to hold it together.
4. Put some sugar on a plate or piece of wax paper. Dip the skewered chesnut into the sugar and roll it around to coat.
5. Place on folded paper towels in 2-quart glass baking dish to microwave. Place on aluminum foil for toaster oven or oven.
6. Microwave on high 8 to 10 minutes or until beef fry is crispy. (Cook in toaster oven or oven about the same time.)
Makes 18 appetizers.
*They came out really good. Even the dog liked them!*
►►

# STEAMED ARTICHOKES

2 medium artichokes
Water
1 lemon slice
Pareve salad dressing

1. Cut the stem off each artichoke. If desired, trim the tops off the artichoke leaves with a scissors.
2. Put about 1 inch of water and lemon slice in a pot. Set artichokes in water. Bring to boil on high heat. Turn heat to low. Cover and cook 45 minutes.
3. Remove from pot. Cool. Place each artichoke on a plate. Pour favorite pareve salad dressing into a small bowl. Serve.
*This can be made in the morning and refrigerated. It is an appetizer and a salad in one.*
►►

**KIDS**

#  CHICKEN A LA CARYN & ELAN

2 fryers, cut up
2 boxes seasoned croutons
1 cup bread crumbs
1 bottle salad dressing,
   pareve (thick "creamy"
   kinds work best)
6 pinches each of:
Seasoned salt
Pepper
Garlic powder
Onion powder
Celery salt
Dill

1. Smash croutons with a cooking hammer or in the food processor. Leave them a little chunky.
2. Mix croutons in a bowl with bread crumbs and seasonings.
3. Pour dressing into a soup plate or bowl.
4. Dip each piece of chicken in the dressing. Roll each piece in the crumbs. Coat well with both dressing and crumbs.
5. Cover a large baking pan with foil. Grease the foil with margarine.
6. Bake in a 350 degree oven for 1½ hours.
►►

#  BAKED POTATOES

2 large baking potatoes
Margarine

1. Wash potatoes.
2. Grease outside of potatoes with margarine.
3. Wrap each potato in aluminum foil.
4. Place on the oven rack and bake with the chicken for 1½ hours at 350 degrees.
5. To serve, unwrap, or make a slit through the foil, push open potato, and add more margarine.
►►

# ◆ FUDGE SQUARES

3 cups confectioner's sugar
¾ cup margarine
⅔ cup non-dairy creamer
12 ounces semi-sweet
   chocolate chips
1 10-ounce jar
   marshmallow "Fluff"
1 cup nuts, chopped
   (optional)
1 tsp. vanilla

1. Combine sugar, margarine, and non-dairy creamer in large, glass mixing bowl. Cover with plastic wrap; poke a few holes through the wrap.
2. Microwave on medium-high for 10 minutes. Stir. Microwave on medium-high for 5 minutes longer. Remove bowl from microwave with an oven mitt carefully—it gets very hot!
3. Stir in chocolate pieces until melted. Fold in marshmallow, nuts, and vanilla.
4. Grease a 13 x 9 inch pan. Pour fudge in and spread it out. Chill until firm. Cut into squares. *This looks like halavah, but tastes like fudge!*
►►

POtpOuRRi

## ◆ EASY APPLESAUCE *Arlene Levin*

KP

1 3-pound bag of Jonathan
   apples, peeled and cored
1 cup water
½ cup sugar
½ tsp. cinnamon

1. Using the food processor, chop apples into small pieces.
2. Place water, sugar, cinnamon, and apples in a pot. Cover and simmer on medium heat for ½ hour or until soft, stirring occasionally.
3. Cool and then refrigerate.
Makes 8 to 10 servings.
*Good with potato pancakes. For those who don't want to peel apples, put through sieve after cooking. This makes a smoother version.*

## ◆ RHUBARB APPLESAUCE *Dorene Benuck*

KP

½ cup water
1 package frozen rhubarb
1 10-ounce package frozen
   strawberries
Strawberry gelatin,
   1 large, or 2 small
   packages
1 medium jar applesauce

1. Boil water. Add frozen rhubarb to water and keep stirring about 20 minutes until mushy.
2. Add frozen strawberries. Mix, then add gelatin and applesauce.
3. Refrigerate until cold.
Makes 6 to 12 servings.
*Refreshing and delicious! People will ask for seconds!*

## BUBBY YETTA'S
## ◆ APPLE KUGEL *Ruth Aberman*

¾ cup flour
½ tsp. salt
½ tsp. baking powder
½ cup sugar
½ cup margarine, softened
2 eggs
1 tsp. vanilla
1 can apple pie filling,
   drained
Cornflake crumbs

1. Sift flour, salt, and baking powder and set aside.
2. Cream sugar and margarine. Beat in eggs and vanilla. Add apples. Fold in dry ingredients.
3. Spoon mixture into greased 1½ quart casserole dish.
4. Sprinkle with cornflake crumbs and bake in 350 degree oven for 1 hour.
*This pareve dish is delicious, fool-proof and versatile. May be served with meat on Shabbat or Yom-Tov, or as a perfect accompaniment to a lox and bagel brunch!*

# APPLE CHUTNEY  *Judith Taylor*

6 large apples, peeled,
  cored, and chopped
2 cups cider vinegar
1½ cups light brown sugar
1 cup raisins
1 cup chopped onions
¼ cup fresh ginger, minced
2 Tbsps. mustard seeds
3 cloves garlic, minced
1 tsp. ground allspice
1 Tbsp. hot pepper flakes
1 tsp. salt

1. Combine all ingredients in a large pot. Bring to a boil, stirring continuously.
2. Reduce heat to simmer. Let simmer for 3 hours, stirring occasionally. Let cool.
3. ALTERNATE COOKING METHOD: After bringing to a boil, place pot in 325 degree oven. Bake, uncovered, for 3 hours, stirring each ½ hour.
4. Transfer to glass or plastic containers. Store in refrigerator or freezer.
Makes 5 to 6 cups chutney.
*Spectacular accompaniment to meat, poultry, or fish dishes! Also great dairy appetizer served with cream cheese and crackers.*

# CURRIED FRUIT  *Hannah Engelman*

⅓ cup margarine
¾ cup brown sugar
4 tsps. curry powder
12 maraschino cherries
1 can pears
1 can peaches
1 can pineapple chunks

1. Melt together the margarine, brown sugar, and curry powder.
2. Drain all fruit. Place in 1½ quart casserole.
3. Add margarine mixture to fruit and bake in 325 degree oven for 1 hour.

## P FRUIT COMPOTE *Karen Sager*

1 large package mixed
  dried fruits (or 2
  6- to 8-ounce packages)
Rind of ½ lemon
1 cinnamon stick
1 20-ounce can cherry pie
  filling
Drain the following well:
1 1-pound can pineapple
  chunks
1 1-pound can Alberta
  peach halves
1 1-pound can pear halves
1 1-pound can apricot
  halves (skinned, if
  possible)
¾ cup sherry

1. Cover dried mixed fruit with water in saucepot. Add lemon rind and cinnamon stick. Cook until tender. Cool.
2. Drain fruits well, but do not drain cherry pie filling. Mix gently with cooked fruits.
3. Add sherry, and place mixture in a large baking dish. Cover and bake in 350 degree oven for 30 to 45 minutes until bubbly.
4. Chill. Serve with meat or dessert.
Makes 12 to 15 servings.
*May serve warm, at room temperature, or chilled.*

## P POACHED PEARS *Janet Resnick*

8 Bosc pears with stems
1 bottle red wine
2 Tbsps. lemon juice
1 cup sugar
1 stick cinnamon
1 vanilla bean
8 candied violets (optional)

1. Peel pears without removing stems.
2. Put wine, lemon juice, sugar, cinnamon, and vanilla bean in a saucepan. Bring to a boil.
3. Add pears to the pan. Add enough water to cover pears.
4. Simmer until tender, about 10 to 20 minutes.
5. Remove pears. Reduce liquid to about 1 cup. Pour over pears. Garnish with violets.
Serve hot or cold.

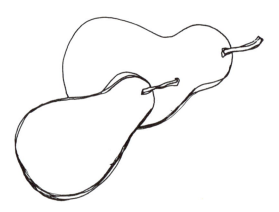

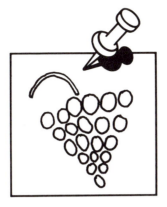

# CANDIED GRAPES *Janet Resnick*

White or brown sugar
Grapes
Egg whites

1. Beat egg whites until foamy.
2. Immerse grape clusters and shake off excess. Sprinkle with sugar.
3. Place on wax paper and refrigerate overnight.

# CRANBERRY ORANGE RELISH *Joan Sohn* ◆P

1 pound fresh cranberries
1 whole navel orange
1 cup crushed pineapple, drained
1¼ to 1½ cups sugar, (to taste)

1. Chop cranberries and orange in food processor.
2. Add crushed pineapple and sugar. Place in bowl or jar.
3. Refrigerate. Can be frozen.
*Great side dish. Easy to make. Can be made days in advance, and tastes better after sitting.*

# CRANBERRY BANANA RELISH *Shirley Steinberg* ◆P

2 3-ounce packages red gelatin (strawberry, cherry, etc.)
2 cups boiling water
1 can cranberry sauce (whole berry works best)
1 cup crushed pineapple with juice (20-ounce can)
2 mashed bananas

1. Mix gelatin with boiling water.
2. Add cranberry sauce. Mix well.
3. Add crushed pineapple and bananas.
4. Chill overnight in bowl.
Mixture will be a solid mold when set. For serving let stand a few minutes and then chop up with spoon into serving bowl.
*Nice accompaniment to any poultry or beef dish.*

# CRANBERRY - CURRANT SAUCE *Janet Resnick*

1 pound fresh cranberries, washed
1¼ cups sugar
1 cup red currant jam
1 cup water
1 cup walnuts, coarsely chopped
2 Tbsps. grated orange peel

1. Combine cranberries, sugar, jam, and water in a large saucepan. Heat to boiling, then reduce heat to simmer. Simmer, uncovered, for 20 minutes.
2. Skim off foam. Remove from heat.
3. Stir in walnuts and orange peel.
4. Refrigerate, covered, overnight.
*Fabulous and festive accompaniment for poultry or meat. Fast and easy as well.*

# SPICED BLUEBERRY JAM *Barbara Ament*

1½ quarts frozen blueberries, drained
2 Tbsps. lemon juice
¼ tsp. cloves
¼ tsp. cinnamon
¼ tsp. allspice
1¾ ounces powdered pectin
5 cups sugar
Paraffin wax, for sealing jars

1. Before preparing jam, sterilize bell jars and lids and keep in hot water.
2. Wash and drain berries (fresh or frozen) and remove stems. Purée berries and measure out 1 quart.
3. In large saucepan, combine purée, lemon juice, cloves, cinnamon, allspice, pectin, and sugar. Stir to mix well.
4. Over high heat, bring mixture to a full, rolling boil. Boil for 1 minute, stirring constantly. Skim off foam.
5. Ladle into hot sterilized jelly jars. Immediately cover with ⅛ inch hot paraffin. Let cool, then cover with lid.
Makes approximately 48 ounces.

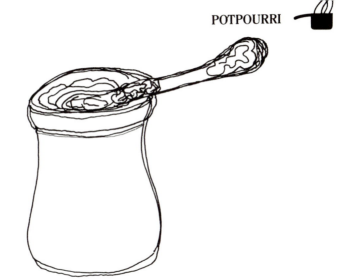

# CINNAMON ROSE JELLY *Barbara Ament*

1¾ cups rosé wine
3 cups sugar
1 package powdered fruit
  pectin
4 cinnamon sticks

1. Mix wine and sugar in saucepan. Bring to a boil. Boil for one full minute, stirring halfway through. Stir in fruit pectin.
2. Pour mixture into sterilized bell jars. Place a cinnamon stick in each jar.
3. Seal jars. Turn upside down for a few seconds. Let cool standing upright. Lids will seal within 24 hours.
Makes about 28 ounces.
*Good on toast or lamb.*

# JALAPEÑO JELLY *Barbara Ament*

1 cup jalapeño peppers,
  finely chopped
1 medium green pepper,
  finely chopped
¾ cup water
¾ cup white wine vinegar
5 cups sugar
1 package powdered fruit
  pectin
2 to 3 drops green food
  coloring

1. Grind or chop peppers together. Place in pan with water and bring to a boil.
2. Add vinegar and sugar; bring to a full boil again.
3. Add pectin and food coloring. Bring to a full boil and let boil for a full minute. Allow mixture to stand for 5 minutes, then skim off foam from surface.
4. Pour into sterile bell jars, seal, and turn upside down for a few seconds. Let cool standing upright. Lids will seal within 24 hours. Finished jelly will be syrupy, not firm.
Makes about 42 ounces.
Serve with cream cheese and crackers.
*Be sure to wear rubber gloves when handling the jalapeño peppers. They will burn your hands and eyes.*

321

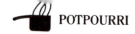 

#  KOSHER PICKLES *Ruth Taxy*

30 pickling cucumbers
½ cup kosher salt
2 quarts water
2 Tbsps. vinegar
4 cloves garlic
2 bay leaves
¼ tsp. mustard seeds
1 tsp. pickling spices
10 sprigs dill

1. Wash cucumbers thoroughly. Arrange in a large glass jar.
2. Boil salt and water in saucepan. Add vinegar, garlic cloves, bay leaves, mustard seeds, pickling spices, and dill. Cool.
3. Pour liquid over cucumbers until completely covered. Loosely cover jar with cheese cloth.
4. Store jar in a cool place for 1 week. "New pickles" may be "done" after five days.

# DILL PICKLES *Jackie Siegel*

**KP**

10 firm baby cucumbers
1 bunch fresh pickling
  dill, washed
3 cloves garlic
Red chili peppers, dried
Fresh peppers, washed
  (optional)
3 Tbsps. kosher salt

1. Use ½-gallon wide-mouth glass Mason jar for pickles. Wash and dry jar well before using.
2. Scrub the cucumbers.
3. On the bottom of jar, place 1 clove garlic, 1 small red chili pepper, 3 strands dill. Put tight layer of cucumbers next. Repeat with 1 garlic clove and 1 red chili pepper on top of cucumbers. Put in another layer of cucumbers and top with garlic clove, 3 sprigs dill, and fresh hot pepper (optional, if you want hot pickles).
4. Add kosher salt. Fill jar with water and seal. Store in a cool spot for three weeks.

# SOUR GREEN TOMATOES *Jackie Siegel*

½ bushel firm green
  tomatoes (approximately)
1 bunch pickling dill,
  washed
3 cloves garlic
1 package dried red chili
  peppers
1 small carrot, peeled
  (optional)
Celery root, peeled and
  cut into 1-inch pieces
Water
3 Tbsps. kosher salt

1. Wash and dry ½-gallon wide-mouth Mason jar.
2. Wash and scrub tomatoes well. Slice into quarters.
3. Place 1 garlic clove, 1 red chili pepper, and 3 strands dill on the bottom of the jar.
4. Pack in tomatoes tightly to middle of jar.
5. Place 1 garlic clove and 1 dried chili pepper in the middle.
6. Pack remaining tomatoes to top of jar. Leave room for remaining ingredients.
7. Place 1 garlic clove, 3 strands of dill, 1 chunk of celery root, carrot, and 1 fresh hot pepper (optional) on top.
8. Pour in 3 Tbsps. kosher salt. Fill jar with water and seal. Place in a cool spot for 3 weeks.

*This recipe doubles, triples, and quadruples well. This and the dill pickle recipe come from Rumania from my husband Mark's grandmother.*

# ABBIE'S AUNT BERT'S FAMOUS EGGPLANT RELISH *Abigail Natenshon*

3 cups eggplant, peeled
  and chopped
⅓ cup green pepper,
  cut up
2 cloves garlic, mashed
1 medium onion, chopped
⅓ cup salad oil
1 cup tomato paste
4-ounce can mushrooms
  with liquid
¼ cup water
2 Tbsps. red wine vinegar
1 tsp. seasoned salt
½ tsp. oregano
⅛ tsp. pepper
1½ tsps. sugar

KP

1. In saucepan over medium heat cook the eggplant, green pepper, garlic, and onion in the oil until eggplant has a wilted appearance.
2. Add tomato paste, mushrooms with liquid, water, vinegar, spices, and sugar.
3. Cover and simmer for 30 minutes or until soft.

*Tastes better the next day, after it has had time to mellow. Can be frozen.*

323

# ◆ CHARLOTTE'S HERRING SALAD *Charlotte Glass*

1 1-pound jar herring in
wine sauce
1 6-ounce jar marinated
artichoke hearts
1 green pepper, diced
1 small jar green olives,
sliced
½ red onion, diced
12-ounce jar chili sauce
½ cup fresh parsley,
minced *or*
1 Tbsp. dried minced
parsley

1. Reserving juice, drain herring and cut into small pieces.
2. Drain artichoke hearts and dice.
3. Combine herring, artichoke hearts, green pepper, olives, red onion, and chili sauce. Use food processor to mix, if desired. Add enough of the reserved herring juice to add flavor.
4. Cover and refrigerate at least 24 hours.
5. Sprinkle with parsley before serving.
Makes 8 to 10 servings.
*Keeps well for two weeks.*

# ● CUCUMBER - DILL SAUCE *Karen Sager*

KP
½ cup plain yogurt
½ cup light sour cream
1 small cucumber, chopped
1 Tbsp. chopped dill weed
Salt, dash
White pepper, dash

1. Combine yogurt, sour cream, cucumber, dill weed, salt, and pepper. Mix well.
*Serve as accompaniment for salmon mousse or other fish.*

# ● "LO - CAL" SOUR CREAM *Sarita Blau*

KP
1 pound cottage cheese
1 to 4 Tbsps. plain yogurt

1. Put cottage cheese in blender. Blend until smooth.
2. Blend or stir in yogurt in the amount desired for tartness.
Makes 2 cups.
*Calorie-reduced. Use on baked potatoes or in place of mayonnaise in tuna salad.*

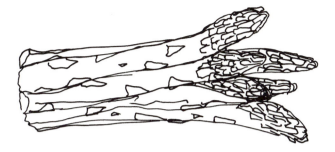

# MICROWAVE HOLLANDAISE *Jackie Siegel* **P**

½ cup butter
¼ cup water
1 to 2 Tbsps. fresh
  lemon juice
Cayenne pepper, dash*
3 egg yolks, slightly
  beaten

**KP**

1. In 1-quart glass bowl combine butter, water, lemon juice, and pepper.
2. Cook on high in microwave 3 to 4 minutes, or until butter melts and mixture boils.
3. With wire whisk or fork beat in egg yolks gradually.
4. Return to microwave at medium low for 30 to 60 seconds or until thickened. (Watch carefully to be sure it doesn't curdle.)
5. Remove. Stir twice. Serve warm or at room temperature.

*Omit cayenne pepper and this becomes a great Pesach recipe.*

# TANGY MUSTARD *Blossom T. Porte* **D**

1 4-ounce jar yellow
  mustard
1 cup tarragon vinegar
6 eggs
¾ cup sugar
½ cup butter
1 tsp. salt

1. Put mustard in top part of double boiler. Pour vinegar over but do not stir. Cover. Let stand overnight.
2. Next day, place pot over hot water and mix mustard and vinegar with wire whisk.
3. Over the heating water (do not let boil), add eggs, one at a time, whisking after each.
4. Add sugar, butter, and salt. Cook, stirring gently, for 5 minutes ONLY.
5. Cool; refrigerate in jars.
Keeps for months.

**P** *Can be made pareve by substituting margarine for butter.*

#  CHINESE CHILI PASTE *Jackie Siegel*

¼ pound hot red peppers
3 garlic cloves, minced
2 Tbsps. soy sauce
2 Tbsps. oil
½ tsp. salt

1. In food processor, finely chop the peppers (discard stems, but keep seeds).
2. In saucepan, cook peppers with garlic, soy sauce, oil, and salt for about 30 minutes, or until paste consistency is reached.
3. Cool. Store in refrigerator.

#  DUCK SAUCE (PLUM SAUCE) *Jackie Siegel*

1 cup plum preserves
½ cup apricot jam
4 Tbsps. vinegar
¼ tsp. salt
⅛ tsp. cayenne pepper

1. Combine all ingredients in medium saucepan. Simmer, stirring occasionally, for about 10 minutes.
2. Cool. Store in refrigerator.

# Ⓜ PLUM SAUCE (MOO SHU) *The Kosher Gourmet*

1 cup brown sugar
¼ cup red wine vinegar
¼ cup red wine
1 30-ounce can purple plums with juice
¼ tsp. ground coriander
⅛ to ¼ tsp. red pepper (cayenne)
¼ cup beef stock
Flaming cognac (optional)

1. In medium saucepan, combine brown sugar, vinegar, and wine. Cook over medium heat, stirring occasionally, until liquid becomes a glaze, about 15 to 20 minutes.
2. Drain plum juice from plums. Set aside ½ cup of the syrup to use in sauce. Pit and finely chop or mash plums. Set aside.
3. Gradually add ½ cup plum juice to the glaze. Add coriander and red pepper. Stir and let cook over medium-high heat, stirring occasionally, for another 20 minutes, or until liquid is reduced.
4. Gradually add beef stock, stirring constantly, and continue to simmer sauce about 20 minutes, or until liquid reduces again.
5. Add chopped or mashed plums, stir well, and continue to cook until plums and liquid combine to make a thick sauce, stirring occasionally, about 25 to 30 minutes in total.
6. If desired, flame a scant amount of cognac in sauté pan. Add to sauce. Cool sauce well. Store in glass jars in refrigerator.
*Serve as a condiment for dipping or brush on Mandarin pancakes before filling with vegetable/meat combinations. If smoother consistency is desired, sauce may be mixed briefly in blender.*

# HOISIN SAUCE *Chris Erenberg*

1 cup dry soybeans
(black salted soybeans
are best)
6 cups water
½ cup sugar
⅓ cup vinegar
1 Tbsp. salt
4 to 5 cloves garlic,
minced
1½ Tbsps. dark sesame seeds
3 Tbsps. chili powder
½ tsp. Five-Spice
seasoning
¾ tsp. cayenne pepper
1 Tbsp. soy sauce

1. Soak dry soybeans in water for 48 hours in uncovered saucepan.
2. Bring soybeans to a boil, skim off foam. Lower heat to simmer.
3. Add sugar, vinegar, salt, sesame seeds, garlic, Five-Spice seasoning, chili powder, cayenne pepper, and soy sauce.
4. Simmer mixture for at least 3 hours, or until beans mash easily. The longer it cooks, the better the flavors combine.
5. Cool. Purée mixture in blender or food processor until it becomes smooth paste. Can add water if too thick.
Store in glass jars in refrigerator. Keeps well.
*The recipe for Hoison Sauce was buried with the Ancient Chinese. This is a tasty, if not completely authentic, substitute!*

#  EGGROLL OR WONTON SKINS *Chris Erenberg*

2 eggs, beaten well
1 cup ice water (Dissolve a few ice chips in cold tap water; water should be *very* cold.)
4 cups all-purpose flour
1 tsp. salt
Flour for kneading and rolling

1. In large bowl, combine beaten eggs and ice water.
2. Combine salt with flour. With a wire whisk, mix 2 cups of the flour mixture into the eggs and ice water. Mix well.
3. With a wooden spoon or by hand, stir in the remaining 2 cups of flour, working from the outside of the bowl to the center until a stiff dough ball is formed.
4. Turn dough onto floured board and knead until smooth and elastic.
5. Cut dough into 2 balls. Cover with cloth and refrigerate for at least 30 minutes.
6. Sprinkle flour liberally on wood board or table. With rolling pin, roll out dough on floured surface until paper thin. This requires time and patience, but if the dough is too thick, the eggrolls you make from it will be too tough! The rolling out gets easier as the dough begins to warm up. Let the dough rest a few minutes if your arms get tired!
8. When dough is rolled to proper thickness, cut into 6-inch squares for eggrolls or 3-inch squares for wontons.
9. Stack squares in layers, either coating each layer lightly with cornstarch, or placing wax paper between each.
Use as needed with filling of choice.
Makes about 24 eggroll skins or 48 wonton skins.

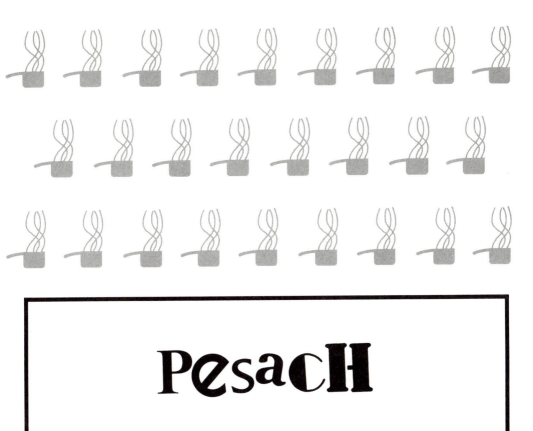

# PesacH

#  SEPHARDIC HAROSET *Phyllis Fischel*

**KP**

1 pound dark raisins
8 ounces dates, pitted
2 cups water
2 Tbsps. sugar
2 Tbsps. honey
Chopped pecans or walnuts
(approximately ¼ cup)

1. Place raisins and dates in a bowl. Cover with the water. Let stand for 1 hour.
2. Add honey and sugar. Chop fine in a food processor or blender. (This may have to be done in smaller batches, approximately ¼ at a time.)
3. Spoon into a heavy saucepot. Simmer over low heat until liquid is absorbed. Allow a long cooking time—from ½ to 1 hour, at least.
4. Remove from heat and place in storage container.
5. Sprinkle with chopped nuts when cool.
Makes 4 cups (enough for two Seders).
*This dark, rich* haroset *has more of the consistency of mortar than the standard Ashkenazi* haroset. *An exciting, sweet addition to the Seder table!*

#  APRICOT HAROSET *Phyllis Fischel*

**KP**

1 cup dried apricots,
chopped
½ cup dates, pitted
½ cup raisins
2 large apples, peeled,
cored, and chopped
Cinnamon stick
½ cup nuts, chopped
Sweet, red wine

1. Place apricots, dates, raisins, and apples with cinnamon stick in a saucepot with enough water to cover. Simmer over low heat until fruits are soft.
2. Drain excess liquid. Discard cinnamon. Cool in mixing bowl.
3. Add nuts and enough red wine to hold all the ingredients together and prevent them from becoming too sticky.
*It's fun to pass a variety of* harosets *at the Seder!*

#  YEMENITE HAROSET *Shoshanah Winer*

**KP**

10 dates, chopped
10 figs, chopped
1 Tbsp. sesame seeds
1 tsp. ginger powder
Red wine
Matzah meal

1. Mix together chopped dates and figs, sesame seeds, and ginger.
2. Add red wine, a little at a time to moisten the fruits and make them more maleable. Add matzah meal, a little at a time, if necessary, to bind the ingredients together.
*A different tasting* haroset.

*(For information and directions to set a Seder Plate, see p. 380.)*

# "CHRAINE" (HORSERADISH) *Robert Dorfman*

KP

1 whole horseradish root
Juice of ½ lemon
White cider vinegar, for
    taste and consistency
1 tsp. sugar
Salt, pinch

1. One to two days before serving, wash horseradish root thoroughly. Cover with water and soak for one or two days.
2. Peel root and remove any brown spots.
3. Grate by hand or in food processor. If it gets dry in the food processor, add a little vinegar to keep it moist.
4. Place in bowl and add lemon juice immediately to keep the white color.
5. Add enough vinegar to keep it moist. Add sugar and salt to taste.

*This makes a very strong* chraine—*excellent when paired with* haroset *between matzot in the traditional "Hillel sandwich" of the Seder. For a milder, red-colored horseradish, add 2 large beets, parboiled and peeled, to the food processor in step 3.*

## ◆ GEFILTE FISH SALAD *Judith Schuster*

KP

1 pound gefilte fish
1 cup celery, diced
1 Tbsp. lemon juice
Salt and pepper, to taste
⅓ cup mayonnaise
3 hard-boiled eggs,
   finely chopped
6 medium tomatoes
   (optional)

1. Break fish into small chunks. Add celery, lemon juice, salt, pepper, mayonnaise, and eggs. Chill thoroughly.
2. Optional: Serve in stuffed tomato and garnish with parsley.

## ◆ ARTICHOKES DELSARDO *Jacqueline Merlin & Janet Resnick*

KP

1 can artichokes, halved,
   drained
Juice of 1 lemon
1 egg
1 cup matzah meal
Salt and pepper, to taste
Oil, for frying

1. Marinate artichokes in lemon juice for about ½ hour.
2. Beat egg with 1 tsp. cold water, salt, and pepper.
3. Drain artichoke pieces. Roll each piece in matzah meal, dip in egg mixture, roll in matzah meal again.
4. Heat approximately ½ inch oil in skillet. Fry coated artichokes in oil, turning as sides become golden.
5. Drain on paper towel and serve.

## ◆ MOROCCAN CARROT SALAD *Chris Erenberg*

KP

6 to 8 large carrots,
   peeled and grated
2 to 3 garlic cloves,
   minced
Fresh parsley, minced
¼ cup olive oil
¼ cup lemon juice
Salt and white pepper
Boston lettuce leaves
Fresh parsley sprigs

1. Combine coarsely grated carrots, minced garlic, and parsley.
2. Mix with olive oil and lemon juice. Add salt and pepper to taste.
3. Let chill. Serve on Boston lettuce leaves. Garnish with whole parsley sprigs.
Makes 4 to 5 servings.
*Grating goes very quickly if you use a food processor.*

# KNAIDLACH *Lottie Weiner*

M

KP

4 eggs, separated
½ cup cold water
1 Tbsp. chicken fat
1 Tbsp. and 1 tsp. oil
1 tsp. salt
1 to 1½ tsps. white pepper
¾ to 1 cup matzah meal

1. Whip up egg yolk with water, then add fat and oil and whip some more.
2. Mix salt and pepper with the matzah meal. Combine with eggs by adding ½ cup first and slowly adding more, up to 1 cup, if needed.
3. Beat egg whites until stiff, but not dry. Fold into matzah meal mixture. Chill 1 hour.
4. Bring water to boil in a 6-quart pot.
5. Wet hands with cold water and shape mixture into medium-sized balls. Drop gently into boiling water.
6. Reduce heat slightly to keep gentle boil. Cover and cook 25 minutes.
*Light and fluffy every time!*

# MATZAH MEAL PANCAKES *Karen Sager*

D

KP

3 eggs, separated
½ cup milk
½ cup sour cream
1 Tbsp. sugar
Salt, dash
½ cup matzah meal
1 tsp. Pesadich baking
  soda (optional)
1 Tbsp. butter or margarine

1. Beat egg whites until stiff, but not dry.
2. In separate bowl, mix together egg yolks, milk, sour cream, sugar, salt, matzah meal, and soda in that order. Combine egg whites and matzah meal mixture.
3. Melt butter or margarine in skillet. Spoon batter, fry, and flip carefully. Serve warm with syrup or jam.

# PASSOVER BAGELS *Vickie Schneider*

P

KP

⅔ cup shortening
1½ cups water
Salt, pinch
3 Tbsps. sugar
2 cups matzah meal
6 eggs

1. Bring shortening, water, salt, and sugar to boil in a saucepot. Add matzah meal. Mix well on stove. It will pull away from sides of the pot. Set aside to cool.
2. When cool, put in bowl and add eggs, one at a time. Mix well after each egg.
3. Drop by large spoonfuls onto cookie sheet.
4. Wet hands and form into bagels by making an opening in center of dough.
5. Bake in 350 degree oven for 1 hour.
Makes 12 to 15 bagels.

## Ⓓ PESACH POPOVERS *Karen Sager*

KP

½ cup butter or
   margarine
¼ tsp. salt
1 cup matzah meal
2 Tbsps. sugar
¼ tsp. cinnamon
4 to 5 large eggs
Peanut oil, to grease tins

1. In 2-quart saucepan, boil butter, salt, and 1½ cups water. Stir to melt butter. Remove from heat.
2. Add matzah meal, sugar, and cinnamon and stir with wooden spoon to make a smooth paste.
3. Stir in eggs one at a time, making sure each is incorporated before adding next.
4. Heat oven to 400 degrees.
5. Spoon mixture 2 Tbsps. at a time into greased muffin tins, or spoon 2 inches apart on a greased baking sheet. Bake 30 to 35 minutes until brown and puffed.
*Serve warm with butter and jam.*
❖ *May be made pareve by substituting margarine for butter.*

## Ⓟ VEGETABLE MUFFINS *Debbie Nathan & Arlene Levin*

KP

¼ cup green pepper,
   chopped
1 cup onion, chopped
½ cup celery, chopped
1½ cups raw carrots,
   grated
6 Tbsps. margarine
1 10-ounce package frozen
   spinach, defrosted,
   chopped, and squeezed dry
3 eggs, well beaten
⅛ tsp. pepper
1½ tsps. salt
¾ cup matzah meal

1. Sauté green pepper, onion, celery, and carrots in margarine for 10 minutes on low heat.
2. Combine spinach, eggs, salt, pepper, and matzah meal. Mix well. Add to vegetables.
3. Spoon into well greased 1½-quart casserole or pan or 12 greased muffin tins.
4. Bake in 350 degree oven for 45 minutes or until firm.
Makes 8 to 12 servings.
*Makes 12 "muffins." Or, bake Arlene's favorite way, as a kugel. Delicious accompaniment to meat or fish.*

## Ⓟ PASSOVER MUFFINS *Mrs. Daniel Chasnoff*

KP

2 cups matzah meal
2 Tbsps. sugar
Salt
1½ cups boiling water
4 eggs
½ cup shortening, melted

1. Dissolve sugar and salt in the boiling water and pour over matzah meal. Mix well and let stand for 5 minutes.
2. Beat eggs. Add eggs and melted shortening to matzah meal mixture. Mix thoroughly. Form patties about ¾ inch thick and 2½ inches across. Place on greased cookie sheet in moderate 350 degree oven 50 to 60 minutes or until golden brown.
Makes 12 muffins.

# PESACH BLUEBERRY MUFFINS  *Arlene Levin*

**P**

**KP**

½ cup oil
1 cup sugar
3 eggs
½ cup cake flour
¼ cup potato starch
¼ tsp. salt
1½ cups blueberries
  (if frozen, defrost
  and drain)
½ tsp. cinnamon
2 Tbsps. sugar

1. Mix oil and sugar.
2. Add eggs and beat together. Mix cake flour, potato starch, salt, and eggs together. Then add blueberries.
3. Pour into muffin tins (with paper liners) until half full.
4. Sprinkle ½ tsp. cinnamon with 2 Tbsps. sugar over unbaked muffins. Bake in 325 degree oven 40 to 50 minutes.
*Easy, fast, and a nice change of pace!*

# PASSOVER "LACHMANIOT" (LITTLE BREADS OR ROLLS)  *Devora Rabkin*

**P**

**KP**

1 cup water
½ cup margarine
1½ cups matzah meal
1 tsp. salt
2 Tbsps. sugar (if sweeter
  bread is preferred)
4 eggs

1. In a medium-sized saucepan, bring the water and the margarine to a rapid boil.
2. Remove from heat. Add the matzah meal, salt, and sugar (if desired).
3. Add eggs one at a time, mixing well with a wooden spoon.
4. Grease hands and form 4-inch balls by rolling the dough between your hands.
5. Put the balls on a greased cookie sheet and place in 350 degree preheated oven for about 25 to 30 minutes.
*They are ready when they look dry and golden.*

## ▣ LAMB CHOP CASSEROLE *Priscilla Sutton*

KP

10 to 12 lamb chops
2 to 3 potatoes, cubed
1 to 2 onions, sliced thin
1 6-ounce can tomato paste
Cinnamon, ½ to 1 tsp.
Allspice (optional)
Salt, to taste

1. Place lamb chops in a baking dish. Cover with potatoes and onions.
2. Place tomato paste and three cans water in mixing bowl. Add spices to taste. Mix and pour over lamb chops, potatoes, and onions.
3. Cover with foil. Bake in a 350 degree oven for 2 hours or until sauce is thickened and meat is tender.

## ▣ LAMB SHANKS WITH SWEET GARLIC SAUCE *Arlene Levin*

KP

4 medium lamb shanks
Freshly ground pepper
2 Tbsps. peanut oil
6 large cloves garlic,
  peeled and sliced
1¼ cups chicken broth
1 cup dry white wine
1 tsp. oregano

1. Season shanks with pepper.
2. Heat oil in sauté pan and brown shanks on all sides. (May have to do this in two batches.) Add garlic with broth, wine, and oregano.
3. Cover and bring to a boil. Reduce heat and simmer gently until meat is tender—approximately 1½ hours.

*Also works well with undivided, large, meaty shanks. Prepare as above one or two days before serving. Slice meat off bones. Shanks may now be roasted for the Seder plate (p. 380). Remove fat from sauce, which will gel when refrigerated. Add sliced meat. Reheat in oven. Delicious addition to Seder—or any—meal.*

# SHISH KABOB (SHASHLIK) *Chris Erenberg & Karen Sager* **M**

**KP**

2 pounds lamb, cut into
  1¼ inch cubes
12 small white onions,
  peeled
12 small potatoes, peeled
12 small plum tomatoes
12 large mushroom caps
1 large green pepper,
  cored and seeded

Marinade:
½ cup red wine
½ cup vinegar
½ cup pineapple juice
½ cup brown sugar
1 tsp. salt
¼ tsp. pepper
1 clove garlic, crushed

1. Combine wine, vinegar, juice, brown sugar, and seasonings in a bowl. Add lamb and allow to marinate several hours in the refrigerator.
2. If onions and potatoes are approximately 1½ to 3 inches in diameter, leave whole, otherwise cut in chunks.
3. Leave mushrooms and tomatoes whole.
4. Cut green pepper into 1½-inch squares.
5. The best method of preparation is to skewer the meat and the various vegetables according to the different cooking times needed. Place marinated lamb cubes on their own skewers; alternate potatoes and onions on skewers; alternate mushrooms, tomatoes, and green pepper squares on skewers.
6. Place skewers on broiler pan or grill, according to cooking time. Potatoes and onions require approximately 20 minutes; lamb approximately 15 minutes; mushrooms, tomatoes, green pepper, approximately 7 minutes.
7. Watch carefully; turn skewers as necessary.
8. Remove meat and vegetables from skewers before serving; arrange some of each kind on individual plates or on a platter.
Makes 6 to 8 servings.
*Shish Kabob (or Russian "Shashlik") is standard Pesach fare in Israel, where it is usually served with rice, which is permitted in the Sephardi Pesach diet. However, it is a delicious and satisfying meal by itself!*

# MEYENA *Janet Resnick* **M**

**KP**

2 pounds ground beef
1 cup onion, chopped
½ cup raw pine nuts
2 15-ounce cans
  tomato sauce
2 11-ounce cans chicken
  broth
9 whole matzot
3 to 4 eggs
Salt & pepper, dash

1. Brown meat, onions, and pine nuts together in a saucepot. Add tomato sauce. Cook down until liquid is absorbed. Set aside.
2. Pour chicken broth into a 2½-quart rectangular Pyrex (the width of a matzah).
3. Line the pan carefully with 3 matzot. Spread one-half the meat mixture on top. Layer 3 more matzot, then the rest of the meat, and top with the third layer of matzah.
4. Beat the eggs, salt, and pepper in a bowl. Pour over the top matzah and chicken broth. Bake in a 350 degree oven for 1 hour.

# M CAPON WITH MUSHROOMS *Karen Sager*

**KP**
1 5- to 6-pound capon
4 ounces dried mushrooms
2 cups boiling water
1 pound fresh mushrooms
3 garlic cloves
½ cup fresh parsley
  (flat-leaf is best)
¼ cup peanut oil
Salt and pepper
Extra peanut oil
  for brushing

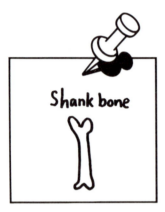

Shank bone

1. Preheat oven to 350 degrees.
2. Place dried mushrooms in a small bowl; cover them with boiling water. Let soak for 1 hour.
2. Line a sieve with paper towel or cheese cloth. Strain soaked mushrooms, reserving strained liquid in a small saucepan.
3. Rinse mushrooms to remove any remaining grit; squeeze dry.
4. Chop prepared mushrooms, fresh mushrooms, garlic, and parsley. (May use a food processor chopping blade.)
5. Heat oil in large skillet. Sauté chopped vegetables. Season with salt and pepper to taste. Set aside to cool. This is the stuffing.
6. Wash and dry capon. Loosen top skin gently. Carefully spread some stuffing between skin and flesh of capon. Spoon the rest into the cavity. (If a more tightly-stuffed farfel stuffing is preferred, mushrooms may be mixed with VEGETABLE STUFFING FOR TURKEY, p. 116.)
7. Skewer and tie capon. Brush with oil, and sprinkle with salt and pepper.
8. Roast on side for 30 minutes. Baste, turn on other side for 30 minutes. Baste. Continue roasting and basting, breast side up, approximately 1 more hour.
9. Remove to carving surface. Let stand while preparing gravy, then carve.
10. Remove excess surface fat from roasting pan. Combine remaining juices with reserved mushroom liquid. Bring to a boil, reduce heat, and simmer 5 minutes. Pass with carved capon meat.

# FRUITED BRISKET *Chris Erenberg* **M**

4- to 5-pound beef brisket
1 onion, finely chopped
1 carrot, diced
¼ tsp. garlic powder
Salt and pepper, to taste
1 cup Concord grape wine
1 1-pound jar fruit
   compote (or equivalent
   in cooked dried fruit,
   drained; reserve liquid)
1 orange, sectioned
1 apple, peeled and sliced
½ tsp. cinnamon
½ tsp. ginger
2 Tbsps. potato starch

1. In large pot, brown meat well on both sides. **KP** Add onion, carrot, garlic powder, salt, pepper, wine, and liquid from fruit compote. Bring to a boil, reduce heat to simmer, cover, and cook for 2½ hours, until just about tender.
2. Add fruit compote, orange, apple, cinnamon, and ginger. Continue cooking until tender, about 1 hour longer.
3. Remove meat and fruit from pot; keep warm. Skim fat from pan juices. Mix potato starch with a little cold water and add to remaining juices. Cook and stir until slightly thickened.
4. Arrange meat and fruit on platter. Pour gravy over meat, or pass separately.
Makes 8 to 10 servings.

# HONEY BRISKET *Adina Torchman* **M**

1 4- to 5-pound brisket
1 14-ounce jar ketchup
3 to 4 onions, sliced
Paprika
Garlic powder
Pepper
2 bags carrots, cut up
3 pounds sweet potatoes
1 12-ounce jar honey
2 pounds dried fruit
2 peels of lemon

1. Place ketchup and onions in bottom of pan. **KP** Place brisket in pan. Season well with paprika, garlic powder, and pepper. Cover and roast for 1½ hours in 350 degree oven.
2. Uncover. Add cut up carrots, sweet potatoes, honey, dried fruit, lemon peel, more paprika, and water, if dry.
3. Roast covered for 2 hours or until done.
4. Check for liquid. Add water and ketchup when necessary.

# VEAL STEW WITH EGGPLANT *Helene Blivaiss* **M**

1 Tbsp. oil
1 medium onion, sliced
½ cup green pepper, chopped
2 cloves garlic, minced
1¼ pounds veal, cubed
1 16-ounce can tomatoes
2 cups eggplant, cubed
1 zucchini, sliced
½ pound mushrooms, sliced
¾ tsp. salt
½ tsp. basil
⅛ tsp. pepper

1. Heat oil. Sauté onion, green pepper, and **KP** garlic until soft (about 5 minutes).
2. Add veal. Cook until veal is no longer pink (8 to 10 minutes).
3. Stir in tomatoes, eggplant, zucchini, mushrooms, and seasonings. Cover pot. Cook until tender (1 to 1¼ hours).
Makes 4 to 5 servings.

## **M** PASTEL *Nancy Goldstein*

KP

1 pound ground beef
2 medium onions, chopped
2 eggs
1 tsp. salt
½ tsp. pepper
2 matzot
Oil
2 cups chicken broth

1. Sauté onion until soft. Brown meat. Let cool and drain off fat.
2. Add eggs and beat well. Add salt and pepper.
3. Soften matzah in water. Oil pan. Fit matzah in pan like a pie crust. Oil crust a small amount.
4. Spread meat in pan and top with wet matzah. Pour a little chicken broth over all. Cover with foil.
5. Bake in 350 degree oven for ½ hour, then add more broth to soften crust. Bake 20 minutes. Then uncover—if dry, add more broth. Bake 10 more minutes uncovered.
6. Cool. Cut into pieces.
Total baking time is 1 hour.

## **M** PASSOVER MEATBALLS *Arlene Levin*

KP

1½ to 2 pounds ground beef
⅔ cup matzah meal
½ cup water
2 eggs, slightly beaten
½ cup onion, minced
1 tsp. salt
¼ tsp. pepper
1 large onion, minced
1 11-ounce can tomato-mushroom sauce
1 16-ounce can cranberry sauce

1. Combine beef, matzah meal, water, eggs, minced onion, salt, and pepper.
2. Shape into meatballs.
3. In large pot add diced onion, tomato-mushroom sauce, and cranberry sauce. Bring to a boil. Add meatballs, reduce heat, and simmer for about 1 hour.
Makes 12 servings.
*Easy, fast, good as family main course or appetizer.*

horseradish

# PASSOVER DAIRY LASAGNE *Fran Fogel* Ⓓ

2 jumbo eggs
1 pound cottage cheese
Salt, to taste
½ tsp. ground pepper
3 large cloves garlic, minced, *or*
½ tsp. garlic powder
1 to 2 tsps. oregano
2 tsps. sweet basil
1 medium onion, minced
3 to 4 whole matzot
Milk
2 10½-ounce cans tomato sauce
4 ounces mozzarella cheese, sliced

1. In a medium-sized mixing bowl, beat the eggs. Add the cottage cheese, salt, pepper, garlic, oregano, basil, and onion. Mix well.
2. Wet each whole matzah with milk until moistened, not soggy.
3. Pour a little sauce into an 8 x 8 inch baking pan, distributing evenly. Layer the remaining ingredients, alternating matzah, cottage cheese mixture, tomato sauce, cheese. Repeat ending with cheese.
4. Bake in 350 degree oven for 45 to 50 minutes.
5. Let the lasagne rest 10 to 15 minutes before cutting.
Makes 6 servings.
If recipe is doubled, only 3 cans of tomato sauce are needed.
*Delicious lunch or dairy supper.*

# PASSOVER CHEESE BLINTZES *Susan Markowitz* Ⓓ

Crepes:
3 eggs
¾ cup matzah cake flour
1½ cups water
½ tsp. salt

Cheese filling:
1 pound cottage cheese
1 egg
½ tsp. salt
½ tsp. sugar
1 Tbsp. cream *or* milk

1. Beat eggs in a bowl. Add flour and water alternately to make a thin batter. Add salt.
2. Pour about 3 Tbsps. batter into a preheated frying pan. Tilt pan in a circular motion to spread batter evenly and thinly.
3. When edges are dry and pull away from the sides of the pan, turn crepe out upside-down onto a towel.
4. Repeat until all batter is used up.
5. Mix cottage cheese, egg, salt, sugar, and milk in a bowl.
6. Spoon 1 Tbsp. filling into center of crepe. Fold in and roll up like an eggroll.
7. Place all blintzes flap side down in a buttered, glass baking dish.
8. Bake in 350 degree oven until blintzes are lightly browned.
Serve with sour cream and jam, or sprinkle tops with cinnamon and sugar when hot.
Use the smallest size non-stick frying pan for making the crepes.
Makes 4 servings.
*You might almost forget it is Pesach!*

## ◆ SPICY EGGPLANT DISH *Jacqueline Meslin*

KP
2 eggplants, sliced and
fried
2 onions
1 green pepper
3 cloves garlic
2 Tbsps. oil
1 28-ounce can peeled
tomatoes
1 tsp. coarse salt
1 tsp. crushed cumin seed
1 tsp. crushed red pepper

1. Chop onion, green pepper, and garlic cloves. Sauté in oil.
2. Add tomatoes, sliced eggplant, and spices. Cook on low heat for 15 minutes.
3. May be served at room temperature.

## ◆ SPINACH RING FOR PASSOVER *Fran Fogel*

KP
4 packages frozen spinach,
chopped
6 eggs, separated
2 Tbsps. margarine or oil
2 Tbsps. cake meal
2 Tbsps. pareve chicken
bouillon in ½ cup
hot water
3 onions, grated
Salt and white pepper
3 large cloves garlic,
minced
½ cup almonds, sliced
Curry (optional)

1. Cook or microwave spinach until separated. Drain well through strainer, or squeeze out excess liquid with your hand. (If necessary, cook gently in frying pan to evaporate remaining liquid.) Place in large bowl.
2. Place egg yolks in mixing bowl and beat lightly. Set aside.
3. Heat margarine or oil in small saucepan until bubbly. Add cake meal all at once and stir with wooden spoon until smooth. Cook a few minutes, then add dissolved chicken bouillon. Turn heat down and stir until mixture becomes a thick *roux*.
4. Add to slightly beaten egg yolks. Return to pot and cook until thick if necessary. Beat with wooden spoon until it is a smooth paste, rich in color and texture.
5. Add garlic, onion, salt, and pepper to spinach. Then add spinach to egg mixture. Stir in the almonds. Add curry, if desired.
6. Beat egg whites and fold into spinach/egg mixture.
7. Spoon into well greased 10-cup aluminum mold. Place mold into a pan with 1 inch hot water in it.
8. Bake in 350 degree oven 30 minutes until firm. Cool 15 to 25 minutes, then unmold. Use knife to unmold. (Might fill center with carrots prepared your favorite way.)
*May be made a day ahead if desired. Be sure to unmold, then return to aluminum mold to store. To reheat, place in oven for ½ hour with some chicken stock poured over it.*

# PASSOVER VEGETABLE KUGELS *Heidi Rosenberg* ◆P

KP

½ cup green pepper,
  chopped
2 cups onion, chopped
1 cup carrots, grated
1½ tsps. margarine
2 packages spinach,
  chopped and cooked
6 eggs, well-beaten
½ tsp. pepper
3 tsps. seasoning salt
1½ cups matzah meal

1. Sauté green pepper, onion, and carrots in margarine for about 10 minutes. Add spinach, eggs, salt, pepper, and matzah meal.
2. Spoon into greased muffin tins until half-full.
3. Bake in 350 degree oven for 45 minutes or until firm. Allow to cool before removing from tins.

*Use pretty platter, and put some vegetables in the middle, surrounded by kugels.*
*This can be made the day before, and baked on the day it is to be served.*

# VEGETABLE LOAF *Helene Blivaiss* ◆P

KP

6 Tbsps. margarine
1 cup onion, chopped
½ cup celery, chopped
¼ cup mushrooms, chopped
1½ cups carrots, grated
¾ cup matzah meal
1 package frozen spinach,
  chopped, drained
3 eggs, beaten
Salt and pepper

1. Sauté onion, celery, and mushrooms in margarine for about 10 minutes.
2. Add carrots, matzah meal, spinach, and eggs and blend. Season with salt and pepper.
3. Place in greased loaf pan.
4. Bake in 350 degree oven for 45 minutes. Let cool for 15 minutes.

*Easy and tasty!*

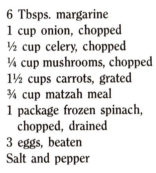

##  CARROT TIMBALES  *Joan Silins*

KP

3 cups carrots, grated
¾ cup matzah meal
2 eggs, slightly beaten
¼ cup onion, minced
1 tsp. salt
2 tsps. chicken fat or
   margarine, melted
2 cans condensed chicken
   soup, undiluted
2 tsps. parlsey, minced

1. Combine carrots, matzah meal, eggs, onion, salt, melted chicken fat or margarine, chicken soup, and parsley. Mix well.
2. Fill greased muffin tin or custard cups ⅔ full.
3. Bake in 325 degree oven 45 minutes or until firm.

Makes 6 servings. For 12 servings, double all ingredients except fat and soup.
*Delicious accompaniment to any meat dish!*

## PASSOVER CARROT PUDDING  *Sarita Blau*

KP

1 pound carrots, grated
½ cup matzah meal
3 Tbsps. potato starch
¼ cup sugar, mixed with
1 tsp. cinnamon and
½ tsp. ginger
¾ cup sweet red Concord
   wine
1 egg

1. Place carrots into large bowl.
2. Add matzah meal, potato starch, sugar, cinnamon, and ginger. Mix well. Add wine and mix well.
3. Add egg, beat and mix very well. If mixture is dry, add more wine.
5. Grease very well a ring mold or casserole or 9-inch round pan.
6. Pour carrot pudding into greased pan. Bake in preheated 350 degree oven for 1 hour.
7. Unmold onto plate for serving.

## CARROT, SWEET POTATO AND APPLE TZIMMES  *Arlene Levin*

KP

3 carrots, sliced
4 sweet potatoes, peeled
   and sliced
3 apples, sliced
½ cup light brown sugar
Salt and pepper
3 Tbsps. margarine
1 cup water

1. Cook carrots in a saucepan with water until tender.
2. Alternate carrots, potatoes, and apples in 2½-quart baking dish.
3. Sprinkle with brown sugar, salt, pepper, and margarine.
4. Add water.
5. Cover and bake in 350 degree oven for 30 minutes.
6. Remove cover and continue baking until top is golden brown.

344

# MATZAH KUGEL *Joan Silins*

3 matzot
6 eggs
½ cup sugar
Salt, to taste
½ tsp. cinnamon
4 apples, shredded
½ cup almonds, chopped
½ cup raisins
Peel of 1 orange, grated

Topping:
¼ cup butter or
  margarine, melted
¼ tsp. cinnamon
1 Tbsp. sugar

KP

1. Crumble matzah and soak in water. Squeeze.
2. In separate bowl, beat eggs. Add sugar, salt, and cinnamon, and beat well.
3. Add matzah, apples, almonds, raisins, and orange rind into mixture.
4. Pour into 1½-quart casserole. Combine butter or margarine, cinnamon, and sugar as topping. Drizzle onto mixture.
5. Bake in 350 degree oven 45 minutes.
Makes 8 to 10 servings.

# APPLE MATZAH KUGEL *Shirlee Kapelusz*

4 matzot
Water
3 eggs
½ tsp. salt
½ cup sugar
½ stick margarine, melted
1 tsp. cinnamon
½ cup golden raisins
2 large or 3 small apples,
  peeled, sliced, and chopped

KP

1. Break matzah into small pieces and soak in water until soft.
2. Peel and chop apples.
3. Drain excess water from matzah, leaving it soggy.
4. Beat eggs thoroughly with a fork. Add salt.
5. To the eggs, add sugar, melted margarine, and cinnamon. Mix. Add the mixture to softened matzot. Stir in raisins and apples.
6. Turn into shallow baking dish. Bake in 350 degree oven for 45 minutes or until lightly browned.
Makes 10 servings.

# APPLE KUGEL *Arlene Levin*

6 medium apples, peeled
  and cut into cubes
1 cup matzah meal
¾ cup sugar
½ tsp. cinnamon
¼ cup oil
1 cup orange juice
5 eggs

KP

1. Mix apples, matzah meal, sugar, cinnamon, oil, orange juice, and eggs.
2. Pour into 8- to 9-inch pan.
3. Bake in 350 degree oven for 1 hour.
Makes 8 servings.

## ◆ MATZAH SPINACH STUFFING *Beth Sair*

KP
7 matzot, broken into
  large pieces
1 cup orange juice
2 onions, chopped fine
2 ribs celery, chopped fine
4 sprigs parlsey, chopped
  fine
½ cup nuts, chopped fine
¼ seedless orange
2 packages frozen spinach,
  chopped
2 eggs, beaten

1. Combine matzot and orange juice in bowl.
Stir well and set aside.
2. Add onions, celery, parsley, and nuts to the
mixture.
3. Chop orange in a food processor into
chunks. Add to mixture.
4. Defrost spinach and add to eggs. Add to
matzah mixture. Stir until well combined.
Makes enough stuffing for 1 large turkey.
*Vegetables, nuts, and orange may all be cut into
chunks, then chopped coarsely in a food
processor. Festive and spring-like for the Seder.*

## ■ MATZAH MEAL STUFFING *Anonymous*

KP
2 small onions, fried
3 Tbsps. schmaltz
3 eggs, separated
¾ cup cold water
½ cup matzah meal
1 sprig parsley
1 tsp. carrot, grated
1 tsp. salt

1. Brown onions in fat (schmaltz).
2. Beat egg yolks.
3. Add water to beaten egg yolks. Add matzah
meal, parsley, carrot, onions, and salt. Fold in
beaten egg whites.
Makes enough to stuff large chicken or pocket
of breast of veal.
*Delicious—try with veal for a special treat!*

# PASSOVER ALMOND TORTE  *Eva Sideman*

8 eggs, separated
1¼ cups sugar
2 cups blanched almonds,
   finely ground, and
   slightly browned
½ cup matzah meal
2 oranges, juice and rind
   chopped in a food
   processor or grinder

1. Chop the oranges with the metal blade of a food processor, or put through a food grinder.
2. Beat the egg yolks well.
3. Add the sugar, almonds, matzah meal, and the orange juice and rind.
4. Beat egg whites until stiff. Fold into orange-nut mixture. Pour into a greased torte pan (10-inch springform works well).
4. Bake in 325 degree oven for 45 minutes.
*Moist and delicious!*

# ALMOND TORTE  *Sarita Blau*

2½ cups almonds
2 Tbsps. matzah meal
8 eggs, separated
1½ cups sugar

1. Grate almonds with nut grater.
2. Stir in matzah meal.
3. Beat egg yolks with sugar.
4. Grease two 8- or 9-inch layer cake pans (round). Flour with matzah cake meal.
5. Beat egg whites until stiff, but not dry.
6. Fold egg whites and almonds alternately into yolks – 4 portions whites to 3 portions almonds.
7. Pour batter evenly into prepared cake pans. Bake in 350 degree oven for about 30 minutes or until they test done.
Frost when cool.
*Good all year round!*

# STRAWBERRY MOUSSE  *Arlene Miller*

1 pint strawberries,
   hulled and sliced
¾ cup sugar
2 egg whites
1 Tbsp. fresh lemon juice
Salt, dash
3 Tbsps. sweet red wine
   (optional)

1. Beat egg whites and sugar until whites are stiff.
2. Add strawberries, lemon juice, and salt to egg white and sugar mixture. Continue beating.
3. Add wine.
4. With electric beaters, start at low speed and increase speed gradually to high. Mix 15 minutes until very light and fluffy.
5. Spoon into bowls. Freeze or keep refrigerated (melts rapidly) until serving.
(May be made ahead and frozen.) Garnish with whole strawberries or grated chocolate. Serve in large glass bowl or individual sherbet glasses. Makes 12 servings.
*Delicious with sponge cake!*

# ⬢ CHOCOLATE HAZELNUT TORTE *Karen Sager*

**KP**

**1st layer: Nut Torte**
1 cup ground hazelnuts
½ cup matzah cake meal
2 Tbsps. potato starch
½ tsp. cinnamon
4 eggs, separated, plus
4 egg yolks
½ cup sugar
⅓ cup sugar
1 tsp. vanilla
Salt, pinch

**2nd layer: Chocolate Mousse**
8 ounces semi-sweet
   chocolate (chips work well)
¼ cup strong coffee
4 eggs, separated
1 Tbsp. brandy
3 Tbsps. sugar

1. Preheat oven to 400 degrees. Grease 10-inch springform pan and dust with a little matzah meal.
2. Mix hazelnuts, cake meal, potato starch, and cinnamon in small bowl.
3. Beat all 8 egg yolks and ½ cup sugar with electric mixer until thick and rich. Add vanilla.
4. Beat egg whites with salt in a separate bowl with clean dry beaters; gradually beat ⅓ cup sugar until whites are stiff, but not dry.
5. Combine hazelnut mixture with yolk mixture. Add ⅓ of egg whites to hazelnut-yolk batter to lighten it; then fold batter into whites.
6. Pour into springform pan and spread evenly. Bake 20 minutes. Do not remove from pan. Allow to cool completely, then spread with chocolate mousse. (Cake will rise while baking, deflate while cooling.)
7. For Mousse layer: Melt chocolate in coffee over low heat, stir until smooth. Cool.
8. Beat egg yolks one at a time into melted chocolate. Add brandy.
9. Beat egg whites in separate bowl; gradually add 3 Tbsps. sugar and continue beating until stiff, but not dry.
10. Mix ½ egg whites into chocolate to lighten. Fold back into egg whites gently.
11. Spread mousse evenly on top of hazelnut torte layer. Refrigerate overnight.
12. Just before serving, remove sides of springform pan. Chocolate may be shaved over the top.
*Beautiful and scrumptious!*

# CHOCOLATE MOUSSE CAKE *Ruth Taxy*

**P**

KP

8 ounces bittersweet
  chocolate
1 Tbsp. instant coffee
¼ cup boiling water
8 eggs, separated
⅔ cup sugar

1. Melt chocolate in double boiler.
2. Add coffee to hot water. Mix with chocolate and then cool.
3. In separate bowl, beat egg yolks with sugar till creamy and thick. Beat chocolate into egg yolks.
4. Beat egg whites until soft peaks form. Stir ¼ of whites into chocolate mix.
5. Fold in remainder of whites.
6. Dust 8-inch springform pan with matzah meal. Pour in ½ batter and bake in 350 degree oven for 25 minutes.
7. In the meantime, refrigerate other half of batter. When baked layer is cooled, pile on refrigerated batter and refrigerate again for several hours.
*Easy, elegant, and delicious!*

# FLOURLESS CHOCOLATE CAKE *Nancy Goldstein* **P**

KP

6 ounces bittersweet
  chocolate
2 Tbsps. strong coffee
6 eggs, separated
⅔ cups sugar (plus 6
  Tbsps. for topping)
¼ tsp. salt
Raspberries or strawberries
  garnish (optional)

1. Melt chocolate in coffee. Stir until smooth. Set aside.
2. Beat egg yolks with ⅔ cup sugar until thick and fluffy.
3. Whip whites with salt until stiff peaks form.
4. Mix chocolate mixture into yolk mixture.
5. Fold chocolate and yolk mixture into egg whites.
6. Transfer ⅓ batter to small bowl and add 6 Tbsps. sugar. Refrigerate.
7. Pour remaining batter into greased 9-inch springform pan.
8. Bake in 350 degree oven 25 minutes. Turn heat off. Leave in oven 5 minutes.
9. While still hot, place on serving platter.
10. Spread chilled, uncooked batter on top of cake.
Decorate around top edges with fruit.
*Elegant all year round.*

*Although these two lovely desserts have similar ingredients, we have included both because their look and texture are different. The variety of flourless cakes should make preparing desserts during Pesach as exciting as the rest of the year.*

**349**

# PASSOVER APPLE NUT CAKE *Diane Kagan*

KP

3¼ cups sugar
4 tsps. cinnamon
Juice of 1 lemon
5 McIntosh apples, peeled,
  cored, and sliced
6 eggs
1 cup peanut oil
2 cups matzah cake meal
2 tsps. potato starch
Salt, dash
½ cup walnuts, chopped

1. Mix ¾ cup sugar, 2 tsps. cinnamon, lemon juice, and apples to make apple filling. Set aside.
2. Beat eggs with 2 cups sugar, beat in oil. Sift together cake meal, potato starch, and salt.
3. Add the dry ingredients to the egg mixture, blending well. Pour half the batter into a greased 9 x 13 inch cake pan. Spread apple mixture over batter. Top with remaining batter.
4. Mix together remaining ½ cup sugar, 2 tsps. cinnamon, and walnuts. Sprinkle over top of cake.
5. Bake in 350 degree oven for 60 to 75 minutes.

*This takes a little time, but tastes like an apple magic cake, and is worth the effort.*

# PASSOVER CHOCOLATE MOUSSE CAKE *Arlene Levin*

KP

7-ounces semi-sweet
  chocolate
½ cup margarine
7 eggs, separated, room
  temperature
1 cup sugar
1 tsp. vanilla
⅛ tsp. fresh lemon juice

1. Prepare cake the day before serving. Preheat oven to 325 degrees.
2. Melt chocolate with magarine in double boiler over barely simmering water. Stir until smooth.
3. Whisk yolks and ¾ cup sugar until pale yellow and fluffy. Gradually stir in chocolate and vanilla.
4. Beat whites with lemon juice until soft peaks form. Add remaining sugar, 1 Tbsp. at a time and continue beating until stiff, but not dry.
5. Gently fold whites into chocolate mixture.
6. Pour ¾ of batter into 9-inch springform pan.
7. Cover and refrigerate remaining batter.
8. Bake cake 35 minutes. Cool completely. (Cake will fall as it cools.) Remove springform. Trim edges with sharp knife.
9. Spread remaining batter over top of cake. Refrigerate at least 8 hours or overnight before serving.

# MARK'S "MAKES YOU FAT AND THAT'S THAT" PASSOVER CAKE *Judy Schuster*

**P**

1 1-pound box matzah
2 cups sweet wine
1½ pounds dark chocolate
1½ cups sugar
1½ sticks margarine
2 to 3 pints strawberries
1 bunch ripe bananas

1. This recipe requires a large pastry brush or a new 1½-inch paint brush, and a square cake pan, approximately 12 by 12, large enough to stack whole matzot. Grease pan with a little of the margarine.
KP

2. Soak matzot in wine approximately 3 to 5 minutes; allow matzot to soften, but not to fall apart.
3. Melt chocolate with margarine over low flame; stir in sugar. Set aside.
4. Slice berries and bananas into separate bowls.
5. "Paint" both sides of a matzah with chocolate mixture. Place in bottom of cake pan.
6. Cover with one layer of sliced bananas.
7. Paint a second matzah on both sides. Place on top of bananas.
8. Cover with one layer of sliced strawberries.
9. Continue to alternate layers in this way: chocolate coated matzah, bananas, chocolate coated matzah, berries. Finish with a chocolate matzah.
10. Pour remaining chocolate mixture over entire stack.
11. Refrigerate overnight.
Makes 24 servings.

# P PASSOVER BANANA CAKE *Eva Sideman*

**KP**

7 eggs, separated
1 cup sugar
¾ cup matzah cake flour
¼ cup potato starch
½ tsp. salt
1 cup bananas, mashed
½ cup nuts, chopped

1. Beat yolks and sugar until creamy.
2. Sift flour and potato starch. Add salt and bananas. Stir into egg yolk mixture. Add nuts.
3. Beat whites with a pinch of salt and fold into cake mixture. Pour into tube pan and bake in 325 degree oven for 40 to 45 minutes. Turn pan upside down to cool.

# MOIST AND EASY
# D PASSOVER LAYER CAKE *Arlene Levin*

**KP**

2 packages chocolate
   cake mix
1 package instant
   chocolate pudding
1 package yellow cake mix
1 cup water
4 eggs
½ cup oil
Shaved chocolate (optional)
Strawberry halves (optional)

1. Mix chocolate cake mix and pudding mix together with the water, eggs, and oil for 2 minutes.
2. Pour the batter into two 8-inch round, greased pans, and bake in 350 degree oven for 35 to 40 minutes. Cool 10 minutes in pan and then take out of pan and let cool completely on rack.
3. Bake yellow cake according to package directions, but pour batter into a greased 8-inch round pan.
4. To assemble: Place 1 chocolate layer on bottom and frost top with package frosting. Place yellow cake on top of chocolate and frost top with chocolate frosting. Place last chocolate layer on top of yellow and now frost entire cake. Can decorate with shaved chocolate or strawberry halves around top border.
Makes 10 to 14 servings.

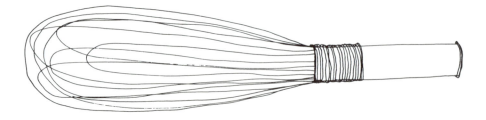

# PASSOVER APPLE CAKE  *Diana Waitzman*

4 eggs
1 cup sugar
½ cup oil
1 cup cake meal
1 tsp. potato starch
6 apples, peeled, cored
  and sliced *or*
2 cans sliced apples
2 tsps. cinnamon
⅓ cup sugar

1. Grease 11 x 9 inch glass pan.
2. Combine eggs, sugar, oil, cake meal, and potato starch.
3. Fill pan with ¾ of dough mixture. Place apples on top.
4. Cover with remaining dough.
5. Bake in 350 degree oven for 45 minutes; test and bake 10 to 15 minutes longer, if necessary.
6. Combine cinnamon and sugar. Sprinkle top with cinnamon-sugar mixture while still hot, if desired.

# APPLE CAKE FOR PESACH  *Beth Sair*

1 cup matzah meal
1 tsp. salt
5 egg whites
1 cup sugar
½ cup cooking oil
¼ cup orange juice
4 cups apples, pared and
  thinly sliced
½ tsp. cinnamon

1. Combine matzah meal and salt. Set aside.
2. Beat 3 egg whites. Set aside.
3. Beat remaining 2 egg whites with ¾ cup sugar, oil, and orange juice, stirring in matzah meal.
4. Fold in beaten egg whites.
5. Spoon half the batter into 8 x 8 x 2 inch pan.
6. Arrange apple slices over batter.
7. Combine remaining ¼ cup sugar with cinnamon, and sprinkle over apple.
8. Cover with remaining batter.
9. Bake in 375 degree oven for 30 to 35 minutes.

# FRUIT NUT MUFFINS  *Sheila Meyer*

3 eggs, beaten
1 cup raisins
1½ cups pecans or
  walnuts, chopped
8 ounces dates, chopped

1. Mix eggs, raisins, nuts, and dates together.
2. Spoon into greased muffin tins.
3. Bake in 325 degree oven 20 to 25 minutes.
4. Put in paper muffin tins after cooling.
*This is a good no-sugar snack all year long. Various dried fruits, nuts, carob or chocolate chips may be substituted or added to this recipe.*

# ◆ "CARMEL" CUSTARD *The King David, Jerusalem*

**KP**

For caramelized sugar:
1 cup sugar
3 Tbsps. water

For custard:
4 cups non-dairy cream
1 cup water
1 cup plus 1 Tbsp. sugar
12 eggs
6 egg yolks

*Individual, oven-proof
   custard cups are required.\**

1. Caramelize sugar by melting 1 cup sugar with 3 Tbsps. water in a small saucepan. Begin with a fairly high flame, stirring constantly to prevent burning. When sugar has dissolved, reduce heat to low. Continue to stir constantly over low flame until sugar turns a light brown color. Cool slightly. Pour enough into each custard cup to coat the bottom.

2. For custard: In a different saucepan, cook non-dairy cream, water, and sugar over medium-low flame. Stir to blend flavors, but do not boil. Remove from heat.

3. In a large bowl, beat whole eggs and egg yolks together with electric mixer or wire whisk.

4. Add to saucepan batter and return to medium-low heat. Stir until mixture becomes thick and rich enough to coat spoon, but do not boil.

5. Fill custard cups. Place cups in a large pan; add water to pan ¾ of the way up the sides of the cups.

6. Bake in preheated 350 degree oven for approximately 1 hour, or until the custard is solid.

7. Cool in refrigerator at least 1 hour, until cool and firm. To serve, cut around edge of custard with a knife and turn upside down on a plate. The caramel sugar will be runny, like a sauce.

*\*Makes 15 servings, using 5-ounce cups; makes 24 servings, using 3-ounce cups.*

*Custards may be stored in their cups for up to one week in the refrigerator. This custard is so rich and delicious, it is difficult to believe it is both pareve and kosher for Pesach!*

*This outstanding recipe was generously donated by Peter Gerstmann, the Executive Pastry Chef of the King David Hotel. Jackie Siegel has successfully adapted it to suit American kosher products and measurements. A half-recipe works equally well. B'tayavon!*

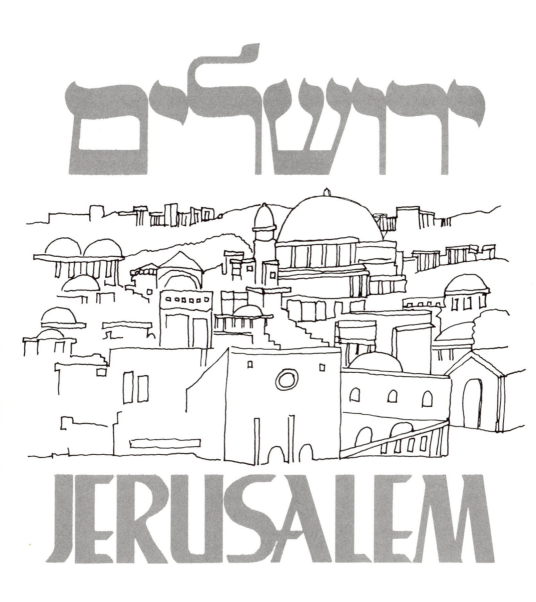

ירושלים

JERUSALEM

## ◆ᴾ MERINGUE MAGIC  *Karen Sager*

KP
4 egg whites
  (extra large eggs)
2 cups sugar
Salt, pinch
1 cup chocolate chips
Margarine to grease pans
Walnuts, chopped
  (optional variation)

1. Using electric mixer, begin beating egg whites on low speed. Increase to medium speed and add ¼ cup sugar. Increase to high speed and continue adding sugar, gradually, ¼ cup at a time. Add salt. Beat until stiff, but not dry.
2. Fold in chocolate chips (or chopped walnuts).
3. Drop by tablespoonfuls onto well greased cookie sheets. Leave space between cookies for spreading.
4. Place in oven. Bake 10 minutes at 275 degrees. Turn down to 225 degrees. Bake 15 to 20 minutes. Watch to make sure they don't brown. The whiter the meringue, the better. Turn oven off, and allow meringues to continue to bake approximately 30 minutes longer.
5. Remove from oven; allow to cool 5 minutes. Carefully remove from sheet with spatula.
*Watch them vanish before your very eyes!*

## ◆ᴾ TOFFEE SQUARES  *Fran Fogel*

KP
2 sticks margarine,
  softened
1 cup sugar
1 jumbo egg
1 Tbsp. vanilla
1 cup matzah cake meal
8 ounces dark chocolate
  candy bars

1. Cream butter and sugar together.
2. Add egg and vanilla, then matzah cake meal.
3. Spread into heavily greased jelly roll pan.
4. Bake in 350 degree oven for 20 minutes.
5. Melt candy bars in microwave or on top of double boiler.
6. Spread evenly and gently over base. Refrigerate for 1 hour to harden, then cut into desired shapes.
*Kids love these!*

# PASSOVER NUT COOKIES   Eva Sideman

P

1½ pounds nuts, ground
2 cups sugar
5 egg whites
Juice from 1 lemon

KP

1. Beat egg whites. Fold in sugar, nuts, and lemon juice.
2. Drop onto a greased pan and bake in 350 degree oven for 15 minutes.

# PESACH MANDEL BROT   Bonny Barezky

P

6 eggs
1½ cups sugar
1½ cups oil
1 cup nuts, chopped
1 cup matzah meal
1 cup cake flour
1 Tbsp. potato flour
1 Tbsp. cinnamon

KP

1. Place eggs, sugar, oil, nuts, matzah meal, flours, and cinnamon in food processor.
2. Shape into rolls and place on waxed paper.
3. Refrigerate overnight.
4. Bake on a greased cookie sheet in 350 degree oven for 30 minutes.
5. Cut into ½-inch slices.
*You may toast if you like.*

# HAZELNUT MACAROONS   Sarita Blau

P

1 cup hazelnuts
1 cup sugar
3 egg whites

KP

1. Grate nuts with a nut grater.
2. Mix egg whites with sugar. Stir in grated nuts.
3. Heavily grease 2 cookie sheets. Preheat oven to 325 degrees.
4. Drop cookie dough by teaspoonfuls onto cookie sheets. Leave 1 to 2 inches between cookies for spreading.
5. Bake in 325 degree oven 20 to 25 minutes until lightly browned. Remove immediately from sheets.
6. Cool on rack or piece of waxed paper.
*Note: The nuts must be grated and fluffy to absorb the egg white mixture properly.*
*This recipe can be divided in thirds.*

Parsley

#  PASSOVER BROWNIES *Arlene Levin*

KP

6 ounces semi-sweet
  chocolate chips
1½ cups margarine
6 eggs
3 cups sugar
3 tsps. vanilla
¾ tsp. salt
1½ cups cake meal

1. Melt chocolate and margarine and allow to cool.
2. Beat eggs, sugar, and vanilla together.
3. Blend in salt, chocolate, and margarine. Gradually stir in cake meal.
4. Turn in well greased 9 x 13 inch pan.
5. Bake in 325 degree oven for 30 to 35 minutes.

# PASSOVER MANDEL BROT *Sarita Blau*

KP

1 cup margarine or butter
2 cups sugar
6 eggs
2¾ cups matzah cake meal
½ tsp. salt
¾ cup potato starch
1 cup nuts, chopped
2 3-ounce bars bittersweet
  chocolate, cut into
  small pieces

Topping:
2 tsps. sugar
1 tsp. cinnamon

1. Cream sugar and margarine
2. Add eggs, one at a time, beating after each.
3. Sift cake meal, salt, and potato starch together. Fold into egg mixture. Add chocolate and nuts.
4. Grease cookie sheet well. Preheat oven to 350 degrees.
5. Form dough into loaves 2 inches wide on cookie sheet. Sprinkle with cinnamon and sugar mixed together.
6. Bake for 45 minutes or until well browned. Slice while warm. Do not toast.

# PASSOVER "POPCORN" *Ricki Elbaum*

KP

4 cups matzah farfel
1 cup chopped nuts
⅓ cup oil
Cinnamon
⅓ cup honey
1 cup raisins

1. Mix all ingredients, except raisins, and spread on cookie sheet.
2. Bake in a 350 degree oven for 30 minutes. Cool thoroughly.
3. When cool, mix in the raisins. Enjoy!

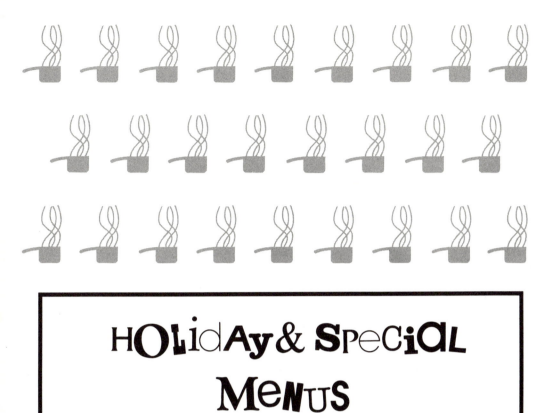

# HOLidAy & SpeCiAL MeNuS

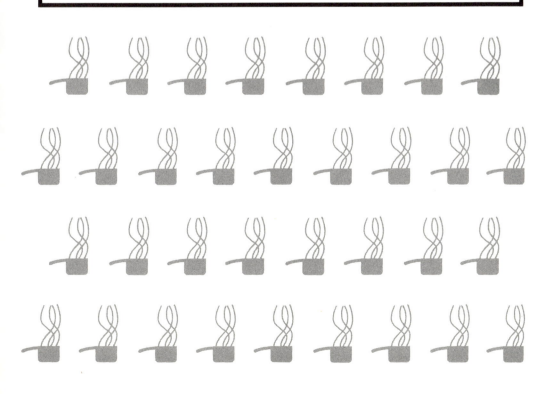

# SHABBAT (THE SABBATH)

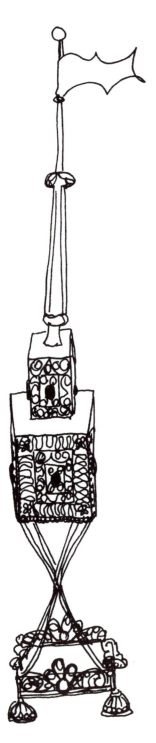

Special meals and Jewish holidays are inseparable. The most important holy day in the Jewish calendar, *Shabbat*, occurs every week, and the Torah commands its observance. The Talmud states that a person who eats three meals on *Shabbat* will be rewarded in the world to come. Traditionally, these three meals are Friday night dinner, lunch following synagogue services on Saturday, and *Seudah Shlisheet* (meaning "third meal") which occurs late Saturday afternoon. Because the kindling of fire and cooking are among the kinds of work forbidden on *Shabbat*, the preparation of all three meals takes place largely on Friday before sundown.

Two important *mitzvot* (commandments) reserved for women relate to *Shabbat*: the lighting of the *Shabbat* candles, which herald the start of the holy day, and the separation of *challah* (portion of bread reserved for an offering in Temple times). The special loaves of holiday bread take their name from this *mitzvah*. Before braiding the loaves, a Jewish woman separates a small piece of dough while reciting a blessing. This small piece is allowed to bake with the loaves, and usually burns, thus representing the offering. Two loaves of challah are served at each *Shabbat* meal, as well as at *Yamim Tovim* (holidays) and *s'machot* (special joyous occasions).

Traditional *Shabbat* foods also include fish, particularly gefilte fish, chicken, or meat, and among Askenazi Jews, chicken soup. Because of the prohibition against kindling fire, Jews everywhere have devised variations of a dish called "Cholent" for the second *Shabbat* meal. This is a hearty stew which is prepared and begins cooking on Friday, but is allowed to continue cooking on a low heat overnight, until it is served for Saturday lunch.

For obvious reasons, *Seudah Shlisheet* is usually a light (often dairy) meal! *Shabbat* ends with the *Havdalah* service which includes kindling a special candle, reciting a blessing over wine, and smelling spices, often passed in a beautiful box like the one pictured here.

# SHABBAT DINNER MENU I ◼M

HERRING SALAD, p. 16, with Crackers
SWEET LITTLE HOT DOGS, p. 284
CHALLAH, pp. 46-47, p. 280
CHICKEN SOUP WITH MATZAH BALLS, p. 61
FRIDAY NIGHT BRISKET, p. 135
KASHA VARNISHKES, p. 173
TOMATOES VINAIGRETTE, p. 77
MONKEY-IN-THE-MIDDLE SALAD, p. 86
GREEN BEANS WITH CELERY, p. 204
MARBLE CHIFFON CAKE, p. 222

# SHABBAT DINNER MENU II ◼M

CURRY DIP, p. 13, with Fresh Vegetables
CHALLAH, pp. 46-47, p. 280
GEFILTE FISH, pp. 21-23
SWEET AND SOUR CABBAGE BORSCHT, p. 62
POULTRY WITH FRESH FRUIT, p. 97, *or*
GLAZED ROASTED CHICKEN, p. 98
FABULOUS RICE, p. 176
BAKED CARROT MOLD, p. 206, *or*
BUBBY YETTA'S APPLE KUGEL, p. 316
BANANA SPLIT TOFUTTI, p. 217
MANDEL BROT, pp. 264-267

# VEGETARIAN SHABBAT DINNER MENU ◆P

HOT OR COLD CABBAGE BORSCHT, p. 63
TIBETAN ROAST, p. 159, with
MUSHROOM & WINE SAUCE, p. 159
ETHIOPIAN VEGETABLE STEW, p. 158
GAZPACHO MOLD, p. 89
SPINACH NOODLE KUGEL, p. 179
Fresh Fruit Platter
CHOCOLATE ANGEL PIE, p. 215
RASPBERRY CAKE, p. 243

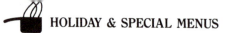 

# **M** SHABBAT LUNCHEON MENU

CHALLAH, pp. 46-47, p. 280
GEFILTE FISH, pp. 21-23
CHOLENT, see recipe below
SEVEN LAYER SALAD, *pareve*, p. 85
CURRIED FRUIT, p. 317
STOVE-TOP BROWNIES, p. 269, *or*
EGG YOLK COOKIES, p. 252

# **D** SEUDAH SHLISHEET (Third Meal)

CHALLAH, pp. 46-47, p. 280
ABBIE'S AUNT BERT'S FAMOUS EGGPLANT RELISH, p. 323
LAYERED SALMON SALAD, p. 74
TUNA MOUSSE, p. 18
EGG SALAD MOLD, (appetizers) p. 20
Fresh Fruit
SUGAR COOKIES, p. 258

# **M** CHOLENT *Gary Siegel*

2 to 3 pounds beef short ribs, trimmed & cut into chunks
1 Tbsp. salt
1 pound dried beans; choose from: lima, pinto, navy, great northern & kidney
4 to 6 cloves garlic, diced
1 spanish onion, diced
½ tsp. pepper
⅛ tsp. chili powder
⅛ tsp. paprika
⅛ tsp. ground cumin
1 Tbsp. olive oil
3 Tbsps. ketchup
4 to 5 potatoes, quartered

1. Place the short ribs and salt into a large stock pot, with 4 quarts of water.
2. Bring to a boil, reduce heat, and cook about 15 minutes. Skim off the fat or scum.
3. Add the beans, garlic, onions, pepper, chili powder, paprika, ground cumin, olive oil, and ketchup. Cook uncovered for 1 hour.
4. Add potatoes and cook another 1 to 1½ hours.
5. Cover and place in 180 degree oven overnight. *Cholent is traditionally served after synagogue for a delicious second Shabbat meal.*

While on *Shabbat* all manner of work is forbidden, on the Festivals work pertaining to food preparation is permitted, with some restrictions. Only cooking of food to be consumed on that day is permitted. When *Shabbat* occurs on the second day of a two-day holiday, or immediately following *Yom Tov*, food may be cooked on *Yom Tov* for *Shabbat*, provided an *Eruv Tavshilin* is prepared. An *Eruv Tavshilin* is a dish prepared before Yom Tov and set aside for *Shabbat*; a special blessing is recited over the *Eruv Tavshilin* before it is set aside.

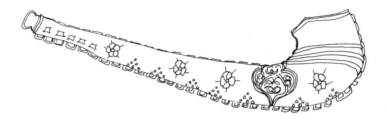

# ROSH HASHANAH

*Rosh Hashanah*, literally "Head of the Year," celebrates not only the beginning of the New Year but also the creation of the world. Most widely known as the holiday on which the Shofar is sounded as a call to repentance, Rosh Hashanah has many interesting food traditions of surprising universality. Honey and fruit symbolize a sweet, fertile, and abundant year. Challah is baked with raisins in special round or bird shapes. Challah and apples are dipped in honey at the beginning of the meal, and a blessing is recited. The head ("Rosh") of a fish or, among Sephardim, an animal, is served in various forms. On the second day, a new fruit of the season is eaten before the *Shehechianu* blessing is recited.

"Gefilte" fish, literally "stuffed" fish, is so called because it used to be stuffed back into the fish skin before cooking. On Rosh Hashanah, it was stuffed into the heads of the fish. Among American Jews today, gefilte fish balls, herring, or sweet pickled fish are more common remnants of the custom. Tzimmes, carrots, sweet fruited dishes, and honey cakes abound. A special confection, *"Teiglach,"* is boiled in a honey syrup, which is then stored and used for dipping and cooking. Bitter or sour foods and nuts are usually avoided.

We are fortunate to have an authentic and outstanding TEIGLACH recipe (p. 364). We offer an original suggestion in our menu for the second day: serve the FRUIT "FISH" to satisfy both the tradition of the fish's head and the new fruit!

## ROSH HASHANAH MENU I (First Day)　Ⓜ

ROUND RAISIN CHALLAH, p. 47
Apple Slices with TEIGLACH HONEY, pp. 364-5, for Dipping
GEFILTE FISH, pp. 21-23
CHICKEN SOUP WITH DILL AND LEEK, p. 60
STUFFED TURKEY BREAST WITH DRIED MUSHROOM SAUCE, p. 115, *or*
ROAST DUCK À L'ORANGE, p. 95
RICE SUPREME, p. 178, with
HONEY-THYME CARROTS, p. 207, in the center
FRUIT COMPOTE, p. 318
TEIGLACH, p. 364
HONEY CAKE, p. 229
CHOCOLATE CHIP DATE CAKE, p. 224

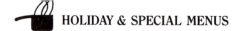 

# Ⓜ ROSH HASHANAH MENU II (Second Day)

ROUND RAISIN CHALLAH, p. 47
Apple slices with TEIGLACH HONEY, pp. 364-5
CHOPPED ("GEHAGDE") HERRING in holiday shape, p. 16
SPINACH FRUIT SALAD, p. 77, (walnuts may be omitted)
TZIMMES WITH KNAIDLACH, p. 134
FRUIT "FISH," p. 69, with
POPPY SEED DRESSING, p. 92
TEIGLACH, p. 364
LUSCIOUS APPLE CAKE, p. 235
CHERRY TORTE, p. 238

# Ⓟ AUTHENTIC TEIGLACH  *Becky Dolin*

3 jumbo eggs, slightly
  beaten in a bowl
2 cups flour, sift before
  measuring
¼ tsp. salt
½ tsp. ground ginger
1 15-ounce box dark
  raisins

Honey syrup:
1 cup honey (1 pound)
1 cup sugar
1 tsp. ground ginger
Heavy 4-quart pot

1. Sift together twice flour, salt, and ginger.
2. Sift ⅓ of the flour very slowly into the eggs, stirring while you sift.
3. Continue sifting all the flour into the eggs, until the dough falls very slowly off the lifted spoon.
4. Lightly flour a work board and a cookie sheet with sifted flour.
5. Pour a small portion of the batter onto the board. Sift some flour over it, and *lightly* knead the dough with one or two dinner knives until it is the consistency of a very light pastry dough. (Flour your hands frequently.)
6. Place a handful of raisins on this dough and lightly knead to incorporate raisins.
7. Divide dough in half. Roll each half into a 12-inch rope approximately ½-inch in diameter. Slice each roll into ½-inch pieces.
8. Flour hands well; roll each piece into a ball. Check to be sure there is at least one raisin in each ball. Add more dough or raisins to the balls to create uniformity. Do not close the balls up perfectly; this will allow honey to seep into the cracks while the balls are cooking!
9. Place formed balls on floured cookie cheet. Continue to repeat mixing and kneading process as quickly as possible with the remaining dough. To avoid tough teiglach, clean hands and scrape work surface between batches; handle dough as little as possible.

Rosh HaShana

Honey

10. Boil 1 to 2 cups water and set aside.

11. In a heavy 4-quart pot, place honey, sugar, and ginger. Cook on high, stirring with a wooden spoon, until it comes to a rolling, foaming boil. (Electric ranges require use of the special wire between the pot and burner to prevent burning.)

12. Drop the balls of dough one at a time into the boiling syrup. (Try to arrange the teiglach evenly spaced in circles in the pot.) Beware of spattering! Return to the boiling point, until honey covers teiglach. Teiglach will puff up. Cover pot, and *reduce heat to medium.*

13. Do not lift lid for 25 minutes. Then, check for light brown color, and stir gently with wooden spoon.

14. Remove pot from heat. Carefully add ½ cup cooled boiled water. Stir every few minutes for 15 minutes to prevent teiglach from sticking together.

15. Strain teiglach into a bowl. Remove, and save all the extra honey to prevent teiglach from becoming soggy. Store teiglach and honey in separate containers.

Makes approximately 90 teiglach.

*Teiglach should have a "cakey-cookie" texture when cut in half. Teiglach honey keeps for years and may be used in any recipe. It is especially good in honey cake, tzimmes, and for dipping apples on Rosh Hashanah.*

*Teiglach was my mother-in-law Rivy's specialty. She learned this recipe from her Russian mother-in-law. Making teiglach is a 3-hour production; however, the results are easy and sweet to eat! Which is why Teiglach is considered a gift of love and is traditionally served at* Brit Milot *and* Bar *and* Bat Mitzvot, *as well as at Rosh Hashanah.*

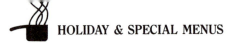
# YOM KIPPUR

*Yom Kippur,* the Day of Atonement, is a solemn day of fasting and repentance, the holiest day of the Jewish calendar. It is preceded by a simple dinner, and followed by an elaborate dairy meal to "break" the fast. Kreplach and chicken are the traditional foods *Erev* (the evening of) Yom Kippur. Cheese, fish, and egg dishes, and sweet yeast pastries are traditional for Yom Kippur Break-the-Fast.

KALETZIN is an unusual Ashkenazi recipe (see opposite page) for a pre-baked, individual, cheese-filled pastry, prepared specifically to be reheated and eaten to break the Yom Kippur fast.

## Ⓜ EREV YOM KIPPUR MENU

CHALLAH, pp. 46-47, or p. 280
CHICKEN SOUP, p. 61, with
GRANDMA IDA'S KREPLACH, p. 378
HONEY CHICKEN, p. 113
CINNAMON NOODLE KUGEL, p. 180
ZUCCHINI CARROT PUDDING, p. 201
SPONGE CAKE, p. 228

## Ⓓ YOM KIPPUR BREAK-THE-FAST BUFFET

KALETZIN, p. 367
SONIA'S HERRING SALAD, p. 16
BORSCHT MOLD, p. 89
BLINTZ CASSEROLE, p. 169
APRICOT CUSTARD KUGEL, p. 183
Bagels & Lox
CREAM CHEESE, p. 309
COTTAGE CHEESE, p. 309
YOGURT, p. 306
CINNAMON COFFEECAKE BRAID, p. 41
CHEESECAKE EL MOLINO, p. 219
MANDEL BROT, pp. 264-267
GRANDMA'S "AIR" KICHELS, p. 267

# KALETZIN *Becky Dolin*

**D**

**Dough:**

1 package dry yeast,
    dissolved in 1 tsp. sugar
    and ½ cup warm water
4 cups flour, sifted
2 tsps. salt
1 cup sugar
1 egg, beaten
½ cup milk, mixed with
½ cup warm water
Extra flour, sifted

**Filling:**

1½ to 2 pounds cottage
    cheese
1½ to 2 sticks butter,
    unsalted

1. Preheat oven to 400 degrees. Butter 2 jelly-roll pans.
2. Put the flour in a bowl. Make a well in center. Pour yeast mixture into well. With your hands, lightly bury the yeast by slowly pushing the flour off the sides of the bowl towards the center. Allow to stand 10 minutes until cracks begin to appear on the yeast.
3. Sprinkle the salt and sugar around the sides of the bowl. Add the egg and the milk/water mixture. Stir with a spoon until all ingredients are absorbed. Dough will be loose.
4. Dust top of dough with a little sifted flour. Cover bowl with towel. Let rise 20 minutes.
5. With floured hands, knead the dough in the bowl. Let rise for another 20 minutes. (Dough may be refrigerated overnight at this point.)
6. Pour dough out onto a floured board. (Dough will be soft and pour easily.) Knead dough, working easily.
7. Cut off a piece of dough and flatten it into a circle 2-inches in diameter and ¼-inch thick. Fill with cottage cheese and 4 or 5 dots of butter. Cover with another circle of dough. Seal by pinching edges. Prick top with a fork, and place on floured jellyroll pan.
8. Continue shaping and filling the same way. Allow plenty of room for expansion between Kaletzin—no more than 6 to a pan.
9. Top each Kaletzin with a slice of butter. Bake 20 to 25 minutes until golden brown. Serve hot. Makes 12 Kaletzin.

*Freezes well either fully or partially baked. To freeze, cool on wire rack, wrap individually in foil, and store in plastic bags in freezer. To reheat, open top of foil, add a pat of butter, and place in 400 degree oven for 20 minutes. My mother-in-law, Rivy Dolin, taught me this recipe, which she learned from her Russian mother-in-law. Kaletzin are traditionally made only once a year—to break the Yom Kippur fast. The house smells sweet as the Kaletzin bake!*

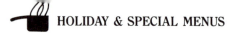

# SUKKOT

The wonderful week-long festival of *Sukkot* has been known by three different names and comprises elements of all three: Festival of In-gathering or Harvest, Season of Rejoicing, and Feast of Tabernacles. As soon as *Yom Kippur* ends, a Jewish family begins building the *sukkah*, a temporary booth with a roof made of *schach* (branches) and open to the stars. The *sukkot* (booths) symbolize both the temporary structures used at harvest time and the temporary dwellings of the Israelites during their forty-year wandering in the wilderness. *Sukkot* are decorated with every kind of seasonal fruit and vegetable, as well as home-made decorations children especially like to display.

Jews fulfill the commandment to dwell in the *sukkah* by eating there during the holiday. It is traditional to serve dishes made from seasonal fruits and vegetables to family and guests.

The *Etrog* (a citron) and the *Lulav* (branches of willow, palm, and myrtle tied together in a special way), represent four kinds of species, and are waved when special prayers are recited throughout the week in the synagogue and *sukkah*. It is customary to make ETROG JAM (p. 370) after the holiday, and to eat KREPLACH (p. 378) on *Hoshanah Rabbah*, the seventh and last day of Sukkot.

The *sukkah* remains standing during *Shemini Atzeret* and *Simchas Torah*, two holidays which immediately follow Sukkot, but no one is required to dwell in it. *Simchas Torah*, literally "rejoicing" in the Torah, is a joyous day of singing and dancing in the synagogue as the yearly reading of the Torah is concluded and begun anew. It is customary to give children apples, raisins, and nuts on *Simchas Torah*.

# SUKKOT DINNER MENU I

**M**

EGGPLANT CAVIAR, p. 14
CHALLAH, pp. 46-47, p. 280
STEW-IN-A-PUMPKIN, p. 371
SPINACH SALAD, p. 76
CHOCOLATE NUT ZUCCHINI CAKE, p. 225

# SUKKOT DINNER MENU II

**M**

CHALLAH, pp. 46-47, p. 280
ISRAELI ARTICHOKE SALAD, p. 78
PUMPKIN MUFFINS, p. 52, with
APPLE CHUTNEY, p. 317
GRANDMA GUSSIE'S STUFFED CABBAGE (as main course), p. 29
FANNY'S POTATO KNISHES, p. 372
DAVIDA'S ZUCCHINI, p. 201
CRANBERRY APPLE CRISP, p. 245, *or*
WALNUT & APPLE PIE, p. 244

# SUKKOT "OPEN HOUSE" DESSERT BUFFET

**D**

PARTY PUNCH (FOR LITTLE OR BIG PEOPLE), p. 35
Coffee
Apple Cider

ZUCCHINI BREAD, p. 44
SQUASH MUFFINS, p. 50

PRAELINE CHEESECAKE, p. 219
RASPBERRY CHOCOLATE TART, p. 242
APPLE CREAM TORTE, p. 238
FESTIVE CARROT CAKE, p. 231

CINNAMON TWISTS, p. 41
BOURBON RUM BALLS, p. 255
SPRITZ COOKIES, p. 252
RUTH'S BROWNIES, p. 269
POTATO CHIP BUTTER COOKIES, p. 253
CHEESE TARTS, p. 254
"MRS. FIELD'S" COOKIES, p. 249

FRUIT ROLLS, p. 289
GRANOLA, p. 290

Seasonal Fresh Fruit and Nuts

# ◆ ETROG JAM *Irene Sufrin*

1 etrog, very firm
2 lemons, very firm
1 cup preserving sugar*
Water

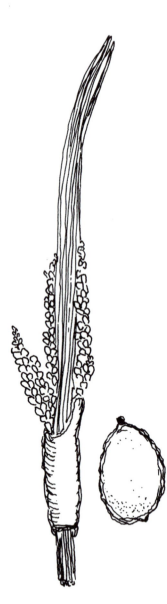

1. Slice the fruit into thin cross sections, removing pits and white membrane as much as possible.

2. Place cut fruit into bowl of tepid water for three days, changing water daily, to remove bitterness. Taste the water on the third day; if it is not acidic, the fruit is ready.

3. Dry the fruit with a paper towel, since water will retard the set of the jam.

4. Place the sugar in a pot, add enough water to cover it, and cook over a low heat. Be careful not to burn the sugar.

5. Add the softened lemon slices and several tsps. of water.

6. When the sugar is syrupy, add the etrog. Continue cooking until etrog gets glossy.

7. Test the jam for a set with a candy thermometer. It should be at 220 degrees. If it is not ready, cook for a few more minutes, then retest.

8. Let the jam cool. Then place jam in sterilized jar.

*If preserving sugar is difficult to find, substitute granulated sugar. Grease the pot and keep the heat very low to prevent burning. Or heat the sugar in a baking pan in a 150 degree oven, stirring through every so often to break up any crustiness that forms on top. Proceed with remainder of recipe.*

# STEW-IN-A-PUMPKIN *Myra Dorf*

1 pumpkin, medium-sized
2½ pounds stew meat
   (Scotch tender roast)
⅓ cup flour
1 tsp. seasoned salt
¼ tsp. pepper
¼ cup oil
1 large onion, sliced
3 packets "Washington Rich
   Brown" seasoning,
   dissolved in 1½ cups
   hot water
2 cloves garlic, minced
2 bay leaves
1 tsp. thyme
½ tsp. paprika
1 Tbsp. Worcestershire
1 tsp. "Kitchen Bouquet"
2 tomatoes, quartered
½ green pepper, chopped
½ cup red wine
1 cup dried apricots
⅓ cup red wine
6 carrots, quartered
3 white potatoes, quartered
3 sweet potatoes, quartered
¼ cup parsley, chopped
10 ounces frozen corn
1 Tbsp. cornstarch,
   dissolved in 3 Tbsps.
   water
Salt & pepper, to taste

1. Combine flour, seasoned salt, and pepper. Coat meat in this seasoned flour.
2. Heat oil in large Dutch oven or soup pot. Brown meat and onions in oil.
3. Add "Washington Rich Brown" seasoning dissolved in water to pot. Bring to boil, and immediately reduce heat to simmer.
4. Add garlic, bay leaves, thyme, paprika, Worcestershire, "Kitchen Bouquet," tomatoes, green pepper, and ½ cup wine. Simmer for 2 hours.
5. While stew simmers, soak apricots in ⅓ cup wine. Open pumpkin at top by cutting circle around stem to make a lid. Clean out pulp and seeds.
6. After about 2 hours cooking time, add carrots, white potatoes, sweet potatoes, parsley, apricots, and wine. Simmer 1 more hour.
7. Add dissolved cornstarch and frozen corn. Simmer 10 minutes.
8. Transfer stew to pumpkin. Bake in 350 degree oven for 45 minutes, or until pumpkin is almost soft.

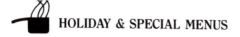 

# FANNY'S POTATO KNISHES *Sharon Dorfman*

**Dough:**
2 cups flour
1 egg
2 tsps. sugar
2 Tbsps. margarine
½ cup warm water
3 tsps. oil
½ tsp. salt

**Filling:**
3 potatoes, peeled
1 large onion, chopped
¼ to ½ cup margarine
Salt & pepper, to taste

1. Blend together all dough ingredients in a wooden bowl or in a food processor.
2. Roll out onto large pastry cloth or floured board. Stretch dough to make it very thin. It will be the consistency of a strudel dough.
3. Cut into circles 2 to 3 inches in diameter.
4. For the filling: Boil and mash the potatoes.
5. Sauté onions in margarine.
6. Add mashed potatoes to onions in frying pan. Add salt and pepper. Blend well with a fork.
7. Place 1 Tbsp. of filling in the center of each circle of dough. Fold over, and pinch the edges together.
8. Bake in a preheated oven at 375 degrees for about 15 minutes until golden.

*My mother-in-law, who came from Poland, made knishes for Shabbat and Rosh Hashanah, sometimes with a meat filling; however, with potato or cabbage filling, they were more traditionally served for Sukkot. By stretching the dough out very thin, she would transform the recipe into strudel dough, which she filled with apples or raisins, cinnamon and sugar, and rolled up jelly-roll style.*

# CARAMEL APPLES FOR SIMCHAT TORAH *Joey & Nathaniel Sager*

1 package caramel candies
1 tsp. to 1 Tbsp. milk
12 apples
12 sticks
Chopped nuts, optional

1. Put water in bottom of double boiler over high heat.
2. Unwrap all the caramels and place them in the top of the double boiler.
3. Heat caramels over boiling or simmering water until they melt. Stir occasionally with a wooden spoon.
4. Add a little milk, if necessary, to make a smooth consistency.
5. Insert a stick into the bottom of each apple.
6. Put out a large piece of waxed paper on a tray. Spread nuts on paper, if desired.
7. Dip and turn the apple in the caramel.
8. Turn the caramel apple in the nuts, if desired. Place on waxed paper to cool and harden.

*We serve caramel apples in the sukkah, too!*

# CHANUKAH

The eight day festival of *Chanukah* commemorates the rededication of the Temple in Jerusalem in the 2nd Century B.C.E. following the victory of the sons of Mattityahu the Hasmonean, led by Judah Maccabee, over the Syrian tyrant, Antiochus IV. Central to the holiday observance is the miracle of the pure oil used to rekindle the holy lamp of the Temple. Although only a single day's supply could be found, the lamp burned for eight days until a larger supply of pure oil could be obtained. Each night of Chanukah, an additional light is kindled in the traditional *Chanukiah*, an eight-branched candelabrum or oil lamp with a movable *shamash*, or ninth light,

from which the others are kindled.

It is traditional to eat foods fried in oil throughout the festival of Chanukah. Potato *latkes* (pancakes) are the prevailing custom among Ashkenazi Jews; *sufganiyot* (doughnuts, often filled with jelly) are the Sephardi custom. In addition, an apocryphal story of Judith associated with the holiday has given rise to a tradition of dairy meals.

Because Antiochus was determined to assimilate (rather than exterminate) the Jewish people, Chanukah is celebrated with an emphasis on children and the commandment to teach them Judaism. It is a wonderful time for including kids in the kitchen!

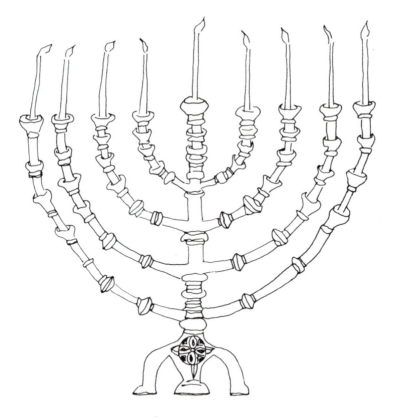

**(D) CHANUKAH DINNER MENU I**

MEDITERRANEAN PLATTER, p. 162
POTATO LATKES, p. 210, with Sour Cream
EASY APPLESAUCE, p. 316
MOGEN DAVIDS, p. 259
HOLIDAY COOKIES, p. 258

**(D) CHANUKAH DINNER MENU II**

SALMON PATTIES, p. 144
LAZY KUGEL, p. 184
Tossed Salad with GREEN GODDESS SALAD DRESSING, p. 92
SUFGANIYOT, p. 257
BOW-TIES, p. 298

# TU B'SHEVAT

*Tu B'Shevat,* the fifteenth day of the month of *Shevat* in the Hebrew calendar, is the New Year of the Trees *(Rosh Hashanah Le'Ilanot).* Although it is the middle of winter for most American Jews, it is earliest spring in Israel, when the sap begins to flow in the trees. It is a time of planting trees in Israel, and a time for remembering and respecting nature and the environment everywhere. Jews traditionally eat a wide variety of fruits, including at least one new fruit of the season. Dried fruits have always been popular in the Diaspora because of the winter season, and some observe the custom of eating 15 different varieties of fruits, symbolic of 15 *Shevat.* Among some Sephardi Jews, the holiday has been called "Feast of Fruits," and 30 to 50 varieties may be served.

## TU B'SHEVAT MENU

**M**

COLD MELON "PUNCH" SOUP, p. 65
ZUCCHINI FRUIT BREAD, p. 43, *or*
BEST GUESS BANANA BREAD, p. 40
CHICKEN CURRY WITH FRUIT, p. 107, with
FABULOUS RICE, p. 176, *or*
ISRAELI CHICKEN, p. 98, with
MOROCCAN COUSCOUS, p. 172
CRISPY NUT BALLS, p. 250
SPOON CAKE, p. 237

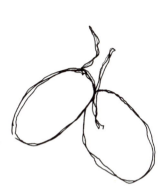

# PURIM

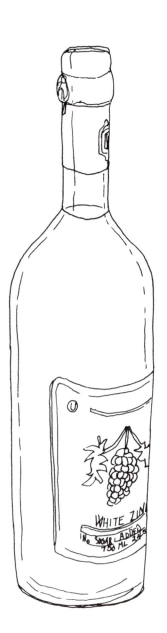

*Purim*, celebrating the story of Queen Esther's rescue of the Jews from a genocidal plot in ancient Persia, has been called a "topsy-turvy" holiday. Everyone wears costumes to synagogue—adults as well as children. It is a *mitzvah* to hear *every word* of the *Megillah* (scroll) of Esther when it is read in synagogue, yet as much noise as possible with *groggers* (traditional noise-makers) is to be made whenever the name of the villain, Haman, is read!

Preceded by the Fast of Esther, on Purim feasting as well as frivolity prevails. The Purim *Seudah* (feast) is served after synagogue or later in the day. Wine is always included, as the Talmud suggests one should become so drunk that one cannot distinguish Mordecai (Esther's heroic uncle) from Haman. According to tradition, Esther was a vegetarian, in order to observe *kashrut* in the palace of the King, and among some Jews, the *Seudah* is a vegetarian meal including a dish with chick peas. Among others, meat-filled *kreplach* are a traditional food, partly because of their triangular shape— the shape attributed to Haman's hat. Challah is sometimes formed into an especially long braid to symbolize the rope from which the villain was hanged. *Hamantaschen* (literally, "Haman's hat") are triangular-shaped, filled pastries prepared especially for Purim. They are included with at least one other—and usually a large variety of—edible treats in special packages for *Mishloach Manot* (literally, "sending portions"). Traditionally, children dressed in costumes deliver the plates, baskets, or boxes of *Mishloach Manot* to friends and neighbors. Food and money are also collected for distribution among the poor. This holiday has obvious great appeal to children. The preparation and delivery of *Mishloach Manot* are traditions children love almost as much as the costumes and carnival spirit.

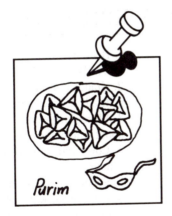

# PURIM SEUDAH 🔷P

CHALLAH, pp. 46-47, p. 280 (double length braid)
GRANDMA IDA'S KREPLACH (as meat appetizer), p. 378
*or* KREPLACH WITH A SLANT (pareve, vegetarian), p. 24
FISH IN PAPER, p. 147
RICE PILAF, p. 176
MARINATED VEGETABLES DELUXE, p. 73
HAMANTASCHEN, pp. 260-263
KORASHKAS (POPPY SEED STICKS), p. 256
Seasonal Fresh Fruit
MULLED WINE, p. 34

# MISHLOACH MANOT BASKETS 🔵D

HAMANTASCHEN, pp. 260-263
POPPYSEED COOKIES, p. 256
EASY CHEESE TARTS, p. 293
PECAN DAINTIES, p. 251
SPICE COOKIES, p. 254
BUTTER FUDGE FINGERS, p. 255
WHITE CHOCOLATE BROWNIES WITH CHOCOLATE CHUNKS, p. 273
NO-FAIL FUDGE, p. 294
ZACH'S CRACKER JACKS, p. 290

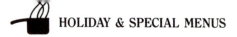 

# ▥ GRANDMA IDA'S KREPLACH *Florence Sager*

**Dough:**
2 cups unbleached flour
½ tsp. salt
2 eggs
1 Tbsp. oil
2 to 3 Tbsps. water

**Filling:**
2 cups cooked beef or
  poultry; leftovers, such
  as brisket or turkey
1 onion, minced
1 Tbsp. oil, optional, for
  sautéeing
1 large egg
Salt & pepper, to taste

1. Beat eggs in a bowl with oil and 2 Tbsps. water. (May mix dough in food processor.)
2. Gradually beat in flour and salt. If dough is stiff, add a little more water.
3. Place dough on a floured board. Knead for about 5 minutes until smooth.
4. Cover with a towel and let rest 20 minutes to 1 hour.
5. For filling, sauté onions in oil, if desired.
6. Grind meat with onions in a grinder, or pulse a few seconds in a food processor.
7. Add egg and seasonings; mix well.
8. Divide dough in half. On a lightly floured board, roll dough out thin, about the same thickness as pie crust.
9. Cut dough into 3-inch squares.
10. Place 1 Tbsp. filling in the center of each square. Fold over diagonally to form a triangle. Pinch edges together, and press down with a fork to tightly seal them.
11. Repeat with remaining dough. (May be frozen ahead at this point. Do not thaw before cooking; add 10 minutes onto cooking time.)
12. Boil 3 quarts of water in a large pot with 1 Tbsp. salt. Drop kreplachs into pot, reduce heat. Cover and simmer 15 to 20 minutes.
13. For fried kreplach, parboil only 5 to 10 minutes. Heat a small amount of vegetable oil in skillet. Fry on each side until golden.
Makes 2 to 3 dozen.
*Serve boiled kreplach in soup. Serve fried kreplach as appetizer or side dish. Kreplach are traditionally served on Erev Yom Kippur, Hoshanah Rabbah, and Purim.*

# PESACH

Food is central to *Pesach* observance, and the *Seder*, a religious service conducted with special symbolic foods around the family table in the Jewish home, is the most universally practiced Jewish ritual. The week-long festival celebrates the Exodus from Egypt and the emergence of the Jews from slavery to freedom and nationhood. The *Seder* (literally "order" of the service) emphasizes the education of children by their parents, and the need for each generation of Jews to reaffirm the centrality of the Exodus to its Jewish identity.

Special dietary laws forbidding consumption of *hametz* (leavening) govern the meals throughout the festival, and provide an added challenge to the Jewish cook. Pesach cuisine has varied throughout the Diaspora, with particularly striking differences in permitted foods between Ashkenazi and Sephardi Jews. Preparation for the holiday begins many days before with the cleaning of the house to remove all traces of *hametz*. (Jewish women traditionally complain that the reason for this observance is to reenact the state of slavery!) The kitchen, appliances, and utensils receive special attention, and separate Pesach dishes are unpacked and prepared. The night before the festival, parents lead children around the house with candles and feathers in a search for the last crumbs of *hametz*. Parents often hide cookies, cakes, or candy to add to the fun. With the last crumbs of *hametz* consumed, real preparation of the *Seder* begins.

As with the other festivals, Pesach incorporates aspects of the spring festivals which preceded it, including the offering of the paschal lamb (whence the name *Pesach*), or first spring lamb, as a sacrifice in the Temple. It is still traditional in many communities to serve lamb as well as spring garden vegetables and fruits at the *Seder* meal. The *Seder* plate contains the special ritual foods displayed or eaten during the service. A separate plate holds three *matzot* including the *Afikomen* (a *matzah* usually hidden *from* the children in Ashkenazi homes, *by* the children in Sephardi homes). Salted water, a reminder of tears shed in slavery, is provided for dipping eggs and greens (although many Sephardim use vinegar). Four cups of wine (or kosher for Pesach grape juice) are poured during the *Seder*, and a separate cup of wine is traditionally left on the table for Elijah, who may come at any time to herald the Messiah, and who, according to many beautiful folk stories, provides for the poor during Pesach. Guests abound at the *Seder* table, for no member of the community is to be without a place or a meal.

Children like to help in the preparation of the *Seder*. We include instructions for the *Seder* plate, as well as a *Haroset* recipe from the KIDS section in the menus that follow, which we hope will facilitate their participation. We hope the recipes in our PESACH section, as well as those marked "KP" throughout the book, will prove helpful, delicious, and fun during the festival week.

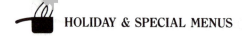

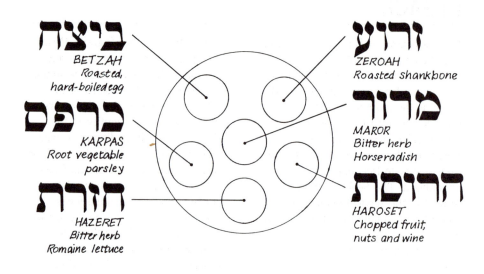

בֵּיצָה
BETZAH
Roasted,
hard-boiled egg

כַּרְפַּס
KARPAS
Root vegetable
parsley

חֲזֶרֶת
HAZERET
Bitter herb
Romaine lettuce

זְרוֹעַ
ZEROAH
Roasted shankbone

מָרוֹר
MAROR
Bitter herb
Horseradish

חֲרֹסֶת
HAROSET
Chopped fruit,
nuts and wine

# THE SEDER PLATE

At least one *Seder* plate is present at every *Seder*. In some communities, each participant or family head has his/her own *Seder* plate, and partakes of the foods directly from his/her plate. In others, there is one symbolic plate, used only by the leader of the *Seder* service, with additional portions of the foods passed among the guests. The plate always contains the following six items:

*1. Karpas:* Part of a root vegetable; most commonly, parsley leaves, celery ribs and leaves, or boiled potatoes. Dipped in saltwater at the beginning of the *Seder* to symbolize rebirth and renewal mixed with the tears and oppression of the past.

*2. Maror:* Bitter herb, usually horseradish root. (See CHRAINE, p. 331.) Represents the bitterness of slavery and oppression. Eaten with *haroset* between two *matzot* in a traditional "Hillel sandwich."

*3. Hazeret:* Another "bitter" herb, usually romaine lettuce leaves, and usually eaten with horseradish.

*4. Haroset:* A dip made of chopped fruit, nuts, and wine. Represents the mortar the Hebrew slaves used to make bricks for Pharoah. Usually the consistency and color of mud or clay, its surprisingly sweet taste represents the sweetness of freedom experienced as a deliverance from slavery. A favorite among children! (See p. 330 & p. 282.)

*5. Zeroah:* A lamb shankbone, roasted in the oven. Represents the paschal lamb sacrificed at the Temple, and refers specifically to the blood of the lamb used to mark the doors of the Hebrews on the eve of the Exodus.

*6. Betzah:* An egg, hard-boiled and roasted in the oven. Represents an additional sacrifice at the Temple. A symbol of mourning, on the one hand, may be a reminder of the destruction of the Temple; a symbol of fertility on the other hand, may be a reminder of spring, rebirth, and renewal.

# SEDER MENU I

**M**

**KP**

ISRAELI HAROSET, p. 281
APRICOT HAROSET, p. 330
CHRAINE, p. 331
CHICKEN SOUP, p. 61
KNAIDLACH, p. 333
LAMB SHANKS WITH SWEET GARLIC SAUCE, p. 336
CAPON WITH MUSHROOMS, p. 338
APPLE MATZAH KUGEL, p. 345
PASSOVER VEGETABLE KUGELS, p. 343
"CARMEL" CUSTARD, p. 354
FLOURLESS CHOCOLATE CAKE, p. 349
HAZELNUT MACAROONS, p. 357

# SEDER MENU II

**M**

**KP**

YEMENITE HAROSET, p. 330
CHRAINE, p. 331
GEFILTE FISH, pp. 21-23
CHICKEN SOUP, p. 61 with
MATZAH BALLS, p. 61
Roast Turkey with
MATZAH SPINACH STUFFING, p. 346
CANDIED SWEET POTATOES, p. 208
DAVIDA'S ZUCCHINI, p. 201
CHOCOLATE MOUSSE CAKE, p. 349
MARK'S MAKES YOU FAT AND THAT'S THAT PASSOVER CAKE, p. 351

# MOROCCAN MEAL
# FOR THE LAST DAY OF PESACH

**M**

SEPHARDI HAROSET, p. 330
LAMB WITH PRUNES, RAISINS, and WALNUTS, p. 122
RATATOUILLE, p. 200
MOROCCAN CARROT SALAD, p. 332
RICE PILAF, p. 176
*NOTE: Sephardi tradition allows
the use of rice during Pesach.*
LA MOUFLETA, to be served several hours after sundown.
*(See recipe and explanation, p. 382.)*
ISRAELI "TURKISH" COFFEE, p. 36

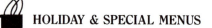
# ❶ LA MOUFLETA *Chris Erenberg*

7 cups flour
2 cakes yeast
¼ cup warm water
1 tsp. sugar
4 cups warm water
⅓ cup oil
Pinch of salt
Melted butter
Honey

1. Dissolve yeast in ¼ cup water with 1 tsp. sugar.
2. Place flour in a bowl, make a well, add water, dissolved yeast, salt, and oil. Mix well.
3. Turn dough onto floured board and knead until smooth and elastic.
4. Grease a flat surface. Make 30 to 40 balls from dough. Cover with a towel and let stand for 30 minutes.
5. On greased surface, flatten each ball into a thin pancake with your fingertips.
6. On hot ungreased frying pan, cook each pancake briefly on each side, until all are cooked. Stack together and cover with a cloth.
7. To serve, soak the pancakes in melted butter and honey.

*La Moufleta is an essential part of the Moroccan Jewish custom called "La Mimouna." In "La Cuisine Juive Marocaine," Rivka Levy Mellul describes this unique tradition she grew up with in her Jewish community of Morocco. At sundown, after the last day of Pesach, families prepared "royal" tables decked with cakes, jams, honey, butter, and stalks of wheat; a special plate filled with flour and decorated with pea pods, coins, and dates, added a rich note to the table. People crowded the streets, going from one house to another, tasting the "Moufleta," symbol of a happy and blessed year, and wishing each other luck and happiness. Arab neighbors joined in the celebration, bringing armloads of cakes, greens, and milk as signs of friendship. Everyone's doors stayed open all night long to anyone wishing to come in for food and blessings. The next day was "picnic day." The evening of "La Mimouna," some families had the custom of preparing yeast which was allowed to rise for 2 to 3 days before using it to make bread. Generally, this yeast was made available to neighbors who had none. This was another proof of friendship and neighborly behavior.*

# YOM HA'ATZMAUT

*Yom Ha'atzmaut* is Israeli Independence Day and celebrates the founding of the State of Israel, the 5th of *Iyar* (May 14,) 1948. It is preceded in Israel by *Yom HaZikaron,* a Memorial Day in honor of Israeli soldiers who have given their lives in defense of their country. It has become increasingly common among Jews in the Diaspora to mark *Yom Ha'atzmaut* by serving a favorite Middle Eastern meal, such as felafel in pita bread. It is many students' favorite school lunch at the Solomon Schechter Day Schools!

# YOM HA'ATZMUT MENU

QUICK BLENDER HUMMUS, p. 15
FELAFEL, below, p. 383
ISRAELI EGGPLANT SALAD, p. 79
Chopped Lettuce, Tomato, & Onion
TEHINA SAUCE, p. 384
KOSHER PICKLES, p. 322
PITA BREAD, p. 384
BANANA CAKE, p. 232
MERINGUE MAGIC, p. 356

# FELAFEL  *Chris Erenberg*

12 ounces dry chick peas
 (garbanzo beans)
8 cups water
5 cloves garlic, minced
¼ cup parsley flakes
¾ cup water (approximate)
¼ cup wheat germ
¼ cup matzah meal
1 tsp. ground coriander
1 tsp. ground cumin
1 tsp. paprika
1½ tsps. salt
½ tsp. pepper
Oil for frying

1. The night before serving, rinse chick peas well in colander. Put in large glass bowl with the 8 cups water. Soak overnight.
2. Next day, drain chick peas in colander and rinse well. Grind in electric food grinder or food processor. Add minced garlic, parsley flakes, and ¼ cup of water to the chick peas. Mix well, either by hand or in food processor.
3. Mix the coriander, cumin, paprika, and salt and pepper with the wheat germ and matzah meal.
4. Add this mixture and another ½ cup of water to the chick pea mixture. Mix until thoroughly blended. Add more salt and pepper, if desired. Let stand for 20 minutes.
5. Form 1-inch balls and fry them in 3 to 4 inches of hot oil until browned and crisp all over. Drain on paper towels.
Makes approximately 50 balls.
*Serve in pita bread pockets topped with a mixture of minced vegetables, if desired, and TEHINAH SAUCE (see recipe p. 384).*

383

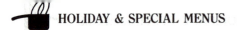

## ◆ TEHINAH SAUCE *Chris Erenberg*

1 cup sesame seed paste
1½ to 2 cups water
⅓ cup lemon juice
1 tsp. salt
1½ tsps. garlic powder
½ tsp. paprika
Pepper, to taste

1. Stir paste before measuring, as it tends to separate. Put in bowl and add ½ the water, stirring constantly. Add lemon juice and stir until all liquids appear thoroughly blended.
2. Add salt, garlic powder, paprika, and pepper. Stir until the spices are well blended with the rest.
3. Gradually add water until consistency of the tehinah is of a pourable sauce.
*Serve as a dressing for felafel "sandwiches."*

## ◆ PITA BREAD *Chris Erenberg*

1 package quick-rising
  dry yeast
¾ cup water
1 tsp. sugar
2 cups flour
1 tsp. salt

1. Dissolve the dry yeast and sugar in the water. Let sit for about 10 minutes, or until the mixture looks foamy.
2. Sift the flour with the salt.
3. Form a well in the middle of the flour. Pour the yeast mixture into the well and stir until soft dough is formed.
4. On a floured surface, knead the dough until smooth and elastic.
5. Let dough rise about 45 minutes in a bowl covered with a towel.
6. Punch dough down, cover, and let rise another 25 to 30 minutes, or until double in bulk.
7. Knead the dough a few times, but do not overwork it. Cut into 8 pieces. Form each piece into a ball.
8. Place balls on cookie sheet (ungreased), cover with a towel, and let rise again, about 20 minutes.
9. Flatten each ball to a thin round shape, about ¼-inch thick.
10. Bake one or two pitas at a time on a floured cookie sheet in a 450 degree oven, about 3 minutes per side. Cool pitas until just warm, put in closed plastic bag for 15 to 20 minutes.
Makes 8 pita breads.
*Cut the round pita in half, and fill the "pocket" with felafel, tehinah, hummus, chopped lettuce, tomatoes, or onions. Pita is also delicious as a scooper for hummus and other dips.*

# LAG B'OMER

The counting of the *Omer* begins on the second day of Pesach and continues for forty-nine days until the fiftieth, *Shavuot*, which commemorates the giving of the Torah. The *Omer* was the grain offering brought to the Temple each year on the second day of Pesach from the first new crop. The days of the Counting of the *Omer* are traditionally solemn, with no weddings permitted, with the exception of *Lag B'Omer,* a day of rejoicing. *Lag B'Omer* also commemorates the end of a deadly epidemic during Rabbi Akiba's time, and honors the sage, Rabbi Shimon Bar Yochai, author of the *Zohar*. In Israel, *Lag B'Omer* is a happy day of bonfires and picnics, and special games for children.

## ISRAELI BARBECUE MENU

MIRIAM'S EGGPLANT SALAD, p. 15
PITA BREAD, p. 384
CARROT SALAD, p. 83
SHISH KABOB, p. 123
EASY COUSCOUS, p. 172
HARISSA, p. 172
TABBOULEH, pp. 79-80
Fresh Fruit
DOUBLE CHOCOLATE COOKIES, p. 248
FUDGY BROWNIES, p. 268

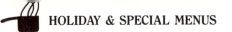 

# SHAVUOT

*Shavuot,* the last of the three great festivals, commemorates the giving of the *Torah* to the Jewish people at Mt. Sinai. An old folk-saying poses the question, "Why is *Shavuot* the best Festival of all? During *Sukkot* you may eat whatever you want, but not wherever you want; during *Pesach,* you may eat wherever you want, but not whatever you want; but on *Shavuot,* you may eat whatever *and* wherever you want!" Among most Jews, it is traditional to eat dairy foods on Shavuot, and the explanations vary. Because Shavuot was also associated with spring harvest, it is the custom to eat a new fruit of the season. Two challahs are often braided into extra-long loaves as a reminder of the two loaves formerly brought to the Temple. Seven-layer cakes and cakes frosted to resemble a mountain are baked in some communities and symbolize Mt. Sinai, the place where the *Torah* was given.

## Ⓓ SHAVUOT MENU I

BOREKAS, p. 158
EDA'S BEET BORSCHT, p. 63
SPINACH STUFFED FISH, p. 140
JONA'S CUSTARD KUGEL, p. 183
STRAWBERRY MOLD, p. 86
CRUNCHY PEAPOD SALAD, p. 76
STRUDEL, p. 237
PAVLOVA DESSERT, p. 216
*(Mound meringue high for Mt. Sinai Cake.)*

## Ⓓ SHAVUOT MENU II

BERRIES & CREAM SOUP, p. 66
SALMON MOUSSE with DILL SAUCE, p. 19
CHEESE BLINTZES, p. 170
BROCCOLI WITH RED PEPPERS, p. 198
UNBAKED FRUIT PIE FOR SHAVUOT, p. 387
COOKIES & CREAM CHEESECAKE, p. 220

# UNBAKED FRUIT PIE FOR SHAVUOT *Irene Sufrin* **D**

Push pastry shell:
1½ cups flour
1 tsp. salt
½ cup butter (cold)
1½ tsps. honey
2 Tbsps. milk (ice cold)

Filling:
3½ cups strawberries
  (sliced fruit or other
  berries or combination)
Honey, to taste

Topping:
Whipped cream, or yogurt,
  or ice cream

1. Sift flour and salt into a mixing bowl. Make a well in the center, and put the butter in it.
2. Cut in the butter with 2 knives.
3. Gently work the butter into the flour with your fingertips until it resembles coarse meal.
4. With a fork, beat together the honey and milk. Add to the flour mixture. Blend together with fingertips, but do not knead.
5. Grease a 9-inch pie pan and heat oven to 425 degrees.
6. Place dough in center of pan. Gently press dough with fingertips to cover the bottom, sides, and rim of pan.
7. Prick the entire surface of the crust with a fork to prevent buckling.
8. Bake for 12 to 15 minutes.
9. Put clean berries or sliced fruit into a bowl. Mix in honey 1 tsp. at a time, tasting to determine how much. Spoon into cooled crust.
10. Top with whipped cream or yogurt and nuts, or serve with ice cream.

*This recipe was included in Irene's Middle School cooking class. The push pastry is ideal for children to make because it eliminates the difficulty of transferring rolled pastry from board to pan. Fresh fruit and cream make this a perfect dessert for Shavuot.*

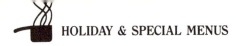

## AMERICAN INDEPENDENCE DAY
 ## 4TH OF JULY BARBECUE

GAIL'S GAZPACHO, p. 64
EMPANADAS CRIOLLAS, p. 30
SALAMI-YOMMY, p. 29
BARBECUED CHICKEN with HONEY MUSTARD GLAZE, p. 109
VEGETABLE PASTA SALAD with MUSTARD TARRAGON DRESSING, p. 72
MOM'S COLESLAW & DRESSING, p. 82
4TH OF JULY MOLD, p. 87
DILL PICKLES, p. 322
DILL TOMATOES, p. 323
Watermelon
COCOA BROWNIES, p. 273

## AMERICAN THANKSGIVING FEAST

MARIANA'S SPINACH DIP with Fresh Vegetables, p. 14
CURRIED PUMPKIN MUSHROOM SOUP, p. 55
*(May be served in individual mini-pumkins,*
*scooped out for a festive soup bowl.)*
GRANDMOTHER'S FAMOUS CRANBERRY BREAD, p. 282
Turkey stuffed with
VEGETABLE STUFFING FOR TURKEY, p. 116
CRANBERRY-CURRANT SAUCE, p. 320
SWEET POTATO PUFF, p. 208
GREEN BEAN-TOMATO AMANDINE, p. 203
STRAWBERRIES & RHUBARB, p. 281
THANKSGIVING PUMPKIN BREAD, p. 282
CRANBERRY PIE, p. 245

# FORMAL DINNER FOR TWELVE　Ⓜ

MAHOGANY CHICKEN WINGS, p. 25
MOCK SHRIMP TOAST, p. 24
CAVIAR MOLD with Crackers, p. 19
Salad of Bibb Lettuce, Artichoke Hearts, and
Hearts of Palm, with VINAIGRETTE SALAD DRESSING, p. 90
BEEF WELLINGTON, p. 138
SPINACH & MUSHROOMS in TOMATO SHELLS, p. 205
CHOCOLATE SACHER TORTE *(pareve option)*, p. 227
PEAR TART, p. 241

# FORMAL LUNCHEON FOR TWELVE　Ⓓ

VICHYSOISSE, p. 59
Mixed Green Salad with
GREEN GODDESS SALAD DRESSING, p. 92
FISH IN PHYLLO, p. 141, *or*
BRIOCHE, p. 142
Fresh Fruit and Berries with
BAVARIAN CREAM MOLD, p. 88
CHOCOLATE MOUSSE IN CRINKLE CUPS, p. 213

# ITALIAN BUFFET DINNER　Ⓜ

HANDFUL MINESTRONE, p. 54
TOMATO-ONION SALAD, p. 78
EGGPLANT, p. 26
SPAGHETTI SAUCE ITALIENNE, p. 130,
with Spinach Fettucini
VEAL PICCATA, p. 118, *or*
CHICKEN PICCATA, p. 95
FRIED GREEN PEPPERS, p. 260
Crusty Italian Bread
CRANBERRY-RASPBERRY SORBET, p. 391
POWDERED SUGAR COOKIES, p. 253

# 7 COURSE ORIENTAL BANQUET *David Hoffman*

A past president of the Chicago area Solomon Schechter Day Schools, father of three Schechter graduates, and member of the Board of Trustees, David Hoffman has enjoyed adapting Oriental cooking to kosher cuisine for many years. David and his wife, Barbara, especially enjoy serving a banquet for 5 or 6 couples to the highest bidder at the annual School Auction. We thank them, and our Food Editor, Myra Dorf, for watching the chef in action to record his methods accurately. David intends that these recipes can be used as guidelines; cooks should feel free to adjust seasonings to suit their own palates. *Plan a leisurely evening of 3 to 4 hours. To facilitate entertaining, have all ingredients ready to stir-fry. Do actual stir-fry cooking while guests wait. This allows time for digestion and conversation between courses, despite a frequently absent host!*

### MENU

LAMB CHOP APPETIZER
ORIENTAL MUSHROOM SOUP
"IT'S NOT SHRIMP" ORIENTALE
SZECHWAN PEPPERCORN LAMB
THREE PEPPER VEAL
FRIED RICE
KUNG BAU CHICKEN (HOT!)
with White Rice
SORBET & FRUIT MEDLEY

# LAMB CHOP APPETIZER   M

24 lamb chops, first cut
½ cup Hoisin sauce*

1. The day before serving, remove fillet (eye) of lamb chop from bone, leaving the rest of the meat on the bone. Set aside the fillets for SZECHWAN PEPPERCORN LAMB (see p. 392).
2. Marinate the lamb bones overnight in the Hoisin sauce.
3. Allow 5 hours roasting time. Spread the bones out on broiling or baking pans. Bake 2 hours in 300 degree oven. Drain fat several times during baking. Baste with Hoisin sauce.
4. Bake 3 more hours at 400 degrees. Continue to drain fat and baste with Hoisin sauce. Makes 8 to 12 servings.
*Serve before the meal with cocktails or a glass of wine to whet the appetites of your guests!*
*For a recipe, see HOISIN SAUCE, p. 327.*

# ORIENTAL MUSHROOM SOUP   M

½ pound meat, diced
½ cup dark soy sauce
4 to 5 cups chicken stock
2 Tbsps. light soy sauce
2 tsps. sesame oil
2 cup assortment of the following, as available:
Tiger lilies
Oriental dried vegetable medley
Oriental mushrooms
Bamboo shoots
Water chestnuts, sliced

1. Marinate meat in dark soy sauce for at least 1 hour.
2. Heat chicken stock with light soy sauce and sesame oil. Add meat. Simmer until meat is cooked.
3. Soak dried vegetables and mushrooms in water approximately 15 minutes until freshened.
4. Add vegetables, mushrooms, bamboo shoots, and water chestnuts to stock. Simmer until flavors blend.
Makes 8 to 10 servings.

# P "IT'S NOT SHRIMP" ORIENTALE

4 packages imitation
  shrimp, defrosted
Oil for frying

Batter for pre-frying:
1 Tbsp. flour
2 egg whites
1 tsp. cornstarch
3 cloves garlic
3 scallions, sliced
4 cups vegetables, sliced,
  including the following:
Carrots
Mushrooms
Peapods
Bamboo shoots

Sauce:
2 tsps. fermented black
  beans
⅓ cup dry sherry
2 Tbsps. soy sauce
1 Tbsp. cornstarch
  dissolved in 2 Tbsps.
  water
1 tsp. apple cider vinegar
1 Tbsp. sugar

1. Mix flour, egg whites, and cornstarch for batter. Dip imitation shrimp in batter.
2. Heat oil in wok or large skillet. Fry shrimp very quickly on both sides (only about 1 minute total). Pre-frying may be done well in advance of stir-fry preparation.
3. Mix sauce ingredients together.
4. Season wok with oil, garlic, and scallions. Add carrots and mushrooms, then bamboo shoots and peapods.
5. Add pre-fried imitation shrimp. Last, add sauce. Stir just until heated, allowing vegetables to maintain their color and crispness.
Makes 10 servings.
*Serve with plain or fried rice.*

# M SZECHWAN PEPPERCORN LAMB

24 lamb chop fillets*
½ to 1 cup mint jelly
Szechwan peppercorns,
  crushed, to taste
1 to 2 tsps. cornstarch
Pineapple & mint leaves,
  for garnish

1. The night before serving, prepare a marinade by warming the mint jelly in a pot.
2. Add crushed peppercorns. Pour over lamb chop fillets. Refrigerate overnight.
3. Drain marinade from lamb and reserve for sauce.
4. Broil or grill the lamb fillets, 5 to 10 minutes on the first side, 5 minutes on the second. Do not overcook.
5. Strain marinade into a pot. Add cornstarch. Heat and stir over low heat, adding more mint jelly if necessary.
6. To serve, spoon a little sauce on each plate. Place 2 lamb fillets on the sauce. Garnish with a pineapple slice and mint leaves.
*See LAMB CHOP APPETIZER, p. 391.*

# THREE PEPPER VEAL  M

2 pounds veal, thinly sliced
Batter for pre-frying:
1 egg white
¼ tsp. sugar
1 Tbsp. cornstarch

Oil for frying
1 large sweet red pepper
1 large sweet yellow pepper
1 large sweet green pepper
4 large mushrooms
4 scallions
1 clove garlic

Light soy sauce:
4 Tbsps. sugar
½ Tbsp. dark soy
½ Tbsp. vinegar
2 Tbsps. cornstarch
¼ to ½ cup water

1. Before guests arrive, cut veal into thin strips. Mix batter of egg white, sugar, and cornstarch. Dip veal into batter and stir-fry in hot oil, 1 to 2 minutes, until veal turns white. Set aside.
2. Slice red, yellow, and green peppers, mushrooms, and scallions.
3. Mix light soy sauce.
4. Just before serving, heat oil in wok. Add ingredients in following order: Garlic, scallions, pre-fried veal, mushrooms, and peppers.
5. Add sauce. Cook until sauce starts to stick to ingredients.
Makes 10 servings.
*Serve immediately with FRIED RICE (see below).*

# FRIED RICE  M

2 cups white rice
1 cup diced chicken
  and/or beef
2 Tbsps. Hoisin sauce*
Peanut oil for frying
½ cup sweet red pepper
½ cup water chestnuts
½ cup bamboo shoots
½ cup scallions
½ cup bean sprouts
2 eggs

1. The day before serving, prepare rice according to package direction. Let rice stand out overnight.
2. Before guests arrive, dice chicken and/or beef. Marinate in Hoisin sauce.
3. Dice red pepper, water chestnuts, bamboo shoots, and scallions.
4. Heat oil in wok. Stir-fry chicken and/or beef. Set aside.
5. Scramble eggs in wok. Chop and set aside.
6. Stir-fry rice in wok. Add diced vegetables and bean sprouts.
7. Transfer to large casserole, making certain to include any oil or juices not already absorbed by the rice. Add meat and egg.
8. Sprinkle a little peanut oil over rice to prevent drying out. Reheat in low oven just before serving.
Makes 10 servings.
❖ *Chicken and/or beef may be omitted for pareve recipe.*
**See HOISIN SAUCE, p. 327.*

## Ⓜ KUNG BAU CHICKEN (HOT!)

3 pounds boneless breast
   of chicken, cut bite-sized

Marinade:
2 egg whites
1 tsp. sugar
1 Tbsp. cornstarch

Oil, for stir fry
8 hot red peppers
2 Tbsps. fresh ginger root,
   grated or diced
6 scallions, sliced into
   1½-inch pieces
1 cup cashew nuts

Sauce:
2 Tbsps. black soy sauce
1 Tbsp. very dry sherry
2 tsps. apple cider vinegar
½ tsp. sugar
2 tsps. sesame oil
½ tsp. cornstarch

1. About 1 hour before guests arrive, mix marinade of egg white, sugar, and cornstarch. Add chicken. Let stand.
2. Mix sauce ingredients, set aside.
3. To prepare for serving, oil wok for stir fry. Always stir-fry over a high fire. (A large skillet may be substituted for the wok, but it may be more difficult to prevent overcooking.)
4. Add to hot wok, in this order: red peppers, ginger root, and scallions. Stir to blend flavors.
5. Add marinated chicken. Cook until tender and white.
6. Add cashews.
7. Add sauce. Stir-fry until hot, but do not overcook.
Makes 10 servings.
*Serve immediately with white rice.*

## ◆ SORBET & FRUIT MEDLEY

For each serving:
3 small scoops sorbet*
1 large lichee fruit,
   from jar or can
2 slices fresh kiwi
Mandarin orange sections
1 large strawberry
Pineapple slices

Arrange attractively on dessert plate. Add a flower, if desired. Serve with fortune cookies!
*Three different sorbets or ices are very festive. See CRANBERRY-RASPBERRY SORBET, p. 291.*

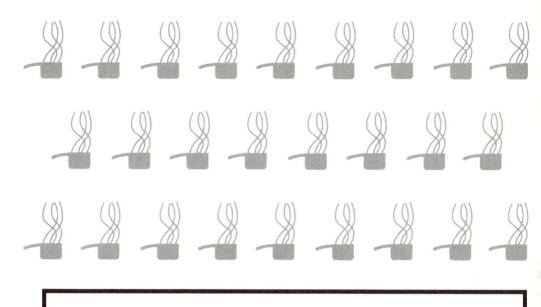

# HOUSeHOLd HiNtS

# HOUSEHOLD TIPS FOR THE KITCHEN

*Heat Lemons* thoroughly before squeezing. This will allow the lemon to produce more juice.

*To soften butter* (without a microwave): Cut butter into pieces, place in deep dish and cover with cold water. Allow to stand 5 to 10 minutes or until soft enough to use.

*Egg Yolks:* Leftover, unbroken yolks can be carefully slipped into boiling water and simmmered until firm. Use as sandwich fillings (with tuna, etc.) or chopped as a garnish on chopped liver, herring, salad, etc.

*Perfect Rice:* Boil the rice with a few drops of lemon juice. The rice will be whiter and grains will separate easily.

*Peel Onions* under cold water, to prevent those tears.

*Egg Whites* can be stored in the refrigerator up to two days, in a covered jar.

*Jam/Jelly in Pastry:* Heat jam to a boiling point before placing on pastry. This will keep the pastry crisp.

*Fresh Bread:* To cut easily, use a hot knife (warm the knife under hot running water, and dry with towel).

*Cabbage and Cauliflower Odors* can be avoided during cooking:
1) Pour a little vinegar on top of closed lid.
2) Place a slice of bread or lemon on top.

*Rapid Cooling:* Do not immerse a hot dish in a bowl of ice; rather, place a dish of ice over bowl or pot of hot food, as cool air descends while hot air rises.

*Good Method for Freshly Brewed Tea:* Boil fresh drawn water. Scald the teapot by pouring in a small amount of rapidly boiling water over the leaves. Stir once or twice, replace lid on teapot and allow to steep for 3 to 4 minutes. Then add more boiling water for the amount of cups required. If the brew is too strong, more hot water can be added. Pour through a tea strainer.

*Turning Out Perfect Cake:* Allow cake to cool 3 to 4 minutes (unless otherwise stated). Place the rack over the tin, hold the rack and tin together with both hands, reverse and rap on the table, then gently lift the tin off the cake. Immediately place another rack on the bottom of the cake and reverse again so that the top of the cake is the right way up. This prevents the wire mesh pattern of the rack from marking the top of the cake.

## LAUNDRY AND CLEANING HINTS

*Beetroot and Wine Stains* on the table cloth will wash out more easily if a layer of salt is sprinkled immediately onto the stain. Club soda is also good for removing stains on carpets and upholstery.

Hannah Engelman

*Tea or Coffee Stains* on a delicate fabric can be removed by applying a few drops of glycerine. Leave for about 1 hour and rinse with cold water.

*Fat or Oil Stains* on light-colored clothing can be removed more easily by covering immediately with flour or baby powder, and gently brushing off after a few hours.

*Shining Crystal:* Wash well in soapy water using an old toothbrush. Then, rinse in either vinegar or a strong solution of washing blue (laundry booster) and water. Polish with crumpled newspapers.

*Flannels or Woolen Clothing:* Add a tablespoon of olive oil to the final rinse, to keep them delightfully soft.

*To Remove Stains from Decanters:* Make up a mixture of 1 part coarse salt to 2 parts vinegar. Shake well, and mix with enough warm water to cover stained area. Leave for a few hours and rinse.

## IMPROVISATION IS THE KEY TO BEING A GOOD COOK!

1. *IF* a chocolate cake turns out too moist, serve it hot with a light chocolate sauce and call it a pudding instead.

2. *IF* homemade cookies crumble badly, use them to make a crumb crust for a fruit pie, or a flan dessert.

3. *IF* your sponge cake turns out flat and hard, cut into shapes with cookie cutters, and sandwich them together with jam, whipped cream, cream cheese and jelly, or whatever you like. Decorate with filling if desired, and sprinkle with candies or flaked chocolate, etc.. Kids will love them!

4. *IF* your cake rises unevenly, level the top by slicing crossways with a large, sharp knife, and turn upside down, using the bottom as the top. Ice.

5. *IF* a cake breaks as it is removed from pan, it could be disguised as a hot pudding and served with hot custard and/or fruit.

6. *IF* a cake sinks in the middle, cut out the center, and fill with fruit, custard, or whipped cream mixed with fruit. Decorate as desired.

7. *IF* a sauce turns lumpy, whisk with an electric mixer, purée in a blender, or press through a fine sieve.

8. *IF* a soup is too salty but not too thick, add a small quantity of instant mashed potato.

# QUANTITIES TO SERVE 100 PEOPLE  *Judy Schuster*

| | |
|---|---|
| Coffee | 3 pounds |
| Sugar | 3 pounds |
| Cream | 3 quarts |
| Whipping Cream | 4 pints |
| Milk | 6 gallons |
| Fruit cocktail | 2½ gallons |
| Fruit juice | 26 quarts—4 #10 cans |
| Soup | 25 quarts |
| Frankfurters | 25 pounds |
| Meat loaf | 24 pounds |
| Beef | 40 pounds |
| Hamburger | 30 to 36 pounds |
| Potatoes | 35 pounds |
| Vegetables | 4 #10 cans |
| Rolls | 200 |
| Bread | 10 loaves |
| Butter | 3 pounds |
| Potato salad | 12 quarts |
| Fruit salad | 20 quarts |
| Lettuce | 20 heads |
| Salad dressing | 3 quarts |
| Pies | 18 |
| Ice cream | 4 gallons |
| Cheese | 3 pounds |
| Pickles | 2 quarts |
| Nuts | 3 pounds |
| Carrots | 20 pounds |
| Lettuce (small salad) | 12 heads |
| Cucumbers | 35 (medium) |

**FRESH FRUIT SALAD:**

| | |
|---|---|
| Grapefruits | 25 |
| Oranges | 25 |
| Cantaloupes | 10 |
| Apples | 5 pounds |
| Watermelons | 2 whole |

# WHAT TO DO WITH LEFT-OVERS FROM SHABBAT  Myra Dorf

*Don't throw away soup vegetables or chicken from soup. Here are some ways to use them:*

*Gravy thickener:* Purée soup vegetables; pour into ice cube tray and freeze. Add as a thickener to sauces or gravies.

*Vegetable Soufflé:* Purée vegetables together; add 2 eggs and 2 Tbsps. of non-dairy creamer. Pour into greased baking dish or ramekins. Bake at 350 degrees for 15 minutes until set.

*Left-over brisket gravy:* Use as the liquid in your meatloaf; also delicious as the base or added ingredient in barbecue sauce.

*Left-over potatoes:* Dice or chop them. Sauté chopped onions, green pepper, and salami in a large skillet. Add diced potatoes and 3 to 6 eggs. Scramble to make "Hopple Popple"!

*Left-over fruit:* Stuff a turkey or turkey breast with over-ripe fruit, e.g., oranges, apples, pears, peaches (a hint from my friend Linda Clark). The white meat will stay moist and flavorful.

If your children will not eat boiled chicken, try these:

## CRISPY CHICKEN

Boiled chicken
1 egg white
½ cup bread crumbs
½ cup cornflake crumbs
Oil
Paprika

1. Bone cooked chicken.
2. Beat egg white until frothy. Combine bread crumbs and cornflake crumbs.
3. Dip chicken into egg white and then into crumbs.
4. Arrange in baking dish and dot with oil. Sprinkle with paprika.
5. Bake at 400 degrees for ½ hour or until crispy.

## WALDORF CHICKEN SALAD

Cooked chicken
2 apples, peeled, cored, and diced
3 green onions, chopped, both green and white parts
½ cup walnut pieces
1 tsp. seasoned salt
3 Tbsps. mayonnaise

1. Cube the cooked chicken. Combine the apples, green onions, and walnut pieces. Add to the chicken.
2. Combine the seasoned salt and mayonnaise. Mix with rest of the ingredients.

# A NOTE ON NUTRITION *Chana Kaufman, R.D.*

Hillel was asked to summarize the laws of the Torah while standing on one foot. Given the same challenge, if we were to define a good diet, our response would be: Eat a variety of foods in moderation.

Variety is important, since no single food or food group can supply all of the nutrients needed by our bodies. By eating many different types of foods, we are more likely to achieve a nutritionally balanced diet. One way of insuring variety is to plan a week of menus for your family. Select foods from each of the food groups, and be careful not to repeat any food too often. Let the children help with this, and post the menu for all to see.

Moderation should be the guide in determining portion size and food choices. For young children, portions should start small, with the child deciding if he or she is hungry for more. Children should be asked to taste everything served, but not forced to eat any one food. Learning to eat a variety of foods in moderation during childhood will help insure good dietary habits throughout life.

Current dietary guidelines advise the reduction of fat (especially saturated fat), cholesterol, sugar, and salt, and an increase in fiber. Of special importance to children and women of all ages is an adequate intake of calcium. Our food choices should emphasize complex carbohydrates, such as beans, peas, nuts, fruits, vegetables, and whole grains, rather than simple carbohydrates (like sugar) and fats. Complex carbohydrates contain many essential nutrients, are low in fat, and are a good source of dietary fiber. Low-fat protein foods include fish, poultry, lean meat, and legumes (beans and peas). Skim milk, low-fat yogurt, and leafy green vegetables are excellent sources of calcium. Oils such as canola and olive are good fat choices, but should be used in moderation.

Instilling life-long, good eating habits goes beyond choosing healthy foods. Mealtime should be relaxed and enjoyable, with emphasis on positive communication between family members. This is not the time to discuss difficult or distressing issues. Eating should be an activity of its own, for the sake of enjoyment as well as nourishment. When mealtime becomes a secondary activity to watching television, driving, reading or writing, we become less aware of our eating behavior. How much did we really eat? What did it taste like? Did we eat until satisfied or until the food was finished?

Food should not be used as a reward or incentive for a desired behavior. As a reward, candy especially can cause children to associate sweets with good behavior. When dessert is served with a meal rather than as a reward for finishing a meal, sweets do not become the central focus. Neither should food be used as punishment. When taken away as a disciplinary measure, food may become all the more desirable to the child being punished. Food may then be associated with behavior rather than hunger. Teach your children to eat when they are hungry, not as a remedy or a reward when they are happy, sad, or depressed.

Make food a positive experience for your family. Get children involved in cooking, shopping, and menu planning. Teach them to read product labels and make wise food choices. The good eating habits they learn as children, will benefit them a lifetime.

# GROWING SPROUTS IN THE KITCHEN   *Irene Sufrin*

Sprouts are great for a kosher kitchen. They are pareve, so you can eat them at a dairy or a meat meal. Add sprouts to salads, soups, and omelets; put them in sandwiches instead of lettuce or relish. Eat sprouts for a snack. One fully packed cup of most sprouts contains only 16 calories (*e.g.*, mung sprouts are 45 calories per cup, and alfalfa sprouts are 9 calories per cup).

Sprouting seeds is a simple process. It begins with dormant or sleeping seeds. You can buy any of these seeds or beans at a health food store: mung beans, alfalfa, lentils, garbanzos, wheat or radish. (Be sure that the seeds you sprout are meant for food, and have not been treated for planting.) The seeds are awakened and germinate when they are provided with moisture, warm temperatures, darkness, and circulating air.

How to sprout seeds and beans:

1. Use a clean, empty jar with a wide opening. A quart jar provides enough room for the sprouts to grow and for air to circulate.

2. Put the seeds in the jar and soak overnight. Use as little as 1 tsp. of seeds or as much as ¼ cup. You can start soaking the seeds after dinner. The next morning will begin Day 1 of sprouting. Keep the jar in a dark place or cover the jar with a paper bag.

3. Rinse the seeds and drain them. Use a wire mesh strainer or cover the jar with a piece of cheesecloth, securing it with a rubber band. Leave the jar tilted, top side down so that the water will drain off. During the day keep the jar covered with the cheesecloth and in a warm, dark place. In the evening repeat the rinsing and draining process.

4. Day 2 and Day 3: repeat the morning and evening process.

5. The sprouting process will take between 60 to 80 hours. On Day 3 you can leave the sprouting seeds in the sun so that the chlorophyll content will increase.

6. Harvest your sprouts by rinsing, draining, and storing them. Place the sprouts in a container and then store them in the refrigerator. They will last 5 days or more.

*This is a fascinating project for parents and kids to do together.*

## INDEX

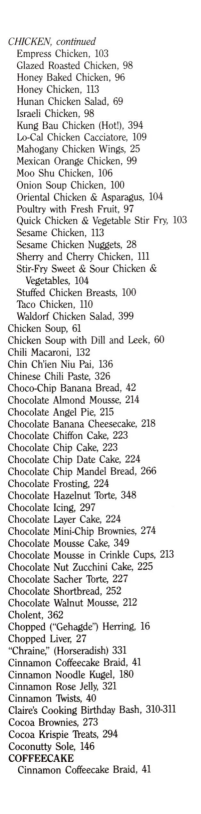

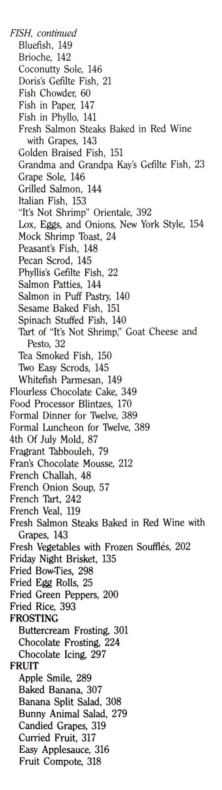

INDEX

# S